HOW TO HUSTLE AND WIN

A Survival Guide for the Ghetto

Part One

SUPREME UNDERSTANDING

Supreme Design Publishing books are printed on long-lasting acid-free paper. When it is available, we choose paper that has been manufactured by environmentally responsible practices. These may include using trees grown in sustainable forests, incorporating recycled paper, minimizing chlorine in bleaching, or recycling the energy produced at the paper mill.

Supreme Design Publishing is also a member of the Tree Neutral™ initiative, which works to offset paper consumption through tree planting.

TreeNeutral

Publisher's Cataloging-in-Publication Data

Understanding, Supreme.

How to Hustle and Win, part 1 : a survival guide for the ghetto / Supreme Understanding ; foreword by Rick Ross.

p. cm.

ISBN: 978-0-9816170-0-8

1. African Americans—Social conditions—1975-. 2. Conduct of life. 3. Social change. 4. Urban poor. I. Rick Ross, 1960- II. Title.

2008901752

Sixth Printing

Visit us on the web at www.HustleAndWin.com

PREFACE

"The devil sure do stay busy" - Somebody's Grandma

Peace! Since we've first published this book, so many amazing things have happened. This should be a great moment - our 10th anniversary edition of a self-empowerment guide that has quite literally changed the world. Nearly every successful artist and athlete I respect has read this book or heard of it!

Bigger than that, there are the millions of people, much like yourself, who may not have a platform (yet!), who have been impacted by this book and the two dozen titles that followed it!

6 DOPE THINGS WE'RE PROUD OF AT SDP

At Supreme Design Publishing, we take pride in producing high-quality nonfiction books. They're well-researched and designed to produce great changes in any reader, through a process of nonformal education inspired by my doctoral dissertation on the learning-centered culture of the Five Percent in America.

When we change lives, we change communities. We've won a few awards and our books earn amazing reviews from all walks of life. This book has been translated into Spanish (by readers!) and will soon be in French. It's used in university courses across the country. It's been spotted in quite a few big artists' videos. Yet i's bigger than rap videos!

Here are six things we're proud to see over the past decade:

1. Getting the blessing of ancestor Dick Gregory as the "change in the wind" the community needed before his transition

2. Contributing to getting political prisoner Mumia Abu Jamal off death row and into general population

3. Assisting former drug kingpin "Freeway" Ricky Ross in his transition to community change activist, educator, and author

4. Empowering hundreds of businesses, schools, community centers, and parents with the resources they needed

5. Ensuring that thousands of Black and brown people (prolly some white folks too) didn't go back to prison, **thanks to a greater understanding of self, allowing them to raise families!**

6. Changing tens of thousands of lives through the gift of self-directed learning and a roadmap to success that works! Ina language most of us can relate to!

YET HERE'S WHAT'S CRAZY...

Our books are banned in prison! Yes, in prison systems across the country. Not just the self-empowerment guide, even science-based texts like *The Science of Self* are banned!

You don't just get a reprimand for reading our books, **you go to the hole!**

Solitary confinement. 23 hour lockdown.

For inhumane stretches of time. For *reading self-help literature?*

WHAT YOU SHOULD KNOW

Here's what anyone should know about these books.

1. **There's never been an incident of violence or unrest related to our books or their readers.** Yet these books are considered a "security threat" because they "threaten the functioning" of some facilities. What functions are being threatened by inmates reading and becoming study-oriented and wanting to improve themselves and help others?

2. **The books don't increase criminality!** Despite the attention-catching headlines, this book shows people how and why NOT to be criminal, and how to live righteously. They explore the risks of poor choices and how to live wisely for a better future. Who does this threaten?

3. **Mental health goes UP when people read.** When they read empowering literature, they are less likely to engage in self-destructive behavior and spend less time stressing and reacting!

4. **Recidivism goes DOWN when you read our books.** When young warriors enter the prison system and encounter our books and the guidance that comes with them, they rarely reoffend! Is this ultimately what threatens the functioning of these facilities? That prisoners don't come back?

5. **Book banning is like slavery!** In fact, since prison remains the only legal form of slavery not abolished by the Constitution or its Amendments, perhaps literate and self-motivated people are indeed a threat to the functioning of the system.

Prisons are profitable - **is recidivism the goal?** Are we being targeted for cutting into the free labor that keeps this industry in business? Who thinks this is wrong?

Is this why Michelle Alexander's *The New Jim Crow* was once banned in prisons as well? Was it dangerous for Black people to learn that prison was modern day slavery because it might shake some out of accepting that lot as their life? What do our books do that warrants them still being on this ban list?

IF PRISON ISN'T SLAVERY, WHY IS LITERACY SO DANGEROUS?

Why are inmates treated so harshly simply for owning *The Science of Self*, a scientific text full of references on geneology, astronomy, and evolutionary history? Or a health text called *The Hood Health Handbook*? Or a history book on ancient Black civilizations?

What do the prisoners forced into solitary as a "security threat group" for owning a book called *Knowledge of Self* or *Black God* have to denounce about themselves to get free? It just sounds crazy.

These books are used in universities and schools, so we're sure they don't espouse hatred - only self love and self development. They're also nonfiction works full of references. So what's really happening here?

We know prison education program push profits over people and typically don't help. Our books do. Is that the problem?

Are educated Black and Hispanic (or Indigenous/Native) people *that scary* - **that books teaching ancestral values and self-empowerment must be** *banned* - **and people who have done nothing else "wrong" must be thrown in 23 hour SOLITARY CONFIEMENT** *simply for having them in their possession?*

LET'S MAKE A CHANGE!

All that to say - time for our books and readers to be given a break!

If you're of moral conscience, you know there's no good reason for any of it.

I considered editing each line that some official had cited as their "evidence" these books could cause problems, but I soon realized I could rewrite the books in full and they'd still end up blocked somehow.

That's when I realized this was a **First Amendment** kind of situation, and predominantly Black and Hispanic people are being stripped of their civil and human rights! Meanwhile, you can find white nationalist literature like *Mein Kampf* in many prison libraries! Something is seriously wrong here!

Rather than spend our time trying to change these books any further, I'd like to raise a demand for prisoners to be given their rights, including the right to educate themselves and read empowering literature that changes lives.

HOW TO GET INVOLVED

Lend your voice against the squashing of literacy among those who can benefit most from it - those incarcerated and with opportunity to truly "rehabilitate" themselves, end recidivism, and help others to grow as they have. You can sign a petition supporting this cause at supremedesignonline.com/petition

At our site you'll find other ways to get involved with our campaign to increase literacy and entrepreneurship everywhere its needed most!

For those without internet access, you can write in at Supreme Design, PO Box 10887, Atlanta GA 30310 with a SASE for a reply by mail.

OTHER WAYS TO SUPPORT SUPREME DESIGN

Supreme Design is dedicated to "Reinventing the World" by raising solutionaries, people who find the answers and apply them to all problems we encounter. We build the future by teaching tomorrow's leaders. We've built a righteous family around our endeavors, and we thank you for your support and companionship.

Want to support our mission? There's plenty of ways to spread awareness and empowerment:

1. Share our social and our site with anyone you think would benefit!
2. Sign up for our emails and share them too
3. Write reviews and comments promoting what we do
4. Join our sales and promotional teams
5. Write a blog or post a video about what you've learned from us!

6. Take people to a bookstore that carries our books
7. Visit a local library and request our books
8. Develop lesson plans or programs using our books
9. Start a bookclub or study group using our books
10. Introduce the books to a college or university professor
11. Donate our books to an indepenent Black school
12. Donate our books to a local homeless or women's shelter
13. Donate our books to halfway house or group home
14. Incorporate our books into your own media projects
15. Mention one of our books every chance you get!

We love when you talk and post about us! Tag us or email us when you do. We want to support you back!

Want early access to everything we do, including our events and book releases? Join our promotional team! You can get an idea of what we're looking for by reading the blogs at our site and following our social media where we post opportunities to work with us!

You can also contribute to our books by sharing your own local solutions and success stories. We have some very specific needs and guidelines! For details on our upcoming projects and what we're looking for (as well as everything above), visit supremedesignonline.com and get started!

HOW TO LEARN THE SOLUTIONARY WAY

Ready to see real change? We do! How? Teaching and learning what works. That's what it means to **#BeSolutionary!**

We started with the curriculum – you all showed us it could be used anywhere – so now we're building an educational system that you can access anywhere – a true school without walls! For our needs!

We're working on homeschooling programs and children's curriculum, as well as real-world learning for adults – teaching industry, science, law, art, and mathematics.

Currently, you can take advantage of their #homeschooling #independentpublishing and #buildyourbusiness programs.

Homeschooling: www.ourbestschools.com

SelfPublishing: www.provenpublishing.com

BuildYourBusiness: www.righteousfamily.com

TSI in its early stages, but growing daily. It's a member of Righteous Family, a business network geared towards entrepreneurship and the rebuilding of our communities. Sign up at righteousfamily.com

START A BOOKSTORE!

Did you know you can start a bookstore for your local community, with as little as $60? Yes! When you visit supremedesignonline.com and take advantae of one of our package deals, you can use the books to build your dream #homeschoolinglibrary or #lendinglibrary.

You can just as easily start a bookstore, out of your living room, the trunk of your car, a rolling cart, an ice cream truck, the corner of someone's barbershop or convenience store, the possibilities are endless.

Why not hit hair salons and festivals with books in your bag? You could even go to door to door like a Mormon, except you're pushing knowledge of self and better health! Who doesn't want that?

The books kinda sell themselves. We even provide you some materials that can help. You've just gotta get yourself out there! Social media is cool, but really getting "social" goes much further! Use your talents to promote yourself as an entreprepreneur because this could be part of your path upwards! You could turn your experience into a book that could sell alongside ours!

Selling books isn't bad money either. For example, our best package deal can make you $520 off an investment of $200. Not bad huh?

Feeling rich-poor? Want to save even more? Use my promo code RIGHTEOUSFAMILY when you order and you'll get 10% off anything at the site, including the already discounted package deals.

Want your own promo code? If you join our sales and marketing team, you can get cashback on your own (discounted) purchases AND 5% of all sales made using your code. You can also help us start some local bookclubs and study groups!

We're putting out a ton of new guides and handbooks to success (in every area of life) so you'll be seeing our books everywhere soon. Why not be a part of the process?

We're really pushing to bring books and self-knowledge back! Remember the days when people discussed books in barber shops and hair salons – and sold them on street corners? We're bringing that era back in a new way – with you! **Let's make it happen!** Peace to the Gods and Earths, and all the Righteous Family across the Universe!

PREFACE TO THE 6ᵀᴴ EDITION

Back in 2008, I had no idea a book like this could become a bestseller. Thousands and thousands of copies later, it's clear that this book is much bigger than that. It's basically spawned a movement, one where people like you actively change entire communities.

When I first wrote this thing, I produced something that was a little different from other books. You see, this is a self-help book, but not really. It's a blend of Black history, urban gossip, hood stories, social commentary, game, business education, relationship advice, and the laws of the universe, all kinda rolled up into one big Swisher.

It's been a few years since this book first came out, so there are some stories that might be a little old by now. But this ain't a damn almanac so I'm not doing updates every year. After all, the LESSONS are gonna be consistent, and whoever I was talking about THEN, there's probably someone in that exact same position NOW.

I made a few updates in previous edition, cleaned up some of the typos (meaning there's still about 53), and added a few notes here and there...but it's 2013, and this book is heretofore being published exactly as is. I'm not exactly sure what "heretofore" means but it sounds right.

On another note, there's a LOT this book covers. I mean, EVERYTHING, from dope to divinity, or from rappers to revolution. But there's also things we don't get too deep on. That's what you'll find in Part Two, in Knowledge of Self, in The Hood Health Handbook, and so on. Yeah, basically, this book is what led to us creating our entire catalogue. Whatever we missed, trust us, we're covering it. (Check www.supremedesignpublishing.com for the latest)

With that said, please enjoy the following book. If you don't like it, you're probably a really fucked up person inside anyway. But hell, you've got a good book in your hands, so maybe reading it can help you.

In solidarity in our struggle,

Supreme Understanding

DEDICATION

To my family. Thank you for your patience and understanding.

To my Almighty Nation, and all those who have assisted me on my journey. Thank you for your guidance and support. I'm paying it forward.

To all my haters. Thank you for the motivation. Without you, I wouldn't be determined to be the best in everything I do.

Foreword

"FREEWAY" RICK ROSS

Thirty **years ago,** I was in the streets when a man who I *thought* was my friend introduced me to cocaine. I ran it…and then I *ran with it.* I was good at what I did. The streets, the government, the media, all said I was responsible for the distribution of cocaine from the west coast all the way to the midwest. An operation, they say, that brought in at least a million dollars a day. I didn't see an end in sight.

Then the inevitable happened.

Thirty years later, things are different…for me at least. I've long since changed my mentality and my outlook on life and success. I eat different now. I haven't even watched television or listened to music in three years. When I started out selling cocaine, I was functionally illiterate – but while held captive, I'd already read over 200 books when a fellow inmate introduced me to a book called *How to Hustle and Win.* It claimed to be "a survival guide for the ghetto." Sounded interesting. In this book, I saw the stories of people I either knew personally or had heard about. But most importantly, I read MY story and the stories of people just like me.

I read about people who were in my same situation, both past and present. I was able to see step-by-step how I could have avoided certain pitfalls. But never one to dwell on my past, I also learned how to capitalize on my successes and natural abilities.

There were things in the book that I was up on, as well as things I had forgotten, so I could confirm the truth of it all 100%. *How to Hustle and*

Win is strictly for the hood. It is a powerful book that every hustler, male or female, should pick up and read. Not only is the book inspirational, but it will also enlighten the minds of our trapped and confused youth. It's rare you come across a book like this.

It was about time somebody taught hustlers how to flip their income into legit business. This was a subject near and dear to my heart, since I owned everything from real estate to movie theaters. In fact, I was nicknamed "Freeway" Ricky because I owned so many properties off of Los Angeles' Harbor Freeway. I learned that part of the game and did it well, but I had to learn the hard way about how this game *really* works. Needless to say, even major players get played…daily.

In prison, I put a lot of people up on game. I saw that Supreme Understanding had the same vision. I know how to recognize a product that has the destiny to change the face of the earth. I always did. Much like I did when I got into the drug game, I read the book and ran with it. I actually began selling copies of *How to Hustle and Win* inside the penitentiary…and I witnessed firsthand the changes it helped people make. The biggest change, I think, is when people start making real sacrifices in the name of Life and Freedom…over Money and Luxury.

Some pursue greatness and claim it as theirs, while others wait for greatness to knock on their door one day. I don't have to tell you that this day hardly ever comes. This being the case, we have to Hustle and Win. I've made many sacrifices on both sides of the wall, both physical and mental. In the end, I *won*. But it wasn't easy. **In order to "win the game," you have to *change it*.** And that's exactly what I did.

I changed my outlook on life – leaving my spirit intact – without ever changing my principles. I've heard some question my actions based upon a lack of understanding of my case, the world at hand, or a severe misunderstanding of the code of the streets. Let me educate you. If you investigate thoroughly, it was *my case* that brought to light how the U.S. Government was *responsible* for bringing drugs into the country. And I took down cops (the "Rick Ross Task Force") who were my enemies (but never my partners). These cops were known for planting drugs on and framing innoce nt people. Taking down these officers, I was able to FREE 150 soldiers from prison.

Yes, I moved a lot of a weight, but I also shouldered some of that very same weight when it came time to be a man. I now take full responsibility for my actions, as well as their repercussions, but I can't live or dwell in the past. I can't talk to you about kilos. I can, however, tell you all about pounds and ounces: *An ounce of prevention is better than a pound of cure.*

Reading *How to Hustle and Win* is part of the prevention. But if you've already found yourself a bit over your head – it can also be the cure. The ghetto is a trap and if you want to survive, it's time for you to take control of your life. Read this book and take your first step out of the grave…and into life. The principles of *How to Hustle and Win* have been my passport to the world, my language, and my livelihood.

– "Freeway" Rick Ross,

American Gangster

Rick Ross is one of the most famous hustlers of our era. Even while incarcerated, his name resounded so firmly in urban lore that rappers have made careers out of impersonating him. He has been featured in dozens of magazines, newspapers, television programs and documentary films. His story is also documented in the sequel to this book, *Rap, Race and Revolution: Solutions for Our Struggle.*

Free as of Fall 2009, Rick Ross has dedicated himself to changing the game he helped create. His many projects include an upcoming book, titled *Diamond Lane,* and a feature film titled *The Life Story of Freeway Ricky Ross.* He is currently looking for artists, actors, and models for future endeavors.

You can learn more about Freeway Rick Ross at his online blog at **freewayenterprise.blogspot.com**

Also make sure to check out his social networking site **www.freewayenterprise.com**, which features the latest in hiphop and urban issues. For all business matters, he can be reached at rickross90746@gmail.com

TABLE OF CONTENTS

PART ONE

FOREWORD 4
INTRODUCTION 10
WINNING THE GAME.. 10
IS THIS BOOK FOR YOU?.. 11
WHAT THIS BOOK IS *NOT*... 12
WHY THIS BOOK WAS WRITTEN 13
2 PARTS – WHAT 4?.. 14
HOW TO READ THIS BOOK 16

WHO ARE YOU?... 18
QUIZ ONE: IDENTITY AND IDEAS 19
THREE KILOS OF COLOMBIAN COKE 21
JAY-Z AND EMINEM: YOU SCARED TO BE YOU?............... 23
26 REASONS TO STAY OUT THE GAME................................. 24
DIRTY MONEY... 28
5 THINGS YOU CAN DO TO GET OUT THE GAME............. 31
CASH MONEY AND BAMBOO.. 32
AKON'S STORY: IT'S ON YOU 33
THE BLAME GAME 35
UGLY ASS FISH.. 36
ARE YOU A NIGGA OR NOT?.. 39
IMAGE IS EVERYTHING? 41
EDUCATION DOESN'T MEAN SCHOOL................................ 44
STUPID IS AS STUPID DOES 48
BLACK IS BEAUTIFUL 51
HUSTLERS CAN BE BRILLIANT.. 53
9 SIGNS WE AIN'T STUPID 54
CAN YOU STAND ALONE?... 57
BORN ALONE, DIE ALONE 59
WHAT THEY LEFT OUT ABOUT SLAVERY 61
DRIVE-BYS AND CADILLACS.. 65
TWO BIG ROBBERIES.. 68
DO THE KNOWLEDGE 70
MENTAL ILLNESSES IN THE BLACK COMMUNITY.......... 72
FIND THE STASH SPOTS 78
THE SUPREME TEAM.. 79
REVIEW 81

WALK THE TALK 83
QUIZ TWO: APPROACH TO LIFE AND SITUATIONS 84
STOP SNITCHIN'.. 86
TELLIN' ON YOURSELF 88
SILENCE IS GOLDEN 89
PULL UP MY PANTS?... 92
26 SIGNS YOU'RE DYING FOR ATTENTION 93
THE WRONG FOODS 95
17 POISONS.. 96
WORD IS BOND 97
THE POWER IN WORDS.. 98
TALKING WHITE 102

THE NAMES WE CALL OURSELVES....................................104
THUG VS. SOLDIER 108
SOULJA 4 LIFE..108
50 CENT: A LIFE OF LIES...114
THE KING OF CRUNK...117
STUCK ON THE CORNER..119
THE XXX YEARS..122
MANHOOD 123
LIFE IS THE BEST TEACHER 124
ADVICE FOR A YOUNG PLAYA..125
TRAPPED 127
HOW TO GO TO JAIL..129
THE "STOP LYIN'" CAMPAIGN 130
PLAYING DUMB..132
REALITY CHECK..133
SUCKERS AND HUSTLERS 134
A FAILURE TO COMMUNICATE...136
FIGURES OF SPEECH..138
REVIEW..144
CHECK YOURSELF **146**
QUIZ THREE: VIEWS AND THINKING................................147
20 COMMON ILLUSIONS..149
PIMPS UP, HOES DOWN...153
911 IS A JOKE...158
THE MIRROR DON'T LIE..161
10 SIGNS YOU HATE YOURSELF..162
HOW DO I LOOK?..163
HUSTLES AND HANDOUTS 165
10 "LEGIT" HUSTLES..166
20 HUSTLING SKILLS 168
THE ART OF THE CON 169
GIRLS GONE WILD..173
THE ART OF WAR..174
SCHEMES AND CONSEQUENCES.......................................176
WINNERS AND LOSERS...178
PRAY AND IT WON'T COME..178
LOSING YOUR MIND..180
IN THE VIP...183
MESSAGE IN A BOTTLE...185
10 LESSONS FROM AMERICAN GANGSTER 188
EACH ONE, TEACH ONE 191
THE ART OF PEOPLE-WATCHING......................................193
THE MOVE BOMBING...195
10 LESSONS FROM THE CLUB 198
RACISM IS ALIVE..201
REVIEW..205
HABITS AND ADDICTIONS..**208**
QUIZ FOUR: VALUES AND PRIORITIES 209
WHAT A WASTE 211
21 DAYS 213
YOU ARE WHAT YOU DO..214
THE FOURTH PATH..216
LAW AND ORDER..219

THE CYCLES OF LIFE 224
A LIFE OF REGRETS 229
JUVENILE "JUSTICE" 231
THE CYCLES OF HISTORY 233
HOW TO DEAL WITH A CRIMINAL CHARGE 235
REVOLUTIONARY LOVE 236
22 GUIDELINES FOR DEALING WITH WOMEN 239
EAT TO LIVE 241
WHO ARE YOU FIGHTING? 245
RACE TRAITOR 245
HOW TO SURVIVE A DYSFUNCTIONAL FAMILY 249
MURDERING FOUR DEVILS 250
DO YOU HAVE AN ANGER PROBLEM? 253
I SMOKE, I DRINK 255
WHY THE POOR STAY WEAK 258
NO PRICE BETTER THAN FREE 261
GUERILLA WARFARE 263
DETERMINED IDEAS 268
WHO YOU WITH? 270
BLACK SKATEBOARDER 271
OUTCASTS 273
TROUBLEMAKERS 275
THEY DON'T WANT YOU 275
REVIEW 277

GUNS AND AMMO **279**
QUIZ FIVE: INFLUENCES AND AWARENESS 280
AT LEAST SHOOT THE FENDER 283
KILLER ANTS 284
TUPAC LIVES 285
YOUNG MONEY 289
STOP CRYIN' 292
BLOODS AND CRIPS 297
KILLING A MAN 301
PAID IN FULL 303
HOW TO GET SMART IN 17 EASY STEPS 306
PAWNS IN THE GAME 308
YOUR SUBCONSCIOUS MIND 311
THE GREATEST… 313
BLOOD DIAMONDS 314
WHO GIVES A F*CK? 315
TO BE CONTINUED 317
REVIEW 318

AFTERWORD **320**
APPENDIXES **322**
ABOUT THE AUTHOR 322
RECOMMENDED READING (PART ONE) 323
BLACK INVENTORS (INVENTIONS A-L) 325
POLITICAL PRISONERS IN THE U.S. 327
HOW TO WIN FRIENDS AND INFLUENCE PEOPLE 329
THE SEVEN HABITS OF HIGHLY EFFECTIVE PEOPLE 330
ARTISTS DON'T MAKE MONEY FROM RECORD DEALS 331
WHAT TO DO IF YOU'RE STOPPED BY THE POLICE 333
WHAT DO YOU DO NOW? 335

Introduction

"Anytime you see someone more successful than you are, they are doing something you aren't." Malcolm X

WINNING THE GAME

As the rapper Jim Jones has said, "You respect my mind, or respect my grind." He was on to something. In this game, you either think smarter, or work harder, if you plan to survive. Otherwise, you might as well kill yourself now. Because this is a dirty game, and it's made to wear you down…until nothing's left. And if that isn't death, what's death?

Now, let's be clear. The word "survive" means getting out, because staying trapped ain't survival in any sense of the word. When I say survival, I'm talking about success. After all, there's nothing less we deserve.

There's no reason you should come up out of all that hell, and not be strong as hell, and smart as hell, at least enough to be successful as hell.

But most of us don't stand a chance in hell of "making it." That's why we live for the moment, focused on the next time we'll ride high, while still living down the lows from the last time things went wrong. While folks on the other side of the fence are eatin the whole pie, it's like we're trapped in a hole, hoping a few crumbs fall over to our side.

And boy, do we fight hard for OUR side. After all, it's all we have. We have to go hard for anything we need in life, and the first thing any man needs is his dignity and self-respect. That's why we'll kill over pride, spill blood for our side, and be the first to ride or die…

Somewhere in the process, we forget that the first time someone told us "ride or die" it was on a slave ship. And the first side, was the west side...of Africa...before we were tricked into taking sides, and takin rides...back when "taking a dive" meant jumping overboard to a cold death before we let them trap us in slavery.

Nowadays, the traps are everywhere, and some of us don't even feel trapped. Some of us are even part of the trap itself...but I can't blame you. We've watched the world abandon us...or so we thought...thinking that the only way to "get right" was to "get it by any means." In the process, we forgot ourselves...and each other.

Little did we know that the world hadn't forgotten us at all. In fact, the poor people of the world – the Black, brown, red, and yellow people of the world – they were waiting on us to rise up. They're still waiting on us to rise up. That's why the world follows every trend set by the Black man. If the Black man of America should ever rise up and demand change, the world would follow. But it would take a great man to take that first step, because most people are followers.

If you're up to it, get ready. It's going to be a long journey.

IS THIS BOOK FOR YOU?

If you're reading this and you're still not sure about whether you're the type of person who would benefit from this book, I'll give you a few hints on how to tell. This book is meant for you if:

❏ You've always been intelligent, but hated school because they only taught bullsh*t.

❏ You see the injustices and wrongs going on all around you, and it's driving you nuts.

❏ You want to change something in the world or in yourself, but haven't figured out how.

❏ You know you're not just another "nigga."

❏ You're trying to turn your life around, but without church or the military!

❏ You're not waiting on Jesus to come back and save you.

❏ You wonder why other people are such followers and hypocrites.

❏ You know there's more to life than this.

❏ You're ALWAYS questioning things.

❏ You're able to take responsibility for the things that are happening in your life (without blaming it on someone else or "the devil")

❑ You're not scared to challenge the things most people believe.

❑ You want better for yourself, your family, and/or your people.

If you responded "yeah" to any of these questions, then do yourself a favor and read this book from cover to cover. If nothing in here sparks your mind, then either you know it all already, or you're braindead.

I tried to make this book an all-you-can-eat for your brain. There's stuff in here that you'll think is stupid, stuff that's funny, and stuff that will make you want to cry or knock somebody the f*ck out. At the end, my goal is to reverse the way we've been destroyed.

Now, this book is *aimed* at young Black men lost in the ghettoes of America. But that doesn't mean other people can't read it and use it. The lessons and information here can apply to *any* person of color...anywhere. After all, we're all going through the same things, whether we know it or not.

WHAT THIS BOOK IS *NOT*

Everybody has expectations about something they're going to read before they actually read it. In school, I assumed every book would be boring, so I didn't really read much. In the process, I missed out on some pretty interesting books.

Then again, I never ran into any books that truly spoke to me and

---

A Note to Everyone Else

Many of the people who pick up this book will not be young men, but parents, educators, loved ones, and other people who are truly concerned about the young men in their lives. If you know how deep the problems are, you won't be turned off or scared by what I'm saying in this book...because you understand why I'm saying it. I want you to read this book so you can know what's really going on, but – more importantly – I want you to get this book into the hands of the brothers who need it most.

Our intellectuals and community leaders would benefit by reading this also, so maybe they'll stop coming up with stupid, misinformed theories that show off how little they know about what's really going on.

As for white people...I'll say this much now: If you're white and you're reading this, either (1) you know this book isn't for you, but you want to find something to start some trouble about, or (2) you know this book isn't for you, but you're genuinely concerned about what people of color are going through...and you want to help.

If you're in the first group, put the book down and go do some yoga. If you're in the second group, then *good for you.* Just make sure you read the whole book (both parts). And don't be turned off by the way things are said. I could say, "The majority of the world's ethnic populations have been decimated by Western capitalist ventures." But, it's much more effective for me to simply say, "White folks have f*cked sh*t up for damn near all of us."

Now, if you're Black and you have a problem with what I just said about white people...you REALLY won't be able to handle what I'm going to tell you in this book. You may want to put this book down so that you, too, can go do some yoga and kiss your dog in the mouth.

---

what I was going through. At least not in school. Later on in life, I learned how to tell if a book would be worth reading.

I'm going to continue saving you some trouble by telling you what NOT to expect out of this book:

This book is NOT a storybook or trashy novel. If fiction is your thing, there are some good stories in this book, so you should still like it...but the stories are all true stories from the lives of hustlers, gangsters, conmen, celebrities, revolutionaries, and racists. On the other hand, if you want to read about steamy church romances and tough guys who are secretly gay, then that's not what this is about.

This book is NOT a church pamphlet. Sure, it has a message. But it's also full of cuss words and criminal activities. If life were different, I'd write it different.

This book is NOT politically correct. There are a lot of controversial topics and ideas in this book. You don't have to agree. I just want you to be able to think about the issues that your schoolbooks left out.

This book is NOT one of those "take power at all costs" books like the *Art of War* or *The 48 Laws of Power*. We've been chasing money and power, and hurting ourselves and each other in the process, for far too long. Change your mind and your body will follow. What do people of color look like following the business model that enslaved and exploited us? We're either going to exploit each other or ourselves. On the other hand, if you develop yourself into a determined, respectable individual with the right mind, success is inevitable.

Finally, this book is NOT a set of spiritual or philosophical ideas that don't work in real life. This book IS real life, and every part of it, including many parts you probably never knew about. This book isn't just about getting money, power, or the right mind, but about transforming yourself so that you can have all that and more.

WHY THIS BOOK WAS WRITTEN

Now let's get into why you picked this book up. Either you already like reading and thought this would be another good book to check out...or this may be the book that gets you BACK into reading.

I was inspired when I first heard Young Jeezy talking about the book he was writing, *Thug Motivation*, to accompany his album of the same name. Jeezy always said he's not a rapper, but a motivational speaker, and I felt him on that. He commented on how most Black youth aren't reading because there aren't many books out there that interest them or address issues that are relevant to them. I felt him on that too. But I waited for the book to drop. And I waited. Another album came out, but still no book. Then I remembered that the wise don't wait for food to rain down from heaven. So instead of waiting for someone else to write a book like this, I wrote one.

Who am I? **I'm you. Before and after.** I've been through almost everything you could be going through, and I say that with some certainty because I've been through a lot (See "About the Author"). I've come out the hell I was born into, as well as the hell I put myself through...and I came out victorious, not a victim. Since I changed my name to Supreme Understanding Allah at 15, I've put a lot of thought and energy into developing a supreme understanding of everything I encountered. My first experience with the culture of Islam taught me that ISLAM means "I Study Life Around Me." By studying, investigating, observing, building with, and listening to others much wiser than me, I've attained the twelve jewels every human being lives in pursuit of:

Knowledge	Freedom	Food	Love
Wisdom	Justice	Clothing	Peace
Understanding	Equality	Shelter	Happiness

I didn't think I'd ever make it to Peace and Happiness. Now that I have, however, I feel like I still have more to do. I'm in the streets daily, working hands-on with the community. I know that sounds like a great thing, but it also means anything can happen to me at any time. I'm okay with that. But I just can't go to my grave not sharing what I've learned with as many people as possible. That's what I've dedicated my life to. So this book is going to help me just as much as I hope it helps you.

2 PARTS – WHAT 4?

Whether you know it or not, you're in school every day, learning from life, and solving the problems it hands you. If you fail the tests, you get another chance to learn the lesson. If you keep failing, you end up a zero. You don't end up WITH a zero. You ARE the zero. Or, worse, you become negative. Now, YOU'RE another problem for everyone else to deal with!

In many ways, this dirty game is a numbers game. T.I. understood this when he recorded "Be Better than Me":

> Ay, it's rules in the game son, learn it young/ When these haters speak yo name, man, burn they tongue/ Never be ashamed of how ya live or where ya from/ You stack a mil, niggas'll see how far you come/ Without a gun, you got somethin'll make 'em bar you son/ That's a million dollar mind, while these niggas is dumb/ Yeah, they gon get outta line, but these niggas is scum/ They outta sight and outta mind 'til

you visit the slum/ Stay down, stay on the grind and your digits'll come/ Bottom line, you gotta shine no matter what you become/ These streets is 40 percent of your mind and 5 percent muscle/ 10 struggle, 10 time, and 35 percent hustle

It's too bad so many of us are bad at math. We're failing tests daily, and many of us didn't even know that we missed the lesson.

Wouldn't it be easier if we could simplify the game into a little book of problems and answers? Or if there was a set of guidelines or formulas that we could use to choose the best paths in life? Or at least if the lessons to life could be clear and straight-forward?

It really can be THAT simple. This book will pretty much give you the game. It will give you every lesson it takes to survive…and to be successful. There's no way I could fit over 120 lessons into one book, and keep it at a length that wouldn't scare most people away. So I put together more than 700 pages of game, then chopped it in half.

This book is organized into chapters based on the nine natural laws of life. You see, life is governed by certain laws that you can't break or escape. Because the universe and everything in it can be described in mathematical terms, the laws themselves are mathematical. Mathematics is a language of laws that is universal, so cultures all over the world have come up with the same ideas throughout history. While many ancient civilizations have come up with a similar set of universal laws, the only one written for young Black people in the streets were given to us by a man named Allah in Harlem during the 1960s.

The Supreme Mathematics were meant to be simple, so that anyone – even a child – could understand. But the principles they described were vast enough to make any scientist's head spin as well. These nine simple concepts covered everything from the development of the physical universe to the personal growth and development of the Black man himself. There's no better way to organize the lessons for a self-improvement book for people of color than by these principles.

The essays included in the five chapters of *Part One* are grouped together based on the first five principles of those nine laws.

These nine laws are:

1. **Mind over Matter:** Be aware. Examine what you know, and how you know it. Know who you are, and where you're going.

2. **Manifestation and Presentation:** Once you know better, do better, speak better, choose better, and live better.

3. **Reconsider and Reevaluate:** Seek understanding. Find clarity, vision, and perspective on yourself, life, and the world.

4. **Create a Culture of Success:** Transform a strong vision into a strong lifestyle and long-term agenda.

5. **Identify your Strengths:** Find your power within, in life, and in the world…and focus on developing it.

6. **Expansion and Distribution:** Broaden your horizons, spread your reach, and find balance in all you do.

7. **Top of the Food Chain…or Pawn in the Game?:** Be yourself, lead yourself, and put the weight of the world on your shoulders.

8. **Kill Yourself So You Can Live:** Eliminate the weaknesses in yourself and the world around you, while developing the strength and discipline it will take to do so.

9. **Seal the Deal:** Choose the best paths, envision the future, ensure survival, and achieve success.

The problem with many so-called "self-help" books is that they're not practical. It's very hard to apply some of those philosophical ideas and cliché sayings to daily life, especially if daily life is a struggle. So the laws by themselves aren't necessarily going to save you life. You have to understand the many life lessons that fall under each of those nine principles. That's the reason why this book is filled to the brim with so much content.

Each chapter covers a variety of issues (women, money, crime, etc.), but the lessons in each book will all fall under one of those nine principles. If you can successfully use these laws to guide your life, you're destined to win before you even begin. *Part One* will cover the the first five principles. *Part Two*, which is titled *How to Hustle and Win, Part 2: Rap, Race, and Revolution* picks up where *Part One* leaves off, and completes the journey with the ninth principle.

How to Read this Book

📖 You can start from the beginning and work your way to the end, or you can find interesting headings in the Table of Contents and hop around from essay to essay. This book can be read in any order.

📖 When you come across a word you don't know, first see if you can figure out the meaning based on the rest of the sentence. If not, grab a dictionary or go to www.dictionary.com

📖 The same thing goes for any person, place, event, or idea that's new to you. Look it up. If you don't feel like grabbing a book, you can start at www.wikipedia.org

- Bring it with you wherever you go. Instead of smoking a cigarette or text messaging when you're bored or waiting for something, *read*.

- Find a partner or two who can get a copy of the book to read as well. When you meet, talk about what you're reading and what you think about it. This develops your brotherhood, your minds, and your ability to communicate.

- Don't hide the book. Unless you're a total pussy, you shouldn't be scared to be seen with this book. If you *are* a total pussy, you're probably getting clowned anyway. Maybe showing people that you're reading a cool book will help keep them from chumping you off so much.

- Take notes. Highlight. Circle important sections. But only if this is *your* book. Otherwise the owner's gonna be pissed.

- Work to understand every idea that is discussed in this book. If you can do that, I guarantee that you'll know more than the average college student.

- I didn't make everything easy. Some of this book is written in very simple language that anyone can understand. Other parts are meant to be more difficult. If this book didn't challenge you, I wouldn't be proud of writing it. I meant what I said about you knowing more than the average college student when you're done. But you'll have to read more than just the funny lists.

- Finally, I didn't make everything obvious. Some of the life lessons in this book have already appeared many times in your life, but you may have missed them. Don't miss the lessons in this book. I may use the Pequot Indians or the Black Mafia to explain a point, but those lessons could apply to everything from a business deal to the check-out line at the supermarket. Keep your eyes open as you read.

THEN · NOW

WWW.HUSTLEANDWIN.COM

YOU GOT ANY FIGHT LEFT IN YOU?

Who Are You?

MIND OVER MATTER

"What lies behind us and what lies before us are small matters compared to what lies within us.

Unless you try to do something beyond what you have already mastered, you will never grow. "

Who are you? Seriously...pretend the finest female you've ever met just stepped to you and asked you that question. You don't know anything about her, so forget about running game by telling her what you think she wants to hear. What would you say?

"Me? I'm _____."

Was that easy? Hard? What did you come up with? Does it describe you as you really are, or what you want other people to see? Was it based on what you do, what you have, or...who you are?

Identity is a difficult thing. Most of us don't even know where to begin in establishing who we are and what we're about. Some of us think we do, only to find out we're just following someone else. For that reason, a lot of us don't know where we're headed in life, or how exactly we'll get there. We also have a hard time dealing with the question "Why?" Why are we here? Why are things in our life the way they are? Why do we do the things we do?

So all of our answers have to begin with an examination of ourselves. Anyway, what better topic is there to study but the person in the mirror?

QUIZ ONE: IDENTITY AND IDEAS

1. **When things go wrong, I...**
   a. find someone to blame.
   b. pray for help.
   c. feel miserable.
   d. get to work on fixing them.

2. **If I was lost in a foreign country, I would...**
   a. look for someone who speaks English and ask them for directions.
   b. look to the sky for a sign.
   c. be nervous as hell.
   d. find a map and figure out where I am.

3. **If I am behind on my bills, I usually...**
   a. have someone who will lend me some money.
   b. wait for some money to come in.
   c. get really jealous of people with money.
   d. find a way to make some money.

4. **To me, heaven is...**
   a. for everyone, no matter what you do.
   b. God's reward for me being faithful.
   c. the only place I'll find happiness.
   d. what I make it.

5. **Racism is...**
   a. what keeps me from being successful.
   b. God's test for Black people.
   c. a thing of the past!
   d. an evil we must continue to fight.

6. **If I could fly, I would...**
   a. steal everything I could and always get away.
   b. go up and meet God.
   c. kill everyone who ever did me wrong.
   d. explore the world.

7. **I got this book because I...**
   a. was told it was a good book.
   b. need to find myself.
   c. liked how the cover looked.
   d. thought the information would be useful.

Explanation

Take a look at how you answered the questions and see which letter you picked more than the others. Before you read the following statements, however, I'm going to offer you this: Although there aren't really any right or wrong answers, your answers tell a lot about you as a person.

You may not like what you find, but don't take it personally. We're all screwed up in one way or another. Life is about the process of perfection, which requires change and growth. You can't grow until you learn your weaknesses.

Mostly As: The "Irresponsibles" These answers describe someone who isn't thinking with their own mind yet. Either they are looking for the approval of others, following others' lead, or blaming their own issues on outside factors or people. In other words, they're always denying responsibility, avoiding accountability, and looking for outside help.

Mostly Bs: The "Faithfuls" These answers describe someone who is highly religious. They believe prayer is the answer for their problems, and often avoid working to solve their problems as a result. They think of everything in religious terms, and rarely use critical thinking or logic to understand what is really going on.

Mostly Cs: The "Emotionals" These answers describe someone who usually responds to situations in emotional terms. They may not spend a lot of time crying, but they are more likely to become angry, depressed, or irrational, than someone who has control of their emotions.

Mostly Ds: The "Originals" These answers describe someone who thinks for himself, solves his own problems, and avoids the pitfalls of the above personality types. These people are usually the most successful in life, because they know how to create their own success. However, sometimes these people can be too intellectual about things.

Sound accurate? Maybe, maybe not. Realistically, you can't be defined by seven questions. But I want you to learn about personality types and the behaviors they produce. Even when something doesn't apply to you, you should be able to learn from it. After all, you may be running with a bunch of "irresponsibles" without realizing it. Just think, if you ever get into some trouble while with one of them, guess who's going to snitch...on you?

The First Principle

"Mind Over Matter" means: Be aware. Examine what you know, and how you know it. Know who you are, and where you're going.

What You'll Learn

- How dirty the game is, and how to hustle your way out of it.

- How to go legit…and get rich.

- How school and learning aren't the same…and which one you need.

- How to avoid being scammed, used, or taken advantage of.

- Who we can blame when things go wrong.

- Where the *new* Black leadership can be found.

- What any man must to do to survive and become successful.

- When to stick to your guns and when to compromise.

- How slavery really went down…and why it matters.

- Which mental illnesses the people around you might have.

- Who is Black…and who is not…and who cares.

THREE KILOS OF COLOMBIAN COKE

Carlos and Rey had sent word through some associates that some big-time drug dealers were going to be in Kansas City, Missouri, and were looking for a buyer. But they weren't interested in meeting with any small time hand-to-hand nickel and dimers. They had big weight, and were trying to unload it fast, but only if the price was right.

Before long, word came back. They had a buyer. Carlos and Rey drove out to Kansas City and set up shop in a motel room on the outskirts of the city. Carlos with his coarse hair slicked back in a ponytail, and the both of them wearing linen suits, they looked like foreigners. When the Kansas City boys showed up, they were four deep, and the two in back were almost certainly carrying big heat.

Rey, speaking with a Cuban accent, played the role of representative, and translated for the weight man, Carlos, who spoke only Spanish. Still, Carlos's gruff demeanor was hard to miss, and it appeared that at any moment he would cancel the deal. The Kansas City boys were big-time pushers, but there was a drought on cocaine that had seriously slowed down their operations as of late. The drought worked out in Carlos and Rey's favor, on the other hand. They were able to demand a ridiculously high price for the three kilos of powder they'd said they'd brought from Colombia by way of Cuba. Rey explained that the prices were high because of the costs of transporting during a time of increased surveillance, and several of the fishing boats they employed in shipping across the waters had been intercepted, resulting in significant losses.

The boys weren't convinced.

Carlos appeared furious. He began yelling at Ray in Spanish, and Ray unsuccessfully attempted to calm him down.

Finally the head of the Kansas City unit intervened.

"All right, all right. Tell him to cool out. Let us sample this sh*t first, and then we'll decide. If it's some high grade Colombian sh*t, we'll f*ck with you."

Rey laid one of the bricks on top of a towel on the motel dresser and pulled out a small knife. One of their guys cut a small hole into the brick, and scooped out some of the powder with the tip of the knife. He tasted it. The deal was sealed. The Kansas City boys handed over a small duffle bag containing 60,000 dollars and they left promptly to get to work.

Unfortunately, there wouldn't be much work for them to do.

Turns out, they'd been stuck with three bricks full of newspaper. There was an ounce of coke stuffed in the corner of one.

$60,000 for f*cking newspaper! Carlos and Rey were laughing their asses off on the drive home.

The lesson? Like the runner who isn't listening when the starter pistol is fired, those who don't pay attention in life are the first to lose. I was told that "knowledge" means to "look, listen, observe, and respect." I was also taught that knowledge was the foundation of everything in existence. It seemed simple: What can you do if you don't know sh*t? If you want to do something, and do it well, you need to "do the knowledge."

So, how observant are you?

"It is impossible for a man to be cheated by anyone but himself."
Ralph Waldo Emerson (1803-1882)

Were there any clues that tipped you off about what was really going down? **Look again**. Did you notice that I spelled Rey's name differently in one place? Well, that's a dead giveaway there's something not entirely true here. Of course, his name wasn't really Rey, or Ray, and of course Carlos wasn't a Carlos. They weren't even Cuban. Just two Black dudes who knew enough Spanish to fake it. Half the time, "Carlos" was just saying random Spanish words really fast. The Kansas City boys had no idea.

They also let "Rey" decide where to stick that knife. If they had "done the knowledge" for themselves, they would've checked a little more thoroughly. But people usually don't do that. They don't count their change to see if they've been cheated. They don't read a contract to see what they're agreeing to. They don't even find out the side effects of prescription drugs before they take them. Hell, people take ecstasy and don't even know that it's usually got heroin, speed, and crack in it! So, before you cheat yourself out of something serious, start with knowledge.

Inspect and investigate.
It's always in your best interest.

JAY-Z AND EMINEM: YOU SCARED TO BE YOU?

Like them or not, Jay-Z and Eminem are two of the most powerful people in hip hop today. Beyond being incredible entertainers, they're highly successful businessmen as well.

But almost ten years back, when I was into the underground hip hop circuit, I remember hearing Jay-Z and Eminem's early music. That sh*t was awful.

Not only was it awful, **nobody was buying it.**

Jay-Z is now a Grammy Award-winning rapper, current president and CEO of Def Jam and Roc-A-Fella Records, co-owner of The 40/40 Club, co-owner of the New Jersey Nets NBA team, importer of Armadale Vodka, and co-founder of the Rocawear clothing line (which he sold in March 2007 for $204 million). He's got a net worth of about $340 million. That's incredible, especially considering the fact he came up in the Marcy housing projects, slinging crack, and never finished high school.

But the first song I heard featuring Jay-Z was a record called "Can I Get Open?" by a group named Original Flavor. Around that time, the hot thing was the rapid-fire delivery of rappers like Das EFX and a young Busta Rhymes, who was then a member of Leaders of the New School. Jay-Z tried that on a couple of songs. Of course, you've never heard those songs, right?

When Jay-Z decided that Speedy Gonzalez sh*t wasn't him, he reinvented himself...as himself. In 1996, he put out *Reasonable Doubt*. Jay's trademark flow caught a lot of attention; the way it would seem like he was just talking to you, baring his soul, but making no apologies. Of course, it's been platinum albums and history ever since.

Similarly, most people have never heard Eminem's first album. He's sold seventy million records, making him one of the best selling rappers of all time. But his 1996 album *Infinite,* where he sounded very different from his later work, didn't even go wood.

Here's what he said about it: "Obviously, I was young and influenced by other artists, and I got a lot of feedback saying that I sounded like Nas and AZ. *Infinite* was me trying to figure out how I wanted my rap style to be, how I wanted to sound on the mic and present myself. It was a growing stage. I felt like *Infinite* was like a demo that just got pressed up."

"If I try to be like him, who will be like me?"
Yiddish proverb

A year later, Eminem put out *The Slim Shady EP.* This time, he sounded a little more like Jay-Z. Again, you probably haven't heard this album.

In 1999, Eminem released *The Slim Shady LP.* Finally, he'd started sounding like the Eminem we're familiar with now. Between the references to gratuitous violence, drug use, and psychotic episodes (all of which were missing from *Infinite*), Eminem begins to show us who he really is, family problems and all. The difference? About 5 million sales.

What does this tell us? Like the aspiring rappers learn in the movie *The Hip Hop Project,* it's beginning to look foolish for us all to rap about the same thing, the same way. **We all have stories to tell that are worth telling, and that applies to music as it does to life.** It just doesn't make sense to try to duplicate someone else's story or style. **Trying to be like someone else, or trying to *be* someone else, is something you're almost definitely going to fail at.** Whether you're rapping or cutting hair, the surest bet is to be yourself, and be successful at that first.

Eminem couldn't be Jay-Z. Jay-Z couldn't be Busta Rhymes. Eminem went platinum being Eminem. Jay-Z went platinum being Jay-Z. And Busta Rhymes maintained that rapid-fire delivery for over ten years and finally went platinum being Busta Rhymes.

You can't fail at being yourself.

26 REASONS TO STAY OUT THE GAME

26. The fall. The only thing worse than riding the bus everyday is going from driving a candy-painted Chevy on 26s to riding the bus everyday. Just remember, it ain't what you got, it's what you get to keep. When you lose, you lose it all.

25. The IRS. When you start taking all that money you making and start making those big purchases, and you can't prove where the money came from…or worse yet, that you gave a huge chunk of that money back to the government, you're either going to see the repo man or the inside of a cell for tax evasion.

24. Secret Indictments. Do you know what a "sealed indictment" is? It means the authorities are indicting you, and you won't know about it until it's too late. They'll have every nickname you've ever used, every address you've ever been at, all of your phone conversations,

and enough testimony against you to have you doing football numbers. By the time you find out, they've collected so much evidence against you that your lawyer would have to cast spells to save you. Why else do you think the Feds have a 99% conviction rate? (Besides the snitches!)

23. The ATF. Everybody I know who has a gun has more than one. If you've got a couple legal guns, they're already watching you. If you've got a couple guns that aren't on paper, you've got bigger problems if they ever find one.

22. RICO. No, not some Mexican dude. The Racketeer Influenced and Corrupt Organizations Act is designed for any of y'all that think you're gonna run a big empire without the white folks trying to crush you.

21. Bionic Dogs. These police dogs can smell anything. And now they're being trained to smell through mustard, cayenne, and all the other sh*t people have been using to hide their drugs. Plus they got cousins that'll bite a chunk out your ass.

20. The DEA. The Drug Enforcement Agency is not playing. With all the extra powers they've gotten since 9/11, they can tap more phones, review more text messages, and monitor more transactions than ever before.

19. Crooked Cops. They'll single you out cause you're Black. They'll steal your dope and sell it to other hustlers. They'll

---

Did You Know?

Average number of months white prisoners serve for a crime: 24 months

Average number of months Black prisoners serve for the same crime: 26 months

Average number of months white prisoners serve for rape: 56 months

Average number of months Black prisoners serve for rape: 70 months

Percent of drivers on Interstate 95 who are Black: 20

Percent of drivers pulled over and searched on I-95 who are Black: 70

Group most likely to be strip-searched or x-rayed by U.S. Customs officials when returning from overseas: Black women

---

plant sh*t on you if they can't catch you doing what they know you're doing. They'll pay people to snitch on you if they can't catch you any other way. And they'll beat the sh*t out of you or shoot you if nobody's videotaping.

18. The FBI. Even though they basically handed over the drug game to the DEA, the FBI ain't off the scene. If you're part of a big criminal enterprise or a large enough drug network, you're on their watchlist.

17. Five-Digit Lawyers. Most hustlers haven't saved up enough money for the first week of a felony trial. You need to ask any lawyer how much they charge to defend on drug distribution charges. I guarantee it's no less than $10,000, no matter what dummy you go to. Now imagine how much it would cost to get a good lawyer who can actually get you off.

16. Six-Digit Bail. Unless you own a house or two, you probably don't have much to offer to cover the whole bail amount. So bond is 10% and it's non-refundable. 10% of $200,000 is how much? Cough it up. Don't have it? Sit in there and prepare your defense.

15. Petty Hustlers. These young boys coming up have no respect for the rules that the old heads observed. Now the game is so cutthroat, you can't trust anyone. I promise you that one of your homeboys will snake you before a stranger does.

14. Women. Any girl you meet hustling is gonna be trouble. Either she's a bad bitch who's gonna use you and waste all your money while f*cking your homeboys, or she's a good girl who will stick by your side and even carry your sh*t...until she gets caught and tells it all.

> "I remember when if you was a hustler you was a winner
> Now that's like rakin' up leaves in the winter
> And that ain't even cool, to miss a few summers"
> Lil Wayne, "Don't Cry"

13. Too Many Chefs in the Kitchen. Unless you find out about a market no one has ever seen before, or create a new one, there's not a lot of room left for you. There's more boys trying to work on one corner than there are Mexicans outside a Home Depot. Unless someone else plugs you in, you're gonna have to fight your way in. And if you're plugged in, plan to pay your plug.

12. The Pyramid. There's only room for a few on the top. There's plenty of disposable nobodies on the bottom. Those are the ones that come and go and nobody notices, slaving away, while the fat cats on top are making millions, moving major weight. Guess who goes to jail first? Oh and, where are you in that pyramid? Let me guess.

11. Itty Bitty Cameras. They're on every rooftop and traffic light in the big cities now. And they can zoom in on the pimple on your nose.

In fact, the "average" American is captured on surveillance camera more than 200 times a day. There are now at least 30 million active surveillance cameras in the U.S., and the numbers are growing. So smile, you're on Candid Camera!

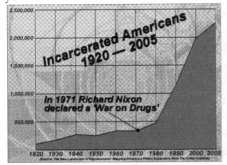

Incarcerated Americans 1920 — 2005

In 1971 Richard Nixon declared a 'War on Drugs'

10. Racism in Sentencing. You WILL get more time than a white boy ever could for the same sh*t. Guaranteed. And if you're on your second strike, don't be a retard.

9. Entrapment. Police informants are selling and buying more than ever before. The police and the other agencies are also recruiting for undercover agents that look more like a hood dude than you do. Bottom line, your homeboy might be a cop.

8. Snitching. You know the routine. They catch two of you, tell each of you that the other snitched and see if you'll snitch for real. Works (almost) every time. If not that, someone who doesn't like you will tell on you when they get caught.

7. Consequences. After you come out from doing some time on a drug charge, you can almost forget about a job or school. It can happen, but it'll be hard. Drugs are considered a crime of "moral turpitude," which basically means you are a convicted dirtbag in society's eyes. Though you already knew a lot of career options are definitely dead though, like being a teacher, doctor, or lawyer, you'll be mad as hell when you get turned away at UPS.

6. Misery. Selling drugs is miserable. If you say no, you're lying to yourself. Who wants to be around addicts all day? Those motherf*ckers are the walking dead, and they're depressing as hell. The worst part is seeing their kids suffering because they keep giving you all their money.

5. Suicide. I don't mean from being depressed. I'm talking about the fact that a lot of hustlers end up getting into their own product. It always starts out real small, but I know a lot of former dealers that eventually became addicts. Ask any old dude that's a heroin addict if they ever sold the sh*t, and see for yourself.

4. No Retirement Plan. How many old hustlers you know? All dead, in jail, or addicted. And there's a few that came home from long bids and they're 45 working as janitors now.

3. The Children. First of all, these little kids are growing up, looking up to you. You may be the only role model they have. If you don't make a change, they'll only follow in your footsteps. And if you have any children of your own, it's gonna feel like sh*t trying to be a daddy from behind them walls. You may not even get any visits, depending on the mother you chose. And if the woman you chose was the type that was with you 'cause you were spendin big paper, she's already found somebody else to pay for her expensive way of life by now.

2. The Alternatives. If you can sell dope, you can sell soap. And I don't mean the kind you trick the smokers with when you're broke and can't afford to re-up. I mean that, if you truly have a hustler spirit, you can hustle anything. There are plenty of legitimate hustles out there for anyone with a little start-up money. Don't say you can't get out the game. If you can flip an ounce, you can flip a house.

1. You're a Pawn, not a King. Sure, you're making money, but look at who most of it goes to. Then look at who will keep most of your sh*t once they've got you. Then look at who the drugs are hurting most. Then look at who is going to jail the most. Then look at who's dying the most. Now look at who put the drugs here. Now look at yourself. Ask yourself where you fit in the equation.

> "By three methods we may learn wisdom: First, by reflection, which is noblest; Second, by imitation, which is easiest; and third by experience, which is the bitterest."
> Confucius

With all that said, you can decide for yourself. Either you can read this information, as well as other lessons throughout the book, and soak up the game that way. Or you can learn about every aspect of the game the HARD way…by going through it yourself. I can tell you now which one will be more painful. But, as always, it's up to you.

You can learn by ear or learn on your ass. Unlike school, however, life teaches the lesson you AFTER you fail the test.

DIRTY MONEY

I ain't gonna sh*t on you just because you sell dope. Personally, I'm against it, but I'd be a hypocrite to condemn something I've done my damn self. And to be technical about it, I'm only against selling the drugs that are literally killing the Black community. After all, pumpin a little weed is not exactly a crime against humanity, especially for someone who doesn't have too many other options.

But let me be clear: Selling drugs should be your last resort, not your first idea. As Jay-Z has said, hustlers hustle out of a sense of desperation, not because of some perverse interest in doing bullsh*t. I know what it's like to struggle. So…I can't knock the hustle.

But, if you're gonna hustle, you need to treat it like the gamble that it is. **No gambler goes into any game, thinking they'll play for ever. They play to get out**. A lot of dope boys, unfortunately, lack that vision. As a result, many of them fizzle out and stay pitchin on the corner til they got so many felonies that they'll be workin at McDonald's at 45…or they move up the ranks and get caught up doin football numbers. Either way, the fast life makes dummies out of a lot of us.

The smart ones are different. They hustle, and they hustle hard. They keep a low profile, and they save their money. They observe the rules to the game, and they don't get caught up in the silly sh*t their partners do. In a few years time, they've stacked enough bread to start a small business or get into real estate. And they're done with the game.

You decide.

> "Niggas in the trap ain't changed in 4 days
> Waitin on a page that's sayin the blow came
> Instead of us just finding more ways to get paid"
> T.I., "Be Better Than Me"

I'm not gonna knock the hustle. At least not too hard. After all, hustlin IS the American way. The Kennedys came up selling bootleg liquor, and I won't even bother to go into all the white families who are wealthy now because their ancestors hustled slaves. So get it how you live, as long as you can live with your conscience. But, by all means, don't plan on getting it that way forever.

This is what hip hop commentator Cedric Muhammad had to say on the subject at www.blackelectorate.com:

> I think a point of reference in Hip Hop would be for us to listen to "Drug Dealer" by KRS-One. KRS-One dealt forthrightly with the historical context in which immigrant and ethnic communities have taken revenue and wealth that they've created illegally and then transferred that into legal, worthwhile organizations, businesses and forms of employment for their own. It's happened with the Jewish community, the Irish community, the Italian community. I can run down the list of ethnic kinship systems that revolved around illegal activity and then eventually over time, there was a transition into what's called legal activity. This is nothing new. Economists study it all the time. People can look at a very good book, *History: The Human Gamble*, by Reuven Brenner. He has written another book called *Labyrinths of Prosperity*, that deals with these dynamics and I think it's very instructive when you look at some of those who may have been convicted criminals or may have been street entrepreneurs who took that money and then put it into the entertainment industry.

Don't forget, though, that when you're Black and building a business empire, you still have to consider some of the same things you would with a drug empire. For example, how do you insulate yourself against RICO charges and the legal harassment any powerful Black man should expect? Cedric Muhammad also offered the following advice to the many rappers who are going through this kind of drama:

> If you're a wealthy artist, then you're getting your money from legitimate business activity, so why would you continue to promote street hustling? Certainly, the hustling mentality is worthwhile as far as the entrepreneurial spirit but if you have a clothing line, you have a barbershop, you have a record label, why would you keep pointing your brothers and sisters to selling crack?

I think that advice applies to anyone trying to go legit. If you're legit, you need to brag about being legit. I love telling people I don't HAVE to do dirt anymore. That's a proud statement, not something I feel funny saying. Not only do you need to project the right image, but you've got to be involved with the right people. Any business hoping to survive an outside attack must be firmly rooted in its community, and connected to the right people and organizations, so that if anything is ever said about that company, everyone will look at the critics or accusers like they're crazy. This applies to individuals as well. It's just like the difference between going to trial with no character witnesses, or going to trial with almost a hundred people willing to testify to how honest and decent you are.

If you still don't get where I'm coming from, check out the spoken word piece "Basic Economics" by Tommy Bottoms on YouTube. You've got to hear it to appreciate it, but here's a piece of it:

> ...It's a very short hop between slinging rock and trading stock/ See, this is basic economics: Buy low, sell high/ Your price determines whether demand meets supply/ See, most of us don't want to admit it or even hear it/ But see, being a drug dealer is the epitome of the entrepreneurial spirit/ See, capitalism breeds capitalists, so if there's demand for a product/ you best believe somebody gonna supply it/ See they've got the right mind, just the wrong grind/...The only way to survive in this society is to have a hustler mentality/ See, as long as you're working for your money/ and your money's not working for you, you'll forever be a slave/...Understand we can't all do it like Dr. Heathcliff Huxtable/ So don't stop hustling, just change your hustle/ See America is designed to get rich/ There's a million and one ways for you to get paid off in this bitch/ And most of them's legit/ Just find a market you want to target, produce a service and(or) product/ And your revenue minus your expenses is going to equal your profit/ See, it's just BASIC ECO-NO-MICS.

Sounds easy enough, right? We all know real life is harder than it looks in the books and movies. But by the time you're done with this book, you'll be able to *Hustle and Win* effortlessly.

When you're in a game you can't win, intend to transcend.

5 THINGS YOU CAN DO TO GET OUT THE GAME

First, launder your money. I could explain more, but it's better if you find someone else who's already done it so they can show you the way. I'll tell you now, you're going to be paying some taxes. Otherwise, the IRS will get suspicious and people will start snooping.

After your money is clean, you can do a lot with it. Here's five things you can do with your money to "go legit."

Start a business. And I don't mean a record label. The DEA knows most of those new labels are fronts for hustlers who never really got out of the game. You're safer opening a laundromat, a used car lot, a tax preparation service, a maid service, or even a construction company. If you're stuck on doin a record label, at least make sure that you keep the business clean, and your artists are actually money-makers (not just old friends).

Buy a franchise. It only takes about $45,000 to start a Dunkin Donuts. And Dunkin Donuts makes money. Guaranteed. So do a lot of other franchises, some of which are more expensive (Burger King, Taco Bell, etc.), and some of which are much cheaper (Jani-King, Roto-Rooter, etc.). Google "recession-proof businesses" if you need some ideas.

Invest in other businesses. Just make sure you make sound decisions. Try to find people who are professional and trustworthy. And make sure their business plan seems like it's guaranteed to be successful. Otherwise you'll find yourself pissed...and I mean *pissed*.

Co-produce a movie. I said CO-produce, which means you're not the only person putting up money. Also, I didn't say direct it, write it, and star in it. Leave that up to the professionals. When you find a project you think will be a hit, work out some numbers on helping to finance it. Those straight-to-DVD titles can make a lot of money, if they're handled right.

Vending machines. Yeah, I know it sounds dumb, but it can work. You just have to buy a lot of them. You buy the machines (about $1,000-$5,000 each), buy the candy and junk food in bulk (that means cases), and set up a route. Then you have your people service that route, stocking your locations with product, and collecting your money. Sound familiar?

It's not about where (or how) you start, it's about where you end up.

CASH MONEY AND BAMBOO

In Russell Simmons' book *Do You!*, he tells of how Baby and Slim, heads of Cash Money Records, got their multi-million dollar distribution deal:

> When a lot of people in the industry first met Baby, they almost automatically assumed that he wasn't the best businessman. He's got a deep New Orleans drawl, tattoos on his face, and more than a few paychecks hanging around his neck...Not the the kind of guy industry suits are usually comfortable around. But Baby got a better deal for Cash Money than any of the suits from Harvard or Howard could have ever gotten. The distribution deal he set up with Universal Records was one of the most favorable I've ever seen. It's become the standard that everyone in the music industry aspires to. What was his secret?
> The answer is that Baby wouldn't compromise his vision.

Russell goes on to tell the story of how Baby and Slim's independent distribution of their music did so well that major labels came knocking, trying to sign them. But these labels wanted to offer them the standard contract, which gives the label most of the money and the least of the risk (see "Artists Don't Really Make Money" in the Appendix). But Baby wasn't going for it. Even Russell himself tried to sign Baby to Def Jam:

> The way it went down was so gangster, he just refused to budge. He told us, "I'll pay you a little fee to distribute my records, but I want to keep the rights to all my masters. Plus loan me a little money on the side while you're at it." It was so outrageous...Someone with a business degree would have never dared ask for those terms. *But Baby didn't know, or care, how the industry worked.* He had a vision and he refused to lose sight of it.

Finally, after watching the two turn down deal after deal, the industry became convinced that Cash Money was holding "a strong hand." Universal came to them and gave them the deal they were looking for.

In Russell's story, Baby and Slim's persistence and determination paid off, despite their total ignorance of business etiquette. Sounds inspiring, but unlikely, right? Especially in light of the other lessons in this book dealing with professionalism, image, and presentation, which tell you NOT to be both stubborn AND ignorant. **Well, it turns out the story is fiction.** After the first printing of *How to Hustle and Win*, I got a few responses from industry insiders about Russell's story. He'd lied. Wendy Day of Rap Coalition told me how she'd personally worked on Cash Money's behalf to negotiate the spectacular deal they'd gotten. Others verified the story. Without the business expertise of Wendy Day, Baby and Slim would have never gotten the terms they wanted. Why? Cause they ain't know sh*t about business! Persistence is good, but persistence alone ain't good for sh*t but getting dissed.

32

So please don't think that you can be successful in business without knowing how the business works, or at least having a competent advisor who does. Why did Russell lie, selling us a formula for failure? I don't know. You figure it out. I *do* know one of the business lessons that Baby and Slim learned afterwards. Before long, their "refuse to compromise" attitude had resulted in the majority of Cash Money's artists leaving the label. Unhappy with their deals, and foreseeing no chance for change, Juvenile, B.G., Young Turk, Mannie Fresh, and others went their separate ways. Even Lil Wayne considered stepping away from the label, looking at significant offers from Jay-Z and others. It was then that the heads of Cash Money realized that – when dealing with other human beings – you must know when to be flexible and bend. They renegotiated with Wayne, offered him the presidency of the record label, and kept their best-selling artist.

The lesson here is that life is not all about money, power, and business. One must be like the bamboo reed. Bamboo is one of the strongest, yet lightest, woods known. However, a constant flow of water is able to break down almost anything. Even rocks are eventually worn away and destroyed by the forces of water and wind. The bamboo reed, however, is strong enough to withstand the current of a river because it remains flexible.

Stick to your guns, but know when to bend.

AKON'S STORY: IT'S ON YOU

Before Akon became an international celebrity, he was a mentor to a rap group I was in, called United Nations. It was called that because it looked like the United Nations of hip hop. There was a Spanish kid, a Vietnamese kid, Akon's brother Omar who was Senegalese, a white boy, one or two others, and I was the token Indian kid. When Akon would come through, everyone would listen intently to whatever advice he gave. I remember him once telling us, that even though there were a bunch of us, many times we would be "on our own." I didn't get it. Anyway, at the time, he was basically a nobody, so I ignored him half the time. I would think to myself, "Who are you? How you gon teach me about this game, and I ain't even heard of you?" That was about 8 years ago, and I learned one important lesson:

You never know who you're talking to.
The bum on the street may be the wisest man you meet, and the
worker slaving away may be king one day.

Since then, I've learned another lesson from Akon: It's all on you. At the end of the day, there's no one you can blame, and no one who is responsible for what happens but you.

In 2006, Akon shouldered the blame for his comments about having more than one wife, which made a lot of high-powered people above him upset (because they also had more than one, and investigations had begun). Akon learned to fall back, and say less. Soon after that, he found himself in even hotter water.

When Akon was performing in April of 2007 in the Zen nightclub in Trinidad, he offered the girls in the audience a chance to win a "trip to Africa" as the prize for an onstage dance contest. The "trip to Africa" turned out to be a dance with Akon. The dance was in the raunchy, "get up on it and grind" style popular in Trinidad, and the film footage was soon making its rounds through the Internet. Why? Because the girl dancing with Akon turned out to be 14 years old.

She sure didn't look 14. And the club was an 18 and over venue. But, in no time, Akon was being called a rapist by the white media. Although the girl looked more than willing, she claimed she "didn't know what was happening." More importantly, she was a government official's daughter. Even more importantly, Akon was a dark-skinned, Black man, and a former drug dealer and car thief. Even worse, he was an ex-convict who was now a millionaire, even owning a diamond mine in South Africa.

First the media attacked him. Then, Verizon Wireless removed his ringtones and decided not to sponsor his tour with Gwen Stefani. Because he was on tour, Akon didn't respond immediately. But when he did, he responded the way a true soldier does. Instead of pointing fingers, crying, or making excuses, he shouldered the blame. In his song, "Sorry, Blame it on Me," he begins:

> As life goes on, I'm startin to learn more and more about responsibility. And I realize that everything I do is affectin the people around me. So I wanted to take this time out to apologize for things that I've done, and things that haven't occurred yet...and things that they don't want to take responsibility for.

Specifically addressing the situation with the teen, he sings:

> I'm sorry for the hand that she was dealt/ For the embarrassment that she felt/ Just a little young girl tryin to have fun/ Her daddy should've never let her out that young/ I'm sorry for Club Zen gettin shut down/ I hope they manage better next time around/ How was I to know she was underage?/ In a 21-and-older club they say/ Why doesn't anybody wanna take blame?/ Verizon backed out disgracin my name/ I'm just a singer tryin to entertain/ Because I love my fans, I'll take that blame

The final chorus is the epitome of how a soldier handles screw-ups: "Even though the blame's on you/ I'll take that blame from you/ And you can put that blame on me." As David Wolf has written:

> Once we understand that life change comes from inside out, and that it is in becoming new that we achieve something new, then we decide to take full responsibility for our lives. The success philosopher Earl Nightingale expressed this understanding when he said: "All of us are self-made, but only the successful will admit it."
>
> You will make incredible progress in your life when you accept 100% responsibility for everything that happens to you. You are where you are and who you are because of one person-yourself.
>
> Take full responsibility for everything that happens in your life. As the saying goes: "When you point your finger at someone, you have three fingers pointing back at you." People accuse others of what they themselves are guilty of.
>
> Winners take full responsibility for everything that happens to them-even when those things seem remote and are not directly attributable to their actions. Taking 100% responsibility for everything in your life transforms you into a new type of person because it forces you to research all "effects" back to their "causes." Understanding "causes" is the science of life transformation.

At the end of the day, it's all on you.

THE BLAME GAME

Mil: Have you handled that business we talked about yet?

Red: Naw, I ain't been able to do that yet.

Mil: What? Why not?

Red: My girl, man. She been trippin. Lockin me out my own house, man. Actin crazy.

Mil: So? What that gotta do with you handling this business?

Red: Is you listenin to me? I ain't even been able to sleep right! I'm sleepin in my car!

Mil: And? How's that keeping you from handling your business? You had two weeks.

Red: Look man, I just told you what's goin on.

Mil: Your girl had you locked out for two weeks?

Red: What? Nah...other sh*t done happened too.

Mil: Yeah?

Red: Yeah, man I ain't bout to be answerin all these personal questions right now.

Mil: Wait. Here's what you don't understand. You failed to handle your business. That affects me. You are being held responsible right now. If you don't understand how that works, let me know. I want to know what's keeping you from doing your job.

Red: I'm sorry man, I'm just under stress. My grandma been real sick.
Mil: That's too bad. I still don't see what that has to do with you handling your business. Why didn't you tell me all this before you took the job?
Red: What? Um, I thought I could handle it.
Mil: So when did you realize that you couldn't?
Red: What? I can handle it. I can handle it.
Mil: Obviously you can't. Because the deadline has passed. I just want to know when all this sh*t started happening and you realized you weren't gonna be done by the deadline.
Red: I don't know.
Mil: Was it that you were so stupid you couldn't figure out that you wouldn't get it done, or so inconsiderate that you just didn't care enough to let me know?
Red: It ain't none of that! See, this is part of the problem! How you expect me to handle business for you when you talk to me like this? This ain't just about me! This is about you too!
Mil: Oh yeah? How did what I'm saying NOW keep you from handling your business these past two weeks?
Red: Man, you know you wrong. You know you wrong. My grandma is on her deathbed!
Mil: Are you being serious?
Red: Man, if my grandma was okay, and my girl was actin right, you KNOW I woulda handled that.
Mil: What about all the other times you didn't handle your business like I asked you to?
Red: There was other sh*t goin on. Man, sh*t is real out here. I don't know what it is. Maybe I'm cursed. Bad sh*t just keep happening to me!
Mil: I see. Well, who am I to expect any different then, right?
Red: Huh?
[BANG!]

**Nothing happens TO you. Everything that happens...
you *caused* it to happen or *allowed* it to happen.**

UGLY ASS FISH

Growing up, I was probably one of the smallest and skinniest kids in my hood. At least I felt like I was. I used to be really self-conscious about it. I spent a lot of time feeling f*cked up about myself.

When I started running with a little group of fellow juvenile delinquents, they were all about brute force. I just couldn't compete. I always seemed to get picked up and tossed somewhere.

So, over time, I learned to use my size to my advantage. Eventually I could squirm out of any grip or hold and regain control. And though I wasn't big and strong, I learned how to be fast. Fast enough to grab a brick or bottle and let you know I'm not playing.

I later learned how to climb fences, scale walls, and climb into windows and openings when no one else could access. Pretty soon, I was invaluable. Anytime we needed to "get in" somewhere, I was the man for the job. Anytime we were doing stick-ups, I was there to go through all the victim's pockets before anyone knew what was happening.

While people may say I was a terrible kid, I think a lesson can be found anywhere. Life teaches us things in the craziest ways. So maybe we can turn all that into a learning moment:

- First, you all should make sure all your windows and doors and entry points are secure before you leave home.

- Second, everything has a purpose. Anything can be an asset if you learn its purpose.

Eventually, I matured and the skill translated to bigger profits. Ten years later, I wasn't robbing anybody. Instead, I was deep in the real estate game and I was working my way into buildings to determine if they were worth buying.

Finding Nemo

The Earth is covered under water on 3/4ths of its surface. The majority of this water is found in the five oceans of the world: the Atlantic, Pacific, Indian, Arctic, and Southern. The ocean is the largest habitat for life on Earth. There are living organisms throughout its entire expanse, from the shallow shores to the deepest trenches six miles beneath the surface.

I'm sure most of us know about the science of camouflage, and how animals (and people) blend in with their surroundings to help them hunt others or avoid being caught themselves. I'm sure you've heard about insects that look like sticks, tigers having stripes to blend in with the tall grasses, and crabs and fish that look just like the coral reefs where they live. But what about when everything is dark, there's nothing to see?

85% of marine life can be found in the top 3,300 feet of water, where there is some light. The space below this area (3,300 to 36,100 ft. beneath the surface) is known as the dark zone. The dark zone is cold (no sunlight), subject to high water pressure (there's tons of water on top of you there, remember?), and nearly barren of food or nutrients.

But the animals that live there, although ugly, are long-lived. Turns out, they are ugly for a reason. These creatures have bodies that are filled with liquid, so that pressure is not a problem for them. Because food is rare, the predators here move slowly so as not to waste any energy, and often wait for food to come to them. As a result, they have large ugly mouths with powerful teeth, while other creatures have different, yet equally unique, means of staying alive.

One example is the dark-colored Anglerfish, which has a head lure that resembles a fishing rod. These lures are lit by luminous bacteria, which they use to bait their prey into their huge waiting mouths. That's right. A glow-in-the-dark fishing rod on its forehead.

It is thought that up to 90% of the animals in the dark zone produce some form of their own light.

Although red light is invisible to most other deep sea animals, the Dragonfish produces a beam of red light from a photophore beneath its eye, to spotlight its prey.

Hatchetfish live in depths where some surface light is still visible. The small hatchetfish is more prey than predator, so it must keep itself from becoming food. As a result, its body is so thin, it is difficult to see head-on. To keep their silhouette invisible from below, they manipulate the light they emit from photophores on their belly to simulate the light from above. Which means, in essence, that it makes itself invisible.

Finally, some squid, shrimp, and worms eject luminous secretions or break off luminous body parts as decoys to throw off their predators when being pursued. That's some impressive sh*t.

What's the point? Everything has its purpose. Even ugliness. So look at what you don't like about yourself, about your life, about the world, and figure out why it's there. Chances are, it's there for a reason. And once you understand the "whys" you can begin using these things to your advantage, rather than as a disadvantage.

Why would a creature living at a depth of about 4,000 ft. have big-ass eyes?

What does a man living in the depths of the ghetto need to survive?

You find a beat-up book on marketing and promotion techniques. How could you use it?

**Everything has a purpose.
Even apparent weaknesses can be hidden strengths.**

ARE YOU A NIGGA OR NOT?

One of the biggest problems we have growing up is figuring out exactly who and what we are. It's called identity and it means the world. Think about this: What if you'd grown up and, all your life, people had been telling you that you were ugly and retarded? What would that do to you? Well, for those of you who know what it's like to grow up dark-skinned around light-skinned people, or light-skinned around dark-skinned people, you have an idea. It makes you feel like something is wrong with you. And of course, you grow up angry. But you also start to believe some of the negative things people say and think about you.

> "It's not what you call us, but what we answer to that matters."
> Djuka (African) proverb

Before long, you're not even trying to figure out who you are, because you've let other people make you. I don't care what you've been told or not told, you've experienced this in some form. Just think back. What ideas did people have about you before you even opened your mouth to speak? What did people say about you that eventually became a reputation? What labels did people put on you that defined who and what you were supposed to be?

As people of color, we have been labeled and put down our whole lives. Some of us just haven't realized it. But all you've got to do is look around. You might be Black growing up in the suburbs, and you think you've got it bad because you've got to deal with those snobby, racist white kids every day, while other Black people think you've got it made. Or you might be Mexican growing up in *el barrio*, thinking you've got it bad because your family's having a hard time getting work, while everyone else says you're taking all the jobs. You might be Filipino, struggling to figure out why the Blacks and Hispanics don't like you, but some of the other Asian people don't either! Or you might be Cherokee, wondering where the hell all your people's land has gone!

Think big. It's bigger than you. Black, brown, red, yellow...we've got a lot in common. And it's not an accident. Our conditions are no mistake. We have different experiences with poverty, but we're all pretty poor in our own way. We all have slightly different experiences with racism, but we all know what it is, and we know it's real. We all know about our own problems, but true knowledge begins when you become aware of the big picture.

> "One camel does not make fun of the other camel's hump."
> Guinean proverb

You'd look real dumb picking on a Puerto Rican or Chinese person. Why? Cause we're not suffering because of *each other*. If you really believe that Mexicans are taking away jobs from Black people, you're as stupid as white people hope you'll be. Realize that we're all being put down…and all by the same people. "Put down" in the sense of being told that we're less than white people, but also put down in the very real sense of being put down at the bottom of society.

"Now who invented niggas in the first place?
And said America is the original birthplace?
Who gettin' 10 - 20 - Life on they first case? My niggas!"
Society, on Trick Daddy's "America"

Just understand this one thing: America made niggas. Without this sick-ass country to blame, there wouldn't be no such thing as a "nigger" or a "nigga." Niggas, Niggers, and Negroes are all a product of this corrupt-ass system. As Tupac said, "I am society's child, this is how they made me, and now I'm sayin what's on my mind and they don't want that. This is what you made me America."

"To deal with this bullsh*t day to day
If I sell some yay or smoke some hay
You bitches wanna throw me up in Pelican's Bay
Call me an animal up in the system
But who's the animal that built this prison?
Who's the animal that invented lower living?"
Ice Cube, "Why We Thugs"

Rich white people think Black people are stupid animals, only good for labor, sports, and entertainment. The old system of slavery was shut down, so new ways were devised. The first is prison, which we'll get into later. We all know who ends up there. The newest form of slavery though, is the way they're working the Mexican immigrants without paying them minimum wage, and without any hopes of ever providing them an education or decent standard of living. There's plenty of Asians being done the same way, except it's sweatshops and prostitution instead of farms and cheap labor.

What does this tell you? Can you see it?

Or are you stuck believing what you've been told?

The truth is that *you* decide how you see yourself, and as a result, you are the only one who can decide who and what you'll be. When you let other people define your reality, you're subject to being as stupid as they tell you that you are. One of the things they convince the stupid among us – Black, brown, red, and yellow – is that we're all different. And by thinking that way, it allows them to tell us that some of us have it better than others. As a result of that, here we are, all of us f*cked up, hating each other instead of the ones who put us in the position we're in. The truth is…as an O.G. once told me, "We all niggas." He was using the word "nigga" to refer to the social conditions we suffer from, under the same system that first called us "nigga."

Today, I've moved past the degradation of being a "nigga" and nothing more. I say we're all Black. Everyone with some color in their skin has that color because their ancestors were Black. If you're light-skinned, it usually just means that somebody in your family tree was raped by somebody white. That goes for you whether you're Puerto Rican, Mexican, Samoan, or Vietnamese. Check your history. We were all Black. So today...as we continue to suffer from that same system...we are all still Black.

It's all about you...but it's also bigger than you.
Your struggle is part of a world-wide struggle.

MOVIE TO SEE

The Untold Story of Emmett Till

If you don't know who Emmett Till was, you must be the type of dude who turns OFF the TV when they start talking about Black history. Emmett Till's story is one every Black person should know, especially the ones who don't understand what's really going on in this great country of ours. The coldest parts about his story, besides his brutal torture and murder, were the way his ignorant-ass uncle sold him out, and how his mother decided to have his funeral held open casket, so everyone could see what white people were doing to our children. If you ain't mad after watching this, you need to check your pulse.

SUPREME THE ASSHOLE ON "THAT BLACK SH*T"

I ain't never heard a dopeboy say to another dopeboy, "There you go, on that hustle sh*t again." I ain't never heard one mother say to another, "Damn, you stay on that mom sh*t, don't you?" But if I had a nickel for every time I heard a Black person say, "Aw, you on that Black sh*t," I'd be nickel-rich.

On that Black sh*t? What else should a Black person be on? Some white sh*t? Some homo sh*t? Some Captain Caveman sh*t? Or how bout some nigga sh*t? If anybody Black tells you to get off "that Black sh*t" do one of two things: (1) Say, "What the f*ck else kinda sh*t should I be on?" or if that doesn't work, then (2) Punch them in the face. After all, anybody who got the nerve to say some sh*t like that ain't bright enough for you to debate history and politics with.

IMAGE IS EVERYTHING?

"They focus on the negative attention
Do something positive, it never get mentioned
(I'm Black!!!) Listen it's a fact

Original man that wouldn't change it if I could, and that's that"
Styles P, "I'm Black"

In the wake of Hurricane Katrina, the Associated Press printed photographs of people holding food while wading through chest-deep water. In the caption featuring a young Black man, he was described as "looting" a grocery store. In the other, a white couple is shown, but they are described as "finding food" from a grocery store.

Google "looting vs. finding" and you should see the pictures. Even Lil Wayne spoke on it in his song "Georgia (Bush)":

> They tell you what they want, show you what they want you to see/ But they don't let you know what's really goin on/ Make it look like a lotta stealin goin on/ Boy them cops is killas in my home/ Nigga shot dead in the middle of the street/ I ain't no thief, I'm just tryin to eat/ Man, f*ck the police and president (Geeoorrrgiaa) Bush

Basketball is a sport where most of the players are now young Black men who come off as "from the streets." Hockey, on the other hand, has always been a white-dominated sport. In fact, the few Black hockey players who have gotten into the National Hockey League have been abused and beaten by the white players.

In basketball, fistfights don't happen often, but when they do, the media and fans say the players are "animals" and should be "ashamed." The players get suspended and hit with enormous fines. Many times, they are looked at as criminals and thugs.

In hockey, on the other hand, there is fighting and roughness in almost every game. In some games, players have even used the hockey sticks to attempt to kill other players. But usually, players who fight are only put a "penalty box" for a few minutes and allowed to go back to playing. The fans love it. They cheer on the fights. It's considered part of the game, and the players are treated like heroes. In July, NHL player Derek Boogaard, an "enforcer" known for his willingness to brawl, opened a "Fighting Camp" in Canada to train teenage hockey players to *fight better* during games.

Keep this in mind, people will judge everything you do based off what they already think of you when they first see you. As a Black man, any ignorant act is going to be seen as "Black ignorance." Any act of violence, even in self-defense, will be called "thuggery." You represent your people, everywhere you go. And the popular opinion is against you and your people. People already think you're ignorant, violent, and good-for-nothing. And I don't just mean white people in America.

"The image of the Black community is horrendous in the world.
The image of Black men in particular is that of a bestial, maniacal and savage group of persons."
Louis Farrakhan

Throughout the world, even among the Blacks in Africa, people only know about Black people what they see on TV. And since they only see MTV, American news, and modern-day minstrel shows like "I Love New York," they think all Blacks in America are ignorant savages. Funny, because all we see about Africans on TV is people living in huts in the jungle, so we think the same thing about them. But Africa is not like that. I've been there, so I know that what they show us is not what all of Africa is like. But when I was there, I met a lot of people who had an even worse stereotype of Blacks in America. Truth is, that's what people think in a lot of places.

Think about this article from the November 16, 2003 issue of the *New York Times* written by a Black American Muslim traveling in Egypt:

> One night during Ramadan, a skinny hustler in knockoff American clothes joined us for dinner. He was one of those 20-something lotharios who haunt downtown Cairo, seducing tourists. After dinner, we sat alone in front of the shop.
> "Do you know the story of Tupac Shakur?" he asked me. I nodded and smiled; I was intrigued that he knew anything about rap and proud that he did. "They killed him in the ghetto," he continued. "I love all the rap, all the niggers."
> My face went hot. I told him he shouldn't use that word.
> "Why not?" he asked. "All the blacks use it. All the blacks have sex and sell drugs like Tupac and Jay-Z."
> Not since grade school had such talk so upset me. "Look at me," I said. "I'm black. I don't sell drugs."
> "Please, don't be upset," the young man said, offering me his hand. "I'm a nigger. I'm a hustler like Tupac."

My brother Diligent experienced the same thing when he went to Mexico and France. Most people he met had never seen an intelligent, civilized Black man before. They expected him to be a stupid thug, and treated him like a king when they saw that he wasn't. This was the kind of Black man they were waiting on. They knew he existed, they just never thought they'd meet one.

You may not realize it, but the ideas people have throughout the world aren't just the rappers' fault, or the white media's fault. Unless you're doing something different, you're part of the problem. Imagine if every African you met was wearing a grass skirt with a bone in his nose. You'd think the jungle stereotype was true.

The same way, when you come off like a dummy, even though you really may be very smart, you're reinforcing the stereotype that they use to make all Black men seem ignorant and savage. You "playing the role" of a gangsta or a hustler is part of their plan to portray ALL young Black men as foolish criminals. Using this stereotype, it's easier to lock away "dangerous" Black men for longer than they would white men. It's

easier to pull someone over for "driving while Black." It's easier to deny somebody a job or promotion, claiming that there's a better white person for the job. It's easier to beat, shoot, and kill a Black man without going to jail.

The worst part is, some of us are so brilliant and sensible, we have to TRY HARD to act as ignorant as we do. We're dumbing ourselves down...for whose benefit?

Let's stop making it easy. Let's stop acting the way they portray us. The world is waiting on us. Let's show them who we really are.

Be yourself, not what they want you to be.

EDUCATION DOESN'T MEAN SCHOOL

"The best-educated human being is the one who understands most about the life in which he is placed."
Helen Keller (1880-1968)

Elijah Poole was one of thirteen children born to a family of sharecroppers in Sandersville, Georgia in 1897. In school, Elijah had barely finished the third grade when he quit school to help his family working in the fields. At 16, he left home in pursuit of something better. In 1931, now living with his family in Detroit, Elijah visited the Temple of Islam to hear a speaker named Master W. Fard Muhammad. Elijah was captivated by Fard's message of Islam as the true divine nature of the Black man and woman.

Elijah joined, convinced his whole family to join, and became active and vocal in spreading the new teachings. Before long, he had become an integral part of Temple of Islam and was appointed as "Supreme Minister," and was told to discard the slave name of "Poole" and change his name to Elijah Muhammad. For the next three and a half years, Mr. Muhammad was personally taught by his teacher non-stop.

When Master W. Fard Muhammad left Detroit in 1934, he gave Elijah Muhammad the sole responsibility of leading the Lost-Found Nation of Islam and "resurrecting the Black man and woman in America." As a final task, Elijah Muhammad, with his third grade education, was sent to the Library of Congress in Washington, D.C., to find and read 104 books that would further assist him in teaching the Black nation.

Over the next four decades of his leadership, membership in the Nation of Islam swelled by the thousands, and temples were built in almost every major city. The Nation had newspapers, books, schools, businesses, and even their own banks and airplanes. By the early 1960s, *Readers Digest* magazine described Mr. Muhammad as "the most powerful Black man in America."

By the mid-1960s, there were more than 60 cities and settlements abroad in Ghana, Mexico, the Caribbean, Europe, and Central America, under the teaching of the Honorable Elijah Muhammad. There had also emerged the leadership of several highly intelligent and powerful ministers, all crediting Mr. Muhammad as their teacher. Of them, two names may ring a bell: Minister Malcolm X and Minister Louis Farrakhan.

Now, what if Elijah Poole had decided to *stay* an uneducated sharecropper?

Did Elijah Muhammad need a college degree to accomplish greatness?

What is the difference between being nothing and being something?

What's keeping you from being great?

No one rises to low expectations.

My Story

I almost didn't make it out of high school. By the fourth grade, I'd already started protesting to my mother, and telling her that I was going to drop out as soon as I was old enough. I hated school. It was bullsh*t. If you can think critically, you've probably thought the same thing at least a few times in your experience with school.

I was expelled from high school during my sophomore year. I didn't plan on going back. But I didn't have a plan. So I went back to school, where during my senior year my guidance counselor told me that I should start looking for work because I wasn't "college material." I might have been a bad ass, but I wasn't dumb. I skipped school, cut class, and did a lot of bullsh*t, but I was reading books and talking about information that most of my teachers weren't up on.

Today, at 26, I have a doctorate in education, while a lot of people my age are still struggling to finish college. I stuck with school, and it's paid off for me. But a lot of the people I went to college with didn't do as well. Half of them didn't graduate (just like in high school), and some of the ones that did are still working dead-end jobs years later.

The way I see it, school and education aren't the same thing. You can make it through life without attending a school, but not without an education. So here's my question: What is education?

Is education getting a high school diploma? A college degree? A refrigerator repairman certificate?

Education is what you make it, and where you find it. You can go to college and learn nothing, or you can know more than a lawyer by the time you're in eighth grade. It's really up to you.

But whether you're getting a PhD (Doctorate in Philosophy) or a PhD (Public High School Diploma), there's a few keys to being successful:

Whatever you learn in life (and learning *is* lifelong), you have to be able to use it to your advantage. You have to: Learn, Interpret, and Apply.

Learn

> "He who refuses to learn deserves extinction."
> Rabbi Hillel

The RZA, one of the most influential music producers in hip hop history, was born into a poor family of 11 children in Brooklyn, New York in 1969. While crack was taking over New York in the 80s, RZA began developing his craft in hip hop. In 1987, he used money he'd made selling weed to purchase a 4-track so he could produce as well as rap.

Teaching himself how to loop samples and make beats, RZA eventually came upon the signature sound that would define Wu-Tang. Using only $10,000, RZA and the eight other members of the Wu-Tang Clan recorded 1993's *Enter the 36 Chambers*.

This album would redefine hip hop and lay the path for a slew of imitators and crews copying the Wu's formula. But RZA almost didn't make it. A few months before they had even recorded the album's first single, "Protect Ya Neck," RZA was on trial for murder. With no money for a bigtime lawyer, RZA depended on himself. He researched on his own, and aided in his defense, which successfully convinced the jury that the shooting death of RZA's victim had been in self-defense.

As Wu-Tang took off, RZA researched other aspects of the music industry beyond beats and rhymes. He proposed an ingenious way to get all the Wu members strong record deals and budgets, while maintaining the Wu-Tang as a group. With RZA doing the negotiations, each member was signed to a different record label in a move the industry had never seen before.

In 1994, his group Gravediggaz was offered their first recording contract. Instead of having his lawyer review it, RZA read the entire document himself, clarified the meaning of a few clauses, made a few changes, and handed it back.

In the late 90s, RZA began teaching himself how to play instruments by watching instructional videos with titles like "Play Piano by Ear," and transitioned to producing cinematics scores for films like *Kill Bill* and *Blade*.

Interpret

A pregnant Black woman lay chained to the bed, fighting to be free. In many ways, this was ironic, as she was a slave, and the child to be born was no other than Nat Turner. Nat's mother had killed all of her other children at birth so that they would never have to suffer as slaves. Now she couldn't stop her master. But Samuel Turner had no idea what he was in for.

Nat Turner grew up much smarter than most of his peers. At an early age he learned how to read and write, and spent much of his time reading the Bible, one of the few books slaves were allowed to possess. But while slavemasters expected Christianity to make the slaves more obedient and passive, Nat Turner read the Bible in a very different way.

By his late 20s, Nat's preaching had earned him the name "The Prophet," and it wasn't long until he began having visions of great change. One day in the fields, his reading of the Bible convinced him that "Christ had laid down the yoke he had borne for the sins of men, and that I should take it on and fight against the Serpent, for the time was fast approaching when the first should be last and the last should be first." By this Serpent, Nat meant none other than whites like Samuel Turner.

On August 13, 1831, there was a solar eclipse, in which the sun appeared bluish-green. Nat took this as a signal, and a week later, Nat Turner's rebellion began. Beginning with a group of only five, but growing to fifty or more rebel slaves and free Blacks, they marched from house to house. They used quiet weapons like knives and hatchets instead of guns, and killed entire families of slaveowners.

Two months later, Nat Turner was finally captured and executed in Jerusalem, Virginia for the murders of 57 whites. His body was flayed, beheaded and quartered, and various body parts were kept by whites as souvenirs. As predicted, it rained after his execution.

The very idea of Nat Turner struck fear into whites for years afterward. After Nat Turner's rebellion, not only did it become illegal to even discuss whether slavery was wrong, the laws against teaching slaves to read were toughened. After all, the idea to rebel had come from a book.

Apply

Frederick Douglass was born into slavery, but managed to learn how to read. He also developed the strength and determination to resist slavery. So he became known as an "ornery nigger" or one who was difficult to "tame." So young Frederick was sent to a "nigger breaker" named Covey, who was known for beating slaves into submission. One day, however, Frederick had taken enough of Covey's whippings and he whipped HIS ass. After getting beat down, Covey never laid a hand on 16-year-old Frederick again.

Sometime later, Frederick slipped away and got free. But even as a free man, he didn't see what he could do to help other slaves...until he began reading. Frederick read so much he soon became known as one of the smartest Black men in the area. He began taking his knowledge and using it to speak out against the evils of slavery. His talent for speaking and commitment to the cause took him all over the country and even to Europe, where supporters paid for his safe return to America.

The white radical John Brown asked Frederick to join in his raid on Harper's Ferry, the only white-led military assault against slavery. Frederick said that his abilities were not in fighting with guns, but with his brains. Frederick Douglass didn't simply POSSESS great knowledge and intelligence...he applied it.

Summary

What's the good in knowing something if you never use it?

What's the good in being intelligent if you never pursue knowledge?

If beating your fists against a wall hasn't torn it down yet, why not try using your head? And I don't mean beating your head against it.

If school wasn't for you, how are you educating yourself?

What have you taught yourself and what will you continue to learn?

One only learns what one teaches oneself.

STUPID IS AS STUPID DOES

There were three idiots who were walking down the road when they came across what seemed like a huge pile of sh*t. The first idiot put his eye in it and said, "Looks like sh*t." The next one put his nose in it and said, "Smells like sh*t." The last one put his tongue in it and said, "Tastes like sh*t." They all looked at each other and said, "Lucky we didn't step in it!"

"It is better to travel alone than with a bad companion."
Senegalese proverb

When I first got that joke, it said "retards" instead of "idiots." I changed it because I thought people would be offended. Well, in this next story, I'm going to say "retarded" a whole lot. But let me be clear: I'm not talking about people who were born mentally disabled. I'm talking about the original definition of the word "retarded," which means "behind in development." And the people I'm going to tell you about are so far behind, it's not even funny.

The other night, I was watching this show called *The First 48* on A&E, and it really made me think. The premise of the show is that most crimes get solved within the first 48 hours, so police and detectives must work quickly to tie up all the loose ends in that amount of time, or less. The show follows local police around after serious crimes, and they show the arrests as well as the interrogations that follow.

This one episode really struck a nerve with me. In it, a 15-year-old Black girl is murdered and burned in a car because she was witness to another murder, and was considering telling the police. Remember "snitching" is a criminal code, which doesn't apply to little girls, old ladies, and concerned community members. But this dude wasn't about to go down for the murder, so he murdered her too.

First the cops found Cheeseburger, who had no alibi, and quickly broke down blubbering in the interrogation room. He led them to Lil Red, who couldn't come up any alibi either, besides saying "I ain't do nothin!" over and over again. Now, these guys were at least 20, 21 years old, and the best they could do was say, "I ain't do nothin!" They weren't even smart enough to ask for lawyers.

"An intelligent enemy is better than a stupid friend."
Senegalese proverb

Finally, Cheeseburger felt like the police were going to charge him with the murder, so he gave up his man, DeAndre. When the cops came rushing for DeAndre, he ran and tossed his gun, but was caught within seconds. You know you can't outrun the SWAT team with smoker's lungs and sagging pants! Once DeAndre found himself in the interrogation room, do you know what his alibi was?

"I ain't do nothin!" "I ain't do nothin!" "I ain't do nothin!" It was like a broken record.

Facing capital murder charges, and not a single brain cell working in his head. And that gun he tossed? It was the damn murder weapon. That's right. He kept the murder weapon. When the police told him about all of the evidence, the witnesses, and even his codefendants turning on him, do you know what he said?

"You got it wrong!" followed by more "I ain't do nothing!"

Of course, they fried his ass.

This episode just made me think about how stupid we're letting ourselves become. It's like we took "I don't give a f*ck" to the wrong level. It makes we worry that some of us don't give a f*ck about being smart, or even being sensible. I mean, who is dumb enough to continue carrying a murder weapon? Who is dumb enough to kill a little girl with dozens of witnesses, and still keep hustling on the same strip? Who thinks it's okay to get charged with murder, and not be smart enough to explain yourself? The dude DeAndre was so simple-minded he wound up basically telling on himself by the end.

Here's the real fun part to the story:

Cheeseburger and Lil Red were actually pretty cooperative. They told the truth, even though it was to save their own asses, but they were still both charged with first-degree accessory murder, which is just about as bad as a normal murder charge. They didn't kill either victim. But they're going to fry too, for f*cking with DeAndre. On another episode, a white guy did damn near the same thing they did (help dispose of the body), and he was only charged with tampering with evidence.

But forget about Black and white right now. Let's talk about normal and retarded. When the f*ck did it become cool to be retarded? When I check MySpace, it looks like everyone's doing it now. Dudes can't even spell the word "money," but they talking bout how much they get…and how they get it. These dudes really be on the Internet (on public record) braggin bout sellin dope, like they've never heard of electronic evidence or secret indictments. Retarded.

But what's even stupider is the way Cheeseburger and Lil Red ended their lives. After all, their lives are basically over. Nobody's coming to visit them or put any money on their books, and they're probably never coming home. These two were actually double-dumb. They were simple-minded enough on their own, but they were even dumber by association with dumb-ass DeAndre.

> "The friend of a fool is a fool.
> The friend of a wise person is another wise person."
> Husia (African) proverb

And situations like this aren't rare. Every day a dozen people go to jail or end up dead because of their retarded friends.

So my advice to you is this: If you ain't retarded, stay the f*ck away from retards. If you are retarded…well, if you are, you ain't even reading this book right now, so who cares?

A stupid person is of help to no one, not even himself.

BLACK IS BEAUTIFUL

"I was born Black, I live Black, and I'm gonna die Black,
probably because some cracker that knows I'm Black – better than YOU nigga –
is probably gonna put a bullet in the back of my head!"
The Spook Who Sat by the Door

Here's an activity for you. Look at the following pictures and figure out

who is Black and who is not. The answers are at the end, as well as whom the pictures are of.

Answers

A. South Indian girl
B. Popular singer from Bangladesh
C. Moi tribal woman from Vietnam

D. Native American man
E. Aeta tribal woman from the
    Phillipines

F. Indian holy man
G. Austrialian Aborigines
H. Emiliano Zapata, Mexican leader
I. Filipino man
J. Brazilian man
K. I forgot to put a picture for K!
L. Andamanese Islanders (Southeast Asia)

M. Mexican man
N. Australian gang members
O. Iraqi man
P. Nicole Richie
Q. Carlos Santiago, Puerto Rican Negro Leagues player
R. Geronimo and other Apaches
S. Baseball player from Panama

Now, who's Black? Everyone in the pictures is Black.

Physically, at least. Some of the people in the pictures may not see themselves as Black, and they may not think Black. Nicole Richie, for example, is someone who doesn't represent Black people. But then again, neither does Condoleeza Rice.

So what did you look at to decide whether someone was Black or not? Was it skin color? Hair texture? Nose, lips?

If you understand that Black people were the first people everywhere on the planet...and that Black people started the first civilizations every where they went...you can understand that Asian, South Americans, and even the Inuit (or "Eskimos") began as dark-skinned Black people. As white people spread, you should also know what they did to the people they found. After years and years of rape...more and more mixed-up people were born, and I mean that in more than one way. As people got lighter and lighter, many of them forgot about their origins. They forgot about the ORIGINAL people, like the Aetas of the Phillipines, the first dynasties of China, or even the first Native Americans. That's why we have great Black authors and historians who have done the work for us. The *African Presence* series of books isn't hard to find, and it tells the story of the early African presence in Europe, the Americas, and Asia. (See "Recommended Reading")

You should also know that Black people don't all have the same type of hair. Many of the Black people of Asia have straight or wavy hair, while other Black groups have the woolly type that most dummies call nappy hair. These two hair types are even in Africa.

Now here's my question: What's the difference between us? I mean ALL of us. All Black people have some very important things in common. And when I say Black, I'm including EVERY kind of Black people. Just think about all these different, beautiful, glorious groups of Black people all over the planet. Now think about what happened to all of them. In addition to being taken over, exploited, and turned into a new kind of people through rape and murder...these people were all taught that Blackness was something bad.

What does that tell you?

Next question: What's wrong with being Black? The same way it's hard to tell a Chinese person – even one from the hood – that they're Black too, it's pretty hard to get some "African-Americans" to be "Black and Proud." It's 2008, and many Black people are still ashamed of their Blackness.

In some parts of India, they would put sesame oil on their babies so their skin would get DARKER, because Black was considered beautiful (in the past). Now, the people of India – even the jet-Black ones – think dark skin is ugly. Now, even in Africa, people buy skin-bleaching creams and blonde hair dye to look lighter and whiter. Wait, there's people who do that sh*t here in America too. If not that, we're chasing after people who are lighter than us.

What does THAT tell you? Wake the f*ck up and smell the (black) coffee.

**Knowing who you are is key in knowing who you'll be.
Start by taking pride in your Blackness.**

HUSTLERS CAN BE BRILLIANT

Jeff Fort was born in Mississippi in 1947. Upon moving to a poor neighborhood in Chicago, Fort dropped out of school after fourth grade, functionally illiterate. At 13, he became involved in a gang that started out fighting off the racist white boys in his community. Fort soon became recognized as the leader of the gang. Under his leadership, the gang adopted Islamic influence and was renamed the Black P. Stone Nation.

By 1965, Fort was controlling a coalition of 21 gangs whom he had united under his flag. Soon after, Fort was able to secure his Nation a federal grant of $1 million for a highly-organized grassroots learning program. In 1969, even President Nixon referred to the Black P. Stone Nation as a community group, and invited Fort to his inauguration.

Of course, the Black P. Stone Nation wasn't all good works. In fact, they controlled a large amount of the drug trade throughout the Chicago area. In 1972, Fort was sent to prison, where he joined the Moorish Science Temple of America. While in prison, Fort renamed the gang the El Rukns and reinvented the gang as a religious movement. This allowed Fort to continue to run the gang from jail, conduct meetings with gang leaders under the guise of religious services, and send orders and messages without surveillance. From prison, Fort continued to control his operations by word of mouth and phone using code. Once out on parole, Fort bought up large areas in the city, expanded his empire, and furthered his political ties.

But in 1982, Fort was sent back to prison, sentenced to 13 years for participating in a drug conspiracy. Undaunted, Fort used his Muslim connections to get in touch with Libyan president Moammar Gadhafi...from prison.

The formerly illiterate Fort was now on the phone speaking fluent Arabic with foreign officials. Fort was accused of making deals with Gadhafi to attack the U.S. on behalf of Libya. Under Fort's orders, several El Rukn members were said to have been smuggled to Libya to enroll in terrorist training, and Fort was negotiating the purchase of a rocket launcher. Dozens of El Rukn members were convicted in the conspiracy, though no actual terrorist acts were committed. Fort was sentenced to an additional 80 years, in order to ensure he could not be released again.

He was shipped to the ADX Florence Supermax prison where he remains today under strict supervision. Fearing that the brilliant Fort could somehow STILL control his gang even under these conditions, prison authorities put him under a "no human contact" order.

Jeff Fort is just one example of how brilliant Black people can be, no matter how little school they attended, or what kind of background they come from. Jeff Fort is an example of the intelligence and ability used in a way that hurt his people, while Malcolm X represents the other possibility (See "True Freedom").

What made Fort so intelligent...and dangerous?

What could he have done if he had completely dedicated his intelligence and ability to changing the hood for the better?

Many of us have incredible potential...too many of us waste it.

9 Signs We Ain't Stupid

The following are 9 ways that Black people, even from the lowest of conditions, show and prove an intelligence you won't find anywhere else:

1. The Numbers Racket

> **Did You Know?**
>
> The revenue that is generated from gambling is more than the revenue that comes from movies, cruise ships, recorded music, theme parks, and spectator sports combined.

Over 70 years ago, in Harlem, Blacks developed an intricate lottery system known as "policy" or "the numbers." Not only were runners responsible for memorizing the bets placed and who placed them (as written records would incriminate many), the people in charge were responsible for orchestrating a lottery system so large that it made millions of dollars from bets that were often as little as five cents. This system was so elaborate and so successful that it was compared to a "street" stock market. In fact, Casper Holstein, one of the founders of the system, came up with it by observing the stock market itself.

2. Pimping

Ultimately, the most successful pimp is the best psychologist. Do you know how cold-hearted and calculating a man has to be to be successful at this game? You have to think at least 3 steps ahead of everyone you have working for you, and understand exactly how to get the desired results from those people. Any real pimp could have just as easily made it rich as a preacher, motivational speaker, or life coach. In fact, many of them – like Bishop Don "Magic" Juan – are getting out of the pimping business to do just that.

Read: *From Pimpstick to Pulpit – It's Magic: The Life Story of Don "Magic" Juan*, by Ann Bromfield and Don "Magic" Juan

3. Cooking Crack

Chef Jeff Henderson was able to take the cooking skills he first learned making crack on motel stoves and eventually become one of the most respected head chefs in the country. Like him, there are young men across this nation who have never taken a chemistry class, but understand the chemical reactions that transform cocaine hydrochloride into a smokeable bicarbonate. They may have failed high school math, but they can work a triple beam, convert grams to ounces, and calculate profits from a re-up while factoring in for potential losses. A dummy can't do that. All a dummy can do is pitch on the block until he's caught by the cops.

Read: *Cooked: From the Streets to the Stove, from Cocaine to Foie Gras,* by Jeff Henderson

4. Going Legit

"Turned a hundred to a million, did it all with game
Turned a hustle to a label, did it all with brains"
Young Jeezy, U.S.D.A.'s "Keep Tellin Myself"

Jay-Z went from hustlin on the block to CEO of several companies. He now commands enough money and power to give "Rocawear" a chance at being the new name of the Nets arena in Brooklyn. But it was the same hustlin skills that allowed him to turn a lump sum into his first album and video (which he financed himself), and then turn that success into an empire. Today, there are thousands of drug dealers going legit, doing everything from starting record labels to buying real estate to producing movies. (See "Cleaning Up Dirty Money" and "10 'Legit Hustles")

5. Drug Distribution

You may not know, but "Freeway" Ricky Ross was once of the best tennis players in his city before he went on to distributing cocaine. What if Ross had taken his talent in tennis, and "pushed it to the limit" as he did his crack-cocaine empire? What if Ross had taken some of his early cash and funded tennis camps instead of crack-houses? What if he had trained tennis instructors instead of dealers? What if he had expanded his business to every major city in the country, like he did with his drug network? For beginners, maybe Venus and Serena wouldn't be the only Black tennis professionals we hear about now. And maybe crack wouldn't be the biggest thing to hit Black America since hip hop. Also, let's not forget about all the ingenious ways hustlers have come up with to transport their product. Imagine if these hustlers took the same skills it takes to create a new stash-box mechanism, and used it to design and patent new inventions that we could all use.

6. Custom Cars

Ride through any hood in America and you'll see cars like you'll never see in a white community. If you've ever watched Pimp My Ride or any car customization show, you know most of their inspiration comes from things Black people have been doing with their cars since pimps were hanging chandeliers in their Cadillacs in the 1970s. Not only that, but it takes a different kind of intelligence to know exactly whats wrong with a car just by listening to it, and to be able to fix it without any special tools. (See *Part Two*, "Old School Whips and Wasted Money")

7. Producing Music

There's another kind of intelligence needed here also. I can write 18 books on 15 topics in 40 minutes, but I can't play a decent drumbeat to save my life. On the other hand, I know people who can't pass their GED who can crank out a beat that takes up 40 tracks and uses 18 samples in 15 minutes. Of course, public schools don't care about the musical intelligence and sense of rhythm it takes to create new dances, produce platinum beats, and sing "Ain't No Sunshine" acapella.

Read: *The Wu-Tang Manual* by the RZA

8. Going "Outside the Box"

Lupe Fiasco wasn't the only dude in the hood doing something different from everybody else. Many people have strayed from the beaten path...and gotten rich. One example is Ejovi Nuwere. Unlike Lupe however, Ejovi wasn't into skateboarding; he was into computers. Like damn near everyone else in the Bed-Stuy neighborhood of Brooklyn, Ejovi grew up around thugs and drug dealers. But instead of pursuing hustling or hip hop, Ejovi got himself into hacking. By the time he was in his late teens, Ejovi had become a career hacker, even committing one of the biggest system break-ins of recent years. By the age of 22, Ejovi was able to fully transition into legitimate use of his skills as a top security specialist for one of the world's largest financial institutions.

Read: *Hacker Cracker: A Journey from the Mean Streets of Brooklyn to the Frontiers of Cyberspace*, by Ejovi Nuwere and David Chanoff

9. Freestyling

Back to music. Many white people don't take rap, or rappers, very seriously. But challenge any English professor to write a decent rap, on any topic, and deliver it on beat. Or even worse, challenge them to freestyle. My bet is they won't be able to do it. Not without sounding like a fool at least. It doesn't just take skill and rhythm to freestyle over a beat. It takes the ability to concentrate and calculate exactly how to begin a sentence, based only a set of possible rhyming words that can go at the end of that sentence, all while sticking to the beat. Most rappers don't realize that when they're doing that, just as most bowlers don't know they have an understanding of the laws of physics. But it's there, just waiting to be used in other ways.

Read: *The Art of Emcee-ing*, by Stic.man of dead prez

There's no shortage of intelligence in the hood. Street dudes are some of the smartest people around. Use it wisely.

CAN YOU STAND ALONE?

I was 15 and it was March. I had plenty of free time, but it wasn't Spring Break. I'd been out of school for almost a month now. I was just plain out of school. After the expulsion, my mother had tried to enroll me in nearly every high school in the country. Everywhere she called, they said no.

I was cool with that.

I was ready to drop out. I'd even made plans. After I'd stopped hustling, my brain had shifted gears to other forms of hustling. I considered buying and selling computers, or sneakers, or even ice cream. I tried to encourage Cortez, who had begun hustling about the same time as me, to go in with me on an Italian Ice cart for the summertime.

My words fell on deaf ears.

Cortez, who would otherwise be down for anything with me, who had even told me he'd take a bullet for me, couldn't follow me down that road. Cortez had resigned himself to his fate. He had no intentions of finding a way out of our urban nightmare. Like a man with cancer, he was tired of the pain, but he was also too tired to fight it.

It seemed like everyone I hung with was kind of weak that way. I mean, I felt strong when we walked 10 deep down the street, scaring the sh*t out of anyone we passed. I felt good when we were all together, drinking, smoking, and talking sh*t like family.

But the more I thought about how all of my friends seemed scared to leave their corners to take trips to New York with me…the more I thought about how they seemed to be scared of new ideas…the more I realized how cut off from the real world we were…the more I felt weak. We all talked about how tired we were of friends dying or going to jail, of being broke daily, and even of our frustration with the police, the government, and the bullsh*t society we lived in. It was hell, and we knew it.

But I wasn't just tired of the hell. I hated it. I was determined to do better. And, even if it meant leaving everyone behind, I had to do what was right for me.

> "I shed tears 'cause I'm told that they'll heal
> To tell the truth I don't know how to feel
> You ever felt alone in a room full of friends?
> Got big plans but you leave 'em in suspense?"
> Rick Ross (the rapper), "Shot to the Heart"

My life went into full bloom somewhere around that time, although there were plenty of seeds that had been planted long before. There were seeds of self-destruction. Seeds of violence. Seeds of alcoholism and dependence. But there were also the seeds of strength and determination.

> ### Did You Know?
> The tsunami that killed millions of people in Southeast Asia may have been caused by the U.S. testing a nuclear weapon in the ocean? In the destruction, the people of the Andaman Islands were nearly wiped out. They were the oldest Black tribe in Asia. The Andamanese were direct descendents of the group of Black people that first settled all of Asia more than 50,000 years ago. They looked just like you. (See "Black is Beautiful")

Out of this struggle, I was born. And through this struggle, I became complete.

As I got older, I learned that I wasn't the only one who struggled with the need for "acceptance"…while still trying to be my own man. In his autobiography *Makes Me Wanna Holler*, Nathan McCall remembers:

> By the time I reached the seventh grade, I'd learned that a dude's life had no meaning unless he hung with someone. You had no identity if you didn't belong to a group. When I first got to Waters, I'd asked classmates the names of slick dudes I saw around school and they always identified them by the group they hung with: They'd say, "That's Li'l Blount. He hangs with Kenny Banks and the boys from Taft

Drive," or "That's Fat Man. He hangs with Leon Bishop and the boys from Henderson Street." Now, at age twelve, I was trying my damnedest to hang loose with a group and get with the styles.

McCall goes on to tell how belonging to a group transformed him:

Hanging with Chip, Cooder, and the others, I grew wilder...In general, hanging out solidified the bond among my buddies and me. Everywhere we went, we traveled in packs of seven to fifteen boys...Through those guys, I discovered the strength and solace in camaraderie. It was a confidence booster, a steady support for my fragile self-esteem. Alone, I was afraid of the world and insecure. But I felt cockier and surer of myself when hanging with my boys. I think we all felt more courageous when we hung together. We did things in groups that we'd never try alone. The group also gave me a sense of belonging that I'd never known before. With those guys, I could hide in the crowd and feel like the accepted norm. There was no fear of standing out, feeling vulnerable, exiled, and exposed. That was a comfort even my family couldn't provide.

After this point, a young Nathan McCall goes on to lose interest in school, soon falling into a life of crime, and ultimately being sentenced to prison. I'm pretty sure you can figure out what happened to most of his friends. I suggest you read the book for yourself though.

But my question here is: Are you scared to stand alone? Do you need to be a part of a group to feel strong and secure? Or can you be your own man?

Keep this in mind. A hyena is a bitch by itself. It can't hunt alone. It has to run with a pack in order to eat, because it takes several weak hyenas to overtake one antelope. Meanwhile, the lion hunts alone.

The weak and fragile must travel in packs.

BORN ALONE, DIE ALONE

"People often say that this or that person has not yet found himself. But the self is not something one finds; it is something one creates."
Thomas Szasz

Marcus Mosiah Garvey, Jr. was born in Jamaica on August 17, 1887. Although he had eleven siblings as a child, all died during childhood except Marcus and his sister Indiana. Garvey's father had a large library, and it was from his father that Marcus developed a strong love for learning. In 1910, he left Jamaica to work in Costa Rica and then Panama. From 1912-1913 he lived in London, where he went to college, and began working for a publication called the *African Times and Orient Review*, which dealt with issues facing Black and brown people everywhere.

Around this time, Garvey had become convinced that uniting Blacks throughout the world was the only way to improve conditions for Black people anywhere. He returned to Jamaica and founded the Universal Negro Improvement Association (UNIA) and African Communities League (ACL), declaring that his goal as President-General was to "unite all people of African ancestry of the world to one great body to establish a country and absolute government of their own."

In 1916, Garvey moved to New York and continued to work as a printer by day, but spent his nights speaking on street corners to any and all who would listen. Realizing that Black people had no visible leaders, he began a 38-state speaking tour.

He challenged the people to redefine their concept of themselves, and to be proud of being Black, which they had never heard before. He told his followers that God was Black as well, and that Black people were the chosen people of God. By 1919, the membership of the organization had reached two million.

> "Black men, you were once great; you shall be great again"
> Marcus Garvey

However, outside forces had created rifts in his organization, which led to splits and infighting.

Unfazed, Garvey set his sights on building an economic base for Blacks by developing trade. He formed the Black Star Line and soon was able to purchase its first ship, which he renamed the S.S. Frederick Douglass.

However, the New York District Attorney's office had begun investigating the UNIA. They couldn't find any wrongdoing, but persisted in their harassment.

Garvey wrote an editorial about it in his newspaper, *The Negro World,* and was jailed until he issued a retraction.

Then, in October 1919, an assassin was sent by the government to kill Garvey. Garvey survived a bullet to his leg and head, and the assassin was said to have committed suicide.

It didn't stop Marcus Garvey. By 1920, the UNIA claimed four million members. On August 1, the International Convention of the UNIA was held and delegates from all over the world came, with over 25,000 people in total, filling Madison Square Garden to hear Garvey speak on the infinite potential of Black people.

Garvey had also begun the Negro Factories Corporation. His plan was to create the infrastructure to manufacture every marketable commodity in every big U.S. industrial center, as well as those in Central America, West Indies, and Africa. Not only that, but there were plans for a grocery chain, restaurants, a publishing house, and several other businesses. (Imagine what could have happened)

Well, what happened?

In late 1919, Garvey was being investigated by the FBI under J. Edgar Hoover, who would soon be infamous for targeting Black organizations throughout America. To accomplish this, the FBI then hired its first five Black agents. When the FBI couldn't come up with anything else, they decided to prosecute Garvey on mail fraud.

Mail fraud!

They created a bogus case with no evidence and witnesses who were caught perjuring themselves, or lying on the stand. Still, in 1923, Garvey was found guilty and sentenced to five years in prison.

Serving his sentence in the Atlanta Federal Penitentiary, he issued the "First Message to the Negroes of the World from Atlanta Prison," where he said:

> Look for me in the whirlwind or the storm, look for me all around you, for, with God's grace, I shall come and bring with me countless millions of black slaves who have died in America and the West Indies and the millions in Africa to aid you in the fight for Liberty, Freedom and Life.

In 1927, Garvey was deported to Jamaica. He continued to work in Jamaica and London, but the millions-strong UNIA had diminished and been dismantled. Since then, there hasn't been a single organization or movement of that size working to improve the lives of Black people worldwide.

Why did Garvey become a leader instead of waiting for one?

What could have easily discouraged Garvey from continuing?

In what ways did Garvey stand alone?

A real man doesn't fear standing alone.

WHAT THEY LEFT OUT ABOUT SLAVERY

In school, all I learned about slavery was that white people bought some poor Black people (mostly naked and fresh from hunting tigers and lions) from the jungles of Africa (where it's mostly naked people and tigers anyway) to do some of the work. Then Abraham Lincoln and the white people in the North decided the slaves should be free. So there was a Civil War, and millions of brave white people died trying to end slavery.

At some point, I felt like things didn't make sense. So I decided to start looking things up. Now I know that 90% of that sh*t was lies.

I wanted to give you the real deal. But I didn't want to do all the work for you. So I wrote up a list of facts about slavery, some of which you may have never heard before. But they're mostly short sentences, meant to inspire you to "do the knowledge." That is, when you see something that intrigues you and you want to know more, look it up.

This is the age of technology, so if you can't make a trip to the library or a big bookstore where you can read for free, look it up on the Internet. The information is out there, just waiting for the right people to dig it up.

I'll start somewhere early:

Christopher Columbus brought Indian slaves back with him when he returned from the Americas, to present to the Queen as a good reason to come to the "New World."

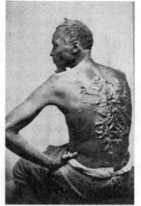

The first Black slaves were brought to the Americas by a Christian trader named John Hawkins on a ship named Jesus.

Queen Elizabeth rewarded John Hawkins by making him a knight. Hawkins chose as his coat of arms the image of a Black man in chains.

Slavery began through Europeans traders doing business with African chiefs, and buying their prisoners of war.

Most African chiefs didn't know what was happening to the people they sold, because the African system of slavery didn't involve dehumanization and cruelty.

As the demand for slaves increased, Europeans worked to create more warfare between African tribes.

When a chief or king wouldn't sell his prisoners to the Europeans, they gave guns to another tribe, and had them kidnap the chief's people.

Many Europeans just skipped the middle man and kidnapped thousands of people themselves.

Black people were held in dungeons on the coast of West Africa, where the men who tried to fight back were thrown together in a small cell to die, while the women who resisted were raped into submission.

I want to stop for a minute while I'm on the subject of Africa. The Africa we've probably seen on TV is a fairy tale. First of all, Africa has millions of people living there. It's NOT just a big jungle full of animals, with a few people running around chasing rabbits with spears. In fact, modern Africa has cities, tall buildings, shopping malls, and – yes – air conditioning. Everyone in Africa is not sick or starving. But YES, Africa is in bad shape compared to America, at least in terms of development. Why? Well, that darn slave trade stole most of the young working-age men and women from African societies. When you take all the young workers away, it hurts the economy and the development of cities, the construction of buildings and roads, and the preservation of traditions and culture. This damage, most of which Africa has still not recovered from, has never been repaid by the countries that did it and got rich from it.

Let's keep moving:

Anywhere from 25-50 million Black people died in the Middle Passage, not counting the slaves who died on American soil.

The historical period of American slavery is called the Maafa, or the "African Holocaust," because of how many lives were stolen and lost (millions more than the Jewish Holocaust).

"Greedy" African kings and chiefs didn't just sell off their own people the way we've been hearing it. *Part Two* gets into all the OTHER factors the history experts don't like to tell you.

Many Blacks jumped off the slaveships or starved themselves rather than become slaves.

The cramped, filthy conditions on the slaveships often resulted in more than half of the people on board to die before they arrived.

So many dead bodies were thrown overboard during the Middle Passage that sharks looking for food still follow that route *to this day*.

Before bringing them to America, slaves were brought to "breaker" islands like Jamaica, where they were stripped of their native culture and beaten until they were "broken in."

Black people resisted slavery fiercely, and whites "made examples" out of many strong men and women to scare the rest into submission. To make an example out of a rebellious slave, whites would tie his arms and legs to four horses and have them run off in different directions at the same time.

Another way they would show the slaves they meant business would be to take a pregnant woman, hang her upside down by her feet, and slit her belly open while she was still alive, and then step on the baby's head to kill it.

Whites also taught slaves to hate and distrust each other so they would not join together to fight for freedom.

Christianity was also used to keep the slaves passive, while Muslim slaves were avoided because they would usually fight or die.

The Pope of the Catholic Church ordained slavery, and used the Bible and the Christian religion to justify it.

Black men and women were shown off, physically "inspected," and bid upon in public auctions. One of the biggest slave auctions became what is now known as Wall Street.

Blacks weren't just beaten and whipped, but tortured and humiliated for even the smallest offenses.

Most of America's cities, towns, and buildings were built using slave labor. Many of today's wealthy white families made their fortunes through slave labor.

The Civil War wasn't fought because the North believed slavery was wrong, but because the industrial cities in the North, which relied less on slaves, were losing money to the South, which was getting rich off slave labor.

Chattel slavery ended in the U.S. 1865, less than 150 years ago, but slavery was allowed to remain in effect for those convicted to prison. (While some countries abolished slavery before the U.S., many others continued the practice well after 1865, and some still do. According to iAbolish, there are 27 million people enslaved around the world.)

All hurricanes and tropical storms that violently hit the Americas begin in West Africa and follow the same path as the slave trade.

Damn, that's a lot to process, huh? Ah sh*t, you might be mad after having read all that. Don't rip the book, please. Just think about how much you missed in school. Think about how much we miss in life by only listening to what others choose to tell us. Remember, there's always more to any story. The people in power withhold the knowledge from us, but they can't keep us from going after it. It takes desire to gain that knowledge however, and that knowledge is always powerful.

Knowledge is powerful. That's why the people with power KNOW, while the powerless believe what they're told.

MOVIE TO SEE

Sankofa

You ain't seen it? It's about slavery, and it's better than *Roots*. And if Sankofa didn't make you want to slap somebody, you can Google *Goodbye, Uncle Tom* online...and THAT sh*t should make your skin crawl. While you're online, you should also check out *500 Years Later* at www.500YearsLater.com.

SUPREME THE ASSHOLE ON "ZOMBIE MOTHAF*CKAS"

If you ain't livin, you're dead, right? Well, some of you jokers are dead and don't even know it. Like a f*ckin zombie. Zombies are dead, but they don't know they should be layin down in the dirt somewhere, so they be up lookin for sh*t to eat. After all, the most basic sh*t a mothaf*cka need to do to live is eat, right? For some reason, zombies want to eat people's brains. That way, more people can be zombies like them…dead and brainless. I've heard that the word "freedom" means having a "free dome" or a free mind. If you ain't got that, you really ain't livin. You're the walking dead…and you don't even know it.

DRIVE-BYS AND CADILLACS

What's Real?

As Maurice Richards drove, his older brother, Irwin, opened fire onto the other vehicle with the assault rifle. As Maurice sped off, the other car eventually came to a stop. The other car had been riddled with bullets, but no one was killed. Maurice and his brother were soon identified by witnesses and arrested. A year later, they went to trial for the incident. Although they were both facing heavy charges, it was 2006, and Maurice also had to get busy promoting his single "Throw Some D's On It."

It became immensely difficult to balance the pressures of dealing with murder charges, while also trying to live the life of the "next" hottest artist. Throwing money around in clubs at night, and spending money meeting with lawyers in the day, this was not the life he'd expected for a rapper.

At the conclusion of the trial, Irwin, 29, was handed a sentence of ten years for attempted murder. As he was only driving, and had no prior convictions, Maurice, or Rich Boy, avoided an attempted murder rap, and was given a suspended sentence.

Dealing with all this certainly helped shaped Rich Boy's philosophy on what being "rich" was all about. In fact, the name Rich Boy was given to him by older uncles who knew him as the son of his father, Rich, and called him "Rich boy" (Rich's boy). It wasn't about money then. But, now, as a rapper, that's what everyone expected.

Rich Boy only went from making beats to rapping about a year before releasing his first album. He used the first single "Throw Some D's" to get the attention of the people, knowing that "what's real" ain't always what's popular. It reminds me of when David Banner released the hit single "Cadillac's on 22s" which had nothing to do with Cadillacs or 22s, and the video was about Emmet Till and the lynchings in Mississipi. Rich Boy has said that, like David Banner, he uses catchy titles to say something of meaning. For example, "Ghetto Rich" and "Let's Get this Paper" aren't about having money, but about the struggles of living Black and poor.

In a June 2007 interview, he explained:

> My name being Rich Boy, I feel like I gotta let the whole world know the definition of money and not on no stuntin' sh*t…It's cool to buy some jewels or whatever, but don't let that be the only thing you want to do outta life. Everywhere I go I let people know that a million dollars is middle class now – but in the hood, that's rich. I used to think a million dollars was rich, too…Material sh*t has no value. There are people who killed somebody five years ago for a pair of Jordans that are probably in a dumpster now.

Appreciating Jail

Similarly, rapper Blood Raw was facing a life sentence right after signing to Jeezy's Corporate Thugs Entertainment label. Now one-third of Young Jeezy's group USDA, he had been snatched up by the Feds at the airport, fresh off a European tour. Blood Raw immediately went from living "the life" to fighting for his life. The Feds, who have a 98% conviction rate, were working to give Blood Raw a mandatory life sentence if found guilty.

Obviously dealing with serious stress, Blood Raw actually appreciated the peace of sitting in the cell, and getting away from the chaos of the streets. It gave him a chance to analyze life and reflect on what truly mattered.

Blood Raw, one of the freshest rap names I've heard in a while, has some background to his name as well. According to him, the "Blood" means the truth, with "Raw" meaning a delivery that's raw and uncut.

As his bio says on his Myspace page:

> It has been stated, one cannot be a true artist without first experiencing pain. If that is accurate, BloodRaw has struggled all of his lifetime to earn the right to be a hip-hop Picasso. That's why my music is so soulful. I have people crying when they hear my music because I'll only spit what I've been through.

In an interview, he explained what he means by "raw, uncut truth":

> I can't forget the struggle. Before I start talking about the money, jewels, and the cars, I got to let people know that it's not really about this – for real.My whole thing is this: Niggas are afraid to say that my old girl or my momma was on drugs, or my daddy wasn't there, or I went to prison at an early age. I've done all of this. I've kept my chest out and

have made no excuses. I grew up in Panama City. It's a real highly drug-infested city. There was never a role model that I know of that came from there. All we knew was the streets. What other option did you have? I say that I am an example...When people really do come from the hood they do everything they can to not go back. If you really weren't there then you don't know the trials and tribulations, so when you get in the game you can start acting all hard and doing all the stupid sh*t because you don't really know what it's like actually being there. I'm not trying to go back.

"Keep It Hood"

The man who introduced the American hip hop audience to the sound of Reggaeton, Noreaga began his career as half of Capone N Noreaga. Both of them named after infamous gangsters, their raps rotated around the gangster images popular in 90s hip hop. But it wasn't necessarily fake.

In 1997, Capone was sent back to prison for a parole violation. While Capone was imprisoned, Noreaga intentionally got himself locked up on a minor charge so he could be with his "blood brother" Capone. Noreage then finished their strong debut album *The War Report* alone. Unlike other rappers who made up fictitious stories, these real events formed the basis for CNN's lyrics.

Since then Noreaga has had several years in the game to observe others' ideas of "keeping it real." In NORE's online journal at www.Hip HopGame.com, he says:

> Man, I had the longest and dumbest argument ever with this asshole from my 'hood yesterday. People get locked up and turn Blood or get with a gang and lose their mind. People don't realize that it makes you look weak. Now if you was with a gang prior to jail and you went to jail and you enforced your gang ethics, that's different. But when you get locked up and turn Blood or Crip or whatever, it turns you into a lame 'cause that's not who you are or who you was prior to your incarceration. People gas themselves up to believe this gang sh*t that doesn't even come from New York. This is a Los Angeles, California thing and when New York people fall into it, it makes our city look like copycats.
>
> I guess what I'm saying is be you and never live in someone else's dreams! Staying 'hood doesn't mean going back to your block and selling crack to the same crackheads you once sold to over 10 years ago. That's not 'hood, that's dumb! Staying 'hood is owning a big-ass house and forgetting to pay your cable bill. Staying 'hood is having a penthouse and all you have to drink is Kool Aid packages. Staying 'hood is going to meetings, talking 'bout millions and realizing that you have an ounce of sour diesel weed on you and you changed how the whole room smelled without even smoking!
>
> I will always be 'hood 'cause being hood is a state of mind and it is not based on being in a certain place. I don't have to shoot no one anymore

or sell any more drugs, ever, and I can still be just as 'hood as ever. Going to jail back and forth doesn't make you a gangster. Making it out the 'hood and still being the same person does.
So remember, who you are is who you are!
Love yourself like jerking off.

Who Came Up With It?

According to Plies, who calls his million dollar jewelry "a bad investment," finances his own videos so he won't have to do what the record label wants (check YouTube for "100 Years"), and won't record with major artists lying about selling dope:

> The term "keeping it real," never came from a nigga that made it out the hood. It's the nigga that didn't make it out that told this nigga, "Hey keep it real, dog!" It's a difference between real and stupid. You can take care of niggas around you if in your heart it's the right thing to do, But if I get f*cked up tomorrow, I'm gonna do this time by myself. These people that supported are going on to the next guy…[In terms of Mike Vick] I've heard, "This nigga stupid, f*ckin with dogs and had all that money." But I've never heard, "That's f*cked up, they ratted dude out." Not standing for something is accepted and I feel like whether you got money or don't, ultimately, standing for something is so important. It's gonna always boil down to me doing what's in my heart…[In regards to people who don't have a background in the streets] I respect a nigga that's never been in the streets even more because he don't spend his down time tryin to convince niggas. Honestly, I don't know no nigga who'd love to be in a shootout every day. I ain't met him.

What's "real" is often what other people have been told to think. Find reality for yourself.

SUPREME THE ASSHOLE ON "MODERN DAY SLAVES"

Maybe you're not a zombie. Maybe you just live on the lowest levels of living…doing what THEY want you to do, thinking what THEY want you to think, living how THEY want you to live. Good for you – You're a slave. A new millennium slave. The worst part is, you're thinkin you're free as a mothaf*cka.

TWO BIG ROBBERIES

The North Hollywood Shootout

In October 1993, Larry Phillips and Emil Matasareanu, were arrested near Angeles for speeding. A search of their vehicle found two semi-automatic rifles, two handguns, over 1,600 rounds of 7.62 mm rifle ammunition, over 1,200 rounds of 9 mm and .45 caliber handgun ammunition, radio scanners, smoke bombs, improvised explosive devices, body armor vests, and three different California license plates. But both spent less than 100 days in jail, and were only given 3 years probation. After their release, most of their seized property was returned to them. By now, you've already realized they were white.

After a string of big bank robberies, Phillips and Matasareanu plotted on their most ambitious heist. After months of preparation including extensive surveillance of their intended target, they loaded almost a dozen rifles and handguns and thousands rounds of ammunition into their vehicle and headed to the bank. They had ordered bulletproof material to make full-body armor, including metal plates to protect vital organs. They had also imported steel-core ammunition for their illegally modified assault rifles and taken the drug phenobarbitol to calm their nerves.

After walking into the Bank of America, they set their watch alarms for 8 minutes, which was the amount of time they estimated it would take for police to respond. But as they walked in, an officer passing by noted their suspicious appearance and called in for a possible robbery. After firing 100 rounds to scare employees into compliance, they were able to get just over $300,000, since that day's money delivery had not yet arrived.

When they exited, they were greeted by dozens of police officers. They engaged the officers in a firefight, spraying armor-piercing rounds into the patrol cars positioned around the bank. Although most of the officers had handguns and some had shotguns, the body armor worn by Phillips and Matasareanu was strong enough to withstand them. Even their helmets and face masks seemed invulnerable.

Several officers were wounded and shot. The pair's modified bullets were piercing through walls and cars. Meanwhile, the officers bullets seemed to be doing no damage. Some officers responded by getting high-powered rifles from a nearby gun shop. Still, Phillips and Matasareanu seemed unstoppable.

18 minutes after the shooting began, a SWAT team arrived armed with automatic weapons. At this point, the two split up. Moving slowly, due in part to the fact that their body armor weighed as much as 3 bowling balls, the pair couldn't get away.

Eventually, Phillips was shot in his unprotected hand and was unable to shoot his rifle. He was then shot by a sniper and killed. Matasareanu was only stopped after an officer shot under the vehicle at his unprotected legs and disabled him.

By the time the shooting had stopped, Phillips and Matasareanu had fired about 1,300 rounds, over 300 various law enforcement officers had responded, Phillips was hit 11 times, and Matasareanu was hit 29 times, and died from shock caused by blood loss.

Troy and Dino Smith's Jewelry Heist

Troy and Dino Smith were brothers who robbed and stole to fund a high-flying lifestyle of partying and luxury. Wherever they would go, they would go hard, including committing home invasions and robberies of big time cocaine dealers. And these brothers were *brothers*.

Known to be clever enough to beat cases on technicalities or escape police by hiding handcuff keys in their underwear, Troy and Dino avoided being caught for twenty years.

In the early hours of the morning, Troy and Dino Smith, with help from two others, broke into a closed down San Francisco restaurant. But their target wasn't in the restaurant. It was next door.

They then drilled a strategically placed hole in the wall connecting the restaurant to Lang Estate Jewelry Store near San Francisco's Union Square. The four then hid in the store's restroom, waiting for the store's employees to open the shop.

When the jewelry staff showed up to open the store, Troy and Dino went into action, tying up the employees at gunpoint. After forcing the manager to open the safe, they began quickly filling their bags with jewelry.

They escaped with an estimated $6 million in jewels—the largest haul in San Francisco history.

What was the difference between these two cases?

What didn't the North Hollywood robbers anticipate?

Which approach was more successful: the strong-armed, forceful approach, or the subtle, thoughtful approach?

Plan for problems or have problems.

DO THE KNOWLEDGE

Bats. Bats avoid obstacles and nab insects on the wing by emitting ultrasonic squeaks and interpreting the echo the sound waves make after bouncing off objects in the environment. This biological sonar, called "echolocation," is also used by dolphins to navigate murky waters.

Sharks. Never play hide-and-seek with a shark because you'll lose. Sharks have special cells in their brains that are sensitive to the electrical fields other creatures generate. This ability is so refined in some sharks that they can find fish hiding under sand by the weak electric signals their twitching muscles emit.

Snakes. Temperature-sensitive organs located between the eyes and nostrils of boas and pit vipers allow the snakes to sense the body heat of their prey. There is one located on each side of the snakes' head, so the animals can perceive depth and strike with deadly accuracy even in complete darkness.

A snake flicking its forked tongue is usually just sniffing its surroundings. A snake uses its tongue to collect particles wafting in the air. The coated tongue is then dipped into special pits in the roofs of the snake's mouth, called Jacobson's organs. There, the odors get processed and translated into electrical signals that are sent to the brain.

Birds. The eyes of insects and birds are attuned to wavelengths of light outside the visible range that humans see in. Birds that appear dull and grey to us are often radiant in colors we don't even have names for when seen in near-ultraviolet light.

Many birds, especially those that migrate, can use the Earth's magnetic field to stay their course during long flights. Scientists think

> **Did You Know?**
> When you take size and only natural weapons into consideration, animals are much more deadly fighters than humans. In fact, a water shrew can kill fish more than 60 times heavier than it, the kick of a hare can kill a polecat, and a praying mantis can devour a hummingbird. However, these "simple" animals are smart enough only to use their most deadly weapons when fighting a "true" enemy, and never when fighting each other. For example, giraffes don't use their forefeet (which can kill lions) on other giraffes, rattlesnakes fight each other without using their deadly venom, and skunks never spray *other* skunks.

these birds might have a sense that lets them "see" the planet's magnetic lines as patterns of color or light overlaid on their visual surroundings.

Cats. Cats have a mirror-like membrane in the backs of their eyes that lets them hunt and move in almost complete darkness. This membrane reflects light after it has already traveled through the retina, giving the eyes another chance to "see" as the photons of light make their second trip through the eye.

Humans. What about humans, the most intelligent of all creatures on Earth? As a child, we were taught that we have five senses (vision, hearing, smell, touch, and taste) but that lesson was incomplete. We have a number of other senses, many of which we are only recently learning about. We have senses that tell us about temperature, balance, and – according to some people – a sense of the future, other people's thoughts, etc. Oh, and let's not forget a sense of humor, common sense, and street sense. So, how many senses do YOU use?

Can you tell when someone is behind you?

Can you sense when someone is lying?

Do you know what to look for to see if someone is "your type"?

Don't waste your senses by remaining blind and unaware of reality.

MENTAL ILLNESSES IN THE BLACK COMMUNITY

Are you mentally ill? Maybe not you, but chances are that someone you know is dealing with some serious issues…and they may not even know it. The following covers several aspects of the history of mental illness in the Black community.

As you read this, think about yourself and the people you know.

Negritude

Benjamin Rush was the racist known as the "father" of American psychiatry. His face still appears on the seal of the American Psychiatric Association. Rush asserted that the color of Blacks stemmed from a disease called "negritude" which derived from leprosy. The evidence of a "cure" was when the skin turned white.

Drapetomania

Another early doctor, Samuel Cartwright, claimed to have discovered two mental diseases peculiar to Blacks, which he believed justified their enslavement. The first one, Drapetomania, was named after Drapetes, a runaway slave. Cartwright claimed that this "disease" caused Blacks to have an uncontrollable urge to run away from their "masters." The "treatment" for this illness was "whipping the devil out of them."

Dysaesthesia aethiopis

Cartwright named a second "disease," Dysaesthesia aethiopis. This disease supposedly affected both the mind and body of Blacks. The symptoms included disobedience, answering disrespectfully, and refusing to work. His proposed "cure" was to force the person into hard labor, which would send "vitalized blood to the brain to give liberty to the mind."

In the modern era, these bogus disorders have been replaced by new disorders. These new disorders are just as popular among doctors diagnosing Black children as the old ones were for slaves. They are ADHD and ODD, and instead of whippings and forced labor, the new treatments are medications that dope our children up into complacent zombies. Oh, and let's not forget that we still have *no idea* how these children will turn out 20 years from now, since the "treatments" are so new. (Just as we're only "now" learning cell phones cause cancer)

"All the trouble in the world is due to the fact that man cannot sit still in a room."
Blaise Pascal (1623-1662)

ADHD, or Attention Deficit Hyperactivity Disorder, basically means, "can't sit still and focus." If you grew up with TV as your babysitter, and never learned how to sit alone and read a book for more than an hour, you're a candidate. The trouble is, that's how most of our young people grow up nowadays. Don't worry. Ritalin and other drugs are here to make you dull, motionless, and ready to "fit in."

ODD

ODD, or Oppositional Defiant Disorder, basically means, "problems with authority." As I've said elsewhere, any member of the oppressed class naturally grows up with a spirit of resentment and frustration towards the powers that be. Millions of people, Black, brown, red, and yellow (and even some pissed-off white folks), are born with this spirit of resistance, and will probably fight until one of three things happens:

1. They are "broken" like a slave or horse, and conditioned to be a "good boy"

2. They end up fighting their way into self-destruction (death, jail, drug addiction, or insanity)

3. They find out about the reason why they're so mad and they fight the only fight worth fighting: **The fight for freedom**

No matter what direction you're headed, they've got some easy solutions for a rebellious kid. Either they send you to an alternative school or they dope you up until you're passive, obedient, and ready to do what you're told.

Post-Traumatic Slavery Disorder

A post-traumatic stress disorder is a mental health problem that results from going through an incredibly stressful ordeal, like being raped or fighting in a war. Often, it leads to depression, unexplained anger, and difficulty managing daily life. Not only that, but it usually remains undiagnosed.

In their book, *Lay My Burden Down: Unraveling Suicide and the Mental Health Crisis Among African-Americans*, veteran psychiatrist Alvin Poussaint and Amy Alexander argue that Blacks in America continue to suffer from a mental health crisis that results from slavery. While things may appear to be getting better for Blacks financially, the authors argue that things are getting worse for us psychologically:

> The psychological effects of what Poussaint and Alexander call "post-traumatic slavery syndrome" that Blacks have managed to hold at bay for so long may finally be catching up to us in 2000, 135 years after

slavery's end. Add to this a potent legacy of dehumanization, including diehard stereotypes about blacks as "cool," intellectually lacking and emotionally uncomplicated creatures – expressed today in UPN sitcoms and BET – and mental breakdown seems all but inevitable.

"Undoubtedly, great strength allowed Black people to survive slavery and discrimination, but the notion that Black men and women can easily handle burdens that would psychologically crush other people has been oversold," the authors write. "The emotional price that they have paid in enduring incredible stresses has been too often dismissed or ignored, and this has hindered the development of mental health services for the Black community."

You already know who suffers the worst:

And guess who has the highest rate of imprisonment, drug use and unemployment? Black young men, of course, the soldiers of the hip-hop nation who amid the distressing statistics are still expected to carry forward the dreams and expectations of the black community. The reality is that far too many of them fail to fulfill these expectations – or find that even worldly success fails to mitigate their despair – so it is hardly surprising that it is they who are suffering most acutely in the current mental health crisis.

Willie Lynch Syndrome

If you've seen the movie *Animal* with Ving Rhames, you know a little about the Willie Lynch speech. I don't know if there was really such a man with such a plan, but I know that it's true today.

I suggest you read the Willie Lynch speech for yourself, just so you can understand how deep it is. The worst part is that it has worked so well, and it continues to work. We keep it working by continuing to dislike and fight each other based on petty differences, most of which we only notice because "they" brought it to our attention.

Just think about how dumb it is for Black people to dislike each other over skin color, considering how we ended up with all these different complexions.

> "(I'm Black!) Whether I'm poor or rich
> Or rich or poor, it's all the same sh*t
> (I'm Black!) Even though my skins kind of light
> That mean my ancestors was raped by somebody white"
> Styles P, "I'm Black"

Think about the gap growing between poor Black people and middle class Black people. We distrust each other, we don't see how we can work together, and we feel we have nothing in common. And in poor communities, we're beefing based on what neighborhoods we're from. We don't own a single street or block, but we're reppin Zones (police zones) and Wards (government districts) like they really belong to us.

Sh*t, in certain cities, you can get killed just because of where you're from. But we're all Black, and suffering for the same reasons. Now tell me that's not sick.

Retardation

According to the definition of retarded, many of us are retarded. Retarded literally means "slow or delayed in development" or "behind." If you're 30 years old and still living with your mama, you're retarded. If you've got four kids and you refuse to stay home long enough to raise them, you're retarded. If you're an adult in need of a job and you don't know how to write a resume or budget your money, you're retarded. And if you're Black and you don't know (or care to know) anything about your people and your history, you're definitely retarded.

Baby Boy Syndrome

In her book, *The Isis Papers*, Dr. Frances Cress Welsing proposes several theories dealing with the psychological symbolism of racism and white supremacy. She examines a number of topics, such as:

- How white people fear being *genetically* wiped out by mixing with other races, so they create racist systems to stay *on top of everyone else*

- How these racist ideas are so deeply ingrained in the white psyche that they manifest in subconscious and symbolic ways almost everywhere

- How, for example, the shape of guns and missiles represent the white man's fascination with sex as a weapon

- How the game of pool represents white supremacy

Welsing explores a number of other topics, but the one I'll address here is the psychological problem that affects our community. She explains that the word "motherf*cker" has some very deep roots in our subconscious mind. She talks about how Black men are stuck in a childlike state, and even when they are of adult age, they want to remain with their mothers. Psychologists call it the Oedipus complex, but Welsing says that's where we got the word "motherf*cker" (See "Names We Call Ourselves"). The movie *Baby Boy* is based off that idea.

Mentacide

Mentacide means to kill one's normal thought processes, essentially to kill one's own mind. Bobby E. Wright, in his book *The Psychopathic Racial Personality and Other Essays*, explains that we are "mentacidal" because we are constantly engaging in self-destructive psychological behaviors and attitudes.

For example, in *Mentacide*, Baruti writes:

It is mentacidal to believe that we are equal (or that they are worth being "equal" to) simply because we have accumulated some meaningless trinkets, have a daily share of the crumbs from the master's table, and have some of the crumbs from the master's table, and have some of the master's children, who psychologically and materially benefit from our oppression and exploitation (whether they are consciously aware of it or not), who are willing to play with us or let us into their sandbox.

Self-Hatred

Do you hate looking at the man in the mirror? Does everything about you bother you? Do you wish you could be somebody else, anybody else? Well then, you may have a serious case of self-hatred. If you're still not sure, see "10 Signs You Hate Yourself."

Stockholm Syndrome

The deeper reason for why people of color love whites so much can be found in two great books: Frantz Fanon's *Wretched of the Earth* and Paolo Friere's *Pedagogy of the Oppressed*.

It's known as Stockholm syndrome. Stockholm syndrome is a psychological response sometimes seen in an abducted hostage, in which the hostage shows signs of loyalty to the hostage-taker, regardless of the danger (or at least risk) in which the hostage has been placed. The syndrome is named after a bank robbery in Stockholm, Sweden, in which the bank robbers held bank employees hostage for six days in 1973. In this case, the victims became emotionally attached to their victimizers, and even defended their captors after they were freed from their six-day ordeal.

Black people were kidnapped for a little longer than six days, so you can imagine that the symptoms are a little more intense. Especially when you consider how we are constantly reminded that they are the best, and we are inferior. After 400 years, you won't just like your victimizer, you won't just want to be like him, you won't just sympathize with him and share his views, you will actually be trying to *be* him or worse.

Being oppressed, we eventually want to identify with the oppressor as a means to no longer feel so oppressed. By (in our mind) pretending to participate on *his* side of the fence, we (in our imagination) end our own misery with oppression. Eventually we really participate in subtle and overt acts of oppression against others, our own, and even ourselves.

"A man who is 'of sound mind' is one who keeps the inner madman under lock and key."
Paul Valery (1871-1945)

Psychological Slavery

Na'im Akbar, in his book *Breaking the Chains of Psychological Slavery*, speaks on how slavery has never left us. Besides the prison system, there is another devastating form of slavery destroying our people. In a nutshell, after the chains were taken off our arms and legs, they were placed on our minds. **Today, we enslave ourselves.**

True Believer Syndrome

True Believer Syndrome is a cognitive disorder that is known to most psychologists as cognitive dissonance. The term True Believer Syndrome was coined to refer to people who continue to believe in things like psychics and cult leaders even after they are shown evidence proving them to be frauds.

For example, when members of Malachi Z. York's Nuwaubian Moors learned that he was convicted of child molestation and other related charges, they cried that he was innocent. When they learned that York himself had pled guilty, they continued to believe in his innocence and fight for his freedom. This fit their pattern, as they had continued to argue for the truth of his teachings year after year, no matter how many times he changed them while denouncing his own old teachings.

The True Believer Syndrome is prevalent in Black churches and organizations that believe in their leadership even after they are exposed as crooks and charlatans. Another example is Bishop Weeks, the preacher who publicly beat the hell out of his wife, Reverend Juanita Bynum. Weeks still has many followers, donors, and supporters, all of whom believe his alibi about being possessed by the devil.

In a world that's designed to strip us of our minds, we can't afford to be crazy.

MOVIE TO SEE

Baby Boy

A story about a young Black man that simply won't grow up and accept responsibility. I've already mentioned this movie earlier, so I'll just let the star of the movie tell you what this film is all about. "If the shoe fits, wear it. Straight up," said star Tyrese Gibson. "If you can't relate to it then you can't relate to it, but you know somebody who is that way. You can't lie. You can't say you've never been exposed to somebody who has lived that kind of life." Co-star Omar Gooding said it's tough to get actual "Baby Boys" to see the reality of their situation:

"I took a bunch of my friends to see the film and when it was done they were like, 'Whew, that was me, I could feel that,' But, other guys, you could still see the mentality, they weren't just like, (shamed look) 'Boy, that was me,' it was more like (happy face) 'Yeah, that was me!' So, they still had the 'Baby Boy' thing. And I was like, (scornful look) "Did you get it, bro?!?""

"Either you're gonna go to see the film and go, 'That's me. I need to change my life.'" said Gibson, "Or, you're gonna be proud of what you do on a day-to-day basis and (see in) the film."

FIND THE STASH SPOTS

Here's an activity.

This is Sammy the Hustler at work.

Can you look at the picture and figure out where Sammy keeps his dope? I'll give you 5 minutes.

Answers

- ❏ It's not in his mouth, and not on his person. That would be stupid.
- ❏ It's not in that paint can, filled with battery acid, but that's where he could throw the dope if the cops pulled up.
- ❏ It could be on a branch of the tree, or in the hole.
- ❏ It could be inside one of those old tires by the fence.
- ❏ It could be on top of the metal guard above the window.
- ❏ It could be behind the faceplate of his radio
- ❏ It could be behind that loose brick above him.
- ❏ It could be under the rock by the tree.
- ❏ It could be under one of the loose pieces of cracked sidewalk he's standing on.
- ❏ It could be somewhere inside the store, where he's worked out a deal with the owner.
- ❏ It could even be somewhere by that old car on the other side of the block, and he may be texting one of his do-boys to come bring it to him.

Actually, there's no dope anywhere in this picture. Sammy the Hustler got out of the dope game two years ago. Now he hustles real estate. He's actually texting a buyer about the vacant lot he's standing near. Sammy the Hustler's going to sell it for $26,000.

Look beyond the ordinary. The man who can't think outside the box stays inside that box forever.

THE SUPREME TEAM

By now, you've probably heard of Kenneth "Supreme" McGriff. Either you've seen his episode of BET's *American Gangster*, or you know about him through the drama between 50 Cent and Murder Inc., which was financed by Supreme. In fact, 50 Cent portrayed Supreme as the character "Majestic" in his movie and book.

Supreme and his nephew Gerald "Prince" Miller allegedly led the infamous Supreme Team which ran Jamaica, Queens through the early 80s. They were said to be over 200 deep, and comparable to the Mafia in terms of organizational structure. But I'm sure you already have heard a little about the infamous Supreme Team. But if you saw the episode on BET, you may have caught a few things that other people missed.

For one, both Supreme and Prince were Five Percenters. In fact, most of the people involved in the beginnings of the Team were. But the rest of the Five Percenters didn't approve of Supreme and the Team getting into drugs. That was against what the Gods and Earths stood for. But Supreme wanted to do what he wanted to do, as did the others.

Another thing you may have noticed was that Supreme and many of the others grew up in a nice neighborhood. In fact, one of the Team's lieutenants, Ronald "Tuck" Tucker, said: "If the drugs weren't in the community, Jamaica, Queens could have been a beautiful place to live. But drugs were easy to get and made fast money. As a seventeen-year-old my thoughts were: Why go to school when I'm making more money than the chairman of the Board of Education?"

Again, Tuck, like the others, did what he wanted to do.

> "It's that middle class nigga, man, tryin to sell dope
> Get caught, turn bitch, and go and snitch on his folks
> Man you wasn't broke, you didn't live in the trap
> You ain't have to turn fed, we don't do it like that"
> David Banner "B.A.N. (The Love Song)"

I don't think it gets any clearer than what Waverly "Teddy" Coleman, another Supreme Team lieutenant said in *Don Diva Magazine*:

> Being down with the Supreme Team was a status thing. I grew up in a good house. I was just attracted to that lifestyle and it was something I wanted to do. I just wanted to be down. I made more money before I got down with the Team than when I got down. [But] it was a movement that I wanted to be a part of. There was a level of respect that the Team commanded and that the Team earned that was intoxicating.

I mean, come on now, the guy was named Waverly! You know he didn't come from the hood! But, as he said, he just *wanted* to be down. Currently, Supreme, Prince, and most of the lieutenants (including Tuck and Teddy) are doing double-digit bids in the feds. They didn't exactly get what they wanted (long-term), but they did get some short-term benefits. Still, the trend continues today.

That sh*t kills me. Every minute, there's a new hustler out on the street doin dirt, who ain't got no business doin dirt. At home, he's got three warm meals waitin, a big-ass bedroom, cable TV, and maybe even two decent parents trying to push him the right way. But that mothaf*cka don't care. His sorry ass thinks he's poor and hopeless too, so he hits the block with people who ain't got half of what he has. They're lookin at him like, "Nigga, go to SCHOOL...you can do better than THIS!" But he's not looking at his NEEDS, he only cares about his WANTS. And his weak ass just WANTS to be DOWN.

And that's how Black neighborhoods like Jamaica, Queens go all the way downhill. Aw, who cares? Do what you want, right?

Know the difference between your WANTS and NEEDS, and live based off your needs.

REVIEW

The principle for this chapter was **Mind over Matter**: Be aware. Examine what you know, and how you know it. Know who you are, and where you're going.

Here are the principles and lessons we covered in this chapter:

Awareness
Don't waste your senses by remaining blind and unaware of reality.
Inspect and investigate. It's always in your best interest.
Knowledge is powerful. That's why the people with power KNOW, while the powerless believe what they're told.
When you're in a game you can't win, intend to transcend.
Foresight
Plan for problems or have problems.
Identity
Be yourself, not what they want you to be.
Knowing who you ARE is key in knowing who you'll BE.
Start by taking pride in your Blackness.
You can't fail at being yourself.
Independence
A real man doesn't fear standing alone.
The weak and fragile must travel in packs.
Learning
One only learns what one teaches oneself.
You can learn by ear or learn on your ass.
Unlike school, however, life teaches you the lesson AFTER you fail the test.
Perspective
It's all about you...but it's also bigger than you.
Your struggle is part of a world-wide struggle.
Look beyond the ordinary.
The man who can't think outside the box stays inside that box forever.
There's no shortage of intelligence in the hood.
Street dudes are some of the smartest people around. Use it wisely.
What's "real" is often what other people have been told to think.
Find reality for yourself.
Priorities
Know the difference between your WANTS and NEEDS, and live based off your needs.
Stick to your guns, but know when to bend.
Purpose
Everything has a purpose. Even apparent weaknesses can be hidden strengths.
It's not about where (or how) you start, it's about where you end up.
Many of us have incredible potential...too many of us waste it.
Responsibility
At the end of the day, it's all on you.
Nothing happens TO you.

Everything that happens...you allowed it to happen or caused it to happen.
Sensibility
A stupid person is of help to no one, not even himself.
In a world that's designed to strip us of our minds, we can't afford to be crazy.
Vision
No one rises to low expectations.

Walk The Talk

MANIFESTATION AND PRESENTATION

"Your true character is revealed by the clarity of our convictions, the choices you make, and the promises you keep. Hold strongly to your principles and refuse to follow the currents of convenience. What you say and do defines who you are, and who you are…you are forever."

When's the last time someone told you something that turned out to be a lie? Depending on how serious it was, it probably changed how you feel about that person, right? After some time, maybe you forgot about the lie and you moved on. What if you found out they lied again? Now, they're a liar as far you're concerned, right?

Some of us are living lies. Some of us are so full of falsehoods that we don't know where the real part of us ends and the fake part begins. There are others of us who aren't living for ourselves, or who aren't living up to our full potential, so we're being untrue in other ways.

A lot this has to do with what other people think of you. People lie and act a certain way to affect how people see them. People half-step because they don't expect as much from themselves as other people expect from them. Either way, we're not stupid. We're doing it for a reason, whether we are aware of it or not. The question is:

Are you getting what you want? Your words, your ways, your actions…are they bringing about the results you desire?

We're going to look at what we say, what we do, how we carry ourselves, and how it affects our outcomes in life. As you grow, you'll gradually eliminate the behaviors that do you no good.

It sounds easy, but usually, the liar doesn't even know he's a liar.

QUIZ TWO: APPROACH TO LIFE AND SITUATIONS

1. **If I tell somebody I'll meet them in ten minutes, I...**
   a. will probably be late.
   b. might get caught up and forget about them.
   c. make sure I leave early so I'm not late.
   d. already know it'll take at least 15 minutes or more.

2. **When I speak to a woman I like, I...**
   a. let her do all the talking.
   b. start talking bout sex as soon as I can.
   c. tell her what I want to tell her.
   d. tell her what I think she wants to hear.

3. **People think I'm...**
   a. a screw-up.
   b. crazy as hell.
   c. bout my business.
   d. whatever I want them to think.

4. **If I made a thousand dollars today, I would...**
   a. probably not know what to do with it.
   b. go ball out and spend almost all of it.
   c. save or invest it.
   d. tell everyone I was rich.

5. **If someone tells me I'm f*cking up in life, I...**
   a. figure f*cking up is not a big deal.
   b. tell 'em to worry bout themself.
   c. listen if it makes sense.
   d. pretend to listen and laugh when they leave.

6. **When I'm around people I respect, I...**
   a. hope that they will notice me.
   b. make sure I really stand out.
   c. carry myself the same way I always do.
   d. try to think and act like them.

7. **My favorite saying (from those below) is...**
   a. I didn't know.
   b. I don't give a f*ck.
   c. I hear you.
   d. I want to do that.

Explanation

Okay, different series of questions, different sets of answers. That means different results, of course. Again, you're looking at which answer you picked more than the others. This chapter deals with behaviors. So if you don't like what you find, it's not impossible to change it.

Mostly As: The "Incompetents" These answers describe someone who just "can't do right." That doesn't mean these people ONLY make bad decisions. It simply means these people spend a lot of time not having a clue about what to do, and making poor choices as a result. Sometimes, these individuals fall upon good situations by accident, but even then, they're not really sure how they got there, or how to make it happen again.

Mostly Bs: The "Ignorants" These answers describe someone who lives like they don't care. While any army needs soldiers like these, a loose cannon is always a dangerous thing. Sometimes these individuals are having a hard time figuring things out as well, but they act reckless and ignorant so they'll seem like it doesn't matter to them. Although they appear strong, they feel they have to act this way because they're having a hard time with life.

Mostly Cs: The "Intentionals" These answers describe someone who usually has a purpose to the words, ways, and actions they choose. They may not always make the most popular choice, but their choices are intentionally designed to bring about the results they want. These individuals usually find themselves in less stupid situations than the others.

Mostly Ds: The "Imposters" These answers describe someone who wants to appear a certain way, whether or not that is really what he is about. They are often so concerned with how others see them that they forget who they really are or what they want to do. These people rarely mean what they say or say what they mean. As a result, it's hard to have any confidence in them.

I won't spend too much time every chapter explaining what you can do with these results. If you don't like what you've found, then challenge yourself to be better. If you disagree with what's been said, then prove it wrong. Either way, the following pages will offer you some insight into how you can do either one.

The Second Principle

"Manifestation and Presentation" means: Once you know better, do better, speak better, choose better, and live better.

What You'll Learn

- Why our people are still selling each other out.
- How to stay out of trouble without having to lie.
- Which ways and actions make you look bad, and which ones are just bad for you.
- How to communicate effectively to make any hustle successful.
- What the words we use *really* mean.
- Why the government is so afraid of *real* Black men.
- How to learn from all of life's mistakes.
- What the differences are between hustlers and suckers, winners and losers, and thugs and soldiers.
- How to get the most of out of life and its experiences.
- What manhood is all about.

STOP SNITCHIN'

There are a lot of decent people in our communities who are upset about the "Stop Snitching" campaign. They think the urban community is threatening everyone in the community to stay silent about the crimes that are happening. That's not what it's really about, unless you're a dummy like Cam'ron (See "Stop Lyin"").

There's one thing you've got to understand about snitches. That is, the most common type of snitch isn't the little old lady who's scared to come out of her house because of the dope boys outside. The most common type of snitch is actually one of those dope boys.

Among the Chinese Triads, there is a blood oath in the initiation of new members that says: "If I am arrested after committing an offense, I must accept my punishment and not try to place blame on my sworn brothers. If I do so, I will be killed by five thunderbolts." If you know about the Triads, you can imagine what them thunderbolts are.

In the Italian Mafia, there's a code known as Omerta. Basically, it means you stay silent when you get caught. You do your bid and you come out with respect for not selling out your family. Well, that's becoming hard to find in our community, isn't it? At an alarming rate, people are being told on, by who? Not the concerned elders and neighborhood watch organizations, but by their comrades.

First of all, the elders and community groups need to be concerned with the conditions that drive our young men to crime instead of wagging their fingers and condemning them while 911 is on hold ANYWAY. At the very least, they could try talking to those young men and women without putting them down, maybe offer some advice or a helping hand, to set them on the right path. Even better, they could take all their concern and use it to fight to change the conditions that drive people like you and me to go down that crooked path. But either way, no matter what they do, they're not the problem.

The problem is that if I sell you an ounce of weed, and you get caught, you can tell on me and get off scott-free so long as I go to jail. As a matter of fact, you can lie and say I sold you some weed even if I didn't. As long as I go to jail, you can go back to the hood and be free.

We all know what's happening when these so-called gangsters get caught with all kinds of guns and drugs, but they're back on the street in a few months. Before long, all of their old buddies are going to jail...to stay. That's not dishonorable, that's despicable. If you're a criminal, take responsibility! Don't sell out the next man so that you don't have to suffer!

Take a look at most of the major Black gangsters who finally got charged with all the dirt they'd done over their 20 and 30-year careers in organized crime...What did they do? They told! And told! And told! And what did it get them? Maybe 5 years off, maybe 10. Wow.

It just goes to show how selfish some people can be, and the amount of trust you can place in someone who's doing dirt with you. Where did this start?

If you ask me, it goes back to slavery (see "Watch Out for the Sellouts").

How many successful slave revolts have you heard about? I can think of maybe two. Nat Turner. Toussaint L'Overtoure. Even the two of them were eventually sold out by their own kind.

There were hundreds, if not thousands, of slave revolts that were stopped or crushed almost instantly because some stupid ass slave sold out his brothers and sisters. These bold men and women were preparing to rise up and fight their masters for their freedom, but almost every time there were one or two slaves who would tell the masters what them "ornery niggers" was up to.

The worst part is, it was usually the field slaves. The ones who suffered worst under slavery, beaten, whipped, worked to exhaustion. Even their children slaved in the hot sun.

But these snitches believed that, if they sold out their fellow slaves, they'd get a worthwhile reward. What did they get? Freedom? Hell no! They usually didn't get sh*t except a pat on the head and the praise, "You's a good nigger, ain't ya?"

Today, our strong Black men are sold out by the weaker ones of our kind. That goes for brothers making big money, as well as brothers out there fighting for the truth. Why? Because they both have the power to disrupt the "status quo" or the way things are in this society. If the hustlers and activists came together one day, and put together their money, their soldiers, and their wisdom...I can't even begin to tell you what could happen.

And that's why snitches continue to exist.

Have some honor. Don't sell out your own people.

TELLIN' ON YOURSELF

If you haven't heard of this organization by now, you probably don't need to, so I won't name names. I'll just call them GMO (as in Get Money Organization). GMO was one of the biggest Black crime syndicates to emerge in recent years. From selling 50-slabs of crack in high school in the 80s, to running an empire spanning eleven states in 2006, the two heads of the organization were doing it big, making over $270 million dollars off cocaine.

The only problem, besides all the drugs and killings, was that these dudes just couldn't keep a low profile. Now, white gangsters – doing the same kind of dirt – run modest businesses like restaurants as fronts and live discrete lives with their families in simple, but expensive, subdivisions. And they try to avoid any unnecessary attention. These guys, on the other hand, had one of their bosses appearing in music videos with stacks of money on a table, and billboards announcing their presence.

It's like they were dry snitching on themselves. Everywhere they went they were flashing money, spending $50,000 a night at any strip club they visited, driving Ferraris and Lamborghinis, and living in mansions. Where was all this money supposedly coming from? GMO had two fronts, a record label that had yet to produce a hit record, and an exotic car dealership that wasn't really a front since they were using the cars to ship their drugs. Did these guys really expect to yell "GMO" and floss millions of dollars worth of jewelry everywhere they went and never fall under the scrutiny of the FBI, ATF, or DEA?

Of course...the inevitable happened. In October of 2006, GMO's two heads, along with seven other members, were indicted and arrested on drug trafficking. In July of 2007, sixteen more were indicted. Even one of my partners got caught up in all the indictments, just because he'd spent some phone time with a few GMO members.

"The government is one step closer to eradicating one of today's most violent and notorious drug trafficking organizations," said a DEA Special Agent. "[GMO] wreaked havoc from coast to coast. Their bold image and in-your-face reputation once propelled them into the media spotlight. Today, we are proud to cast an ominous cloud over this once-thriving criminal network."

"The Get Money Organization once had billboards...boldly proclaiming that the world was theirs," said the U.S. Attorney. "This indictment is a rejection of that claim...The government is shutting down [their] once-flourishing drug empire."

And ever since the indictments began, almost everyone who was screaming GMO just a year ago when GMO was makin' it rain, poppin' bottles with them in the strip club...all of a sudden they've stopped screaming. All of the hotheads and loudmouths that yelled GMO from the rooftops are quiet as a mouse now while their leaders sit in cells awaiting their fates. Just goes to show you...

It's not always a good idea to attract attention to yourself.

SILENCE IS GOLDEN

Allah

Mayor John Lindsay was walking the Harlem streets with Allah, the leader of the Five Percenters (See *Part Two*). The Five Percenters were a group of Black and Hispanic youths who had embraced Allah's teaching that they should see themselves as Gods, and act accordingly. It was a summer in the 1960s, and Allah's movement was growing. He needed the Mayor's help to secure a building for his young Gods.

As they walked, Akim, one of the young Gods approached Allah with a joint in hand. He attempted to pass it to Allah. Allah looked at the young God and then down at the joint. He responded, "Oh, I don't do that."

Akim was dumbfounded. Allah and the Mayor had passed him by now, but he was stuck in his place, confused about what Allah had said.

He knew Allah smoked. In fact, he has smoked with him before. Was Allah lying? Was he lying to save face in front of the Mayor?

He thought carefully and critically.

It was clear now. Allah had said "I don't do that." And he didn't.

Smoking on a public street, especially in front of the Mayor? Who in their right mind *would* do that?

Now Akim felt dumb. He passed off the joint and sat down to think, determined to learn how to be "discrete."

You can be honest without telling on yourself.

Assata

Since May of 2005, Black revolutionary Assata Shakur has been classified as a "domestic terrorist" by the FBI, which has offered a $1 million reward for assistance in her capture.

Assata Shakur, godmother of Tupac Shakur, was highly active in the Black Power movement throughout the 1970s. First a member of the Black Panther Party, and then the more militant Black Liberation Army, Assata was charged with every crime the prosecutors could pin on her:

✢ charged with armed robbery of Hilton Hotel in New York City, 1971 (case dismissed, 1977)

✢ charged with bank robbery in Queens, 1971 (acquitted, 1976)

✢ charged with bank robbery in the Bronx, 1972 (hung jury, 1973)

✢ charged with kidnapping of a drug dealer, 1972 (acquitted, 1975)

✢ charged with murder of a drug dealer, 1973 (case dismissed, 1974)

✢ charged with attempted murder of policemen, 1973 (case dismissed, 1974)

She beat every bullsh*t case. Finally, Assata was charged with the murder of New Jersey state trooper in 1973. The irony is that she was the one they were planning to kill. Even though there was strong evidence showing that she was shot with her hands up in the air, and that Assata never fired a gun that night, she was convicted and sentenced to life plus 26 to 33 years, to be served consecutively.

Of course, Assata suffered numerous abuses while imprisoned. Sick and underfed, she might have died in prison. But on November 2, 1979, she escaped. Assata was rescued from the Clinton Correctional Facility for Women in New Jersey, under mostly unknown circumstances. What little is know is that three members of the Black Liberation Army came into the prison fully armed and got her out.

No one, including the guards, was injured during the prison break. Charged with assisting in her escape was her brother in the struggle, Mutulu Shakur, stepfather of Tupac Shakur. Two others were also charged. Partly for his role in the jailbreak, Mutulu Shakur was added to the FBI's Ten Most Wanted Fugitives list, where he remained for the next four years until his capture in 1986.

After her escape, Assata lived as a fugitive for the next several years. The FBI put out "wanted" posters throughout the New York/New Jersey area. Meanwhile, her supporters hung "wanted" posters of their own. Their posters said "Assata Shakur is welcome here."

By July of 1980, FBI director William Webster complained that the search for Shakur was not going well because local residents refused to cooperate. Even the crackheads and snitches weren't telling.

> "Silence is also speech."
> Fulfulde (African) proverb

With the help of her supporters, Shakur avoided capture by the FBI for five years. In 1984, she was granted political asylum in Cuba and slipped out of U.S. jurisdiction.

The seeds for Assata's revolutionary attitude was planted in her early childhood. In her autobiography, *Assata*, she wrote:

> I was to be polite and respectful to adults, but when it came to dealing with white people in the segregated South, my grandmother would tell me menacingly, 'Don't you respect nobody that don't respect you, you hear me?'

Assata spends much of her book, which she wrote while living in Cuba, explaining her philosophy as a "Black revolutionary" in America.

One thing she doesn't spend time explaining, however, is the workings of the Black Liberation Army. She also says very little about the details of the crimes she was accused of committing. Finally, she says almost nothing about her jailbreak. She doesn't tell who was involved, how it was done, or how she avoided being captured.

Usually, people tell it all in their autobiographies. And since Assata was now safe in Cuba, where the Cuban government loved her and would not send her back to the U.S., why not tell that story? Wouldn't you want to tell everyone how you broke out of prison? Especially if you didn't have to worry about it getting you in trouble?

Why doesn't Assata tell those details? Because the people that were involved, and there may have been many, don't deserve that. Assata Shakur is not alone. Her struggle is interwoven with the lives of countless others. Although she is almost free (living in exile), many others who helped her are now political prisoners. Many others are still on the run. Many others are not known about.

Remember, your life is not a single thread, hanging alone. It is part of a vast fabric, woven so tightly that one thread cannot be removed without damaging the whole fabric.

Also remember, whether it's your life or the lives of others that is at stake, you must show discretion.

Sometimes it's best to just keep your mouth shut.

Take a break.
Put this book down for a minute.

Do NOT go back to reading this book until you do one (or more) of the following things:

- ❑ Call somebody who is going through some rough sh*t and make sure they are okay.
- ❑ Eat something that your body is telling you it needs, or drink some water.
- ❑ Wrestle, spar, or slapbox someone to make sure you "still got it."
- ❑ Take a walk through your neighborhood and see if somebody needs help with something.
- ❑ Clean up a part of your house, or organize some f*cked up part of your life.
- ❑ Tell somebody about this book and what you're learning. Invite them to come read it.
- ❑ Give this book away to somebody who needs it and get another copy for yourself.
- ❑ Cook something good, and make enough to share. Invite people.
- ❑ Check yourself out in the mirror and pick something to improve.
- ❑ Identify ten positive things about your life and stop forgetting them when you're stressed.
- ❑ Tell somebody you love them, cause it might be your last chance.

This has been a PSA from 360 and SDP.
Once you're done, carry on.

PULL UP MY PANTS?

In almost the same way that the NBA issued rules that no sportswear, sunglasses, headgear, exposed chains or medallions may be worn at league-sponsored events after that brawl that spilled into the stands, Black men are once again being targeted for their clothing. This time, a number of city officials and community leaders are trying to ban sagging pants in cities across the nation. In one city in Louisiana, the style carries a fine of as much as $500 or up to a six-month sentence. The claim is that young people are exposing their body parts. But I've never seen a Black man show his ass cheeks by sagging his pants. Still, the laws are gaining support. But this time, it's not white people targeting Blacks. The majority of the people pushing for these new laws are Black. They're Black, they're old, and they believe that the youth can be "saved" if they tighten their belts.

> "I keep it gangsta, and why should I change that?
> F*ck you old mothaf*ckas tryin to change rap
> But ain't you the same cat
> That sat back when they brought cocaine back?"
> Ice Cube, "Gangsta Rap Made Me Do It"

Here's a question: Do you respect your elders? It's not that simple, right? The average young man on the streets nowadays respects the elders who have earned his respect, but he's not gonna bow down in front of every old man and woman who crosses his path and tells him to pull his pants up. Why? Because when the elders tell us to pull our pants up, they never ask why we let them sag in the first place.

They say it's a prison style. They say the homosexuals would have their ass exposed to let the other inmates know they were "available." That may be true, but that theory just seems a little out there. All I know is that they take your belt and shoelaces when you get locked up. So a lot of people hit the block, fresh from jail, with no laces and pants hangin' off their asses.

But it doesn't matter. The elders who condemn the youth, their fashion sense, their musical taste, their values – these elders won't exert any effort to understand these youth, to help these youth make legal money, to help these youth with their very adult problems…basically, **the elders don't respect the youth.**

I know how a young dude on the block feels when an old preacher-lookin' guy tells him to pull his pants up without asking him how he's doing. Cause I was that young dude on the block. And that old man never did *anything* for me. His values weren't my values. His life wasn't my life. And his world, his reality, his understanding, wasn't mine. Yet he felt entitled to "put me in my place."

92

Truth is, most of us don't know why we wear our pants low. Some of us do it to fit in. Some of us overdo it for attention. But most of us do it simply because it's a style. It's a style that communicates how young poor people feel about this world they're in, this world that's given up on them, this world that doesn't give a f*ck about them.

Presenting yourself to this world in a way that the world has deemed unacceptable and inappropriate – or "ghetto" – is just another way to say to this world, "Kiss my Black ass."

Not that everyone who exhibits those kind of behaviors knowingly feels that way about the world. A lot of us have a sense that we're being sh*tted on by the world, but we can't put our finger on it well enough to be able to explain it.

If I say anything to somebody about their pants, the best advice I have is this: Don't wear anything so loose or so low that you can't run at full speed if you need to. Plain and simple.

Be you, by all means.
But don't look so stupid that the right people don't respect you.

---

26 SIGNS YOU'RE DYING FOR ATTENTION

"Where there is no shame, there is no honor."
Ethiopian proverb

Here's a list of things that people do in public to let people know they're crying to be heard and dying to be seen. If this sounds like you, it means one of two things. Either (a) you don't care what other people think about you because this society ain't gave you sh*t, or (b) you are trying extra hard to get noticed by people in this society, and looking real foolish in the process. Either way, you need to step your game up. Cause I'm tired of watching people make an ass of themselves.

1. You attempt to publicly holla at a girl, or physically grab her to stop her, and then curse her out when she disses you.

2. You walk down the street with a group of loud people who take up the whole sidewalk, scaring the hell out of white folks and elderly people.

3. You yell out the name of your gang or set in a place where nobody cares, like a shopping mall.

4. You go to a quiet place like a bookstore or movie theater, and talk real loud like you own the place.

5. You talk so loud on your phone that everyone can hear about the stupid drama you've gotten yourself into this time.

6. You go out with a white girl and insist on showing her off like she's some kind of trophy.

7. You try to get tough with someone who has the power to fire you or arrest you.

8. You encourage your child to yell cuss words or booty-shake for your friends' amusement.

9. You wear a James Brown perm, blonde dreads, multi-colored hair, or a "Boosie fade" (and you're not Lil' Boosie).

10. You act "extra-Black" or "extra ghetto," depending on who's watching.

11. You encourage your girlfriend to wear slutty clothes, so you can show her off.

12. You're always saying "Watch this" or "Hey y'all, listen to this."

13. You approach a female who is in a relationship, or – even worse – actually with her date, and aggressively try to get her for yourself.

14. You ghostride, do a burnout, or do a donut in front of a crowd of people who don't know you, and don't care.

15. You act mad with the police when they arrest you for doing some ignorant sh*t you knew you shouldn't have been doing (like the above).

16. You act all wild like you want to fight somebody, but then pretend someone is holding you back.

17. You act tough because you're with a bunch of dudes who you know will fight for you.

18. You come out wearing one of those outfits you saw on the *Pimps Up, Hoes Down* DVD.

19. You come out looking drunk or high and smelling like weed or liquor to inappropriate places like work, church, or court.

20. You rap or sing out loud in public for no reason, especially if you're singing along to music only you can hear on your headphones.

21. You dance to a beat that only you can hear on your headphones, or – even worse – only in your head.

22. You make prank calls.

23. You act like a little bitch when you ain't the center of attention.

24. You floss big jewelry – real or not – and hope nobody outshines you.

25. You put rims or a sound system on an old junk-ass car and show off like you're doing it big.

26. You blow all your money on your friends when you're behind on your own bills.

Only a baboon shows his ass and laughs about it.

THE WRONG FOODS

> "I'm skatin on ice like Christy Yamaguchi
> Catch me in the Chevy, eatin blowfish sushi"
> Young Dro, "Rubberband Banks"

Eat the wrong part of a Japanese blowfish and you can die within hours. Everyone who eats it knows that. But they eat it anyway.

Blowfish contains tetrodotoxin, a potent neurotoxin that can kill a human in no time. But for many Japanese, blowfish (also called pufferfish or fugu in Japanese), is an expensive delicacy enjoyed on special occasions. The responsibilities attached to preparing fugu for eating are quite serious. If prepared wrong, the diner **dies within hours.**

A fugu chef must be able to safely dissect the fish, label its edible and poisonous organs and prepare the meat and skin to meal-ready quality all within 20 minutes, with no mistakes. Every time. And that's just for the training.

It's not easy. The most deadly organs of the fugu look almost identical to other organs that are to be eaten as delicacies. Even with all the training, **hundreds of people die every year** from consuming improperly prepared fugu. The poison paralyzes the muscles while the victim stays fully conscious and eventually dies from asphyxiation. There is still no antidote.

Fugu, which translates literally as "river pig" is part poison, part pleasure. The skin is poisonous, the liver is highly poisonous, and several other parts of the fish are equally dangerous to humans. There are even non-lethal quantities of the poison that will remain in the prepared flesh of the fish. Diners say this leftover poison gives "a special desired tingling sensation on the tongue."

This leaves me to wonder: **Is it THAT good?** I mean really, is it worth dying for? According to most people who've eaten it, it's usually pretty bland and – at best – tastes a little like chicken. It's actually the sauces you dip it in that make it seem good.

Would you spend anywhere from $30 to $100 on a small plate of fugu?

Does eating fugu seem stupid to you? Why?

So what level of poison or toxicity is allowable for you? 60%? 23%? 8%?

Anyone who dies eating something they know contains any amount of poison deserves whatever happens. But that's the way we live, isn't it?

We may not eat "river pig," but we eat the "city pig." We eat food that everyone knows will kill us, some of which is so nasty even the Bible said don't eat it. Some of us even snort a little powder here and there, figuring that "a little bit" won't hurt us. There's tons of other things that we take in that are no good for us. And we're killing our bodies and our brains slowly. With some things, like the fugu, the little bit of good in it just can't make up for the bad. And that goes for anything we take in. Sometimes it's better NOT to take the "good with the bad," especially if there ain't enough good to be found!

A "little bit" of good doesn't make something bad worthwhile.

17 POISONS

Here's a few things I'm sure have killed some part of your mind, your body, or your community already:

1. Reality TV shows that make celebrities out of ignorant assholes, sluts, and drug addicts that personify the worst traits in our people.

2. Daytime talk shows that make all relationships involving Black people seem completely dysfunctional and circus-like.

3. Modern-day minstrel shows where Black actors embarrass themselves by mocking how "ghetto" Black people act for the amusement of white people.

> **Did You Know?**
> The average American eats at McDonalds more than 1,800 times in their life. Worldwide, more people can identify McDonald's golden arches than a Christian cross. Over 114 murders have occurred in McDonald's restaurants. Of course, fast food diets have probably killed millions more.

4. Vaccinations and other shots that actually pose a risk of you catching the disease you think you are being protected from.

5. Destructive emotions like lust, greed, envy, or hatred.

6. Red meats that contribute heavily to health problems like cancer, heart disease, and high blood pressure.

7. Religious denominations that encourage poor people to give up what little money they have with the hopes of being rewarded somehow.

8. Religious denominations that teach tolerance and patience to people who are suffering and being taken advantage of.

9. Religious denominations that claim to change the world when the community where they are located is still in shambles.

10. Food or drinks that are high in chemical content, or mostly composed of ingredients the average person cannot pronounce.

11. Eating habits that involve fast food more than once or twice a week.

12. Any food or food product involving pork or a pork-by-product (especially something really gross like chitterlings or lard).

13. Blue juice (there's nothing in nature that you can consume that is that color).

14. "Get rich quick" schemes and programs that focus on promising dreams to poor people who don't have the business sense to know better.

15. Malt liquors and spirits that are marketed specifically to the Black community.

16. Any drug that permanently damages your brain or body, including many prescription drugs.

17. Weed with any "special" or unknown added ingredients.

Be careful what you take in. Everything that's good TO you isn't good FOR you. And too much of anything is never a good thing.

WORD IS BOND

What constitutes a lie? If you tell your mother you're going to graduate, and you know you aren't, that's a lie, right? Is it a lie when someone asks you where you've been and you make something up? Is it a lie when you promise to go out with a young lady and then change your mind to go out with someone you like better?

> "One falsehood spoils a thousand truths."
> Ashanti proverb

Put yourself on the receiving end. Think of how you'd see it if you were that other person. In most cases like these, you've violated someone's trust in you, and…you're lying.

Back in the old days, a person could bond a friend out of jail on the strength of their reputation. Their word was the bond. Reputable people could bond out on their own reputation. That's known as being released on your own recognizance. How many people do you know that have been able to get bonded out of jail without putting up a cash bond or offering their house or something of value as collateral?

What happened to honesty? What happened to integrity? Have we been lied to so much that we don't value the truth anymore? Some of us lie when we don't even have to. Some of us don't keep our word, when it would be easy to do so.

We say we'll be there at 3:00 pm. We show up when we feel like it.

We tell someone we won't do something, knowing we're going to do it…probably as soon as they walk away.

We do something and say we haven't…even when it's obvious.

We get caught lying…and still insist we're not.

We get criticized for not keeping our word…and we make excuses.

We've all done it. I know I have. But what does this make people think about you? How many people have dismissed you or stopped f*cking with you because of these lapses?

As Tony Montana says in *Scarface*, "All I have in this world are my balls and my word, and I don't break them for nobody!"

Think about what Tony meant. Why was his word important?

Your reputation is based off how real you are. If you're known for saying one thing, but doing another, you're just not a real dude. You can try to explain, but people see through your bullsh*t.

A man who has no integrity, no honor, is like a slithering snake, surviving only by slipping out of the grips of one situation after another, due to his slickness…until finally, he meets his end by slipping into a trap from which he cannot escape.

"Every violation of truth is not only a sort of suicide in the liar, but is a stab at the health of human society."
Ralph Waldo Emerson

The ninth commandment is "You shall not bear false witness against your neighbor" (Exodus 20:16). Stephen Crotts addressed this commandment with these words:

> I write in praise of true words/…Marriage vows kept/ Membership vows maintained/ Appointments met on time/ Fair descriptions/ A person's word their bond/ I write in praise of honesty/ A pure life/ All being what it seems/ A firm handshake, eyes that meet in sincerity/ Clear conscience and sound sleep.

How would other people rate you on your integrity?

How dependable would other people rate you on your word?

You ain't worth sh*t if your word ain't worth sh*t.

THE POWER IN WORDS

"A wise man hears one word and understands two."
Jewish proverb

In Islamic tradition, Allah says "*Kun faya kun*," which means, "Be and it is." In John 1:1 of the New Testament, most Bibles say, "In the beginning was the Word, and the Word was with God, and the Word was God." But better translations say the Word was "divine" or having the power of a god, not that it was God himself. What's the point? Words have power. Words have the power to make real things happen…and those who can fully harness the power of the spoken word have the power to change minds, change lives, and change the world.

This is what Minister Louis Farrakhan was talking about when he spoke with Gil Noble about how language is used to change the perceptions of our people:

I talked about how the word 'Negro' was used and how limited that term was and how the Honorable Elijah Muhammad used the term "Black" in such a way that it developed in us a body and the nervous system that connected us to our people all over the world.

So that when something was done in the Congo, years ago, in the killing of Patrice Lamumba, there was a demonstration by Black people at the U.N. When Martin Luther King was murdered a hundred cities were set on fire because we had developed a nervous system that allowed us to feel the pain of one another through the language that the Honorable Elijah Muhammad used.

So the enemy stepped up his studies of us. He wanted to know what was it and who was the leader that ignited us to burn up a hundred cities when all of the people that were burning the cities were not followers of Martin Luther King Jr.

They concluded that it wasn't a specific person that was causing this as much as it was the way the media was used. It had given us as a people one shared attitude toward white people and toward what we called 'the establishment.'

These attitudes hardened into a system of belief that all of us shared, no matter where we were in America – a belief about police; a belief about government; a belief about white people – that was very real. That attitude and belief grew into ideology – a common idea – that all of us shared and we had become a national community, even though we were in different groups; different churches and mosques, etc, there was something that bound us altogether.

When the enemy saw that television had served that purpose and the name "Black, Brother and Sister" had caused us to see ourselves as kin to people of color all over the world, they decided after the assassinations of Malcolm and Martin and the departure of the Honorable Elijah Muhammad, they had to change language.

They started that by again using the term 'minority.' Once we accepted the terminology, 'minority', a certain frame of mind came with accepting that language.

The fact that we are the 'majority' was destroyed. Then we became the 'disadvantaged.' Then we became 'the largest minority in America.' Then we became 'African Americans' and there we've stayed – 'minority, disadvantaged, African Americans.'

But what happened to us as a result of accepting that language? It killed the nervous system that the language of Blackness created. Then, every television show with Black as an adjective describing it, such as 'Black

News' in New York; 'Black Journal,' 'Black Star' program in Baltimore, every city had something "Black" as a description of the main noun, and so 'Black Journal' became 'Tony's Journal;' and 'Black News' was eventually taken off the air. "Black Star" was gone. Now you have no program anywhere on television with the name "Black" in front of it.

So the subtlety of the enemy, in deceiving us, was that he knew the value of language and that if you shift the language you shift perceptions. What he did was to create the death of our nervous system that connected us as a family. Then we could become tribes and kill one another and not feel the pain of our Brothers in the Caribbean, our Brothers in Brazil or our Brothers in Africa.

We began to be less and less global and more and more narrow in our focus, to be narrower right down to gang and tribes in terms of denomination and organization, and kill each other throughout America and not really feel the pain.

"One word can change a nation."
Five Percenter saying

In the movie *Malcolm X*, you'll see that one of the first things Malcolm realized on his journey was that all the definitions for the word "black" were negative or related to evil, while all the definitions for "white" were related to ideas of good and purity.

It's pretty clear if you just think about it:

Blackball	White-out
Black Plague	Whitewater
Black magic	White magic
Black sheep	White House
Black cat	White lie
Blacklist	White Christmas
Black market	White noise
Blackmail	White lightning
Black-hearted	White flag

Noticing the obvious negative qualities in the "black" words above and the positive connotation to the "white" words, I decided to look up the two in the dictionary as Malcolm X had. Here's some of what I found in the 2006 *Random House Unabridged Dictionary*:

black

1. lacking hue and brightness; absorbing light without reflecting any of the rays composing it.

2. characterized by absence of light; enveloped in darkness: *a black night.*

3. (*sometimes initial capital letter*)

    a. pertaining or belonging to any of the various populations characterized by dark skin pigmentation, specifically the dark-skinned peoples of Africa, Oceania, and Australia.

    b. AFRICAN-AMERICAN.

4. soiled or stained with dirt: *That shirt was black within an hour.*

5. gloomy; pessimistic; dismal: *a black outlook.*
6. deliberately; harmful; inexcusable: *a black lie.*
7. boding ill; sullen or hostile; threatening: *black words; black looks.*
9. without any moral quality or goodness; evil; wicked: *His black heart has concocted yet another black deed.*
10. indicating censure, disgrace, or liability to punishment: *a black mark on one's record.*
11. marked by disaster or misfortune: *black areas of drought; Black Friday.*
13. based on the grotesque, morbid, or unpleasant aspects of life: *black comedy; black humor.*
14. (of a check mark, flag, etc.) done or written in black to indicate, as on a list, that which is undesirable, sub-standard, potentially dangerous, etc.: *Pilots put a black flag next to the ten most dangerous airports.*
15. illegal or underground: *The black economy pays no taxes.*
17. deliberately false or intentionally misleading: *black propaganda.*
18. *British.* boycotted, as certain goods or products by a trade union.
19. (of steel) in the form in which it comes from the rolling mill or forge; unfinished.

white

1. of the color of pure snow, of the margins of this page, etc.; reflecting nearly all the rays of sunlight or a similar light.
2. light or comparatively light in color.
3. (of human beings) marked by slight pigmentation of the skin, as of many Caucasoids.
4. for, limited to, or predominantly made up of persons whose racial heritage is Caucasian: *a white club; a white neighborhood.*
8. lacking color; transparent.
9. (politically) ultraconservative.
10. blank, as an unoccupied space in printed matter: *Fill in the white space below.*
13. *Slang.* decent, honorable, or dependable: *That's very white of you.*
14. auspicious or fortunate.
15. morally pure; innocent.
16. without malice; harmless: *white magic.*

Subconsciously this has an effect on us: Black is bad. White is good. There's no escaping the message in that.

This message is a fundamental part of American society. Everywhere you go, you can't miss it. It's even a basic part of how and what we are taught in school. As G. Kalim has written in *The Five Percenter Newspaper:*

> I know that you youngsters don't like school and I know why. There was a time when I didn't like school either, because all they did there

was make everything white good, and I ain't white...You are inundated with an educational process which promotes their whiteness and demotes your Blackness. The same thing happened in my time, which is why I was so rebellious.

Messages like this are everywhere in our society, and they affect us daily. Think about it. What do you think about when you hear the word "McDonald's"? Most of us probably get hungry. I'm hungry just from typing it, and I don't even like McDonald's!

It's called subliminal programming. Over the years, we've become programmed to respond in certain ways to the things we hear. During slavery and for a long time afterwards, white people made a big deal out of never calling a Black man a "man," and always addressing grown men as "boy" and "son."

What did this do to Black men? What did it make them begin to think and feel after years and years of hearing it?

What are the messages we hear now?

Where are they coming from, and what are the purposes behind them?

Wait...what about the messages we are sending to ourselves and each other?

Everything that's said has more meaning than it seems. Choose your words carefully, and listen thoughtfully to what you hear.

TALKING WHITE

"Ebonics" is the name given to the way many Black people speak. Basically, it means "Black English." Black English is another dialect of Standard American English, just like American English ain't the same as British English or Australian English. But hey, it's Black, so it's not acceptable in America. Anyway, all Black people don't speak Black English. In fact, there's always a few kids in any Black school that get ridiculed and picked on for "talking white." Everyone can tell that they're speaking differently, and it sounds a lot like the way white folks talk on TV.

Usually these kids were raised in a house that didn't allow "that ghetto talk," or the parents were either very educated...or very white. But the kids that "talked white" didn't just talk differently. Their whole style was different. And it showed. So let's not get it twisted. People who speak proper English didn't get dissed just because they talked proper. They were usually also pretty lame. But guess what? They usually became pretty successful.

Why? Well, they learned a very basic principle without knowing it. If you want to be successful in France, then you need to speak French. I've met tons of people over the years who say they want to own their own businesses, but they can't speak proper English. Sometimes, it's hard to understand them if you're not from the exact f*cking neighborhood where they're from.

There's nothing wrong with speaking how you're comfortable when you're home. Trust me, when I'm with people I'm comfortable around, I cuss, I use slang, I might even say a few words that don't exist. But when I step in that office, or that presentation room, I know how to speak the language of business.

I'll tell you about an old business partner of mine who had $10,000 to invest into a small business opportunity. I'll just tell you how it went, and you try to put yourself in his shoes. Two people come in with their business proposals, hoping to get your money. Here's how it goes.

Joshua Jones comes in wearing a suit, but it looks like his pants are sagging for some reason. Why the hell are his suit pants sagging? His tie isn't tied correctly, so it just looks like an ugly knot. He hands you his proposal, gives you "dap" because you're Black and he assumes you're "cool," and says to you:

> Okay, homeboy. We got the connect from a dude overseas. Straight drop. He got like fitty cases of fresh Ones waitin, just waitin, for me to say the word. He want thirty, Ima give him twenty-fie tho – we gon let em go for sixty. It ain't gon cost but like fie extra each to set it up cause niggas want em. Tell me I ain't workin with something!

Next, Henry Henderson comes in with a simple suit, but it looks like it fits him well. And either he knows how to tie a tie, or somebody did it for him. He shakes your hand limply, and you can tell he's fresh from the suburbs. He begins:

> According to market analysis, there's a great deal of interest in the urban market for Nike Air Force Ones. I've found a wholesaler in China who's willing to sell them to me at a significan't discount of thirty dollars per pair. If we factor in costs for marketing and distribution, we can sell them at sixty dollars retail for a profit of about twenty dollars per pair, which would give us a gross return on your investment of $15,000.

Who would you rather do business with? Most likely, you'd trust Henderson with your money. Why? He's obviously got some mastery of the language of business, the language of money, and he's comfortable in that world, no matter what else he might do outside of the office.

But...if you have a keen eye for business, and you could look past how he said what he said (which most people can't do), then you'd know Joshua Jones had a better proposal. How much better? Do the math. He would have made almost $20,000 instead of the $15,000 Henderson promised.

**People rarely just look at what you're saying;
they are usually looking at how you say it.**

THE NAMES WE CALL OURSELVES

We have some serious issues with identity. We're so screwed up on who and what we are, we let other people define us. Historically, those "other people," have been whites. Most of us are familiar with the names white people have called people of color. Man, there's so many, you could go on forever!

Black people have been called everything from coon, darkie, and porch monkey to jigaboo, tarbaby, and some other names that I don't even understand. Hispanics were spics, wetbacks, or mud people, depending on where you came from. Asians were dotheads, gooks, chinks, or towelheads, also depending on where you came from.

These names were intended to dehumanize us. By addressing us as less than a man, we were made to feel subhuman, or less than human. However, you only give a name power when you respond to it. And there's one name in history that has acquired more power than any other.

That's right. Nigger.

At some point during slavery, Blacks adopted the use of the word nigger to take the sting off it. Basically, it meant less when whites said it because Black people could use it as well. So nigger (which the southern whites would sometimes say as "niggah") became a powerful word in the Black community.

And over time, we forgot about its origins and its purpose. And it became standard.

Here we are now…It's hard to convince someone white about why you still use that word today. And white people are really mad that Black people can call themselves "nigga," but they can't. Some of them don't get it. Some others really would love to call you a nigger and not get punched, so they've started saying it as "nigga," like "all the rappers say."

When people like Kramer and Don Imus make their racist comments, they're not isolated crazy white folks. What makes white people so uncomfortable is that this is how a *lot* of them think, but they're smart enough never to say those words, at least not in public. These same white people are mad that you can say "nigga" but they can't.

So what's going to change? Allow white people to call anyone a "nigga" as well? Or finally start letting go of a word with a foul history? I know how hard it is for some of us to talk without using the word. That's understandable. But we can't use that excuse forever.

Anyway, the problem is deeper than that. One of my brothers once told a young dude in Jersey that he was God by nature because he was a Black man. He looked at him like he was crazy and told him, "Nah, I'm a NIGGA...nigga!"

That type of thinking is common, just like in the 60s when Blacks would call each other "brother" and "sister." There was always somebody who'd yell back, "I ain't your f*ckin brother!"

That's the problem. The problem isn't that we use a word with a f*cked up past. It's how we think. And it's not just us. It's everyone who has been made to feel subhuman. There are Mexicans who call themselves wetbacks. There are women who call themselves and each other bitches. But it's not everyone!

As Ludacris' character said in *Crash*:

> It's just Black people demeaning other Black people, using that word over and over. You ever hear white people callin' each other "honky" all the time? "Hey, honky, how's work?" "Not bad, cracker, we're diversifying!"

Makes you think about how we see ourselves, huh? Based off the sh*t we call ourselves, it ain't looking too good.

Here are some of the things we call ourselves and each other...and why.

Animals: We call each other by every LOWLY member of the animal kingdom out there (cat, dog, snake, rat, bitch, monkey, bird, duck, pigeon, pig, hog, chick, etc.). Are we really subhuman? Who was the first person to call us animals? Think about it.

While we're on the topic of animals, I've been hearing people calling themselves "gorillas" lately. Okay...I know it goes back to strong-arm pimps who were said to be "gorilla pimping," but it's become popular *recently* as a result of 50 Cent and G-Unit.

The story behind this is pretty twisted, but I'll keep it short. G-Unit was originally "Guerilla Unit," as in a unit of "guerillas." Guerillas are the revolutionary soldiers who typically fight for their people and overthrow governments. The white folks at the record label were threatened by that kind of thinking. They don't want soldiers! They want monkeys...who sing and dance! So they made 50 change the name to "Gorilla Unit," as in a unit of big black apes who can entertain white folks. Great work, 50!

Pimp: What's funny about this word is that most of the dudes who call themselves pimps would actually be considered "tricks" in the pimp game (See "Pimps Up, Hoes Down"). Sleeping with six different girls does not make you a pimp, especially if you're breaking bread to do so.

Most real pimps don't even deal with their girls sexually. A pimp is a man in control of himself and his finances. That eliminates 90% of the young boys claiming "pimp" nowadays, huh?

Thug: Before Tupac, a thug was another word for a goon. A mindless muscle, especially in criminal endeavors. Now it's a lifestyle. See, if everyone who was a thug, goon, or gangsta had something that was really worth fighting for and killing for, I wouldn't say sh*t. Tupac's definition of thug described a Black man who was willing to fight for what he believed in, not just an ignorant dude willing to kill another Black man behind a little bit of money.

> "Let me say for the record, I am not a gangster and never have been.
> I'm not the thief who grabs your purse. I'm not the guy who jacks your car.
> I'm not down with the people who steal and hurt others.
> I'm just a brother who fights back."
> Tupac Shakur

Note: The word "thug" actually comes from India. It was the name of a bloodthirsty gang that killed all their victims. These Thugs had their own symbols, hand signs, rituals and slang. Look it up: Thugee cult of India

Goon: People been sayin this word pretty heavy every since Plies hit the scene. Gradually, the word "goon" is becoming the new "thug." In the same way, it was originally a word for dumb criminal muscle, basically a guy who does the dirty work for the smart guy who's really running the operation. Wow, that's really shooting for the stars, huh? If you *have* to use a word you heard from someone else, at least have the aspirations to call yourself a f*ckin boss, not a f*cking worker!

I mean, I've got some goons I can call when I want to take care of a "problem," but I still hope they're trying to be something bigger than a goon someday!

Boy: That's your boy, huh? Read the *Isis Papers* by Francis Cress Welsing. Or watch *Baby Boy*.

> "What does the Black man call his woman? Mama.
> What does the Black man call his friends? His boys.
> What does a Black man call his house? The crib."
> Narrator, *Baby Boy*

Some of us gotta grow up and be men. Think about it...almost every rapper nowadays is "Lil" this or "Young" that. I'm talking about grown men, 30 and up, callin' themselves by kids' names. Doesn't that make you think about how we see ourselves?

That's why it's good to hear people saying "I'm a grown ass man" more often nowadays.

Motherf*cker: You ever heard of an Oedipus complex? Look it up later. For now, see above. Anyway, the ones who really "f*cked" our mothers were the slavemasters raping them. Me, personally, I don't wanna f*ck your mama or mine.

G: G used to be short for God. Now it's short for Gangsta. Out of all these things I've listed here, the only name I've ever called someone that made them MAD was "God! Think about it. A "nigga" getting mad because someone called him God!

Gangsta: A "gangster" was a mob dude like Al Capone or Lucky Luciano. We supposedly appropriated that image and made it our own. But a gangster is supposed to be someone who *controls* an operation, not a goon who *serves* in an operation that is bigger than him. And drugs is bigger than you. It's CIA big. When you start controlling your own life, and the lives of people around you, that's Gangsta. Oh wait, no...that's God.

Oh…I didn't forget about the ladies. They're just as screwed up as us:

Dime, Silver Dolla: Women think their worth is measured on a monetary scale. Are their looks what determine their value? And is that how they're gon' measure it? In monetary terms? That tells you a lot about their values. But I guess it kinda makes sense, since most of the "dimes" and "silver dollas" out there would look like rusty nickels if they didn't spend most of their paychecks on their appearance.

Bitch: A term given to Black women by white men and made popular in the 17th century. She was seen as a sexual being, good for breeding and animalistic pleasures. And they call themselves that because it's cute. It's just like nigger. If a man says "bitch," it's a problem. But a woman calls herself "bitch" and feels good about it. Stupid.

Diva: It kills me when women call themselves a diva. She don't sing opera. She's not a diva. A diva is another word for an "operatic prima donna." (I looked it up) The other meaning of "prima donna" is a temperamental, conceited person. And she's wearin' that like a badge of honor?

That's all for now, if you can think of any more, add on.

_____: _____

_____: _____

_____: _____

We define ourselves and our reality.

THUG VS. SOLDIER

The thug, like the soldier, is both respected and feared. What's the difference between a thug and a soldier (or warrior)?

✦ A soldier fights for the people. A thug fights against the people.

✦ A soldier does whatever is necessary to protect his people. A thug does whatever is necessary to protect himself only.

✦ A soldier takes care of his woman and children. A thug avoids his woman and children.

✦ A soldier plans for tomorrow. A thug lives for today.

✦ A soldier respects those who have more wisdom and experience. A thug only respects those whom he fears.

✦ A thug is a threat to the community. A soldier removes threats to the community.

✦ A soldier doesn't relax during a time of war. A thug takes more breaks than anyone else.

✦ A thug loves material things and the pleasures they bring. A soldier loves the people and the values he holds dear.

✦ The powers that be are scared of soldiers rising up in the Black community. The powers that be are happy about thugs destroying the Black community.

✦ A soldier fights for a reason, and is not motivated by his emotions. A thug has no idea who he should be fighting or why, so he is usually driven by emotion alone.

Finally,

✦ A soldier needs guidance from higher authorities, and will fight as directed. A warrior has the fight within him, and will continue regardless to whom or what. A thug doesn't listen to anybody, and his actions show it.[1]

When you fight, fight for a reason.

SOULJA 4 LIFE

COINTELPRO

The infamous Counter Intelligence Program was started by the U.S. government in 1956. The COINTELPRO program was kept secret until

1971, when a group of radicals broke into FBI offices and stole documents and other evidence. That same year, FBI Director Hoover announced that COINTELPRO had been shut down.

COINTELPRO was made to stop the growth of almost any person, group, or organization that the American government didn't like, but they paid special attention to Black organizations. According to official FBI documents, the program was designed to:

- "prevent the coalition of militant black nationalist groups"

- "to prevent violence on the part of black nationalist groups"

- "to prevent militant black nationalist groups and leaders from gaining respectability"

- "to prevent the long-range growth of militant black nationalist organizations, especially among youth" and

- "to prevent the rise of a messiah who could unify and electrify the militant black nationalist movement"

According to Brian Glick in *War at Home*, COINTELPRO used a broad array of methods, including:

1. Infiltration: Agents and informers didn't just spy on political activists. Their main purpose was to discredit and disrupt the organizations. The FBI sent in agents who would join the organization only to spy and gather information, or cause chaos and confusion between its members. Meanwhile, the FBI and police exploited the fear of infiltration to smear genuine activists as agents.

2. Psychological Warfare from the Outside: The FBI and police used hundreds of other "dirty tricks" to undermine progressive movements. They planted false media stories and published bogus leaflets and other publications in the name of targeted groups. They forged correspondence, sent anonymous letters, and made anonymous telephone calls. They spread misinformation about meetings and events, set up pseudo movement groups run by government agents, and manipulated or strong-armed parents, employers, landlords, school officials and others to cause trouble for activists.

3. Harassment through the Legal System: The FBI and police abused the legal system to harass dissidents and make them appear to be criminals. Officers of the law gave perjured testimony and presented fabricated evidence as a pretext for false arrests and wrongful imprisonment. They discriminatorily enforced tax laws and other government regulations and used conspicuous surveillance, "investigative" interviews, and grand jury subpoenas in an effort to intimidate activists and silence their supporters.

4. Extralegal Force and Violence: The FBI and police threatened, instigated, and conducted break-ins, vandalism, assaults, and beatings. The goal was to frighten supporters and disrupt their movements. In the case of radical Black and Puerto Rican activists (and later Native

Americans), these attacks—including political assassinations—were so extensive, vicious, and calculated that they can be considered a form of official "terrorism."

The program went after a broad spectrum of civil rights groups; targets included Martin Luther King, Malcolm X, Stokely Carmichael, Eldridge Cleaver, Allah (Clarence 13X), and The Black Panther Party. This information was made public in 1976. However, no government program stepped up to fix all the damage that already had been done.

Did You Know?
There were over 40,000 pages of FBI documents on Malcolm X? To this day, only about half have been declassified for public knowledge. There are also three whole chapters that were cut out of the Autobiography of Malcolm X. These chapters, are now held in the safe of a Detroit attorney who bought them for $100,000, and very few people have seen their contents.

This left hundreds of political prisoners in jail, hundreds left physically and mentally wounded, and dozens living in exile. Although COINTELPRO was supposedly shut down, most people are sure it still exists, only under another name.

Recently, many have come to learn about something known as "Hip Hop Police," a very real segment of law enforcement targeting young Blacks, especially those associated with the hip hop culture. Rappers aren't the only ones targeted for jail time and assassinations. Young Black men of all shapes and sizes are being entrapped by a slew of informants and agents that are taught to dress like, talk like, and act like, "niggas from the hood."

After the murders of Biggie and Pac (by still-unknown assailants) failed to brew into an East-West war (as it had been hoped), operations intensified. Recent reports reveal that several city police departments have "special units" dedicated to the new Black activists for this generation: Rappers.

"Damn...and I sure miss Pac
Ever since that boy died, all the rappers done stopped
talkin bout real sh*t, but if they don't, their records flop
And they get chased by the hip hop cops"
David Banner, "So Special"

I've heard that we have now transitioned from COINTELPRO to RAPINTELPRO, as rap is the only voice for today's generation of young Black people. In fact, one of the COINTELPRO memos, dated March 4, 1968, said that no political activist or person with an ideology that was perceived as a threat to the establishment "should have access to a mass communication media."

Whether you like it or not, rappers are the loudest ones speaking nowadays. But that's why most of the rappers being pushed and promoted nowadays are young, dumb, and saying absolutely nothing. The powers that be fear the powers in the music.

As James Muhammad said:

> Just like they had counter intelligence programs to deal with Malcolm X and Martin Luther King Jr. years ago, the FBI and CIA have a way to deal with the leaders in the hip-hop generation. Sometimes, they arrest you. Sometimes, they create an environment that facilitates murder. Still, in certain cases, the aim is to steal time. Before you know it, **you awake one day with very little life left to do something for your people**.

A number of Hip hop activists like Davey D and Troy Nkrumah have made it clear that we continue to be targeted. Nkrumah, of the National Hip Hop Political Convention, has spoken about a report from the NYPD that named several Black entertainers who were under surveillance:

> Many popular artists are being followed, reported on and tracked for "political" reasons. That report sited the influence these artists would have if they started becoming political and started speaking on political issues. We are talking about people like, Jay Z, P-Diddy, Alicia Keys, just to name a few that were spied upon by the Rap Police. Another report came out of Miami a few years back showing the surveillance of other popular rappers.

This is going on everywhere, making it a "systemic" problem. A systemic problem is one that is so widespread it can't be stopped in just one place at a time. It is part of a bigger system that must be stopped altogether. From New York to Detroit to Miami to Atlanta to L.A. to Texas, it's going down.

Cedric Muhammad, of the *Black Agenda Report* website (www.BlackAgendaReport.com) reported:

> In the year 2000, I was actually present at Congress for the hearing surrounding the Rap-A-Lot investigation. The Houston police department, the IRS, the DEA and the FBI, all had James Prince and the rapper Scarface and really the whole 5th Ward of Houston, under surveillance, in their hearings. I'm sitting right there. They're giving me paperwork. I'm actually able to see who the undercover agents were. They admit that they had close to 400 informants inside of the 5th Ward that were related to this investigation. So, I think eventually they arrested Scarface on some possession of marijuana charge. Does that really warrant 400 informants and FBI, DEA, the IRS?

But why crush hip hop? Is it all about Black people getting money? No. It's deeper than that. They don't care if you getting "stupid money" and stayin' stupid. They're worried about something else.

As Bradley Gooding said in "Poor Righteous Teachers: The Story of the FBI and the Five Percenters," the reason why the FBI and COINTELPRO couldn't crush the growth of the Five Percenters was because they knew how to destroy political movements, but not cultural movements. So, ever since the birth of hip hop, and especially since the conscious rap of the 1980s, the people in power have sought to destroy the cultural movement that is hip hop...because it is dangerous.

When Public Enemy, KRS-One, and the Poor Righteous Teachers were making young Black people want to change their lives, educate themselves, and fix their communities, it became clear how dangerous hip hop was. That's why gangster rap was ushered in right away, with the help of powerful men like Jerry Heller (see "The Cycles of History"). And since Tupac was killed, everybody's been too scared to say anything.

And when they do, either their albums flop or they're getting shot. That's why I was sad, but not surprised, when I learned what happened to Soulja Slim.

Soulja Slim

Soulja Slim was born in the Magnolia Projects of New Orleans on September 9, 1977. After changing his name from Magnolia Slim to Soulja Slim upon joining No Limit Records, he produced a number of underground and mainstream hits with No Limit until he formed his own label in 2002.

On November 26, 2003, Slim was shot several times in the face and chest in front of his mother's home in the 7th Ward of New Orleans. According to Nik Cohn's book *Triksta: Life and Death and New Orleans Rap*, some of Slim's so-called "friends" stole the Rolex from his wrist before making the news public. Other "friends" raided his studio and stole his clothes, shoes, and the laptop containing his next album. Slim was buried in the leather camouflage outfit he wore for the cover of his 1998 release "Give It 2 'Em Raw" to symbolize the fact that he was a "Soulja 4 Life."

Soon, the police and the media spread rumors that there was a $10,000 hit placed on him by No Limit Records.

22-year-old Garelle Smith from the St. Bernard Projects in the 7th Ward was named as the likely hit man. Smith was arrested on December 30, 2003 and charged with Slim's murder. The gun that was used to kill Slim was a police-issue .40 caliber Glock semi-automatic pistol that Garelle Smith allegedly stole from the home of a New Orleans police officer. Ballistics tests determined that the gun was used in the killing, but for some reason the charges against Smith were dropped in February 2004. Slim's killer has still not been found.

So…Execution-style murder? An attempt to place blame on a "rival" record label? A police officer's gun? Suspect released? No killer found? Hmm…Who killed Soulja Slim, and why?

Of course, the media presented Slim's murder as his own doing, stating: "The Nov. 26 murder eerily echoed the violence of his profanity-laced songs, which told of gangs, drugs and drive-by shootings."

His stepfather had another side to the story. He said envy of Soulja Slim's swift rise might have motivated the killing. He said the performer's dark themes weren't meant to incite violence, but rather to expose the chaos of "ghetto life" so it might be cured. To prove his point about his stepson's character, he added that Slim broke no laws after ending a four-year prison stint in 2001 for a parole violation. But Soulja Slim wasn't just trying to "get his sh*t right," as he rapped in the song "Street Life." He was saying some dangerous sh*t. Just take one look at one of the kind of music he was making before his murder:

> "We talk a lot about Malcom X and Martin Luther King Jr.,
> but it's time to be like them, as strong as them.
> They were mortal men like us and everyone of us can be like them.
> I don't want to be a role model. I just want to be someone who says,
> "This is who I am, this is what I do. I say what's on my mind."*
> Tupac Shakur

One of my favorite Soulja Slim songs is "Soulja 4 Life," which was re-released on dead prez and the Outlawz compilation album, *Can't Sell Dope Forever*, as "Soulja Life Mentality."

On it, Slim raps:

> Money in the bank dawg, dem haters don' like dat/ Bitch this ain't the slave days, us niggas gon' fight back/ You crackers can write dat all up in the magazines/ Put me on a TV screen and I'm gon' say the same things/ You can call me racist, Black man in this white world/ I'm sick seein' sell out niggas married to these white girls/ Knowin' they the enemy, can't never be no friend of me/ I just get my dick sucked, nut in they mouth instantly/…Black man kill a Black man, it's cool they lovin dat/ Black man kill a white man and they sentencin' him to death/ White man kill a black man, they scream about self-defense/ Break it down to manslaughter, with all of the evidence/ Ever since I been here, been nothin' but sin here/ I done backed up out the game, just to pursue my career/ So I'm gon' say this loud and clear, mothaf*ck the white man/ Ku Klux Klan talk sh*t, but they don't wanna start sh*t

Does his death make sense now? Can you imagine how dangerous those ideas are in the South? Black people in the South, New Orleans especially, have always been on some gangsta sh*t. The mentality Soulja Slim had adopted in his last years had explosive potential, especially if those ideas caught on and spread like wildfire. Now ask yourself the question. Who killed Soulja Slim, and why?

> They fear the uprising.
> They know that one man can change everything.

MOVIES TO SEE

The Recruit; Spy Game; The Bourne Trilogy; The Good Shepherd
The CIA is deep. Enough said.

50 CENT: A LIFE OF LIES?

50 Cent was born into poverty as Curtis James Jackson III in Queens, New York on July 6, 1975. Today, he's one of the richest and most powerful Black celebrities in the country.

I can't lie. 50 Cent is smart. He may look like a big ass goon, but he's no dummy. According to *Forbes Magazine*, 50 earned $41 million in 2005 (mostly from record sales and branding deals that included a clothing line, a line of sneakers, a street lit book line, and a video game), ranking him eighth on the *Forbes'* list of the world's 100 most powerful celebrities. More recently, Coca-Cola bought VitaminWater for $4.1 billion, earning Curtis Jackson about $100 million since he bought a percentage of the company in 2004. You can't argue about whether or not 50 is a good businessman.

He definitely has an impressive resume: This man went from slinging crack at twelve to having a net worth of at least $200 million and living in Mike Tyson's old mansion (which he bought in 2003 for $4 million and is now selling for $20 million). That's one hell of a businessman.

But we know that businessmen aren't known for their integrity and honor. They lie. They cheat. They steal. And they continuously scheme to increase their profits.

Curtis has admitted that his target audience is suburban white kids, so that's our first clue that he's not being entirely real with us. How much of his persona is really him, and how much is part of the business plan? We know what the suburban white kids want from Black people: Angry, dangerous gangsters that vent all of their frustrations for them, in ways they could never imagine doing in their quiet, privileged lives.

So is 50 who he presents himself to be? We know that, other than a small time drug offense where he served an eight month boot camp sentence, 50 has no major convictions. According to one of his old business partners, it's all for show: "Yeah 50 sold drugs, but 'I'ma kill you' and all that sh*t...he don't do that. He ain't never shot nobody, cut or stabbed nobody... nothing like that. None of them niggas [are like that], from Banks to Yayo," stated 50's old friend and partner Bang 'Em

Smurf. Smurf claimed that G-Unit's superthug persona is an image and a marketing tool the Queens emcees have used to get to the top.

In his own autobiography, *From Pieces to Weight*, 50 admits, "Most of the niggas out there who talk gangsta and thug sh*t in raps don't really want to be a part of the stuff they're putting on their records."

Really? Maybe the whole "50 Cent" persona is made up, considering that he lifted the name from a real Brooklyn thug who used to rob rappers, right before Curtis released his first single "How to Rob an Industry Nigga" in 2000. There's even a full-length DVD out about *The Real 50 Cent*, Kelvin Martin.

It gets deeper. According to that *Forbes* article I mentioned earlier:

> Fiddy doesn't smoke marijuana or drink alcohol--often filling up an empty bottle of Hennessy with iced tea to drink on stage--and he's never viewed music as a passion. "I've never been obsessed with it," he said. "I never got into it for the music. I got into it for the business."

Wow. So he pretends to drink Hennessy and smoke weed, as he claims in songs like "High All the Time"? That's not gangsta. But what 50 does isn't meant to be truly gangsta. It's all for show. And who's he aiming to please? White people.

But wait...he *did* get shot nine times, though. Right?

Wrong. According to the official police report, 50 was NOT shot nine times, or even five, which would have tied him up with Tupac. Tupac really did get shot five times and live, and that definitely helped get him more recognition and respect. Maybe that's what 50 was thinking about when he lied. According to his police report, which you can look up at www.mediatakeout. com, the truth is that he was only hit by three bullets.

A liar, huh? What about a snitch?

Well, I'm sure you know he brought down the Murder, Inc. empire that

```
.CAR010C              NEW YORK CITY POLICE DEPARTMENT            01/24/03
OCAR10M                ABBREVIATED UF61 INQUIRY                   19:04
                     YEAR: 2000 / PCT: 113 / NUM: 005204
_ STAT: COMP: 005204  DAY: THU  FR DT: 05/24/00 FR TIME: 11:20 (RPT DT: 05/24/00)
        P.LAW: 12010   PDCODE: 109  OFFENSE: ASSAULT 1F          JURIS: 00
        ADDR1: 140AVE & 161 ST       LOC: STORE UNCLASSIFIED
        ADDR2:                       PREM: OTHER
_(VICT: NAME: JACKSON, CURTIS )      SEX: M  RACE: BLACK          AGE: 24
  01/01 ADDR: 140-56 161 ST QUEENS , NY
        TEL#: ( 718 ) 528 - 1441     ACTN:
VEHI:   #:           STATE:    YEAR:     MAKE:      MODEL:
        COLR:
PROP:   MV:     CU:     JL:    CL:    WP:    OF:   TV:    HG:    CO:    MS:
WEAP: TYPE:                                 MODEL:         MAKE:
  01/01 DESC: SMALL BLK HAND GUN            COLOR: BLACK
PERP: NAME:                         SEX:      RACE:              AGE:
        HGT:  '      WGT:     EYE COLOR:     HAIR LEN:     FAC HAIR:
_ DETL: 01/02  _ WITH: 01/01
  REPORTER STATES THAT UNK TWO PERPS IN A BLUE OR BLACK VEHICLE DID BLOCK HIS
  CAR AS HE ATTEMPTED TO MAKE A U TURN.PASSANGER DID GET OUT OF THAT VEHICLE
  WALKED OVER TO THE FRONT OF THE COMP'S VEHICLE AND PULLED OUT SMALL BLK
  HANDGUN AND FIRED MULTIPLE SHOTS (THREE SHOTS HIT THE VECTIM) ON THE RIGHT
  P3 = EXIT / ENTER = PROCESS / 'X' TO EXPAND / 'N' FOR NEXT / PF11 = CLEAR
  INQUIRY WAS SUCCESSFUL ...
```

produced Ja Rule, 50's arch enemy. Murder, Inc., it was revealed, was financed by Kenneth "Supreme" McGriff, a drug kingpin 50 seemed to be obsessed with. When whatever relationship they had went sour, it went *real* sour. How did 50 get back at him? Did he go after them with a "Fully Loaded Clip"?

No! He just put out a song or two naming their names and started a rap beef by attacking their artist Ja Rule (for making "singsong" rap, which is what 50 started doing shortly thereafter).

When the Feds questioned him about it, he told them to listen to his lyrics for clues. Then, as the investigations began and the beef escalated, G-Unit took out a restraining order against Irv Gotti and the rest of Murder, Inc. Before long, McGriff went down hard.

As if the snitching, lying, and pretending weren't enough, 50 goes even further in being a dancing monkey for white people with money. According to one website discussing 50 and G-Unit, 50 changed the name from Guerrilla Unit to Gorilla Unit "because he felt guerilla was too military." I doubt it was *his* decision.

> "Twelve monkeys on stage, it's hard to tell who's the gorilla/ You should have stayed as a drug dealer"
> Common, "Start the Show"

And when Kanye West was brave enough to say "George Bush doesn't care about Black people" in response to Hurricane Katrina, guess who jumped to defend Bush? Curtis said, "The New Orleans disaster was meant to happen. It was an act of God. I think people responded to it the best way they can. What Kanye West was saying, I don't know where that came from."

Only thing true about this guy is that he's a true slave.

This guy sounds more and more like somebody's telling him what to say and do the more you learn about him. And think about it. When Black people listen to him, what's the direction the music and the messages push us to: *Guerrilla* Unit (movement of revolutionaries) or *Gorilla* Unit (bunch of f*cking monkeys)?

As Kenneth "Supreme" McGriff, who was recently sentence to life in prison, said about him:

> That cracker is pimping him. He ain't nothing but a motherf*cking house nigger who set everything, set us back 150 years. Next thing he gonna be doing is macaroni and cheese commercials.

What's your opinion of an individual who lives like this? Why?

Note: In Fall of 2009, 50 Cent and Robert Greene finally released their book, The *50th Law*. It's decent advice for any aspiring entrepreneur, but you can tell they've been influenced by the work of other *(ahem)* "urban self-help" authors. In fact, Greene admitted that there were two versions of the book. I could say more, but I don't want 50's lawyers on me. Anyway, in the book, Curtis confesses, "50 Cent is a person I created. Soon it will be time to destroy him and become somebody else."

A bad reputation is a death in itself.

A 2012 AFTERWORD ON 50 CENT

When we released the third edition of How to Hustle and Win, a lot had changed. Many of the "young rappers" I talked about who "just came out" had come and gone and were already forgotten. I tried to update their names with newer young rappers who fit the same description, but by the next printing, those rappers were gone too. So I quit, and left it as is, figuring everyone would get the message regardless. I tried to catch up on some of the historical things that had changed, but the messages were the same, so I left the essays the same. And, with the exception of a few corrections, I didn't plan on doing any more edits to this book. But since I first published *How to Hustle and Win*, one of the things my readers always talk to me about is this article on 50 Cent. They love it, because it throws dirt on a dude that a lot of people love to hate. And I stand by it, because much of it needed to be said. But I've got an additional lesson to pull from the life of 50 Cent, one that I'm proud of. A while back, I sent this book out to a close friend of 50's, who shared it with him. From what I understand, he wasn't too thrilled about his portrayal. And since that time, I swear I've seen him transform in the public eye. He still put out a lot of the same music, and kept up a beef here and there for publicity's sake, but that brother nearly starved himself to play a cancer patient for the movie *Things Fall Apart*, which I discussed in *The Hood Health Handbook*. And then he got on his humanitarian thing. He committed to feeding a billion hungry children and ending hunger in Africa. And he put his money where his mouth was, dedicated the proceeds from his Street King energy drink to the cause. And he actually went to Africa to get into the hands-on part of the work. He went on a Twitter rant, talking about how f*cked up things are for poor children in Africa, appealing for his fans to get involved.

And most recently, he's suggested that he's going to start changing his lyrics, talking about real social issues that he's became aware of since his "pilgrimage" to Kenya. So I commend him, and it would be unjust of me to allow this 5th edition to go to print without adding this addendum. The lesson here? People can change. Support them when they do! It'll motivate more of us to change for the better when we see others being supported for the changes they've made. When we continue to hate on people who are clearly trying to do better, we're not helping the problem. In fact, we're giving the ones who are changing a reason to say "Well f*ck it then." One example is Soulja Boy. After he got a copy of this book, where I also talk about him pretty bad, he started his own path to redemption. He started with tweets attacking racism and the military industrial complex. Nobody supported him. He did a song called "Third Eye Open" and people said he was throwing up gang signs instead of realizing he was trying to find "consciousness." And ever since he did all that, his buzz got killed. It's no accident. If you want people to change, you have to be prepared to support them! Otherwise they'll fall off, or return to doing the same bullsh*t you criticize. Fortunately, 50's got enough bread to sustain this positive kick. I salute him for even taking that RISK though. And I hope his transformation continues, and I hope books like this can continue to influence others to do the same. Speaking of which, yall saw this book in that "Deeper than the Ocean" video by Future, right?

THE KING OF CRUNK

You can't miss Lil Jon when he appears. Whether he's promoting his energy drink, Crunk Juice, or doing a cameo in a video, Lil Jon is the undisputed king of hype in the South. He became famous introducing the world to crunk music, which took over airwaves from "Put Ya Hood Up" in 2001 to "Snap Yo Fingers" in 2005. He's been everywhere from Subway commercials to the *Chappelle Show*, doing his trademark routine. You know what it is, dreadlocks swingin, grill shining, screaming "What?!" "Yeaaaah!" and "Okaayyy!" at the top of his lungs.

At this point, Lil Jon is still one of the most recognized faces in hip hop across the world.

But what most people don't know about him is that he's not anything like what you see on TV. All that screaming and acting crazy? That's a performance.

In real life, Lil Jon goes home to a quiet life with his wife and kids. Behind those sunglasses, his eyes show his calm and intelligence. Yes, intelligent. Matter fact, after he graduated from Douglass High School in Atlanta in 1989, he went on to pursue a bachelors and masters degree. But like other college graduates in hip hop (like Master P or David Banner) you'd never be able to tell. I have some friends who went to high school with Lil Jon. He was a DJ then also. But Jonathan Smith was also a total nerd. Normally, people wouldn't f*ck with somebody like him, but he threw the livest house parties around. And while his parents were gone, every teenager in Atlanta was partying at his house. It was there that he learned what it takes to keep the crowd hype.

Now he's taken that skill and turned it into an image that people will remember even after he's long gone. But that image only comes out when it's time to perform. When that 12-pound, 73-carat "Crunk Ain't Dead" chain comes off his neck, he's humble, well-spoken, and family-oriented. Some people, on the other hand, don't know how to "turn it off." They're a thug in the streets, so they stay a thug at a job interview…and don't get the job. Or they're calm and intelligent, but don't know how to show another side when they're around a group of wild knuckleheads. That's how you get eaten alive. It's a successful man that knows how to wear the mask, as well as when to take it off. It's also an honest man who reveals, as Lil Jon does, that his "crunk" image is not who he really is in his personal life.

Wear the right face at the right time.

STUCK ON THE CORNER

It was almost like the little crew of guys who hung out a few blocks from my house took me on as their pet project. They made it their mission to teach the fresh-faced wide-eyed Indian kid to ice grill, slapbox, wrestle, climb fences, play the dozens, and of course, roll a blunt and smoke weed.

I've never turned down a learning opportunity. So it wasn't long before I was running with the stick-up kids, them in it because of need from poverty, me in it out of a want for adventure.

It also wasn't long before the newness of it wore off, and everything in this world began feeling natural, and everything outside of this world became increasingly foreign. And of course, it wasn't long until I was being frisked or running from cops daily. We did a lot of stupid sh*t. Like running across the hoods and roofs of rows of parked cars, or playing chicken by tying our shoes in the middle of busy roads, or playing  manhunt in abandoned houses and jumping off roofs and out of windows. Scaling the ledges and fire escapes of apartment buildings and jumping from rooftop to rooftop sounds really stupid and dangerous, doesn't it? We *loved* it.

Throwing rocks and empty beer bottles at people and cars from the roofs of people's homes sounds cruel and deranged, doesn't it?

Fun, fun, fun.

Insulting each other's mothers until somebody was ready to fight?

Pure entertainment.

I'd already begun drinking when I was about 12 or 13, but this new set of circumstances introduced me to a much more diverse, and more regular, enjoyment of hard liquor. Boone's Farm, Mad Dog 20/20, Thunderbird, all the cheap sh*t, basically. We were young winos I guess. Forty ounce bottles of St. Ides and Olde English 800 littered the church steps where we hung out nightly, interspersed by the occasional 32 oz. Magnum from the days when all you had was a dollar to spend. Oh, how could I forget the most phenomenal drink ever invented? Cisco, otherwise known as "Liquid Crack."

You would think that anything nicknamed Liquid Crack wasn't fit for human consumption, and with the way it rolled around in the bottle like oil instead of splashing like a normal liquid, it was clear that it really wasn't.

But in many ways, we weren't fully human. In a way I'd later learn Frantz Fanon had put it succinctly, we were functioning on a subhuman level...and proud of it. Drinking daily, sometimes alone so I wouldn't have to share my liquor or my moments of clarity, freestyling huddled around a pause tape playing on a small boombox, fighting tooth and nail over petty bullsh*t, and smoking five or six participants to a single blunt of low-grade weed, and then eatin' bullsh*t snacks from the corner store or the wing spot...This is the way life was to be until I left New Jersey, and this was all there was to life. To simplify things, I even put it all in an easy-to-follow table below:

Life in Jersey City, circa 1995-96		
Activities	Foods	Drinks
Freestyling	Buffalo Wings/ Fried Chicken	Red or Blue Flavored "Drinks"
Slapboxing/Wrestling	Large French Fries	50 Cent Sodas
Random Crime	Hot Chips/Spicy Pickles	Cheap 40 oz. beers (St. Ides, OE 800)
Drinking/Smoking	Pork Products (Pork Rinds, Pickled Sausages, Slim Jims)	Cheap Wine (Thunderbird, Night Train)
Talking Sh*t	Sunflower Seeds	Hard Liquor (Hennessey, Alize, Seagram's Gin)

And that's really all there was to life.

What have I learned from looking back? Besides the fact that I was on the way to cirrhosis of the liver, or an ulcer from all that spicy bullsh*t, I've realized that I had boxed myself in completely. There were certain things you just couldn't do or say in the hood because they were outside of that "box."

I started trying to convince my partners to come out to New York City with me. It was just a train ride away, and I knew there were a ton of fine females out there to holler at. They weren't with it. So I tried the mall. These motherf*ckers didn't even want to hit the mall. At least, not more than once every month or two. It ain't like we had sh*t better to do. We were just stuck on our corner.

> "Life shrinks or expands in proportion to one's courage."
> Anais Nin (1903-1977)

And they wouldn't admit it, but they were scared to try anything else. When I reported that I'd met some girls on one of my solo trips to a neighboring city, and that these girls wanted to meet them, they all talked a good game about how it was gonna go down. When the time came, smoking a blunt took precedence over making the trip.

Eventually, I started heading out to Manhattan on my own. I'd go out there and drink my liquor, smoke my cigarettes, and take in all the sights. I'd flirt with the girls, talk to strangers, and made a few friends and a few enemies. And it was invigorating. I finally felt alive, being let out of my cage. It was those early trips out of Jersey City that gave me the desire and the confidence to leave the North altogether to move down South by myself at 16. And life ain't never been the same since.

It takes courage to leave your corner.

MOVIES TO SEE

Boyz in the Hood; Always Outnumbered, Always Outgunned; Gang Tapes

Boyz in the Hood is the classic story of coming of age in the ghetto. The most significant point in the film, for me, is the knowledge that father Furious Styles drops on the young men from the hilltop overlooking the hood.

Always Outnumbered is based on a book by Walter Mosley, an excellent Black author. It's a classic story of a Black man doing what's right in the hood, against all the odds.

Gang Tapes is pretty interesting. It's supposed to be footage from a videocamera that some young gang members stole and used to record every thing going on in the hood. If you pay attention, you'll get the message out of it.

THE XXX YEARS

"Good judgment comes from experience, and experience comes from bad judgment."
Barry LePatner

This is your life. From ages 0-13, it's all about physical development. You're learning the basics (hopefully) about how to function in this world, but you won't be doing much yet.

From 13-17, it's like prep. You might THINK you're doin it big, but you're just getting your feet wet.

From 17-25, these are some of the most important years of your life. These are what I call the XXX years. Not because they'll be XXX-rated (though they might be), but because of the three Xs: eXperience, eXperiment, and eXplore.

> **Did You Know?**
> Puberty reshapes brain structure? That's why adolescence is so emotionally unpleasant. Hormones like testosterone actually influence the development of neurons in the brain, and the changes made to brain structure have many behavioral consequences. Expect emotional awkwardness, apathy and poor decision-making skills as regions in the frontal cortex mature.

eXperience: During this time, you're going to learn a lot about life…the hard way (See "Life is the Best Teacher"). As long as you're intelligent enough to avoid the traps that will get you killed or sent to prison, you shouldn't be scared to live life. Some of your lessons you'll pick up by listening to people who can coach and mentor you (See "Each One, Teach One"), but others you'll simply have to learn through hard experiences.

eXperiment: An experiment of any kind begins with an idea tha is tested through trial and error. Most experiments involve a little bit of guesswork, a whole lot of predictions, and a gang of dissapointments. This may be the time in your life when you want to try all kinds of new sh*t, and see what's for you and what's not. Have fun. Break the mold. Take calculated risks. Do what no one else has done. That way you won't have regrets when you're 30 and 40. Just don't do no homo sh*t.

eXplore: While you're experimenting with life and people, why not see what the world has to offer you? When I was 18, I started buying Greyhound tickets and making trips to see the country. That inspired me to start taking advantage of AirTran Airline's Xfares discount, which allows young people to fly for super-cheap rates. I suggest you do the same. Get out of your box. Travel. Meet new kinds of people. Go places you normally wouldn't go. You may discover something that will profoundly affect the course of your entire life.

Explore, Experience, Experiment.

MANHOOD

"I take this time to write this missive, that you might better understand, therefore better endure, the long suffering of becoming a man without ever learning what or who you are in the present scheme of things."

Rober H. deCoy, *The Nigger Bible*

Manhood is about a lot of things. Problem is, most of us never find out what those things are. So we play around at it, for 10, 20, 30, even 40 years...never fully becoming grown men. I was going to write a long essay on what it means to become a man. I was going to write about choices, and independence, and maturity, and patience, and almost a hundred other things.

Then I remembered something I'd learned back in school could do the job just fine. I just happened to be paying attention in high school English Literature when the professor showed us Rudyard Kipling's poem *If*. It may sound crazy, but this poem from 1895 could help a lot of us out today. It goes:

If you can keep your head when all about you
Are losing theirs and blaming it on you;
If you can trust yourself when all men doubt you,
But make allowance for their doubting too;
If you can wait and not be tired by waiting,
Or, being lied about, don't deal in lies,
Or, being hated, don't give way to hating,
And yet don't look too good, nor talk too wise;

If you can dream, and not make dreams your master;
If you can think, and not make thoughts your aim;
If you can meet with triumph and disaster
And treat those two imposters just the same;
If you can bear to hear the truth you've spoken
Twisted by knaves to make a trap for fools,
Or watch the things you gave your life to broken,
And stoop and build 'em up with wornout tools;

If you can make one heap of all your winnings
And risk it on one turn of pitch-and-toss,
And lose, and start again at your beginnings
And never breathe a word about your loss;
If you can force your heart and nerve and sinew
To serve your turn long after they are gone,
And so hold on when there is nothing in you
Except the Will which says to them: "Hold on";

If you can talk with crowds and keep your virtue,
Or walk with kings – nor lose the common touch;

Did You Know?

You could learn a lot about America from Harry Holzer's 10-year survey of attitudes among Black males toward employment. In 1979, as the decline in factory jobs set in, researchers asked Black men whether they had a better chance making a living illegally or legally. Sixty percent preferred to stay legit. When Holzer's team asked the same question again in 1989, that number fell to 40 percent.

If neither foes nor loving friends can hurt you;
If all men count with you, but none too much;
If you can fill the unforgiving minute
With sixty seconds' worth of distance run -
Yours is the Earth and everything that's in it,
And – which is more – you'll be a Man, my son!

Manhood is not easy, but the conscious decision to truly become a man is one of the most important steps.

LIFE IS THE BEST TEACHER

I've probably been through more women than I should admit. Fortunately, I've been smart enough not to rack up any baby mamas or STDs along the way. But good condoms can't save a man from everything. Over the past several years, I've been through just about every bad relationship you could imagine. It seemed like I kept experiencing the same drama, time after time. Just as soon as one problem would go away, I'd find myself with a new set of issues to deal with. For a while, I blamed the women I was meeting. When I realized a man can only blame himself for the sh*t he goes through in life, I started looking for the real reasons behind my problems.

What I saw was that every time I didn't learn from a bad relationship, I was bound to encounter the same drama the next time around, like a class I kept failing and having to take over again. Once I learned the lesson, I avoided the problem from then on. It took me several years, but I finally learned enough to situate myself in the best relationship I've ever been in. Finally…**no more drama**. Smart, sensible, secure, AND she's fine as a motherf*cker.

But here's a recap of six relationships I had to go through before getting where I am now, minus the countless smut stories and flings in between. (I'll include some of those stories in *Part Two*) I've noted the problems I experienced in each relationship, and the lessons I learned:

Relationship	Problems I Experienced	Lessons I Learned
Misha (1997-1998)	She doesn't share any of my interests She's young and immature She's still trying to find herself	Don't be with someone too young to appreciate you
Nia (1998-1999)	She's ten years older than me, and nags me like my mother She's insecure and always jealous She's hardheaded and uncomfortable with change	Don't be with someone old enough to be your mom.
Princess (2001-2002)	She doesn't share any of my interests She's not trustworthy She's used to a completely different type of dude	Don't be with someone who doesn't share any of your interests.
Amber (2003-2004)	She's still trying to find herself She's not trustworthy	Don't be with someone who is with you to "try

	She's used to a completely different type of dude	something different."
Anisah (2004-2005)	She's insecure and always jealous She's hardheaded and uncomfortable with change She wants to be in charge	Don't be with someone who always wants to be in charge.
Kay (2006-2007)	She's still trying to find herself She's hardheaded and uncomfortable with change	Don't be with someone who thinks they're too smart or too good to change and grow.

If you noticed, every time I actually learned something, I didn't experience it again. Any time I missed a lesson, I experienced the problem again and again until I learned. Life is like this, whether it's in terms of love, business, or any other area. As philosopher George Santayana said, "Those who do not learn from history are bound to repeat it."

You *will* repeat a class you don't pass.

ADVICE FOR A YOUNG PLAYA

Here are 15 tips on presentation and appearance. In many situations, the first impression is the last impression. Just as you can blow your chances with a female by having the wrong approach, you can shut yourself out of thousands of opportunities in life by having a f*cked-up presentation of yourself.

1. **To begin, cut them damn fingernails down.** I'm not saying you need to start getting manicures. But I'm tired of my palm bleeding every time I give a young dude a strong dap.

2. **Check your breath often.** Nobody wants to talk to you, and you can't figure out why? Do people seem to move away when you start talking? It's obvious. There's nothing worse than the sh*tmouth. Keep gum and mints on you at all times. You can check your own breath by running your finger down your tongue or coughing into your hand.

3. **Stop feeling yourself (or your girl).** Public groping of yourself or anyone else is just not acceptable in today's society. It makes you look like a deviant that needs to be locked away somewhere before he rapes an old lady.

4. **Stop spitting in public.** Especially if you can't clear your chin. It's bad enough leaving nasty globs where other people walk, but even worse when you get some on yourself. At least spit discretely into some bushes.

5. **Adjust your walk.** You can't take that pimp bop, gangsta swagger, hunchback goon shuffle, or George Jefferson monkey-walk with you

everywhere you go. I'm not saying walk like you have a stick in your ass. I'm saying tone it down when you go other places where it's not the norm. Like your job.

6. **YOU DON'T NEED TO SCREAM TO COMMUNICATE!** Stop all that yelling and loud-talking in places where you supposed to keep a low voice. It just looks bad when you see a hoodrich dude in a nice restaurant for probably the first time...and he's making himself look like a real jackass by talking so loud everyone from the chef to the valet can hear him. Even worse if he's can't pronounce sh*t on the menu. You also don't look cool when you're on the bus talking loud on phone...especially if it's personal business. Even worse, if you're using Bluetooth. Because then you look like a weirdo talking to himself.

7. **Enunciate.** Yes, e-nun-ci-ate. That means speak clearly. If you're with your people, and everybody talks the same way, that's one thing, but nobody wants to call Customer Service and hear somebody who sounds like they got marbles in they mouth. Again, know when to switch it up.

8. **Learn the etiquette.** If you're in a proper kind of place, like a fancy restaurant or a job interview, you need to follow the correct etiquette. You ain't Chris Tucker or Martin Lawrence, so the sh*t ain't funny when you just start making sh*t up and lookin ignorant. If you don't know what to do, read up on it or ask questions beforehand.

9. **Observe the dress code.** If it says "business attire," wear that. Don't wear a white tee with a suit jacket over it. And no matter where you are, even if you work at a fast food place, please don't ever try to sag some slacks or dress pants.

10. **Stop telling on yourself.** Stop making drug transactions over your phone. Stop wearing graphic t-shirts that promote drugs while you have drugs on you. Stop reporting to your job or your probation officer high or drunk. Stop telling people what you're going to do to them before you try to do it.

11. **Take your fights outside, preferably out back somewhere.** If you really want to fight, that is. Fighting indoors seems cool if there's fifty of y'all and three of them, but fighting indoors is usually also a sure bet that a few of y'all will get locked up and charged with assault and destruction of property.

12. **Two words:** Vi-sine.

13. **Get a belt.** I'm not knockin a dude saggin his pants. I'm knockin the dude who does dumb sh*t and can't get away because his pants keep falling down while he's trying to run.

14. **Use common sense.** Whatever you do, if you know it's something you shouldn't be doing, be discrete. Don't promote and advertise your bullsh*t. If you're with your girl and you want to look at some ass, look at it while she's distracted. Not while you're trying to get the girl's phone number by pretending she's a long-lost cousin. Unless you're a redneck, we don't look at our cousins' asses.

15. **Think ahead.** You get three strikes with the criminal justice system today. Don't waste them on petty sh*t. Nobody respects someone doing 25 to life for repeated shoplifting.

Image counts. Make sure the impression you leave with people is the one you want them to have of you.

SUPREME THE ASSHOLE ON "DIRT-BOMB MOTHAF*CKAS"

Two words: HY-GIENE. Your neck ain't supposed to be four shades darker than the rest of you. And the corners of your mouth and eyes ain't supposed to be white and crusty. Them bird baths ain't cutting it. You need to scrub hard. Get some steel wool and some dish detergent if you have to. And put some lotion on. And when you brush your teeth, do the front AND the back of your teeth. And your tongue. Like Ghostface said, stick the toothbrush all the way to back of your throat if you have to. That's where all that halitosis is at. Or maybe it's that rotten ass tooth you won't go to the dentist about. While you fixin yourself up, do something about those razor bumps. It looks like ostrich skin under your chin. Two more words: WEIGHT LOSS.

TRAPPED

The "trap" is Southern slang for a neighborhood where there's only one way in and one way out, making it easy to hustle out in the open while avoiding police raids. Dopeboys see the "trap" catching addicts, or catching suckers who aren't from around there. Some take the "trap" idea to the next level and believe that they could trap police there as well.

THE GAME IS COLD.

Basically, the hustlers see themselves doing the trapping.

On the other hand, a few of us see the trap for what it is…and who's really being trapped.

After all, who lives in the trap? Who's stuck in the trap from 5 pm to 5 am? Who can't leave their trap because the boys from that other trap want to do something to em? Who is never going to make it out of the trap? And finally, who MADE the traps we stay in? Who created those conditions?

There's a shirt I like that says: Prison, Parole, and Probation are TRAPS. If you can't see how, this must be the first page you've read in this book.

Do you know how many people sentenced to death row become exonerees when DNA evidence shows they never committed a crime? Do you know how many of those people were Black? As a side note, do you know how many of these people went to death row because their alleged crimes were against a white woman?

Do you know how many kids are being tried as adults, and being sentenced to adult prisons? Do you know how many of those kids are Black?

Do you know how big the differences are between the punishments for Black people committing drug offenses and white people committing drug offenses?

Do you know why?

I've never heard it better than the way Charshee McIntyre put it:

> I place the practice of imprisoning African Americans, particularly the males, in the founding father's structural design of this nation...From the beginnings of this nation, we, African Americans, have lived (and do live) with the fear that if we do not end up in prison or in some other form of institution, someone in our families will. I claim that our incarcerations occur not because of criminality or accidents of injustices but due to the structural design of this nation. Institutionalization became the ultimate solution in which Whites address the problem of having free Blacks in this country.[2]

With that being said, I want you to look back over this essay and consider this: Am I being trapped, or am I trapping myself? The simplest way to look at it is this: the powerless and simple-minded are trapped easily because they eagerly walk into the trap, expecting nothing. On the other hand, intelligent and powerful people often trap themselves by refusing to do what they know they can and should do.

Some of the brothers I hustled or hung with in Jersey were brilliant. We could have started businesses or moved to Atlanta, where jobs were available (then). But I was the only one who made it. Why?

Some of us feel trapped, when we are the ones trapping ourselves.

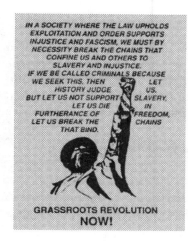

IN A SOCIETY WHERE THE LAW UPHOLDS EXPLOITATION AND ORDER SUPPORTS INJUSTICE AND FASCISM, WE MUST BY NECESSITY BREAK THE CHAINS THAT CONFINE US AND OTHERS TO SLAVERY AND INJUSTICE. IF WE BE CALLED CRIMINALS BECAUSE WE SEEK THIS, THEN LET HISTORY JUDGE US. BUT LET US NOT SUPPORT SLAVERY, LET US DIE IN FURTHERANCE OF FREEDOM, LET US BREAK THE CHAINS THAT BIND.

GRASSROOTS REVOLUTION
NOW!

HOW TO GO TO JAIL

If you're going to jail, don't let it be over some dumb sh*t like being a millionaire dogfighting with snitch friends, or trying to get into the dope game because you want to go from driving a 2005 Toyota to a 2007 Bentley. Don't go to jail because you feel like somebody disrespected you, and you reacted out of emotion. And please, PLEASE don't go to jail over a white girl. If you're gonna go to jail, there's only one reason I see fit:

Fighting injustice.

Now, there's smart ways to do that, and there's dumb ways.

Most of us are angry or plain misguided. So listen. Don't think you're making a statement by going to jail over some bullsh*t. I'm tired of hearing "Free Scotty" and "Free Junie" when these dudes are only doing 6 months for slapping their girlfriends. Second, it's not smart to get locked up for "going off" on the system like Brian Nichols…because no one will even know what the hell you thought you were fighting for.

Instead…if you put in enough work in the community, working to change people's minds, and working to change the community itself…that's enough to get their attention. You'll join great company, like all the Civil Rights leaders who did time fighting for what they believed in. Or all the free Blacks who went to jail trying to help slaves get free. Or the thousands of political prisoners who are in jails across America today. Here's a few names of Black political prisoners that you should know about:

Jalil Muntaqeem	Lorenzo Stone Bey	Phil Africa
Albert Nuh Washington	Mark Cook	Richard Mafundi Lake
Charles Sims Africa	Mumia Abu-Jamal	Robert Seth Hayes
Herman Bell	Mutulu Shakur	Sekou Kambui
Kojo Sababu	Ojore Lutalo	Sundiata Acoli

You can even read statements from each of them at the *Prison Activist* website (http://PrisonActivist.org).

> "This is dedicated to my motherf*cking teachers, Mutulu Shakur, Geronimo Pratt, Mumia Abu Jamal, Sekou Odinga, and all the real OGs, we out…"
> Tupac, "White Man's World"

There's a bigger list of political prisoners in the U.S. in the appendix. Hit em up. Then again, some of us don't even write to our own flesh and blood once they're locked up.

"You can jail a Revolutionary, but you can't jail the Revolution."
Huey P. Newton

Contact one or two them, if you're not already writing somebody in prison. It'll let them know that there are still young people on the outside who are interested in what they were fighting for. It will also give you a chance to develop your writing skills if they aren't where you want them to be, as well as give you a chance to learn more about what's really going on in this country of ours.

Even if you fall, fall for a good reason.

THE "STOP LYIN" CAMPAIGN

As an OG interviewed by the producers of the *Criminals Gone Wild* DVD explains, the "stop snitching" code was for criminals, not regular civilians:

> There's this thing about snitching and I want to get to that. Cause I've been thinkin about this for a while. And it needs an OG to talk about it. When I was coming up, it applied to me and my boys. If we did a crime together, and one of us get busted, we didn't tell on the other one. If somebody does something to somebody in your family and you ain't gon snitch, then that means that you gon get at that nigga…You didn't snitch because you didn't want the police to get him, cause YOU wanted to get him. It wasn't just you didn't snitch cause you didn't want to tell. "Snitchin" is for a criminal. If you ain't a criminal then that sh*t – "don't snitch" – don't apply to you…
>
> I recently seen an interview with this cat Cam'ron where he said if he found out he lived next door to a serial killer, he wouldn't tell police, he would just move away. So what he's saying is that he don't give a f*ck about your or me. That killer could kill your mother, my mother, and he ain't gonna say nothin. That mothaf*cka's out of his mind. What he really should have said is, 'If I knew a serial killer was livin next door to me, I'm gon get my boys and we gon go over there and take care of that mothaf*cka.'
>
> Okay, I could understand you don't want to call the cops on him, but you need to go over there and take care of him. Because next, that mothaf*cka might kill somebody in your family. You don't let nobody come into your community and do something to your family, or any of your friends' families, and don't do nothin about it. You better snitch, or you better get at that nigga whoever did it. If you don't do nothin about it, they gon come back and do it again. They gon think it's alright to come to your household or your block and do whatever the f*ck they want, because you ain't gonna snitch and you ain't gonna do nothin about it either.

But then again, Cam'ron is the same guy that pointed the finger at Jay-Z for getting him shot in DC, so his word ain't worth a one-ply sheet of used toilet paper. The point is, if you aren't policing the community, and making sure innocent people feel safe, those innocent people are ALLOWED to get outside help.

But a lot of us are stuck on a code we don't even understand. We're just saying whatever everyone else is saying. And we're gonna lose behind that kind of simple-minded thinking too. I know a brother who did 5 years behind some sh*t he had no part of. Guess why he thought he shouldn't clear his name? And you know the dudes who did it left him in there to rot. Just think about all the innocent brothers goin to jail, for takin the blame for some sh*t they weren't even responsible for. Guess what? That's part of the plan. If you or your organization gets powerful enough, pretty soon somebody will come around who will do some bullsh*t that will get YOU in trouble. And guess what else? They WON'T take the blame, AND they'll expect YOU not to give them up.

With that said, I've heard enough about the "Stop Snitching" campaign anyway. I've got something a lot better to campaign for. How about "Stop Lying"? As Pimp C said before his demise, "Stop lyin to these kids....Tell it like it is."

Here's the basics of the "Stop Lyin" campaign:

1. Stop actin like something you're not, because you'll get found out some day, some way.

2. Stop actin like some sh*t is all good, when it's not. That's why our kids are all f*cked up now, followin the wrong sh*t.

3. Stop becoming different people depending on who you're around.

4. Stop telling one group of people one thing, and another group something else.

5. Stop talking about sh*t you know nothing about, or tryin to act like an expert in some sh*t you barely understand.

6. Stop labeling yourself with descriptions that don't really fit you. For example, you ain't a "hustler" if your hustles never pay off. You ain't "getting paid" if you don't have more money than you did a year ago. You ain't a "gangsta" if you ain't runnin no organization. And you ain't a "pimp" if you ain't makin money sellin pussy. Think about it this way: You ain't "fightin" if you just getting your ass whupped and not getting no punches in. That's not called "fighting." That's called "getting beat up." Get it?

7. Stop giving people bad advice, especially if it's something that didn't work for you.

8. Stop making excuses for your own failures.

9. Stop telling yourself it's okay to be a half-assed f*ck-up.

10. Stop bein nothin and thinkin you somethin.

11. Stop trying to be what you think other people want you to be.

12. If you're smart, stop trying to "sound dumb," and if you're dumb, stop trying to "sound smart."

Tell it like it is, and act like yourself.

PLAYING DUMB

Now…I know you're thinking, "Damn, Supreme, shouldn't somebody dumb try to get smart? Ain't that a good thing?"

Yeah, it is a good thing to try to GET smart. That's not the same as trying to "sound" smart. Trying to "sound smart" usually occurs in one of the following four situations:

1. When you get stopped by the police, and you try to act like a good college student so the officer won't search you for weed.

2. When you're at a job interview, and you're trying to fake it.

3. When you're tryin to pull a chick that's "out of your league."

4. After you've learned some sh*t, and you feel like telling everybody.

Let me just tell you now, in all of the above situations, that "smart" sh*t won't really work.

With the police officer, he already knows whether he plans on searching you when he stops you.

With the job, you're either qualified or not.

With the female, she can smell your perpetrator cologne from a mile away…and the sh*t stinks. Step your game up. That "expert opinion" won't get you any pussy.

And in the last case, it's one of two possibilities:

1. The people you're talking to already know about the sh*t you're saying, or

2. The people you're talking to don't know about none of that sh*t, but they don't like all them big words you're using. They think you're tryin to show off, and you're making them feel dumb and small.

So here's my advice: Be yourself. There's no reason to try to use big-ass words now, or talk down to people. The people who love you will listen to what you're saying a lot more if you speak to them the way they're used to. That doesn't mean you've gotta do all the dumb sh*t you used to, just that you've gotta show them you're growing up…one day at a time. You just can't go from ignorant to genius in 2.5 seconds.

In fact, when I was 15, I explained most of the lessons I learned by comparing life to pussy or dope. Nobody thought I was trying to "sound smart" and everybody – even older people – started coming to me for advice.

But the truth is that most of you aren't really dummies. Most of you are f*cking brilliant, and you've just been dumbing yourself down all this time. Out of everyone who reads this book, at least 75% of y'all were the smartest kids in your class back in first and second grade. Sometime after third grade, a lot of you started shutting down, not giving a f*ck, and dumbing yourselves down. You probably had plenty of different reasons, but that's not what's important now. You're here now. You know now. You know you're smarter than a lot of the people you deal with, but you probably don't know how to break out of that box you put yourself in.

It's actually not as hard as you'd think. You have options. I'll put them in order, from easiest to hardest:

* Do what the others do, but think the way you choose.

* Start slipping in little bits and pieces of what you're learning and hope that some of the other fish will bite.

* Start slowly changing the company you keep, so that you can be around people who understand and accept the real you.

* Wake up one day and decide to be yourself, your real self, and knuckle up on anyone who has a problem with it.

No matter what path you take, don't switch up overnight, cause your eyes are open now. You're always going to have to speak the language of the people you talk to. And above all, nobody wants to hear preaching, even religious people. They just go to church for the music.

Finally, as Malcolm X said in his *Autobiography*:

> You have to be careful, very careful, introducing the truth to the Black man who has never previously heard the truth about himself, his own kind, and the white man…The Black brother is so brainwashed that he may even be repelled when he first hears the truth. Reginald advised that the truth had to be dropped only a little bit at a time. And you had to wait a while to let it sink in before advancing the next step.

The Earth wasn't made in a day (or 6).
Change will come, but give it time.

REALITY CHECK

You AIN'T rich if you can't buy the house without a loan…or if you only have a nice car, but live in an	You ARE rich if you have the money for the house, but you use your company to buy it and you spend nothing.

apartment.	
You AIN'T the man when you have control over a little pussy or money.	You ARE the man when you're in control of bigger things than pussy or money.
You AIN'T rich just because you have nice gear and kicks.	You ARE rich if the company that makes the gear and kicks pays you to wear them.
You AIN'T "big-time" just because kids and a few broke folks respect you.	You ARE "big-time" if politicians and executives respect you.
You AIN'T real if you act like a thug in the streets, but like a nerd around your mom.	You ARE real if you act like a nerd *all* the time.
You AIN'T powerful if you gotta spend money for people to like you.	You ARE powerful if people spend money on you, hoping you will like them.
You AIN'T a major player if you can die tomorrow, and nothing will change.	You ARE a major player if you die tomorrow, and ten more people rise up to continue your work.
You AIN'T smart if you keep getting caught, but never get convicted.	You ARE smart if you flip your money into something legit, so you don't have to worry about being caught.
You AIN'T happy if you have to drink, smoke, party, and f*ck to take your mind off your problems.	You ARE happy if you know how to solve every problem you have.

Be real with yourself and others. You may get away with lying to others, but the worst crime is lying to yourself.

SUCKERS AND HUSTLERS

> "There are only two kinds of people in the whole wide world, grifters and suckers...
> [With suckers,] let their stupid brains stay asleep in their chump world.
> Keep your own brain honed to razor sharpness in the secret world of con."
> Iceberg Slim

Iceberg Slim inspired a lot of people. Not only was he the reason why almost every rapper from Ice Cube to Ice-T put "ice" in their name, but his books inspired a legion of young hustlers in the same way that the movie Scarface inspired most of the dope dealers of the 80s and 90s. Most people missed the bad endings and the tragic truths contained in Slim's book like they did with Scarface, but I guess that's how 85% of people look at life anyway, huh?

In fact, Slim wrote: "Chumps prefer a beautiful lie to an ugly truth."

And as Robert Greene, author of *The 48 Laws of Power*, says about this quote in his online blog:

> The sucker wants to believe certain things about life and so projects these wishes on to the real world, seeing what he wants to see, not what is. A hustler thrives on reality, ugly or unpleasant--finds his poetry in the real. He sees the whole table and plays it as it lays.

Greene uses quotes from Iceberg Slim's classic novel *Pimp* – like the one above – to illustrate some of the major qualities that separate true hustlers from marks and suckers. Here are seven others:

"No point in getting upset about the unknown. Only suckers do that."

> A hustler has to deal with danger and risk. It's part of the game. You cannot control it all, nor would you want to. Chaos, unknown factors are not something to be anxious about. They represent opportunities for new angles, new hustles. The sucker cannot stand the unknown and so either fouls up by getting impatient and over anxious, or retreats to a false world of security and the known.

"Stop letting your mind leapfrog like a screwy sucker."

> A sucker's mind moves all over the place, forgetting the order of things and making chaos where there is none. Hustlers have to stay cool and focused on the chain of events as they unfold, the various angles that are being played, with the possible reactions. A hustler never forgets where the 8 ball lies and how to get to it methodically.

"I don't lag my bills like a sucker."

> Suckers have the wrong relationship to money. They try to save pennies here and there, or grasp for the big kill that has all the odds stacked against it. Money brings out all of their neuroses. A hustler understands money. It is a tool for power, for con, and a resource for pleasure. And he always knows the odds.

"Don't get foxed out of your bankroll. The con is made for everyone, you know."

> Anyone is susceptible to being conned. The wisest hustler can suddenly fall for the worst tramp and lose all of his money on her. The hustler is aware of his own weaknesses and openings to con. This awareness is his edge. A sucker thinks he knows it all and cannot be fooled. That is his fatal flaw.

"Never forget that a grifter's word has to be like a gold bond to his associates."

> Honor among thieves, in other words. Lower-level hustlers forget this and the importance of reputation. They get lost in the moment and screw the wrong person. Greed should never trump consideration for your credibility. If you don't understand the subtleties of this, you are a sucker.

"I went to the phone to call the Goddess. I walked away from it. It was a sucker play to call her so soon."

> Impatience is the hallmark of the sucker, and it is never clearer than in matters of seduction. He can't wait to call, spilling out his guts with a confession of love, or trying to reveal how eager he is to impress and please. Emotion trumps strategy. Patience and time is the hustler's creed. "I play for time and see what happens," says Elizabeth I, the great hustler Queen of England.

"...you blew your top like a mark. You should have stayed cool and figured some con with me to separate that sonuvabitch from a few grand."

> Anger is deadly and stupid. In a competitive and dangerous world, anger is a great temptation. But only a sucker gives into natural anger at the state of things by reacting with rants and outbursts. The hustler plays the bigger angle and gets revenge on the target by hitting him in his pocketbook, or his reputation. Anger is not repressed but properly channeled.

Sucker or Hustler? Mark or Con? Victim or Survivor…better yet, Victim or Victorious? It's up to you. The weak are often weak because they choose to stay asleep. It's up to you to think differently.

All of life is a choice. Choose the highest road.

SUPREME THE ASSHOLE ON "FOUL-MOUTH MOTHAF*CKAS"

Curse words aren't all bad. Sometimes you need to use one or two (or twenty) to get your point across the right way. Still, if you can't talk for a whole day without cursing, there's something wrong with your vocabulary. Basically, you don't have one. Go get a thesaurus and learn you some words. After all, sometimes it's better to call someone a "pompous, incestuous ingrate" than a "bitch-ass mothaf*cka."

A FAILURE TO COMMUNICATE

A drug lieutenant and his crew of soldiers returned to the boss's house after a long mission of punishment and retaliation. "How we doing?" asked the boss. "Boss," replied the lieutenant, "I've been putting in serious work with the goons, on all your enemies on the westside."

"What?" yelled the boss. "I don't have any enemies on the westside!"

"Oh," said the lieutenant. "Well, you do now."

They say poor communication is the number one killer of relationships. And that's true for more than just "love" relationships. That includes business partnerships, friendships, and just about anything that requires more than one person working on something. Usually, things fall apart because of a failure to communicate clearly.

16 Tips for Effective Communication

Here are 16 tips that will help you communicate better, and accomplish your goals with ease:

1. **Ask what that need to be asked; say what needs to be said**. You can't blame anyone else if it's *your* fault something wasn't known.

2. **Don't take everything so damn personally**. That dude who won't give you change for a five may not be disrespecting you. He doesn't speak English. Now stop acting like a two-year-old.

3. **Shut the f*ck up sometimes.** Especially when someone more qualified is talking, or when you're hearing some sh*t you can use.

4. **Think twice before you respond.** Otherwise, you're likely to say some sh*t you wish you hadn't. And once it's said, you can't really take it back.

> "The best way to keep one's word is not to give it."
> Napoleon I (1769-1821)

5. **Might ≠ Will.** When someone says they "might" do something, it doesn't mean they "will," and you shouldn't say you "will," when you really mean you "might."

6. **Raising your voice never helps the situation.** It doesn't make you look tough either, since the coldest, hardest people are the most low-key. It just makes you look emotional.

7. **Never tell somebody who you'll go and tell.** Not on the streets, and not on the job. It just won't work out. If you're gonna bring someone else in, don't make an announcement beforehand.

8. **Paraphrase.** That means you can clear up a lot of miscommunication if you just repeat what you think the other person is saying, in your own words. You might see that a person doesn't always mean what YOU think they mean.

9. **Explain yourself.** Don't expect people to understand something you ain't tellin em, or to go along with something that they don't see.

10. **Compromise.** Find some common ground, something you both agree on or something you both want, and work from there.

11. **"Peace" don't mean pussy.** There is always a time and place that calls for showin your teeth. If you let too many violations slide, it's not long before everybody's playing you for a chump.

12. **Empathize.** That means try to see it from the other side. Consider what they're dealing with, and try to understand. And let them know you can see that before you ask them to see your side.

13. **Shut the f*ck up again.** You're probably *still* talking too much. How you gonna learn anything? 2 ears...2 eyes...only 1 mouth.

14. **Develop your vocabulary.** It doesn't matter how you learn new words, but learn you some. Matter fact, work on your English all the way around. That way, you'll sound smarter and you won't be spelling baby words like "paid" and "money" wrong on your MySpace page.

15. **Typing ≠ Texting.** Speaking of Internet users, learn how to use punctuation. You see these groups of words here, with periods at the

end? These are called sentences. Use em if you want people to understand you. Also, typing in all capital letters = SCREAMING.

16. Finally, stop using them tired-ass **catchphrases and clichés**. Just cause a rapper said it doesn't mean that you can say it every few minutes now. If you got your own catchy, slick sh*t to say, that's cool. That's called creativity, and it's what keeps those slick-talkin pimps in business. On the other hand, sayin something you heard someone else say is weak and followish. See, that's a word I made up. Followish. That's originality. Try you some.

Poor communication eliminates chances for opportunities, while effective communication multiplies them.

FIGURES OF SPEECH

"My metaphors are dirty like herpes, but harder to catch
Like an escape tunnel in prison, I started from scratch"
Immortal Technique, "Industrial Revolution"

While we're on the subject of words and language in this chapter, I thought I'd hit you with an English lesson. If you missed class the day they went over "figures of speech," here's some basic information on the different uses of figurative language. Try to apply what you learn here. Even if you ain't a rapper, it'll step your talk game up.

Metaphor – a comparison of two different things based on a quality they share. Examples: Tupac's "Me and My Girlfriend" or Common's "I Used to Love H.E.R." are whole songs based on metaphors.

Simile – a comparison of two different things using the word "like" or "as." Examples: "Her ass was as soft as two pillows stuffed with marshmallows," or just about any Lil Wayne lyric using the word "like."

Hyperbole – creative exaggeration. Examples: "Stacks to the ceiling" or any other rap lyric where rappers talk about money they don't have.

Personification – giving human qualities or behaviors to a non-human thing. Examples: Young Dro rapping, "My trunk bumpin and shakin, it got the Holy Ghost;" Tony Montana screaming, "Say hello to my little friend!" or Lupe Fiasco saying "Hip hop saved my life."

Onomatopoeia – words that sound like the action they describe. Example: "My guns go bam-bam, your guns go pow-pow"

Alliteration – repetition of a beginning letter sound. Examples: Papoose's song "Alphabetical Slaughter" If you ain't heard it, you need to go find it on YouTube.

Cliché – an overused phrase or saying. Examples: "It's all good;" "I'm Rick James, bitch!" or "It's off the hook."

Oxymoron – a compound word or set of words that contradicts itself. Basically, the meaning of one word cancels out the other word. Examples: "Jumbo shrimp" "Military intelligence" "Fox News" "White nigga" "Easy life" "Good dope" "H.N.I.C." "Homo thug" "Big baby" "Reality TV" "Underboss" "Pretty boy" "Baller on a budget" "Hoodrich" "Black Christian"...

What? What did I say wrong? Oh, *that*. I meant to type that. You're a Black Christian (or a "Brown Catholic")? You're an oxymoron.

Don't you know where you got these religions? Don't you know the slavemasters required their slaves to attend church services, or encouraged their slaves to hold their own "slave services," hoping that Christian beliefs would make them more soft and obedient?[3] Don't you know that the Spanish conquistadors pushed priests on the people to help extend their influence and control? Yes, Black or brown, as always, we've been done the same way.

Just think about it: Christianity was the most effective tool in making the slaves passive enough to KEEP them from rebelling. The whole idea of a heaven waiting for those who suffer on earth is something the people in power made up. They made it up and gave it to the people who got overpowered...it happened the same way everywhere white people went.

"First they had the Bible and we had the land. Now we have the Bible and they have the land."
South African saying

Think about it. In slavery, white slaveowners worked hard to brainwash Black people with many ideas, such as:

- The idea that Blacks were powerless and inferior, while whites were the ultimate source of power and authority (being closest to the white God and white Jesus).

- The idea that one group of Blacks was better than another.

- The idea that there was a heaven waiting for everyone who starved and suffered on Earth, but didn't fight back.

- The idea that there was a hell waiting for everyone who fought back against the hell they were given on Earth.

One of the main tools used to brainwash Blacks in this system was Christianity. According to slavery historian, Herbert Aptheker, white people used the Bible to back up everything they did to Black people. The slaves were given what is called "slave religion," and "the aim of this instruction was to breed meekness and docility."

According to another historian, Kenneth Stampp, who wrote *The Peculiar Institution*:

> Through religious instruction, "the bondsmen learned that slavery had divine sanction, that insolence was as much an offence against God as against the temporal master...and they heard of the punishments awaiting the disobedient slave in the hereafter." This teaching of heaven and hell was used to instill a fear of rebellion against whites, who were being made out to be the closest thing to God, if not God himself.

It was taught that "the moral virtue of a non-resistant spirit was a favorite theme of southern ministers, when they preached to slaves." William Parker, a freed man, recalled: "The preachers of a slave-trading gospel frequently told us, in their sermons, that we should be 'good boys' and not break into master's henroost, nor steal his bacon."

That's right, boy! You better not steal dat bacon! Stampp goes on to say, "They heard, too, that eternal salvation would be their reward for faithful service." They were taught that their Christian behavior would "jump the present life" and go on "to furnish them with all the requisite conveniences for the next."

So while Christianity planted the fear of a vengeful God who demanded submission of a slave to his or her master, it also pacified and contented the slave with the promise of a better life after death.

That means your life is gonna SUCK now, but if you don't act up, you'll go to a magical place when you die! With ponies, and golden streets, and pretty ladies!

Sucker.

According to Frederick Douglass:

> Trained from the cradle up to think and feel their masters were superior and invested with a sort of sacredness, there were few who could rise above the control which that sentiment exercised.

That must explain why Black folks in church are so damn scared of white people!

So "Black" and "Christian" just shouldn't go together. That's too screwy. You can't be *all about* being Black and be *all about* Christianity as well. It's really a conflict of interests. But you can definitely be an "American Christian"! If you still don't get it, maybe you need to go back over the past two chapters (especially see "Suckers and Hustlers").

Okay, well what about those of us who weren't enslaved by Europeans, forced to accept their religion, and then tricked into believing that the white way was the best way? Well, if you're Hispanic, that's not YOU! Why? Because, your people went through all of that too! And almost the exact same way, except you're the descendant of two oppressed groups instead of one. Then again, Blacks in America have some Indian blood too, don't they? Anyway, here's some history on the roots of Christianity in Latin America.

Ponce de León arrived in Boriken (Puerto Rico) in 1508. By 1510, the Spaniards were trying to enslave the Taino, and the Taino weren't havin it.. The Taíno revolted against Spanish enslavement and also against their forced conversion to Christianity. And those two went hand in hand.

The Spanish established in the colony the "repartimientos" and the "encomienda" forced labor system, which were implemented later in the rest of the empire…that is, all of Latin America. The "encomienda" consisted on the granting to the Spanish colonists of a certain number of natives (between 30 and 300) to be instructed in the religious teachings of the Catholic Church. The natives were supposed to work in the mines or in the lands of the colonist during their indoctrination. The Spanish royalty promised freedom to the natives once they were certified as full fledged Christians. So if you wanted to get free, you had to change your whole culture up and accept that white God named Jesus. But here's the trick. There was no freedom waiting for those hopeful natives. The Spaniards never planned to let them free. In fact, they soon realized that a Christian slave was the most obedient slave. Why? See above! When you believe that your reward is waiting in heaven AFTER you suffer on earth and die, you'll never fight for what's right! It worked everywhere!

You see, the Spanish wanted to erase any trace of Taíno culture and traditions. They wanted a full internal and external transformation of the Taíno. And one of the best methods to do so was a compulsory indoctrination in Catholicism. The Taíno were also being required to learn Spanish as well as the "proper" ways of interacting socially. Their names were changed after baptism to Spanish ones and their social structure being changed. The Spanish wanted to eliminate the figure of the bohíque and other customs that the Taino had in common with indigenous people throughout the world, like oral traditions, councils of elders, socialist economies, etc. And today, many Puerto Ricans are mestizo because in those days the Catholic priests were in favor of marrying off the daughters of Taino Chiefs to the second sons of Spaniards to avoid blood shed. In all reality, what this did for them was obtain large tracks of land from the Natives and free labor. That religious preaching had NOTHING to do with helping or "saving" people. How the hell can you be saved by someone wicked? Especially when your people were better off beforehand?

When Francisco Pizarro was granted permission to conquer Peru in 1529, the Inca (king) Atahualpa sent a messenger, Cinquinchara, to study the Spaniards and see what they were about. Cinquinchara informed Atahualpa that they were small in numbers, less than 200 men, and had Indians bound with "iron ropes." Atahualpa asked what to do about the men, and Cinquinchara replied that the Spaniards should be killed because they were evil thieves who took whatever they wanted and were "supai cuna" or "devils." He recommended trapping the men inside of their sleeping quarters and burning them to death. But this didn't happen. When Atahualpa met with Pizarro to confront him about the rumors of enslavement, rape, and murder, Pizarro lied, denying everything and saying they had come as servants of God to teach the natives the "truth about God's word." He said he was speaking to them so that they might "lay the foundation of concord, brotherhood, and perpetual peace that should exist between us, so that you may receive us under your protection and hear the divine law from us and all your people may learn and receive it, for it will be the greatest honor, advantage, and salvation to them." Bullshit! And guess what? Atahualpa didn't dig any further into the accusations.

The next time they met, Pizarro brought Friar Valverde, who explained the divine reasons why the Spanish had come to Peru, and even Athualpa's first lesson in the Catholic religion. After doing so, he handed Atahualpa a Bible, hoping that he and his men would immediately convert to Christianity (in preference to being considered an enemy of the Church and Spain by the Spanish Crown). Atahualpa stated that he was no one's bitch and asked who made them boss. Friar Valverde pointed to the Bible, saying that it contained God's word. Athualpa took it, shook it close to his ear, and asked "Why doesn't it speak to me?" He then threw it aside. And this gave the Spanish all the reason they needed to take Athualpa hostage and take over the land by force. And as they raped and pillaged, Friars like Valverde taught religion.

As Mansio Serra Leguizamon wrote to the Spanish Crown about the people of Peru:

> I wish your Your Majesty to understand the motive that moves me to make this statement is the peace of my conscience and because of the guilt I share. For we have destroyed by our evil behaviour such a government as was enjoyed by these natives. They were so free of crime and greed, both men and women, that they could leave gold or silver worth a hundred thousand pesos in their open house..So that when they discovered that we were thieves and men who sought to force their wives and daughters to commit sin with them, they despised us. But now things have come to such a pass in offence of God, owing to the bad example we have set them in all things, that these natives from doing no evil have turned into people who can do no good.. I beg God to pardon me, for I am moved to say this, seeing that I am the last to die of the Conquistadors.

And the same thing happened everywhere in Latin America. Mexico is another example. Today, almost 90% of Mexico considers themselves Roman Catholic ("Roman" huh? Doesn't that tell you something?). But even as recently as the early 1900s, things were different. The leaders of the Mexican Revolution of 1910 realized that the European Catholic Church were major players in keeping the Mexican people oppressed. Their political influence was undeniable. Upon realizing this, Mexican leaders began working to eliminate this influence. While there were 4,500 priests (most of them of white) "serving" the people before the rebellion, by 1934 there were only 334 priests licensed by the government to serve fifteen million people, the rest having been eliminated by emigration, expulsion and assassination. By 1935, 17 states had no priest at all. In 1937, the Pope issued the third complaint about the persecution of the Mexican Church. By 1940 the Church had "legally had no corporate existence, no real estate, no schools, no monasteries or convents, no foreign priests, no right to defend itself publicly or in the courts, and no hope that its legal and actual situations would improve. Its clergy were forbidden to wear clerical garb, to vote, to celebrate public religious ceremonies, and to engage in politics," but the restrictions were not always enforced. That same year, open hostility toward the Church began to cease with the election of Manuel Ávila Camacho (1940-46), who made a deal with the Catholic Church. And the people fell back to sleep.

"The clergy, this unrepentant traitor, this subject of Rome, this irreconcilable enemy of native liberties, in place of finding tyrants to serve and from whom to receive protection, will find instead inflexible laws which will put a limit on their excesses and which will confine them to the religious sphere."
Flores Magón, Manifesto to the Nation, The Plan of the Mexican Liberal Party (1906)

Where does this leave you. I'm not saying every Christian is an idiot, so don't take it personally. I can fully understand why most people who read this book are gonna be Christians. It's not like you *chose* that religion. Most likely, you were born into it. And it's pretty hard to shake something you've been taught since birth. Especially if you've been coerced with fear of eternal damnation!

So I don't expect you to wake up overnight, but let this be food for thought. After all, if the church was all we needed to get right, you wouldn't even be reading this book. Sh*t, you might need to buy a few copies of this book, and leave them in one of the pews at your local church. Just set it down somewhere people will see it.

**You can't serve two masters.
A real man refuses to be a walking contradiction.**

REVIEW

The principle for this chapter was **Manifestation and Presentation**: Once you know better, do better, speak better, choose better, and live better.

Here are the principles and lessons we covered in this chapter:

Wise Words
Everything that's said has more meaning than it seems. Choose your words carefully, and listen thoughtfully to what you hear.
Have some honor. Don't sell out your own people.
People rarely just look at what you're saying; they are usually looking at how you say it.
Poor communication eliminates chances for opportunities, while effective communication multiplies them.
Sometimes it's best to just keep your mouth shut.
You ain't worth sh*t if your word ain't worth sh*t.
You can be honest without telling on yourself.

Wise Ways
A bad reputation is a death in itself.
Be you, by all means.
But don't look so stupid that the right people don't respect you.
Even if you fall, fall for a good reason.
Wear the right face at the right time.

Wise Actions
Image counts. Make sure the impression you leave with people is the one you want them to have of you.
It's not always a good idea to attract attention to yourself.
Only a baboon shows his ass and laughs about it.
Tell it like it is, and act like yourself.

Wise Choices
A "little bit" of good doesn't make something bad worthwhile.
All of life is a choice. Choose the highest road.
Be careful what you take in. Everything that's good TO you isn't good FOR you. And too much of anything is never a good thing.
Be real with yourself and others. You may get away with lying to others, but the worst crime is lying to yourself.
It takes courage to leave your corner.
Manhood is not easy, but the conscious decision to truly become a man is one of the most important steps.
They fear the uprising. They know that one man can change everything.
We define ourselves and our reality.
When you fight, fight for a reason.
You can't serve two masters. A real man refuses to be a walking contradiction.

Growth and Development
Explore, Experience, Experiment.
Some of us feel trapped, when we are the ones trapping ourselves.
The Earth wasn't made in a day (or 6). Change will come, but give it time.
You will repeat a class you don't pass.

UNACCEPTABLE   ACCEPTABLE

UNACCEPTABLE   ACCEPTABLE?

Check Yourself

"Every thought we think is creating our future."

Understanding is the best thing you can get out of any experience – good or bad. We all know that whatever doesn't kill you only makes you stronger, so we might as well live like we're not scared of setbacks. But that doesn't mean we move through life making the same dumb mistakes over and over again, and then shaking it off like nothing happened.

Life is about growth and development, change and transformation, reconsideration and reevaluation. As we live, we learn, and as we learn, we live better. If you're not following that process, I can't imagine how deep a hole you must've dug for yourself by now.

There's nothing wrong with making mistakes. But how much do you learn when you do? When you fail at something, are you able to figure out why? Do you understand your thinking process?

One of my partners – he's not a pimp – but he can pull any female he sets his mind on. I'm always amazed by the quality (at least physically) of the females he has around him at any given moment. And he doesn't spend a drop of money on them either. In fact, these women know he's not committed to them, and yet they remain and do whatever he wants them to do. How does he do it? How does he know exactly what to say and do?

His answer? Psychology. He understands how people think.

Realizations about life aren't always crystal clear, because understanding takes time. But if you're 25 and you can't understand what's going on in other people's minds (or your own), you're probably having a real hard life.

It's time to learn how to understand *everything* going on around you.

QUIZ THREE: VIEWS AND THINKING

1. An illegal alien is...
    a. a Mexican who is trying to sneak into our country.
    b. someone who enters a country without permission.
    c. one of those little green men from another planet.
    d. I don't know.

2. The message of the movie *The Matrix* was...
    a. machines can take over the world if we let them.
    b. we are being lied to and need to wake up.
    c. there was no message.
    d. I don't know.

3. I think the creation story in the Bible...
    a. isn't something I should question.
    b. is a myth.
    c. makes perfect sense.
    d. I don't think anything about it.

4. The best way for me to do 199 X 3 is...
    a. with a calculator.
    b. (200 X 3) - 3
    c. 199 + 199 + 199
    d. 199
        <u>x 3</u>

5. Usually, rappers and other celebrities...
    a. are great inspirations or role models.
    b. are not really what they present themselves to be.
    c. can teach you exactly how the game goes.
    d. are rich, so money talks.

6. When a female I like is ignoring me...
    a. I move on to another female who won't.
    b. I rethink my strategy.
    c. I don't leave her alone until she pays attention.
    d. I don't even notice.

7. Money is...
    a. the root of all evil.
    b. a resource.
    c. the key to happiness.
    d. money.

Explanation

You already know what it is. No need to keep explaining.

Mostly As: The "Lazies" This is someone who doesn't really like to figure things out for themselves and develop their own understanding. Instead, they take the "lazy" approach and take on an idea or an interpretation they may have heard somewhere else, or one that seemed like the easiest way out. The problem with that approach is that the easy way isn't always the best way. An analogy for this is the student who copies answers "hoping" to get an A.

Mostly Bs: The "Clear" This is someone who thinks rationally and clearly, not to mention critically. One of the essential qualities of good thinking is to question the ideas that everyone else has so that you can arrive at your own understanding. This type of individual employs effective thinking in their approach to life. An analogy for this is the scientist who know's what he's doing.

Mostly Cs: The "Crazies" This is someone who isn't actually crazy in the clinical sense. Instead, the screwed-up ideas present in the world today have driven this individual to some real crazy thinking. Keep in mind that insanity is really all about seeing the world in an illogical manner, and doing things in a way that simply doesn't make sense. An analogy for this is the man who thinks he's a woman, or the Black man who thinks he's white.

Mostly Ds: The "Hazies" This is someone who really doesn't care for all that thinking business in the first place. With or without a cloud of weed, this individual's brain remains in a fog, and they like it that way. It's not that they employ lazy thinking; they simply don't want to think at all. This attitude is very unproductive for any endeavor where success is desired, and is often dangerous. An analogy for this type is the blind man driving on a busy street.

The Third Principle

"Reconsider and Reevaluate" means: Seek understanding. Find clarity, vision, and perspective on yourself, life, and the world.

What You'll Learn

- How to see reality for what it *really* is.
- Which common illusions keep us confused and making unwise choices.
- What the pimp game can teach anyone about life and hustling.

- How to see yourself for you who you really are…and should be.
- What skills any hustler needs to survive.
- Why strategy is essential for life and any hustle.
- How to tell if you're really happy with yourself and your life.
- What the pimp game can teach you about life and business.
- Why you shouldn't believe everything you hear, read, or see.
- How racism is still alive and well…and what that means for us.

20 COMMON ILLUSIONS

I don't want to admit it, but I kinda like this show, *Criss Angel Mindfreak*. I can't lie. That sh*t is pretty cool to watch, like how he'll let himself get crushed by a steamroller, or stick his arm up someone's ass and throw the peace sign up out of their mouth…and what makes you keep watching sh*t like that is how REAL it looks. Of course, it's all an illusion…and we know that, since it's on TV and it's entertainment.

But illusions are everywhere…and most of us miss em. I've been very careful in studying life around me over the past few years and I've noticed a lot of sh*t that ain't really what it appears to be. I thought I'd share 20 common illusions:

Illusion #20: Money can buy you happiness. I don't even need to explain this one. Just read up on the life story of anyone who's really rich. They're on drugs, they're miserable, they hate themselves and their family, and they want to run away from life. Not to mention their cousin Ray-Ray keeps asking for money.

> "Being happy is better than being king."
> Hausa (African) proverb

Illusion #19: We have 'original sin.' A lot of the stuff they teach you in church is just plain silly. How could the same white people who tell us they're not responsible for slavery (because their grandfathers did it, not them) give us this religion that says we're all cursed because of what somebody did thousands of years ago? If you believe in all the sins in the Bible, then you should go stone yourself and everybody else right now.

Illusion #18: We can have 'the good life.' People look at their own messed up childhoods and dysfunctional families and dream about perfect families and perfect lives. Nothing in this world is perfect. That's the nature of an imperfect world. The beautiful thing about a healthy life or a healthy family is being able to get over the problems you will have, not *never* having any problems at all.

"Look, bet all you see is tats, money, grills, and chains
But if you scratch the surface you can feel the pain
Names change, but the situations still the same"
T.I., "Da Dopeman"

Illusion #17: There's power in prayer. Yeah right. Really, any idea involving a person hoping and waiting for magical, miraculous thing to happen and make things better is pretty stupid. Even if things somehow "accidentally" go right once in a while, you'll ignore whatever you did to make things better or worse, and your performance never improves. That's like playing basketball, but not working on improving your technique, because you think it's all in God's hands.

Illusion #16: There is a perfect woman. You're looking for a woman who looks like Nia Long, gets nasty like a two-dollar freak, gets paid like Oprah, and cooks like your big auntie? You keep waiting on that and you'll end up with a woman who looks like Oprah and gets paid like a two-dollar freak. Love is a bout accepting and embracing someone's imperfections, not trying to bag a supermodel with your stankin ass.

Illusion #15: Ballers have money. A lot  of these dudes BAAAALLIN at the club and the strip club, makin' it rain and so on, ain't REALLY got no money. Half of them are ambitious dudes TRYIN to get into the music industry and tossin around what they call "flash money" in the hopes that people with real money will notice them and f*ck wit em. The other half are 9 to 5 ass motherf*ckas that saved up their whole check from UPS or Target so they could feel like a king for one night out the month. They'll worry bout that light bill later.

Illusion #14: The rap game is real. It's like WWF. The white folks who run it are behind most of the beefs anyway. And since when do real gangstas issue threats on songs that might take weeks or months to come out? And if you believe that dudes are gettin spins and radio play cause of talent, you're REALLY lost. You ever heard of payola? It's how some of these wack-ass hits became hits. You can try to get in the industry and get big too, but I hope you ready to give up your values, give up your image, give up some money, or give up some ass (oh, you didn't know half of the industry was gay?). As Jay-Z says on "Ignorant Sh*t":

> They're all actors, lookin' at themselves in the mirror backwards/ Can't even face themselves! Don't fear no rappers/ They're all, weirdos, DeNiros in practice/ So, don't believe everything your earlobe

captures/ It's mostly backwards, unless it happens to be as accurate as me/ And everything said in song, you happen to see/ Then, actually, believe half of what you see/ None of what you hear, even if it's spat by me/ And with that said, I will kill niggas dead

Illusion #13: 'Model chicks' are really pretty. That chick you met last night ain't really that cute. She ain't got no pretty face, that's makeup and weave. She ain't got no perfect body, that's some designer jeans that hold her ass up and a bra that works magic. If she's spent some real money, she might have gotten some surgery or at least some booty shots. Speakin of surgery, that chick might not even be a chick.

Illusion #12: Rappers are rich. A lot of rappers are broke. Face it, a lot of these dudes failed math in school. They got stuck with deals that gave em big advances to show off with, but left em scrapin for crumbs when the record sales were done. But who's gonna listen to a broke rapper? Of course he's lyin. He gotta lie so you'll wanna buy his sh*t and get him at least halfway out all that debt. (See "Artists Don't Really Make Money" in the Appendix)

Illusion #11: Bling is worth it. Or rented rims. Or rented jewelry, or rented Lamborghinis for the weekend. There's also a lot of fake and bootleg stuff out there. A lot of the Prada shoes you see are really Fradas, and a lot of the platinum chains are really stainless steel from the Korean jewelers in the flea market. You really need to floss that hard?

Illusion #10: A good job = A good life. Them middle class dudes in business suits ain't really got they sh*t together either. A lot of them bought big ass houses and cars they can't afford on payment plans that cost just a little bit to start out and increased a whole lot as time went on. And their jobs are the type that might fire you the moment you stop making them enough money. You're basically a paid slave, and they can even take that away whenever they feel like it. Then you're back on the bus with a briefcase full of resumes. How you gon tell your golf buddies that the repo man took your sh*t?

Illusion #9: Trends will last forever. For example, platinum was some stupid sh*t to buy if you bought you some while it was hot. Everybody else was wearin white gold or some platinum-plated sh*t and gettin the same amount of attention. But you spent $100 per GRAM (if you bought the real sh*t) for some dull ass metal that's basically out of style now. What are you gonna do with that now? Wear it with that ugly-ass Coogi sweater? Speaking of which, I wonder what everybody did with their spinners?

Illusion #8: Magic pussy. The idea that pussy is something new and incredible every time you get it is a f*ckin illusion. That's just your dick lying to your brain. If you f*ck three different broads in your lifetime, then you've just about experienced all that pussy's got to offer. Ain't no magic pussy out there with superpowers. Unless you count inflicting a slow death as a superpower.

Illusion #7: The "superior" white man. White people ain't smarter than you. They're just more connected. In this country, even the dumbest white person can sound like other white people, no matter how dumb they are; while a smart Black child is gonna be treated like a retard just because he talks Black. Stop tellin yourself you can't do sh*t because you failed out of school. There's tons of successful white people who probably don't even know how to read. But they can pretend, hustle, and make sh*t happen. The reason you can't do sh*t is cause you stay sittin on the couch or the porch with your boys eating Doritos.

Illusion #6: School + Hard work = Success. Speaking of being "smart," the whole idea of school and hard work equaling success is pretty much an illusion too. I know plenty of folks who graduated from school with me years ago, and they still ain't found no job. A college degree don't guarantee you sh*t nowadays. Sure, it can help if you got a game plan for how you gon use it, but otherwise you foolin yourself.

> **Did You Know?**
> 85% of movie actors earn less than $5,000 a year from acting!
> The average yearly salary of a DJ you listen to on the radio is only $20,000!

Illusion #5: Milk and meat make you healthy. Milk don't do a damn body good. Maybe a cow's body, but not yours. The same with meat. If everytime someone gets sick or pregnant, they tell you to cut down on meat, don't it make sense that sh*t was bad for you the whole time?

Illusion #4: Thugs everywhere. I'm not sayin all thugs are fake, I know plenty of real certified thugs who don't compromise or backpedal for nobody. I'm talking bout the dudes who look and talk like thugs who hit the gay club when they go out of town. Some of em got turned out in jail, and some of em was gay from the start. None of em should be allowed to live near a school zone.

Illusion #3: Taye Diggs. I don't mean dude specifically, but dudes who fit his PROFILE. This kind of dude is a "downlow" situation waiting to happen. I understand some women out there want a guy who always smells good, wears cashmere turtlenecks, goes to church regularly, and knows how to order wine. But a lot of good dudes just weren't raised like that. And a lot of booty-bandits were.

Illusion #2: A "true" religion. Man, this may be the biggest illusion of them all. Do I even need to explain? I'll just say a few basic things that speak volumes. First, most of us got our religion from white folks.

White folks don't even believe in their religion for anything other than a social network. Meanwhile, this sh*t they gave you had you believin in heaven after slavery, and nowadays it's heaven after poverty. Even your black preachers are just usin it to get rich or get ahead or get pussy. The only fools who believe that God will help them are the fools who never seem to get any help.

Illusion #1: The American Dream. Now, if this ain't an illusion I don't know what is. This is supposed to be the land of opportunity. For who? Everyone but you. This country was built off the blood, sweat, and tears of Blacks, Indians, Mexicans, and even the Chinese. Now, everyone who bought into the dream is doin a little better, right? Wrong. Y'all sold out. How the hell I look getting exploited and then joining up with the asshole who exploited me? And then who do y'all exploit? The ones who ain't sold out. Seems like there's only a few of us left. But that's what America, and the Dream, is all about: Exploitation. That's what capitalism, our whole economic system, is all about. And you can believe in that equality sh*t if you want to. In this country you ain't equal to sh*t but your net worth.

Understanding is seeing things for what they really are, not what they appear to be.

PIMPS UP, HOES DOWN

Anthropology: The study of humans

Sociology: The study of groups of people and their interaction

Psychology: The study of the mind

Archaeology: The study of the evidence of past cultures

Genetics: The study of genes and heredity

Genealogy: The study of ancestry and lineage

Biology: The study of life

Ethnology: The study of ethnicity and race

Omnology: The study of everything

Pimpology: The study of understanding the female psyche to the point of being able to control and manipulate a woman

Pimp or Be Pimped

According to Pimpin Ken, in *Pimpology: the 48 Laws of the Game*:

> "Purse first, ass last" is the motto of pimpin, the very foundation on which pimpin is built. What separates a pimp from a trick is that a pimp completely flips the game. A trick pays a ho for the pussy, but a ho doesn't get to f*ck a pimp until she pays him.

According to its standard definition, a pimp is "a man who procures clients for a prostitute." That means that, by definition, the majority of pimps are white. They are the owners of massage parlors, strip clubs, escorts services, and brothels.

But according to Ice T, any employee is functionally a hoe for his or her pimp, the boss. Using the example of a rapper or singer, he explained the analogy:

> The producer says "hmmm you look nice...you gonna make me some money" and he dresses his ho up pretty and flashy and he puts him or her out there on the music track. When she or he is all used up and can no longer make him money, he moves on.

With this philosophy in mind, Ice T believes one should either be the best hoe they can be and get to a point where they can pimp themselves, or choose to be a pimp and pimp others. In the DVD *American Pimp*, Ice T admits that he can neither rap nor act. He says he's not very talented in either skill. But when he was going after his first record deal, he sold himself to the label executives, convincing them that they'd be stupid not to sign him. It worked. Ice explained that, during the years that he recorded for that label, he was a hoe. "But," he adds, "I was a good hoe, because I knew I was a hoe, and I knew what my job was." But a hoe, naturally, works until they're used up. So if a hoe wants to survive, they've got to move up in the food chain somehow. After selling millions of records for his label, Ice T began selling himself to movie executives the same way he had to the music industry. After appearing in a few feature films and dozens of straight-to-video titles, he sold himself onto the show *Law and Order: Special Victims Unit*, where he remains one of the main characters today.

It's Lonely at the Top

A pimp can never show weakness to his women, and must constantly be cold and on alert. So although pimps appear to be in control, every pimp – in a sense – becomes a whore to his prostitutes. A pimp's main job is to know his prostitutes inside and out, without letting them completely know him. As Iceberg Slim said, "A pimp is the loneliest bastard on earth. He's gotta know his whores. He can't let them know him. He's gotta be God all the way."[4]

As one hoe explained about her pimp:

> He would just snap. Like his whole expression would change. One day he came to my motel room to beat my ass. He came over just to beat my ass. And made it clear that he came over to beat on me. He said he had some extra time on his hands, that he didn't have anything to do, so he wanted me to know that he knew I was thinking about doing something stupid. And I was too. I was thinking about leaving him

again. The last time I left him, I ended up in Cleveland....He beat me until I blacked out....But he was like that. He could be so much fun one time, silly and playing around and the next minute, he could be something else, somebody you don't want to f*ck with.

I even tried my hand at the game for a minute. It didn't give me nothing but small money and big headaches. At the end of the day, I just couldn't bring myself to beat this girl into gettin me bread. For the short time that I was doin it, I was miserable. The lifestyle – with all the parties, strippers, and wild episodes – may have seemed fun on the outside, but I was dying inside. As I thought about the path I'd taken, I realized that I didn't know any happy pimps. They were all dead cold, fire hot, or just plain room-temperature miserable.

My brother Sincere Truth, once a pimp himself, had this to share:

Sincere's Views on the Game

I have known numerous pimps (a lot of them actually prefer the term entrepreneur) in my lifetime and heard stories about many others. While a handful, such as Tanelli (deceased from Cleveland) and Ken Ivy aka

Pimpin Ken (alive from Milwaukee), were classy guys, most are not.

People like Bishop Don "Magic" Juan of Chicago, Seymour of Chicago (nice guy) and Goodgame of Cleveland either directly or indirectly may influence people to think that the pimp life (or as classier pimps call it, the sporting life) is a glamorous lifestyle. But if you look beyond the jewelry and the pimp cups, a person will find out that 90% of the time, pimping leads to a mental and physical death.

People need to realize that most pimps are not successful. Most pimps are "suckas" for drugs. Most pimps are not rich and the ones that are, usually were extremely cruel, either physically or mentally (not all pimps are woman beaters). Certain pimps such as Bishop Don "Magic" Juan, by his own admission, were known to beat women with bullwhips, twisted hangers (commonly called pimpsticks) among other things and then make them stand in a bathtub naked for hours and then pour lemon juice on their wounds.

A pimp/racketeer from Cleveland known as Scatterbrain (one of the few pimps who could also be classified as a gangster) was known to beat women with water hoses. He also put hangers on the stove, waited until they got red-hot, and burned them. He even tied one woman to the back of his car and dragged her down the street (the character of Scatter in the classic film "Superfly" was based on him). I personally have seen a pimp (I'll leave his name anonymous) tell his "bitch" to put her leg to the curb and then he climbed on top of his car and then jumped on it.

Most importantly, it is important that people understand the end result for most pimps and hoes. Most of them do not live over fifty (drugs, violence, insanity, and now AIDS takes its toll on them). Most of the others end up in prison. Pimps like Bishop Don "Magic" Juan, who have become fixtures in movies and television shows, are the exception and not the rule. Of the scant few pimps who make it to old age, a lot of them are drug addicts. Some continue to pimp as some hoes look at them as father figures. (But who in their right mind wants to pimp in their golden years?) Pimping is hard work. The saying "Pimpin' ain't easy" is based on fact.

Some become bar owners. Some become stickmen or flunkies at after-hour joints. A large percentage of them are raving lunatics in psyche wards and nursing homes (hence mentally dead), while some start pastoring churches. I must also note that I do know a 73-year-old former pimp in Cleveland that owns a successful construction company. But once again, that is the exception, and not the rule.

Oh, the scant few women that are exploited by pimps (the hoes) that make it to old age, a lot are also drug addicts. Some "square up" and get married. Some become business women, because the pimp game made them business savvy. Some become pimping lesbians. Some are also in the psyche ward, while some become overly dramatic, ultra-religious members of a church who "shout" all of the time and will give the pastor their last dime. (The irony is that the pastor is sometimes a former pimp himself.)

Successful pimps (in my opinion) can be grouped together with corrupt politicians, preachers, psychics and conmen, because they strive to manipulate and exploit the weaknesses of the people for their personal benefit.

By no means would I recommend that you enter the pimp game (some of you are going to do it anyway) but, if that is what you're going to do, be aware of the traps that are in the streets.

Also, you should know that you don't have to use pimp game for only an illegal enterprise. You can use certain aspects of the game in relationships and the business world. As far as relationships, the average "square" has a shameful sense of inferiority and has a tendency to put the wisdom (woman) over knowledge (man) A pimp, on the other hand, knows that he is the "catch" and he always puts himself (knowledge) over the woman (wisdom). In a proper relationship, the man (knowledge) is number one, the woman (wisdom) is always number two. However, you can't get to three (understanding) without the two.

In the business world, you can also use the pimp game. Pimps are very business savvy (they are truly entrepreneurs). They possess an innate ability to remain "cool" under pressure. And whatever they say out of their mouth, they stand by it. This can be applied to the business world. You need to be savvy to make money (if you are in retail your savvy has to be uncanny). When a bad situation develops, a good businessman does not panic. He weighs his options, looks at the pros and cons, and then makes logical decision. A good businessman stands by what he says because his word is bond. If your word is your bond, you will succeed in all of your undertakings.

If You're Still Interested

If you're sincerely interested in learning more about the dirty game of pimping, you should read the following books. They'll take you deep into that world.

The Naked Soul of Iceberg Slim by Iceberg Slim

Pimp by Iceberg Slim

Whoreson by Donald Goines

From Pimpstick to Pulpit by Bishop Don "Magic" Juan

The Pimp Game: Instructional Guide by Mickey Royal

Pimpology: The 48 Laws of the Game by Pimpin Ken

On the other hand, if you're just interested in getting pussy, that has nothing to do with pimping. In fact, most pimps don't do a lot of f*cking. (as you'll see by reading the books named above). In a pimp's mind, "First you get the money, then you get the honey." But...if all you want to know is about getting sex, then you can read "How to Get Pussy" in *Part Two*. Then you may want to try the following titles:

The Art of Macking by Tariq Nasheed

The Art of Seduction by Robert Greene

MACK Tactics: The Science of Seduction Meets the Art of Hostage Negotiation by Christopher Curtis

**Understand your position.
Play your role accordingly.**

911 IS A JOKE

See if you can figure out what the following two stories have in common.

911

In May 1969, Alex Rackley, a twenty-four year old member of the New York chapter of the Black Panther Party, was tortured and murdered because Party members suspected him of being a police informant. A number of BPP members had taken part, and three Party officers eventually admitted guilt. George Sams, the man who identified Rackley as the informer and then ordered his execution, claimed it was under the direct orders of leader Bobby Seale himself. It later came out that Sams was himself the informant and agent provocateur in the employment of the FBI.

A Joke

At a sexual assault trial, a young woman was so traumatized she couldn't bring herself to repeat on the stand what her attacker had said to her. "I won't force you, Miss," said the judge. "Just write down what he said on this slip of paper and I'll pass it along to the jury." The woman took the paper and wrote, "I want to f*ck you until you die."

The judge read the note and directed the bailiff to give it to the foreman of the jury. The jurors passed the note silently among themselves. Finally a woman handed the note to the last juror, a man who been sleeping through much of the proceedings. She shook him awake and passed him the slip of paper.

He read it, smiled at the courteous juror, and stuck the note in his pocket.

"Sir, you must give that paper to me now," the judge ordered.

"I don't think so, your Honor," the man replied. "This is a private note from this lady here to me."

9/11 is a Joke

If you looked at the last two stories, and deduced that the common theme had something to do with messages or communication, you're a smart dude. Both stories illustrate the need for people to look at both the message AND the messenger. But the best example of a message from a shady source is something we've been hearing about for over seven years now. If you still believe in all the sh*t you've heard, I feel sorry for you. For the rest of us, 9/11 is the perfect example of why you should always question WHO is telling you something, and WHY they are telling you. Here's a list of facts you can look up on the internet that show why. These facts show that there's a big difference between what we've been told, and what was really going on. Towards the end, we can start looking at WHY:

The U.S. had begun planning to go to war with Afghanistan and Iraq long before 9/11.

While Iraq has vast supplies of oil, Afghanistan produces 85% of the worlds opium supply. This opium is used not only to make heroin, but most pain-relief drugs as well.

Osama Bin Laden, who normally takes credit for any attacks he ordered, said he had nothing to do with 9/11. He blamed it on people "inside" the American government. Months later, a suspicious new video was released where Osama took credit.

One of the planners was caught more than once before the attacks, and suspected of "terrorist activities," but the FBI had him released each time.

Many of the 19 hijackers were seen before the attacks, partying, drinking alcohol, and getting lap dances at strip clubs, though that's something Muslim "extremists" wouldn't do.

Many of the 19 hijackers were seen AFTER the attacks, living in other countries, though they're supposed to be dead.

NORAD air defense planes could have been called to stop the planes or shoot them down, but they were ordered to "stand down."

In the weeks before the attacks, the World Trade Center was sold on a short-term lease. The attacks made the new owner a lot of insurance money.

The twin towers fell in a way that has never happened before with any steel building. The only way a building that size could fall straight downward so fast is in a controlled demolition.

In fact, another building, Building 7, was never even hit by a plane, but fell straight down in 6.5 seconds. No explanation has been offered.

At the Pentagon, a third plane is supposed to have crashed into the empty side of the building. But there were no engines, wings, or plane parts to prove it at the crash site. In fact, the only video of that area shows what looked like a bomb going off.

In World War II, German dictator Adolf Hitler bombed his own government building and blamed it on Poland. He used this "attack" as an excuse to go to war with Poland so he could take over their land.

In World War II, the U.S. knew the Japanese were going to attack Pearl Harbor. But the U.S. allowed (or helped) it to happen because they needed a reason to go to war. Look up "kamikaze pilots" and see the similarities.

Many similar events, known as "false flag" operations, have been created throughout history to justify the desire of the people in power to go to war.

The resulting war didn't just boost Bush's popularity rating from 30% to 70%, it also helped our failing economy. Before 9/11, America was in a recession. But the wartime economy changed all that, especially with all the money Bush demanded from Congress and other governments. Today, our war with Iraq alone costs $720 million dollars a day. One day in Iraq could pay for a full year of college for more than 63,270 Black students. One day in Iraq could feed every starving child in the world for more than 16 days. One day in Iraq could vaccinate every child in Africa and South America for measles and save millions of lives.

In the first few months of the war with Iraq, not only did millions of dollars worth of national treasures disappear from their museums, but a delivery of $9 billion dollars, in cash, was declared "missing."

Since the war with Iraq has not resulted in lower gas prices for common citizens, who do you think is benefiting? Where do you think this money is going?

Also, the fear generated by the "attacks" has allowed the U.S. to make major changes to our government, including passing the PATRIOT Acts, which take away many of our Constitutional rights.

The government now has powers that it never had before, and is using them to arrest and imprison more people than ever before. (see "26 Reasons to Stay Out of the Game" and "The War On Terror")

Another Message with a Mission

COINTELPRO was active in its efforts to "intensify the degree of animosity" between the Black Panthers in Chicago and the Chicago gang, the Blackstone Rangers. These included sending an anonymous letter to the Ranger's leader, Jeff Fort, claiming that the Panthers wanted to take his life. This act was a strategy to bring about "reprisals" or retaliation against the Panther leadership. In Southern California, similar actions were taken to exacerbate what was called a "gang war" between the Black Panther Party and another Black organization called the United Slaves. Violent conflict between these two groups, including shootings and beatings, led to the deaths of at least four Black Panther Party members, and several members dropping out of both groups. FBI agents claimed credit for instigating the violence between the two groups. In this case as well, government agents sent messages to United

Slaves leadership in the name of the Black Panthers, in order to prompt antagonism, hostility, and violence.

Consider the messenger before you consider the message.

MOVIES TO SEE

Long Kiss Goodnight; Fight Club; Star Wars: Episode II: The Phantom Menace; Shooter; V for Vendetta

All of these movies tell the true story of September 11th. Basically: Our government creates chaos to gain more power over scared people. Black and brown people become the targeted scapegoats.

If you don't get it, you never will.

THE MIRROR DON'T LIE

Life is mathematics...yeah, just like the class. That is, if you can't work out the problems at the most basic level, you'll be stuck repeating that same "class" until you demonstrate mastery of those kinds of problems.

YOU'RE NOW LOOKING AT THE CAUSE OF ALL YOUR PROBLEMS

WWW.HUSTLEANDWIN.COM

If you're successful, you get to move on.

Eventually you'll be tackling the kind of problems Einstein couldn't deal with. But that's life. Life is about progression, growth, development, etc...NOT repeating the cycles we have already completed.

I am currently observing myself on a number of levels. This is known as metacognition. In Supreme Mathematics, it is represented as the number 11, or "Knowledge Knowledge." That is, I am taking on an awareness of the way my mind works. I am learning about how I think. In many ways, this process is critical to self-awareness. You'll have a great deal of difficulty finding peace with yourself and your reality until you are actually aware of yourself on a psychological level.

As for me, I am, for the first time, taking into account all of my flaws. Not flaws that one or two people have tried to point out to me (because those can be personal, meaning they only bother those one or two people). I'm talking about the flaws that I am sure are making my life harder. I'm sure they're real, because I've taken the time to pay attention and seriously observe myself and others.

For example, I am very impulsive. I also have a temper. So I sometimes say or do things that I shouldn't have said or done. That's something I'm working on now.

But what's amazing is how long it's taken me to figure that out. No matter how many mistakes I made because of my impulsiveness…no matter how many problems I created for myself…I could never see that it was me. The whole time, I refused to look in the mirror. I couldn't see it because I didn't want to.

As a result, I kept going through the same bullsh*t over and over again. It's only now, now that I have looked at myself, that I can begin making the necessary changes.

I've never cared much about what people thought of me. I'm not self-conscious like that. But that doesn't mean I should have been ignoring all the times when people told me I was impulsive. It took me being self-aware – looking at myself in the mirror – to finally see it for myself.

So next time you want something to think about, take a look in the mirror. Hopefully, you can see clearly and honestly enough to know what you need to work on. But I also hope you can see all the greatness within you as well. As Nas raps on "You're the Man":

> Forty-five in my waist, starin at my reflection/ In the mirror, sittin still in the chair like my conception/ When everything around me got cloudy/ The chair became a king's throne, my destiny found me/ It was clear why the struggle was so painful/ Metamorphosis – this is what I changed to/ And God, I'm so thankful

Don't be self-conscious; be self-aware.

10 SIGNS YOU HATE YOURSELF

> "(I'm Black!!!) I got to show my homeboys love
> First thing we learned in the hood was homeboy love
> (I'm Black!!!) And I'm that if I ain't nothin else
> (I'm Black!!!) I'm beautiful, I love myself"
> Styles P, "I'm Black"

A great scholar, Albert Memmi, in *Dominated Man: Notes Toward a Portrait*, proposed:

> In every dominated man, there is a certain degree of self-rejection, born mostly of his downcast condition and exclusion…When the objective conditions are so weighty and corrosive, how could we imagine that they will not result in some destruction, that they will not warp the soul, the behavior and even the physiognomy of the oppressed man?

Another great scholar, Tupac Shakur, in his song "White Man's World," said the same thing:

Proud to be Black, but why we act like we don't love ourselves?/ Don't look around busta – Check yourselves/ Know what it means to be Black, whether a man or girl/ We still struggling, in this white man's world

Here's ten signs that suggest you're one of those "dominated men" who hates yourself because of this white man's world:

1. You're constantly trying to change or hide things about your physical appearance, especially the "Black" features.

2. You treat your body like a trash dump instead of a temple.

3. You lie about your life and your past, either to hide things or make things seem better than what they are.

4. You're always finding things wrong with yourself or your life.

5. You cut yourself, talk down on yourself, or think about killing yourself.

6. You find yourself hating people who are a lot like you.

7. You don't want to be Black, and you may even try to use other words to describe yourself.

8. You try to avoid or get away from your own people.

9. You'd rather be drunk or high than thinking about your life.

10. You can't honestly say, "I love myself" without feeling funny.

The man who has been taught not to like himself is doomed to destroy himself.

How do I Look?

As executive chef at Café Bellagio, of the famed Bellagio hotel in Las Vegas, Jeff Henderson has gained quite a reputation among the world's rich and elite. His talent in the kitchen have earned him a good deal of fame, but perhaps some of that fame can also be credited to the fact that Jeffrey Henderson was one of San Diego's most successful drug dealers.

Henderson's autobiography *Cooked: From the Streets to the Stove, from Cocaine to Foie Gras*, details his transition from cooking crack cocaine in Corningware Pyrex pots to cooking oven-roasted striped sea bass with savoy cabbage and fingerling potatoes infused with chive olive oil.

Growing up in inner city California, Henderson started hustling at an early age. Before long, he was buying kilos of cocaine, cooking up the product in motels, and supplying the city with hundreds of thousands of dollars worth of crack. He enjoyed his earliest experiences in Vegas bringing his squad of dealers to gamble in Ceaser's Palace with Louis Vuitton bags full of money, where they would be picked up by limos and treated like kings, gambling 30 Gs at a time. All that came crashing to an end when, at 23, he was caught, and sentenced to nearly 20 years in prison.

There, he was assigned to washing dishes in the prison kitchen, where he learned to cook from his fellow inmates. Upon his release, he relentlessly pursued his goal of being a chef. But the same people who treated him like a VIP when he was a Vegas high-roller wouldn't give him a chance when he came looking for a job in the kitchen.

In the five years following his release, he'd worked his way up from minimum-wage dishwasher to a sous-chef at one of the best restaurants in L.A. But no one in Vegas seemed to care. And it wasn't just because he was Black. In his words:

> My cooking resume was impeccable, five stars across the board, but their enthusiasm had a way of drying up as soon as I told them I had spent time in federal prison for drug trafficking. On the outside, I was what was acceptable for a Black man in corporate America: clean shaven, earring hole covered up; I even toned down my walk so that I wouldn't swagger and come off as ghetto during interviews -- I've got a pretty good stroll. Still, it always came down to me being a felon.

How did Henderson finally get in?

He stepped his game up considerably. He assessed his situation and changed his approach. Here, he describes how it went:

> The night before my Caesar's interview, I snooped all over the hotel to put my game plan together. If I saw some cooks walk into the casino, I would roll up on them.
> "Hey, how you doing?" I'd say. "My name's Jeff Henderson. Can I talk to you for a second? I'm thinking of moving up here. What's it like? What's the chef like?"
> It was a reconnaissance mission. Since I'd have to prepare a tasting meal for the executive chef, I planned to base it on the foods he liked. I wanted to make my mark by showing up for the interview with the full menu in my briefcase. So when he says, "Hey, this is nice," he doesn't know that I've already been on his property eating his food. The cooks tell me he likes Italian, so I go to the Caesars Italian restaurant, Terrazza, and have the Veal Milanese. I even chatted up some of the hostesses to get a feel for the hotel politics.
> By the time I walked into the man's office, I was comfortable, confident. It was a huge room decorated from one end to the other with Roman-style artifacts, the walls covered with pictures of prize fighters. The man behind the desk was a smooth middle-aged Italian from New York with black hair slicked straight back.
> And here I was, this black motherf*cker in a $150 Brigard chef's coat made of Egyptian cotton. I went right into my hard sell, telling him that I was ready to go to work on the spot. I told him straight up: "Look, Chef, I've done some time. I learned to run a kitchen in prison. But my resume speaks for itself."

I think he liked my aggressive approach. In Vegas, like in prison, you have to be tough to run a kitchen. If the cooks sense any sign of weakness, they'll run you over, tell you how to do your f*cking job. "Mr. Henderson," he said. "Did you ever kill anyone?"

"No, sir."

"All right," he said. "I want you to cook me dinner on Friday. Write up a menu."

I opened my briefcase, showed him the menu I'd already typed up and brought along with me, and told him that instead of giving me the usual ninety-day probation period, just to give me a month.

Be aware of your situation, and set up your approach with that in mind.

HUSTLES AND HANDOUTS

There's a lot of people out there now who are more into handouts than hustle. They don't know the first thing about getting that guap and keepin it, which is why we've got some rich people in the hood, but most of us ain't wealthy. See, "wealth" is when you have generational money, coming down from father to son, and so on. Most of us that are getting that bread right now won't even be able to put our kids through college, which is gonna force them to have to hustle too. And they'll end up repeating that same bullsh*t cycle.

After all, we don't hustle like Trump and Rockefeller. We hustle like pimps and rock-sellers. We get easy money, and spend it like it will always be there. Then we learn that easy money is risky money. But we learn that the hard way, don't we?

I'm not really that big on being a millionaire, nowadays, as I've already walked down that road and didn't care too much for it. But I figure I'll teach you a couple things bout "real" hustlin. I'm not talking bout the kind of hustlin you hear in songs like Yung Joc's "Coffee Shop" and Rick Ross' "Everyday I'm Hustlin" (drug money comin in easy). I'm talking bout the kind of hustlin you see in the videos for those same songs (getting paid off everything from owning car washes to selling hair products). Those rappers ain't no dummies. Which one (the song or the video) do you think REALLY tells the story of how they get their money now?

> "I had to make my own living and my own opportunity...
> Don't sit down and wait for opportunities to come; you have to get up and make them."
> Madame C.J. Walker

As Chamillionaire said at the end of his song "Won't Let You Down":

See, rich people ain't going to tell you how to get paid/ And broke people act like they the richest people in the world/ Always tellin people with money how to get it/ Always spendin money that they thought they was gonna get./ Always buying things they can't afford./ Stop making excuses./ If chronic smoke makes him sleepy, he's gonna tell ya he got chronic fatigue/ If liquor makes him drowsy, he gonna say he got that grey goose disease/ If women keep taking his money, he gonna tell ya it slipped off his sleeve/ Whatever your weakness, stop making excuses please/ You should not be on couch or in house, you should be en route/ If you gotta ask where, then that's the reason you ain't got nothing/ You don't know how to listen, go get it

This is a recent conversation I had with one of the young dudes in my neighborhood:

Supreme: Why ain't you workin?

Kasim: Ain't nobody tryin' to hire me.

Supreme: Where have you gone?

Kasim: Man, to the mall, to every restaurant, everywhere.

Supreme: That doesn't sound like "everywhere" to me. Have you tried a construction site?

Kasim: Once, but they just looked at me like I was a thug.

Supreme: How were you dressed?

Kasim: Like a thug I guess.

Supreme: Okay, so now what?

Kasim: I guess I'ma have to hustle. I need to eat, you know?

Supreme: You eatin just fine at home, you sure you don't just want some fresh clothes?

Kasim: Okay, you got me. But how else I'ma get money?

Supreme: Dope money's just a short-term loan. You pay it all back in lawyer fees or jail time.

Kasim: Well then, you tell me something better than hustling.

Supreme: If you say you can hustle, *you can hustle.*

Kasim: Man, you *just* said…

Supreme: There's *other* hustles out there, if you know *how* to hustle. If all you know how to do is post up on the block and wait for the money, you ain't really got no hustle anyway. But if you got some real hustle about you, there's a ton of ways to make legit money *without* goin' to jail.

Many have dreams, but few choose to wake up and work hard enough to make them real.

---

10 "LEGIT" HUSTLES

Here's ten of the hustles I shared with Kasim:

	Requirements	How to Do It	$	X	Profit Margin
Buy and Sell Cars	In-depth knowledge of cars; free time; tools; access to a tow truck; friends who like to work on cars	Buy old cars or junk cars from folks having hard times, elderly people, or salvage auctions at low prices, fix them up and resell them	$ $ $	X X	If you get the cars and parts at less than half of what they're worth, and do the work yourself, you should double your money
Real Estate	Decent credit (or your own money); ability to learn quickly; a car	Buy old houses or land in areas that are rising in value, fix them up and resell them	$ $ $ $ $	X X X X	If you buy the houses at 30- 50% of their value, you can turn $20K into 40K or more
Recycle Pallets	Knowledge of where to get used wood pallets; access to a truck	Buy the pallets from warehouses and other places. Take them to companies that buy pallets.	$	X	Pallets will cost you nothing,, repair them and resell them for 5 to 10 bucks a piece
Recycle Bulk Paper	Knowledge of businesses that use lots of white paper; a vehicle	Arrange with businesses to pay you a small fee to recycle their paper. Bring the paper to companies that buy used paper.	$	X	The paper comes to you free, and the business even pays you. You get up to $10 per pound (on average a 100 pounds a trip)
Whole-sale Apparel	Knowledge of wholesalers and discounts; a network of people who buy clothes	Buy the clothes cheap and find people who will pay a little more for it. Or you can start taking deposits and orders.	$ $ $	X X X	Depends on what you're selling. But if you have the right kind of people buying, you can make a lot of money.
Ghost-write Papers	The ability to think and write on a college level; Internet access	Put up flyers or spread the word on college campuses. Tons of lazy (or dumb) students will pay you to write their papers for them.	$	X X	From $3 to $10 per page, depending on the length and difficulty of the assignment (as well as how good you are).
Throw Parties	Access to cheap alcohol; friends who'll help; a network of people who like to socialize and party; pretty girls	Come up with a party idea, propose it to a club. Offer to either collect on the door or on the bar. Provide either the alcohol, the entertainment, or both. Or just throw "rent" parties at your house.	$ $ $ $	X X X X	Depending on how many people attend, and how much you're charging to get in (or for drinks), anywhere from $100 a night to $2,000+.
Recycle Scrap Metal	Knowledge of where to find used scrap metal; strong arms; a vehicle	Pick up the metal and bring it to plants where copper, aluminum, steel, iron, or brass is recycled.	$	X X	Depending on the type of metal, its quality, and how much you have, anywhere from .05 to .50 a pound

	Skills/Materials	Strategy	$	X	Profit
Sell CDs and DVDs	A computer with a CD burner and a printer (or a connect on bulk product)	Either make your own CDs or buy them in bulk. Hustle but be careful. You can also have people pay to advertise their business on your CD/DVD.	$ $	X X X X	From $2 to $8 per CD/DVD, not counting ads. But if you're bootlegging, watch out for cops and angry rappers, because you could lose it all.
Create Wearable Art	Creativity; a network of people who buy clothes; paint (or airbrush); wholesale shirts and jeans	Buy blank clothes, decorate them so they're flashy and fly (or take requests), and sell them to the type of people who will make other people want to get their own.	$ $	X X	Depending on the quality of materials you use and the demand for your product, you can make anywhere from $10 to $40 on a t-shirt or pair or jeans
Take Pictures	A steady hand; a digital camera; a computer with a good printer and photo paper (or print at a local Rite Aid or CVS)	Find a place you can use as a studio (or pick out some great locations). Print up business cards or flyers for your services, market to the right people, take good pictures, and ask for referrals	$ $ $	X	Photography typically pays per hour of studio time, so think in a range from $20 to $60 per hour, depending on your skills. You can also get paid at clubs and events if you work with the promoter.
Sell Candy/ Water/ Etc.	Knowledge of where to buy candy or water in bulk; a cooler or trunk; two legs	Buy a lot of something people want or need, and sell it somewhere that they'll want or need it (like water at a park in the summer)	$	X X	Depends on what you're selling. For every $20 invested, expect to make anywhere from $30 to $60 back.

Key $: Start Up Costs **X:** Risk Factor

With enough drive and ambition, anyone can become their own boss.

20 HUSTLING SKILLS

And here's 20 skills I told Kasim he would need to be successful in any kind of hustle:

1. Buy low, sell high.
2. Supply must meet demand (sell what people want).
3. Reward repeat customers.
4. Reward referrals (word of mouth is the best advertisement).
5. Don't do "credit."
6. Get out and grind like your life depends on it.
7. Scared money don't make money.
8. If it's legal, advertise.
9. Sell your product like you believe in it.
10. Don't get discouraged when you don't sell.
11. Diversify your products so you won't suffer in a drought.

12. Find a market that works for you.

13. Tell people what they want to hear, but don't lie.

14. Develop a reputation for honesty and dependability.

15. Be available whenever people need your services.

16. The early bird gets the worm

17. Offer volume discounts (the more they buy, the less they pay).

18. Work your way up the food chain (go from retailing to wholesaling).

19. Reinvest your profit, instead of wasting it.

20. He who works like a slave, eats like a king.

You can find more on the principles of true hustling in Hotep's book *The Hustler's 10 Commandments: A Collection of Corporate Best Practices, Ancient Wisdom, and Guerrilla Tactics for Today's Independent Minded Entrepreneur.*

You either look inward or outward for what you want.

THE ART OF THE CON

Ali had seen the game before. A shady-looking guy in his mid-30s shuffled around a pea between three small cups on a piece of cardboard while about a dozen people watched. Ali had heard of the shell game before, but he knew it was a scam.

But as Ali passed by, a young man approached and bet $20. Ali figured the guy was bound to lose and be upset, so he watched. Instead, the young man found the pea and doubled his money.

With that, Ali started to change his mind. Was it possible? Perhaps he could win as well, he thought. Before anyone else could jump in, Ali bet $20. He lost the first time, but the guy offered him a second chance for only $10. He was unsure about another wager, but he believed he had figured out a foolproof strategy to win. He bet his $10 and won. Even with this win, Ali was still down $10. The guy challenged him not to back out now…"I'll triple whatever you bet" he offered.

Ali wasn't just convinced that he knew how to win by now, but he was thinking of how good he'd feel when he tripled the $100 he still had in his pocket. It was the last of his money, and he needed it to buy groceries, but Ali wasn't worried about losing. He'd see another man win, and even he had won already. He was about to get $300.

But he lost. With nothing left to gamble, Ali walked away angry, ashamed, confused...and broke.

Ali wasn't a hustler, even though he thought he was. Ali was hustled. He was a mark, a vic, or a sucker, as they say in the game.

Some of my Favorite Scams

There's thousands of cons, or "confidence tricks" that have been used successfully by hustlers and conmen over the years, from selling the Brooklyn Bridge to tourists to establishing fake businesses to trick people out of their personal information. In an attempt to keep it brief, I'm just going to focus on a few of the most popular cons in the Black community. Once again, whether it's legitimate or illegitimate, we can see that it takes a great deal of intelligence to "make it" as a Black man in today's world.

Before I begin, though, let me say that the following is for informational purposes only. In no way am I suggesting that you use any of these techniques on other people!

Get-Rich-Quick Scheme

Get-rich-quick schemes are so varied they nearly defy description. Everything from fake franchises, real estate fraud, psychic hotlines, fortune tellers, quack doctors, miracle pharmaceuticals, faith healing, charms and talismans are part of the dirty game. Variations include the pyramid scheme, Ponzi scheme, Matrix sale, and Multi-level Marketing. Some examples include hustling Pre-Paid Legal, Tahitian Noni, the YTB "travel agencies," and ACN online "malls."

The Advance Fee Fraud

The advance fee fraud (or the 409 scam or Nigerian scam), takes advantage of the victim's greed. The basic premise involves enlisting the mark to aid in retrieving some stolen money from its hiding place. Anyone trying this has already fallen for the essential con by believing that there is really money to steal. One recent example is the Black money scam (look it up so nobody tries it on you). The mark is made to think that he or she will gain money by helping crooks get huge sums out of a country (the classic Nigerian scam) or past the eyes of authorities. As a result, the mark cannot go to the police without revealing that he planned to commit a crime himself.

This fraud is related to check fraud, which – like credit card fraud – is a dirty way for a con artist to make money off a greedy mark, while ruining the mark financially. Similarly, people shopping for bootleg or stolen merchandise, illegal drugs or firearms, or any other "dirty" purchases are unable to report being swindled to the police. That is, unless you think it's smart to run to the cops complaining about being scammed out of your money on a drug deal.

The Romance Scam

Nowadays, the Romance scam can be found on Internet dating sites. The con finds a lonely loser through a personals website or an instant messenger program. The con then works hard to play the role of their mark's fantasy mate and to develop a romantic relationship, which leads to promises of marriage or a meeting.

However, after some time the mark learns that his Internet "sweetheart" is stuck in her home country, lacking the money to leave the country to be with the mark. The con artist (often really a man) then begins either asking for money to be sent, or turns the scam into another type of fraud by offering fake checks in exchange for the needed cash.

> ### Did You Know?
> A scientist named Royall Rife came up with a cure for cancer in the 1920s, but the American medical industry saw it as a threat to all the money they were making off a sickness that 'couldn't be cured.' Rife was killed, all of his work was destroyed or 'lost', and everyone who supported him was threatened into denying any knowledge of his cure.

The Badger Game Extortion

The badger game extortion is usually done to married men. The mark is pushed, sometimes under the influence of drugs or alcohol, into a compromising position, such as an affair or a homosexual or immoral act. Then the con artists threaten the mark with public exposure of his acts unless blackmail money is paid. Be careful of scandalous women!

Insurance Fraud

Insurance fraud is a scam in which the con artist tricks the mark (which can be an individual or a business) into damaging, for example, the con artist's car, or injuring the con artist themselves (in a manner that the con artist can exaggerate). The con artist fraudulently collects a large sum of money from the mark's insurance policy, even though they intentionally caused the accident (See "Schemes and Consequences").

The Abuse of Charity Scam

The con-man may pretend to have some injury or disadvantage to gain sympathy (and donations) e.g. a panhandler in a wheelchair, the woman with kids along the freeway off-ramp or the fake youth football team from the poor neighborhood. The most entertaining part of these frauds is when the day is done and the scammers pick up their props, walk down the street to their cars, and drive home.

The "Just $5" trick is an abuse of charity scam where the conman approaches the victim and asks for "just $5" to help them achieve some goal that is almost within reach. The conman shows some cash to prove they have "almost enough" and usually adds some props to add credibility: carrying a car part that needs repair/replacement or carrying a gas can (because the car ran out of gas and the wife and children are waiting). There are variations on this scam, such as the "Just Got out of Jail" version, or the "Help Me Get Home" version where the conman is trying to get to another state.

The Pigeon Drop Technique

The pigeon drop technique involves a pair of con men working together, one of whom is set up to look poor and the other one to look wealthy. In one version the wealthy man pretends to lose something valuable at an expensive place like a fancy restaurant, and he offers someone there, like a waiter, a huge reward. The poor man finds it (he has it already), and offers to give it to the waiter for a few hundred dollars. In the other version, the poor man leaves behind something that looks valuable, like a violin, and the wealthy man offers to buy it from the waiter for a huge amount when he sees it. When the poor man returns, the waiter offers him a few hundred dollars for it. Either way, the result of this scam is the two con men are a few hundred (or thousand) richer (minus the cost of whatever crap they sold), and the mark is left with something worthless.

> **Did You Know?**
> Fifteen people are known to have been crushed to death tilting vending machines towards them in the hope of a free can of soda. Nothing's free!

This con has transformed into a more common, but less dignified, version, which is the hawking of fake jewelry to tourists and other gullible people.

The Shell Game

Three-card Monte or "Follow the Lady," are based on the same principles as the ancient shell game. The trickster shows three playing cards to the audience, one of which is a queen (the "lady"), then places the cards face-down, shuffles them around and invites the audience to bet on which one is the queen. At first the audience is skeptical, so an inside-guy places a bet and the scammer allows him to win. This is sometimes enough to entice the audience to place bets, but the trickster uses sleight of hand to ensure that they always lose, unless the con man decides to let them win to lure them into betting even more. As you can see in the story above, the mark loses whenever the dealer chooses to make him lose.

Summary

What does this have to do with you? Well, many of us who think we are hustlers are really the ones being hustled. The best part of this hustle is that we think we're winning even when we're losing. The people running the dope game, like the shell game, make you believe you could win by showing you what other people have "won." They don't tell you that many of those people were part of their game. And they don't tell you that you only win until they decide to take it all away. And since most people don't learn from the mistakes of others, they play the same game, thinking they may be able to win even though almost everyone else loses. Ali grew up in a religious household where they believed that you can pray and get something out of nothing. But in the real world, you can never get something from nothing. It's physically impossible. It takes something great to make something great. Anything that looks better than that is an illusion. But we fall for it every time, even though we – like Ali – say we know better.

Know better, do better.

GIRLS GONE WILD

Joe Francis is the 32-year-old multi-millionaire kingpin of the *Girls Gone Wild* video empire, worth an estimated $100 million. He built his business from the ground up, selling tapes of naked and often barely legal white girls wilin out in "Raw! Real! Uncut!" action in college and spring break towns across the country.

But today he was the one being filmed. Held at gunpoint, laying face down with his pants around his ankles, he moaned, "My name is Joe Francis. I'm from Boys Gone Wild, and I like it up the ass." For added effect, a pink vibrator was resting in the crack of his ass.

It was the work of small-time hustler Darnell Riley. Darnell had a dirty past, but had used his quick tongue and good looks to con his way into high society. Before long, he was partying in Hollywood and dating Paris Hilton. For a Black man with a criminal record, Darnell thought he was making big moves. But even a friend of his said "Darnell was fascinated by glamour and all the Hollywood bullsh*t. He thought he'd make it somehow, but he was criminally minded."

On the night of January 22, 2004, Riley entered Joe Francis's Bel Air mansion, and made the infamous tape. Then, Riley took Francis's Rolex, a video camera, a painting, some Louis Vuitton bags, and $1,500 in cash. He then drove off with Francis bound and gagged in the trunk of Francis' Bentley. He dumped Francis and the car sometime later, and they were discovered by security guards.

But Francis didn't know who it was that did this.

He didn't even know Darnell Riley's name until he started comparing notes with his friend, Paris Hilton. Francis was being extorted for

$500,000, but he learned that Darnell had been blackmailing Hilton for $20,000 a month. Darnell had 12 hours of footage of her having sex with various men, smoking weed, and even calling two Black men "dumb niggers" behind their backs. This was actually the incident that broke up the partnership between Hilton and Nicole Richie – who is actually Black. Darnell hadn't told Francis who he was, but he was bold with Hilton. And what he told Hilton, Hilton told Francis. Francis put two and two together and pointed the finger at Darnell, who was soon arrested.

There's something all these people have in common. That's the fact that everything done in the dark will one day come to the light. Darnell Riley thought he was getting away with blackmailing two celebrities and living "the good life" off extortion money. But eventually, he not only exposed himself as a conman, but as the extortionist in both cases.

Paris Hilton had put her own slutty business out there without help several times. But these tapes confirmed that she wasn't just a slut, but she was a racist as well.

Finally, Joe Francis may seem like the victim in this case, but this is a perfect case of irony as well. After all, he's the man that's made $100 million putting young dumb girls on tape embarrassing themselves, and possibly ruining their chances for a normal adult life. You can't exactly live a normal life once everyone's seen you on a *Girls Gone Wild* DVD. And Darnell's lawyer says there's more dirt than you'd think. He claims Darnel and Joe Francis were actually in a relationship, and the film was one of their sex tapes!

Whatever is done in the dark will one day come to the light. Whatever you do, make sure it is something you wouldn't mind everyone knowing about.

THE ART OF WAR

In the excellent *Makes Me Wanna Holler*, Nathan McCall writes:

> Mo Battle taught me chess by explaining its philosophical parallels to life. "You can understand the game of chess if you understand the game of life, and vice versa," he said. In life, the person who plots his course and thinks ahead before he acts, wins. It's the same with chess."
> One day, I made a move to capture a pawn of his and gave Mo Battle an opening to take a valuable piece. He smiled and said, "You can tell a lot about a person by the way he plays chess. People who think small in life tend to devote a lot of energy to capturing pawns, the least valuable pieces on the board. They think they're playin' to win, but they're not. But people who think big tend to go straight for the king or queen, which wins you the game." ...The most important thing that Mo Battle taught me was that chess was a game of consequences. He said that, just

as in life, there are consequences for every move you make in chess. "Don't make a move without first weighing the potential consequences," he said, "because if you don't, you have no control over the outcome."

I'd never looked at life like that. I seldom weighed the consequences of anything until after I'd done it. I'd do something crazy and then brace myself for the outcome, whatever it happened to be. I had no control over the outcome and no control over my life. When I thought about it, that was a helluva stupid way to live.

But on the chessboard, I eventually saw that I could predict – and, more important, control – outcomes if I considered the consequences of moves before making them. That gave me a whole new way of looking at things.[5]

As you can see in the movie *Fresh*, the game of life is a lot like the game of chess. Smart moves lead to smart outcomes. But there are a few things you should remember:

- White ALWAYS moves first. Every other game has a roll of the die, a flip of a coin, or some other method for determining who should go first. Not Chess. White will always be one move ahead. Because Black starts late, it must work harder than white to win.

- All it takes to make good predictions (just like the kind the psychics make for $2.99 a minute) is a rational mind. You simply have to look at the factors that are already in play, and then figure out all the possible circumstances, meaning the different things that could occur. With practice, this becomes easier. Before long, you'll be able to predict anyone's next move with ease.

- You need patience. A good game is a challenge that may take a long time to finish. An easy game doesn't make anyone a better player.

- A lowly pawn – if played correctly – can take out anyone, but a pawn can never become a king. Even when the pawn makes it to the end of the gameboard (rare), it can be upgraded to become any other piece – except a king.

- Reconsider and reevaluate regularly. That means you have to constantly look at what's going on to decide what to do next. You may have started out with a great plan, but if everything has changed since then, it's time to replan. Also, if your gameplan ain't workin, why would you stick to that plan?

- Even kids play by the rules. Why? Because if you don't start out by learning how to play by the rules of the game, you'll never be ready to play with the big boys. Too many of us are adults now, still trying to play by kid rules.

■ If you want to win at this game, or any game, you can't have any fear. You can't fear death, loss, or sacrifice. You've got to be ready to lose everything, even though you'll play smart enough so you don't have to.

The 1875 poem, *Invictus* (meaning "Unconquered"), also captures the spirit of fearlessnesss one must have in this dirty game called life:

Out of the night that covers me,
Black as the Pit from pole to pole,
I thank whatever gods may be
For my unconquerable soul.

In the fell clutch of Circumstance
I have not winced nor cried aloud.
Under the bludgeonings of Chance
My head is bloody, but unbowed.

Beyond this place of wrath and tears
Looms but the Horror of the shade,
And yet the menace of the years
Finds, and shall find me, unafraid.

It matters not how strait the gate,
How charged with punishments the scroll,
I am the master of my fate:
I am the captain of my soul.

Life is chess. Learn from the game.

SCHEMES AND CONSEQUENCES

"I believe that everything that you do bad comes back to you.
So everything that I do that's bad, I'm going to suffer from it.
But in my mind, I believe what I'm doing is right."
Tupac Shakur

The Robbing Drug Dealers Scheme

Mega, even after going "inactive" from the Rolling Sixties gang, was still a rider to the heart. Having left L.A., he had left a lot of that "old life" behind. But old habits die slow, you know? Around the time I met him, Mega made most of his money pushing pounds of Cali weed. But every once in a while, the weed game would dry up, or he'd take a loss somewhere in the shipment process. And when funds were low, the guns would show.

But Mega wasn't goin after "innocent people". He robbed crack dealers. These guys loved to throw their money around and show off. And they were scavengers. They fed off the death of Black people. The way Mega saw it, there was nothing wrong with taking advantage of people who were doing the Black community wrong. If it was easier, he said, he'd be robbing jackleg preachers too.

Mega would get a couple of good-looking girls together, and set up any interaction through them. By the time ol' girl was done spittin her game, the dude would either want to purchase some weight, or purchase some pussy. Either way was fine with Mega. She would set it up, and he would come set it off. I don't know how you get robbed in your own garage, but it's happened to a couple of folks you may have heard of. The thing these guys never realized was that when they were throwin money around and showin off how much they had, there were consequences for that. When they were leeching off the Black community – at least how Mega saw it – there were consequences for that.

And one way or another, these dudes got played because they couldn't see far enough into the future. They couldn't look past the idea of getting paid or getting laid and that's how they got played. Life is chess. The more successful player is the one who can see further ahead in the game.

> "Men are not punished for their sins, but by them."
> Elbert Hubbard (1856-1916)

The Car Insurance Fraud Scheme

On cue, Mega hit the brakes. All four passengers in the car braced themselves as they were rear-ended by the Escalade behind them. It had been raining, and the slick roads not only made it difficult for the large SUV to stop before hitting them, but it also caused Mega's Coupe De Ville to careen straight into a ditch off the road.

The driver of the Escalade hadn't been hurt badly. Fortunately for him, the vehicle hadn't flipped over, as they often do in these kind of accidents. EMS arrived shortly thereafter and transported Mega, Tamil and two others to the nearest hospital. They didn't look hurt badly, but they had to be dragged out of the vehicle by emergency workers. The two Cadillacs were both banged up pretty bad. But Mega's car had been wrecked on both ends from the rear impact and the forward dive into the ditch.

Of course, this had all been planned in advance. The accident had been mapped out almost to a tee. An accident in such weather made sense, plus the wet roads concealed any evidence that Mega had slammed on the brakes. All four passengers of the car were eventually awarded hefty settlements for their medical bills, chiropractic treatments and therapy, and the damage done to the vehicle, which was declared a total loss. The insurance company couldn't even tell that the engine was on its last legs, and they paid much more than the Coupe De Ville was worth.

But what Mega and Tamil hadn't planned for were the long-term consequences. Years after the accident, their backs continued to give them problems. The damage that had been done was permanent. Even with chiropractic treatments, which they would now have to pay for out of pocket, the pain and discomfort would persist. A plot for a few thousand dollars now, in hindsight, didn't seem so bright. Life is chess. The more successful player is the one who can see further ahead in the game.

There are consequences for every move you make, and every action you take.

WINNERS AND LOSERS

Winners spend hours on the Internet researching, making contacts, and promoting their businesses or causes.	Losers spend hours on the Internet looking at music videos on YouTube and leaving cute comments on MySpace.
Winners take twenty dollars and turn it into forty.	Losers take twenty dollars and spend it on a one-blunt bag of purple kush.
Winners get settlements from a relative's death or an insurance claim, and open businesses.	Losers get settlements from a relative's death or an insurance claim, and buy a new car.
Winners travel and explore the world.	Losers don't even watch the Travel channel.
Losers hope and pray they'll "make it" one day.	Winners have a game plan, so they know how and when they'll get there.
Winners take risks...calculated ones.	Losers take risks, but never check the odds.
Winners hang with other winners, and share their stories.	Losers hang with other losers, and compare their stories.
Winners criticize themselves for their own failures and shortcomings.	Losers criticize everyone except themselves, and blame others for their failures and shortcomings.
Losers have champagne taste and beer money.	Winners have beer taste and champagne money.
Losers hope to find happiness in money, prestige, or material possessions.	Winners find happiness in the relationships they have and the good they do for others.
Winners write TV shows and design video games for kids.	Losers watch TV and play video games like kids.
Losers look at winners and say, "Man, that could be me!"	Winners look at losers and say, "Man, that could never be me!"
Losers waste what little money they have on bullsh*t.	Winners make a lot of their money selling bullsh*t to losers.

A man's orientation in the game of life plays a major role in whether he wins or loses.

PRAY AND IT WON'T COME

"The sailor does not pray for wind, he learns to sail"
Gustaf Lindborg

One of the primary characteristics of our self-realization as God is the fundamental understanding of cause and effect. E. Franklin Frazier in his classic research into man's spiritual and religious culture described "magic" as an individual's belief that some sort of formula could be used to achieve real effects. That is, a magical object, incantation, or belief, could decide what would happen in physical reality.

Those who believe in magic would, for example, recite a prayer for rain. If it did rain, the belief in the power of the prayer and the gods/belief systems with which it was associated would be affirmed and reinforced. If it did not rain, fault would be attributed to the practitioner who would find some flaw in either their recitation, themself, other unforeseen circumstances, or the stronger magic or will of evil spirits plotting against the needs of the practitioner. To cite a modern example, think about bowling. When a bowler rolls the ball, he prays or says his "lucky words," hoping for a strike.

- If he gets a strike, he feels like his prayer works.

- If he doesn't, he blames it on his roll, the ball, or other factors.

But he never figures out that his prayer didn't change anything. So...how far have we come?

As they say in the film *What the Bleep Do We Know?*, people today, with all of our scientific advances and technical knowledge, still retain a "backwater" concept of God and spirituality. Prayers are nothing more than the magic tribal people subscribe to. They have no real effect. There is no mystery God. As Min. Farrakhan has said, rain is real. How can you attribute a real effect to such unreal causes (Mystery God)? Anyone who is aware of the water cycle should have abandoned the theory of God "making" it rain. However, I have heard grown people describing fog over a cemetery as "spirits," loud thunder as "God's anger," and disasters like Hurricane Katrina as "God's will" This is not to mention the childlike beliefs that praying for prosperity (or tithing for prosperity) will somehow relieve the poor of their financial conditions, or that elderly people are really cured of their ailments in those mega-churches with the charismatic white evangelists.

> "I prayed for freedom twenty years, but received no answer until I prayed with my legs."
> Frederick Douglass

Don't get me wrong, our MINDS do have power. We CAN affect reality with our thoughts, especially our own health. Studies have shown that people who are able to focus their minds can channel their thoughts to heal themselves and improve their own lives. But studies have NOT shown that religious people can call on an unseen God to help them out in real affairs with any degree of success. Even the Bible says, "God helps those who help themselves."

> "Stop the mindless wishing that things would be different. Rather than wasting time and emotional and spiritual energy in explaining why we don't have what we want, we can start to pursue other ways to get it."
> Greg Anderson

So rather than pray for my desired results, I introduce causative stimuli or action to produce the inevitable effects. In simple English, I put in the work needed to make it happen.

> "For life is a chain, cause and effected
> Niggas off the chain because they affected
> It's a dirty game, so whatever is effective"
> Jay-Z, "Minority Report"

**There is no better aid to clarity in life
than understanding the law of cause and effect.**

LOSING YOUR MIND

I Didn't Say It

Dan Barker, former preacher, and now co-president of the Freedom from Religion Foundation, says in *Losing Faith in Faith: From Preacher to Atheist*:

> You believe in a book that has talking animals, wizards, witches, demons, sticks turning into snakes, food falling from the sky, people walking on water, and all sorts of magical, absurd and primitive stories, and you say that we are the ones that need help?

Sounds like the words of Mark Twain, who said: "A man is accepted into a church for what he believes, and he is turned out for what he knows." Another minister, Rev. Donald Morgan said, "If you eat sausage, you are better off not knowing the inner workings of sausage factories, and if you are a Christian, that of the Christian church."

Don't look at me! I didn't say it!

The Joke

Eleven Christians and one atheist are hanging on a rope. If one of them does not let go of the rope, it will break and all of them will die. The atheist says he will sacrifice himself and let go because the Christians are such good friends that they would all grieve too much if one of them was to die and wreck their lives. He finishes his speech and the Christians are so touched by his generosity that they all begin to clap.

The Reality

> "The inhabitants of the earth are of two sorts:
> Those with brains, but no religion,
> And those with religion, but no brains."

Abu'l-`Ala' al-Ma`arri, poet of Ma`arra

Okay, all religious people aren't that brainless. But, if you really think about it, religious people are taught and trained NOT to think. When you are raised up in religion, you grow up believing and having faith as a way of life. But when you "believe" you have no way to KNOW if your belief is true. That's why people say "believe" means to "be lied" to.

"I do not believe in belief."
Edward M. Forster (1878-1970)

Faith is "belief in things unseen," and religious people swear that's all you need in life. I don't get it. If you're not supposed to use your rational mind, and our infinite intelligence isn't useful, why do we have brains? Don't religious people expect you to use your brain to pick between the 500 religions out there, and decide to get "saved"?

"Worship God. It's easier than thinking."
Chapman Cohen (1868-1954)

"A true idea has no need of any faith."
Ken Harding

As my brother Supreme Scientist Allah has written:

If we are capable of determining whether or not to be a slave to 'Jesus', why aren't we capable of successfully determining the best for ourselves in other matters in life? The answer is simple: we are! However, this is feared by [religious people], because thinking for ourselves will ultimately result in acting by and for ourselves. This would surely threaten the slaves' dependency on his master.

Wow, makes you think doesn't it?

Or are you just going to "keep the faith"?

Not a Joke, But it Could Be

"If you were taught that elves caused rain, every time it rained, you'd see the proof of elves."
Anonymous

This isn't a joke, but you might think it is. I was riding the bus one morning, and this cute female happened to be sitting next to me. I started getting at her, and she was obviously feeling me. Halfway through the bus ride, we passed by a cemetery. It was cold outside, and some fog had gathered above the cemetery grounds. She saw this and said, "Look! Do you see that? Those are their spirits."

I turned around and looked at her like "Are you retarded?" I didn't say that though...because she was cute. I said, "No, that's just fog." She wasn't havin it. She swore she'd seen spirits.

I said, "You know how when it's cold in the morning, there's water vapor in the air?" She was clueless. "No, I ain't heard of that," she replied. She continued, "Don't you believe in God?"

I couldn't believe it. As we went back and forth, I realized this 20-year-old high school graduate didn't understand the goddamn water cycle. That's some sh*t you learn in fourth grade.

You should NOT be 20 or 30 still thinking that lightning and thunder are "God's anger" or that rain "comes from God." You should know fourth grade science.

As far as the people 40,000 years ago who didn't understand fire, rain, and earthquakes, I can see why they came up with Gods to explain all that. That's where those "God in the sky" ideas came from, you know: People who didn't know sh*t.

In the words of scientist Richard Feynman in *Superstrings: A Theory of Everything*:

> God was invented to explain mystery. God is always invented to explain those things that you do not understand. Now, when you finally discover how something works, you get some laws which you're taking away from God; you don't need him anymore. But you need him for the other mysteries. So therefore you leave him to create the universe because we haven't figured that out yet; you need him for understanding those things which you don't believe the laws will explain, such as consciousness, or why you only live to a certain length of time—life and death—stuff like that. God is always associated with those things that you do not understand.[6]

It's the new millennium. You can look up anything you're curious about. You ain't got no excuse to be thinking that the Earth is spinning on God's fingertip.

Think for yourself, or be a slave to others' imagination.

SUPREME THE ASSHOLE ON "LAZY ASS BASTARDS"

It's always a mothaf*cka who ain't doin nothing to better his life who's whinin bout, "Aw, man, life is just so hard...Niggas just don't want to help." Ain't you heard that "God helps those who help themselves"? That means: Stop waiting for some white man, your mama, or even that mystery God, and go help yourself. If you don't get up off your ass, and stop layin around eatin Doritos and playin Xbox, you ain't gonna get sh*t outta life.

I was reading in one of the Ripley's *Believe It or Not!* books about this old Black dude who did surgery on himself using a knife, a drill, and some screws. He fixed his own rib cage. What the hell have you fixed lately? Have you even fixed yourself a decent meal lately? I mean a meal, with the vegetables on the side, not a sandwich. Back to Ripley's. I read about this other Black dude named Ivory Hill who had a wooden stake stuck in his head. It went all the way through. But dude just took his ass to a hospital somehow. He ain't lay around waiting for help. My point is: Anything is possible...but you gotta start by getting your ass off the damn couch!

In the VIP

Justin just knew he was gonna catch something nice tonight. He had a plan. The plan was so perfect, there was no way he was going to be at home beating his dick again tonight, he thought. First, Justin had promised to change the oil in his lawyer uncle's 745i BMW for only $50. That way, Justin was able to keep the car overnight at his house, where he had said he'd do the job. *

Of course, Justin took the car out that night. But before hitting the club, he stopped at his cousin Mike's house and borrowed one of his freshest outfits, by promising him to drive him around next time he had the BMW. Just before heading for the club, he stopped by the bank and went through the trash bin located next to the ATM machine. After a few minutes of searching, he found what he was looking for. Satisfied, he sped off towards Club 730.

Since the bouncer was an old friend from high school, Justin was admitted to the VIP section where some local rappers were tossing around "flash money" so they'd seem like they'd already made it. Justin got into the mix on the strength of his look, and before long, he was popping bottles he hadn't paid for. In almost no time, all this shine helped Justin secure the attention of Valerie.

> **Did You Know?**
>
> Approximately $25 million is spent each year on lap dances in Las Vegas. America spends $10 billion on pornography every year – the same amount it spends on foreign aid.

Valerie had a face like a top model and a waist like a pop bottle. She'd been dancing nearby another baller-type who was ignoring her, so when Justin called her over, she came quickly. She saw Justin's Gucci glasses, his iced-out chain, his $400 jeans, and knew she liked what she saw. So did Justin. Her breasts were nearly popping out of her shirt, and her ass, even in jeans, looked like a pillow with a rubber band round the middle. She was almost like a thick Beyonce.

Speaking of rubber bands, that's just about when Justin pulled out his stack of a hundred ones. He had just cashed his check from working double-shifts at UPS, and the hundred singles were going to have to last. At least until Valerie was drunk enough to leave with him. So Justin spread it out, tossing up occasional showers instead of full-on making it rain. But the singles on the ground kept Valerie's attention because she was sure Justin had more. With a chain like that, he had to.

Fortunately, by the time Justin was running low, Valerie was ready to go. They left Club 730 together in the 745, and Valerie nearly lost her mind pressing buttons and playing with all the technology inside. Justin thought she seemed a little ditsy, but she was fine enough to not care.

The way her long hair fell over her bare shoulders, the way she batted her long lashes, the way she smelled like fruit and flowers…and money. Maybe Justin had found a sugarmama.

But Justin couldn't take her to his house. Justin still lived with his mother. Of course, Justin lied and said his house was too far away. Valerie didn't want to bring him over to her place either, saying that she didn't "know him well enough." So they pulled up to a dingy motel. Justin, almost out of cash, was forced to pay for the room on his mom's credit card. He was a little worried, but got his confidence back after thinking about Valerie, who was drunk and grinding against him as he paid. Valerie looked like she had some magic pussy, Justin thought.

Upstairs, Valerie pushed Justin into the room and tossed him on the bed. Shutting the door, she began removing her clothing while Justin's heart raced with excitement. He grew rock hard with anticipation.

Then…as Valerie dropped her push-up bra, filled with tissue paper, Justin realized Valerie's breasts weren't full or round. They were actually small and sagging. And her stomach was rippled with stretchmarks, almost like a shriveled-up prune.

Then her jeans came off. And her ass fell apart with it. She wasn't wearing buttpads or anything. It was just that her jeans held her ass in a shape she didn't naturally have. Her ass went from "lovely lady lumps" to "loose lard" in five seconds flat. Justin was crushed. But he was determined to get some pussy now. But when Valerie took her panties off, Justin thought he could smell a 6-month-old tuna fish sandwich that someone left behind a radiator somewhere. He almost quit then, but his dick wasn't ready to say no.

As politely as he could, Justin asked Valerie to take a shower first.

Five minutes later, when she emerged, the smell was almost the same, but now her weave was frizzy, her makeup had washed off, and her fake lashes were gone. Without all of this, Valerie looked more like Fantasia than Beyonce.

At this point, Justin finally gave up. He told Valerie's drunk ass to get dressed while he went out to start the car. That's when Justin learned that the car had been stolen. Meanwhile, Valerie learned that the diamond chain she was about to steal was stainless steel…and the Gucci glasses were actually Cucci. By the end of the night, they learned that they were both broke and both still lived with their mothers, as that's who they had to call to pick them up from the motel.

**Getting caught up in initial appearances
is the fastest road to disappointment.**

MESSAGE IN A BOTTLE

The four of us sat huddled around a rickety kitchen table in Sun's apartment, perched on black milk crates or unstable plastic lawn chairs. On mine, the long jagged cracks that spread throughout the chair nearly separated the front right leg from the seat, causing the chair to wobble violently anytime I shifted my weight. Juan and GQ were both Hispanic, and Timothy and Jesse were Black, leaving me the "other". Sun was not far, fishing for something in his disheveled bedroom. Clouds of smoke wafted through the dilapidated second-floor apartment. We had just finished smoking our third blunt for that afternoon, and were still passing around another too-large bottle of straw-gold elixir.

As I took a hefty swig of the beer, Timothy complained loudly, "You're getting f*ckin backwater all in the bottle! You need to learn how to drink!"

"A little spit won't kill you, you nasty motherf*cker," I retorted, as I took another long drink.

"F*CK you, you little Hindu bastard!" he shot back.

The others chuckled.

Just then, Sun emerged with his trusty boombox, laid it upon the table, and inserted a black beat tape. Both the cassette and the radio were marked with graffiti letters scrawled in silver paint marker to identify Sun as the owner. We sped through the tape until stopping at a beat we could all agree upon, and commenced freestyling as in a traditional cipher. We kept up *tradition* too: traditionally drunk and high...even Sun was traditionally wack and incoherent with his old drunk ass.

As the cipher died down, and we relished in our highs, Sun was again fishing around in his room. Yet he was much faster this time, as if something in there was somehow placed according to some system of organization amidst the other chaos and filth. Though the beat tape continued to play, the apartment was extraordinarily quiet. Sun's live-in girlfriend and babymomma, Gwen, was gone for the day with the kids, save one. Sun had just put the two year old, nicknamed Fat, to sleep by giving him a good sip from the forty ounce. And with Gwen gone, there'd be no raucous fights between her and Sun, where he'd confess that he'd rather f*ck a dirty goat than her, and she, in turn, promised to cut his dick off while he slept.

I felt an odd silence sweep over the room when Sun revealed the object of his search. It was a black binder, filled with neatly handwritten and photocopied pages, and kept immaculately clean. I knew he'd pulled it out after smoking with us on other past occasions, but for some reason, I simply hadn't taken an interest in its contents until now. Hesitantly, I asked, "What is that sh*t?" Sun quickly answered, **"This isn't sh*t. This is my book of life."**

I had no idea what the f*ck he was talking about. What *life* did this mothaf*cka have? Certainly not one that needed any kind of book to accompany it. Sure, Sun occasionally imparted tidbits of wisdom to us, but we were half his damn age, so he never seemed *that* wise. It seemed a wise man would keep the company of other wise men, not a ragtag group of juvenile delinquents.

I was still attempting to decipher the significance of what he'd called it when I asked if I could take a look inside. He agreed, warning me only that it would be "the deepest sh*t" I'd ever come across, and that I couldn't play with the information I'd find within. I was dismissive, but he was right. To this day, *he was right*.

The first page I flipped to had the letters of alphabet accompanied by symbolic meanings. It looked like mumbo-jumbo, but something else on the page caught my interest. In the upper right corner there was a small drawing of a man encased in a circle much like that drawing by Da Vinci, except that by his arms, legs, and head were written the letters:

A – L – L – A – H.

It made sense almost instantly. It was like an epiphany, minus the angels. Man was God, Allah. Arm, Leg, Leg, Arm, Head – Man in his completion – 360 degrees. Sun only allowed me to skim a few more pages before taking the book away – but I was hooked from there.

In many ways, Knowledge of Self was the answer to the questions I'd already had, but no one could answer. I'd suffered for much of my youth because of my highly intellectual nature. I couldn't find reasonable answers to my questions regarding racism and theism, and I was exhausting myself trying to find them. By the time I was 15, even though I spent a lot of time in the streets, I spent equal time reading up on the culture and racial identity of the Egyptians, the Babylonians, and the Mayans, as well as the tenets and beliefs of Confucianism, Buddhism, Taoism, Islam, and even f*ckin Zoroastrianism, which I think went out of practice hundreds of years ago.

The search was both fruitful and fruitless. I gained plenty of knowledge, but little or no understanding. And my high school teachers, even Mr. Smith, couldn't really meet the needs of a 15-year-old who'd read damn near the whole Bible, and was attempting to make sense of it on his own. My mother, of course, couldn't quite relate either. When I couldn't sleep because I didn't understand the forces behind racism or the scientific possibility that God didn't exist, she'd just offer some hokey-poke answer like "Nobody knows that, son, so don't worry about it," or simply shoo me off to bed again. I actually had begun questioning God around the time I was in third grade, when the religion classes at St. Aedan's School required us to read Biblical text. Anyone who's read the Bible knows that sh*t don't add up. There are contradictions everywhere. Not to mention all the stuff that supposedly happened all the time back then and never seems to happen for real nowadays.

I remember my first "incident" in a religion class occurred about three months into me being skipped into third grade, when I asked the teacher: If Jesus died and rose as a "spirit," why did he need to:

Did You Know?

George Washington, our first president, paid $250 for a slave he bought by mail order? President and Founding Father Thomas Jefferson had children by one of his slaves, Sally Hemmings? Abraham Lincoln said he didn't care about whether Blacks were free or slaves, and that he only freed the slaves to help him win the Civil War and reunite the Union? "Great people." my ass!

- Roll the rock to the side to get out the tomb?

- Change clothes to hide from the Romans?

- Eat fish and honey? (Look it up)

If Jesus was so great that he died and came back, why didn't all the other great people, like:

- Slave-saving Abraham Lincoln?

- Tree-chopping George Washington?

- Peace-loving Dr. Martin Luther King, Jr.?

Of course, that didn't go over well. And it only got worse from there.

"I distrust those people who know so well what God wants them to do because I notice it always coincides with their own desires."
Susan B. Anthony (1820-1906)

Eventually, I completely dismissed the myths of Christianity as mystical, magical mumbo-jumbo. I soon began questioning the idea of God as a whole, beginning with the question of why I suffered so much, though I had done no wrong. I believed God was a tyrant, before arriving at the idea that maybe God was a figment of everyone's imagination, like an imaginary friend.

So, at about age 11 or 12, I devised a simple experiment. For some time, God had been giving me horrendous advice in my prayers. I tried praying to St. Jude instead, and that worked out a few times, but he had a pretty high failure rate as well. So I wondered if God's "voice" was just my own voice, and all that advice and guidance had just been what I had *believed* God would have wanted me to do. So I tried praying to God, except I wanted God to sound like Papa Smurf and say the most ridiculous things I could concoct. Of course, it worked.

Me: Dear Lord, please tell me what to do about my family's troubles.

God: Well...you've got to smurfiddy-smurf 'til your smurfs aren't unsmurfy.

Me: Goddamnit, I knew it!

It still took me a few years to completely dismiss the notion of a Mystery God, but that day basically cinched the deal. From there on, I either spent my time ignoring God or being mad at him, whoever or whatever he was. Because whatever or wherever he was, he evidently wasn't looking out for – or even communicating with – me. I was waiting for a sign.

Who woulda thought that God would finally appear as a drunk 30-year-old with broken furniture? Laugh if you want...but without that brother, there'd be no Supreme Understanding.

A lesson can be anywhere. Some you find, some find you.

---

10 LESSONS FROM AMERICAN GANGSTER

You know a lesson can be found anywhere. If you watch any movie with an eye for what's REALLY going on, you can learn some things. Here are ten things you can learn from the movie *American Gangster*:

1. Awareness

The dope game, like any criminal enterprise, is bigger than you. Frank Lucas is well aware of it. Halfway through the film, he comments on how Bumpy Johnson didn't own his business – a white man did – so a white man owned him. By the end of the film, Frank knew that his going to prison wouldn't change anything in the streets. He knew that he was simply a small part of a business that went much higher than him. The cops are part of it, the courts are part of it, the politicians are part of it, and the Mob is part of it. A man like Frank Lucas isn't a king in a jungle like this. By the film's end, we see what kind of animal he actually becomes.

Do you know where you fit in the game of life?

2. Humility

When Frank's brother starts wearing flashy suits, he tells him he doesn't really look good – he looks "like a clown." He explains that "The loudest one in the room is the weakest one in the room." Frank isn't like that. He's humble but confident. He's rich but lowkey. In real life, Frank Lucas would monitor the strip he controlled from a beat-up Chevy, wearing a fake beard, a long wig, and dark glasses. "I'd sit there in Nellybelle and watch the money roll in," he said in an interview. "And no one even knew it was me. I was a shadow. A ghost." In the film, Frank keeps a low profile and avoids attention until his wife convinces him to wear a flashy chinchilla fur coat and matching hat. When he sees the negative attention it brings, he burns it and goes back to his business suits. Today's hustlers are a little different, to say the least. Just make it easier for the Feds to indict, I guess?

3. Discipline

All around Frank Lucas is drugs. But you'll never see him do a single drug himself. In the film, you won't really see him touch any, cut or cook any, or retail sale any with his own hands. When Frank learns that his driver, his brother, has drugs in the trunk of their car, he bashes his head against the window and fires him. He treats everyone who shows a lack of discipline this way. In fact, another of his brothers gets hooked on the drugs they're selling and starts losing control. With no internal discipline or focus, this brother begins wrecking Frank's life.

4. Ingenuity

While dealers like Nikki Barnes were paying $35,000 a key for cut heroin, Frank found a way to get pure for only $4,000 a key: He went straight to Southeast Asia and cut out the middle men. Few people of this time would have the ingenuity and intelligence to run an operation like his, much less to figure out a way to ship in large amounts of heroin in the coffins of dead U.S. soldiers. And how many of you would be ready to hop on a plane to a country on the other side of the globe, much less the jungles of a country that's in the middle of a war?

5. Leadership

Leadership can be good or bad. While Frank Lucas ran his operation with strong leadership, and did his best to eliminate the weak links, it's very hard to treat people like family and do business as well. Especially when the business is dirty. Frank not only paid by losing most of his family, including his own mother and wife giving up on him, but he saw his young nephew get killed trying to follow in his footsteps.

6. Greed

In the film, Nikki Barnes is like a competitor to Frank. But Nikki buys Frank's heroin, cuts it four or five times and sells the weaker product with the same "Blue Magic" name. Frank stops him, and asks him why he doesn't just sell it as is, since he'll still make more than enough money? The reason of course, is Nikki's greed. But Frank is greedy as well: He does run a drug empire, remember? Even when he is warned "success has enemies," Frank works twice as hard to be twice as successful. Even when he has an opportunity to get out of the game, he won't. Even though he is advised: "Quitting while ahead is not the same as quitting." Even when his wife suggests that they leave while they can, he won't. In the end, he loses it all.

As Lucas said in an interview 30 years later:

> There wasn't gonna be no next Bumpy. Bumpy believed in that share-the-wealth. I was a different sonofabitch. I wanted all the money for myself . . . Harlem was boring to me then. Numbers, protection, those little pieces of paper flying out of your pocket. I wanted adventure. I wanted to see the world.

7. Karma

> "Because you have drowned others, you were drowned."
> Rabbi Hillel

You reap what you sow. Frank Lucas and Nikki Barnes are both "free" men now, if you can call their lives free. They snitched on enough people to reduce their sentences significantly. But I can't imagine what it feels like to get out of prison and see the hell that you have helped create. Especially since things are even worse now. Not to mention that they're broke and can't show their faces on most streets.

Recently, a reporter for *New York Magazine* got Frank Lucas and Nikki Barnes to do an interview together, marking the first time they've spoken with each other in 30 years. They spoke on a number of things, such as how their lives have turned out (they're both pretty poor now, with Frank Lucas recently being described as "the old man in the fake Timberland jacket" and Nikki Barnes being unable to show his face again on the streets of Harlem) as well as the damage they realize they've done:

> **Nikki Barnes:** No one should be elevated because of what they did in the drug business. The way we operated—there was a lot of violence, like, ten to twelve homicides, to keep the whole operation running. You can't glorify that. It's not something Frank or I would tell any of our children to get into.
> **Frank Lucas:** Absolutely right, Nick.
> **Nikki Barnes:** Heroin wreaked a lot of havoc and a lot of pain in the black community. I shouldn't have done it. Maybe I was aware, but I just didn't give a f*ck. I wanted to make money, and that's what I did. Looking back, I wouldn't have made those decisions, but it's a hell of a lot different and much easier to sanitize yourself after the fact.

8. Influence

You're being influenced right now. Constantly we are presented with things that push us in one direction or another. When Frank worked under Bumpy Johnson, he absorbed everything...and over time it came out. Anything you take in will come out somehow. In the same way,

Frank's nephew – a promising ballplayer – was influenced so much by watching Frank that he quit baseball to try his hand at the dope game.

9. Handling Conflict

There are three major ways to handle a conflict: Diplomacy, Strategy, and War. Watch the film and look at how Frank uses each approach, and when he uses it.

10. Purpose

Why are you here? What are you here for? In many ways, Frank Lucas did as much good for the people as one of his junkies. He didn't want kids to start doing heroin but they did. He didn't intend for heroin to become an epidemic in Black America, but it did. He didn't mean to provide a model for drug distribution for future groups to copy, but he did. His purpose, as he saw it, was only to "get rich" (see "American Dream"). He had no vision of the war going on in America, even though the Civil Rights Movement and the Black Power Movement were all around him. The way I see it, you can die poor, or you can die rich, but you're all gonna die…if you're gonna live and die fighting, why not fight for something worth fighting for?

With all that said, what do you get out of movies, songs, and shows? Is it just entertainment? Or can you see the life lessons unfolding? If you can't relate everything you see back to your own life, you're missing a big part of the picture.

**Everything can be a learning opportunity if you let it.
The world unfolds in layers of meaning.
Keep looking and you'll see it all around you.**

EACH ONE, TEACH ONE

When Dr. Dre left N.W.A. to start Death Row Records, he was on his own. Having nobody to tell him how sh*t was, he learned the game the hard way: through experience. Somehow, he emerged successful, dropping one of the most celebrated albums ever with *The Chronic*. On *The Chronic,* Dre's first solo venture, he took a risk by sharing the spotlight with a young unknown with a funny name: Snoop Doggy Dogg. Dre had decided to take on Snoop as a protégé, and mentored him on the ins and outs of the rap game.

Dre taught Snoop everything he had learned about the music industry. As a result, not only was Snoop incredibly successful (bringing more money back to Dre), but he avoided many of the mistakes other guys in his position were making. While young gangsta rappers fell off left and right, Snoop managed to last – and remain highly successful – for over a decade after Dre first took him under his wing.

"He who learns, teaches. He who teaches, learns."
Ethiopian proverb

In fact, having people like Snoop under his wing improved Dre's own gameplan. It turns out teaching someone else is the best way to learn.

When a six-year old rapper named Kid Murder hit the stage rapping with the confidence of a grown man, Snoop Dogg took interest the way his mentor had once taken interest in him. He gave the boy a new name – Lil Bow Wow (after himself) – and began educating him on the traps to avoid and the paths to take.

Years later, Bow Wow has been one of the very few rappers who didn't fall after childhood. While Kriss Kross, ABC, Quo, and dozens of other kid rappers have disappeared, never to return, Bow Wow has managed to carry his success into adulthood. The number one reason being that he found a mentor...or a mentor found him.

They say: "When the student is ready, the teacher will appear." As you learn, and find others to guide you towards growth and success, don't forget that one day, somebody will be looking for you as well.

In *Young Gifted and Black*, Theresa Perry explains how slaves felt once they learned how to read:

> Becoming literate obliged one to teach others. Learning and teaching were two sides of the same coin, part of the same moment. Literacy was not something you kept for yourself; it was to be passed on to others, to the community.

T.I., in his song "Praying for Help" says the same thing about sharing the life lessons one has learned:

> I ask how can a man who's done so much, be treated so unjust/ Cause I tried to inspire the folks/ You wanna condemn em cause they sell dope/ Well man, show em the ropes/ Be a father or a football coach/ A role model or a symbol of hope/ Take another approach/...Can't you see they only do what they know/And you wonder why they don care no mo'?

Lil Wayne talks about youth looking for guidance as well, when he says on "Don't Cry":

> Why we gotta kill our own kind when we rise?/ Got me lookin' down the ladder now, when I climb/...Pullin' up on my nephews/ And they don't wanna drive/ They wanna learn how to work the tool/ And who am I not to do the duty? Just think/ Their pops' advice gets sent through black ink/ And that stinks, but homey, that's real/ And in the hood, even steak smell bad on the grill

Whether or not you're ready to find a mentor or teacher for youself, there are probably dozens of kids out there who could benefit by you taking the time to talk to them. Just make sure you teach them how to avoid falling victim, and not simply how to fake it until they fall.

Find a teacher; be a teacher.

THE ART OF PEOPLE-WATCHING

There used to be these commercials on TV where they would wreck cars with crash-test dummies in them, to show you why you should wear a seat belt. Right after the dummy's head flew through the windshield in slow-motion, the screen would read: "You could learn a lot from a dummy."

You sure can. If you want to learn something while having a good laugh, just watch stupid people. You can see these real-live dummies in motion on the bus, on the street, in the club, or even at your job. They are walking lessons...on what NOT to do.

I try to sit back and do some people-watching at least once a week. I pick a spot and I just post up. Sometimes I write down what I've noticed or learned. Here are a few observations and lessons I picked up one week by just watching or dealing with other people:

1. People you've been treating like crap can turn out to be your only friends when you're in a time of need. Then again, some people can't handle being treated any other way.

2. Kindness is not a weakness. But being naïve is.

3. Look at this nut. White people must do drugs because they don't have enough problems.

> "Wherever we look upon this earth, the opportunities take shape within the problems."
> Nelson Rockefeller (1908-1979)

4. People don't understand what life is about, so they wander around all clueless. You can see on their face that they don't get it. Life is a series of problem-solving exercises and compromises, broken up into chapters by intense moments of victory or misery. If people could see that, they wouldn't be lookin all goofy every day.

5. Another missed call. Women only wish you were their man until you really are.

6. Another indecent proposal via text message. I'll pass. Sex is better when you feel like you'll want to lay next to that mothaf*cka afterwards. Not jump up and wash off like you've been contaminated.

> "Owned by CA, State Property/ Just like the year 1553"
> Ice Cube, "Why We Thugs"

7. This dude needs to stop collect calling me four times a day, to tell me all this silly sh*t happening in the jail. Man, jail = slavery. Any time you're ready to jump hoops for a snack cake, you've either become a slave or an animal.

8. This dude's got on a hat that says "M.O.B." M.O.B. huh? If it's Money Over Bitches, what's over Money?

9. What was she thinking? That "play then pay" scam don't work on me. You know, that scam women run, where she acts like a wonderful girl with no problems at first? Then one day, she mentions a financial problem that "just" popped up (*sure*), knowing the man will come to her rescue...get the f*ck outta here!

10. Another missed call. I'ma let this one go. Most girls silent auction themselves to the highest bidder. That is, the one guy (out of all the guys who have gotten her number) who offers the most attention, or most expensive gifts/dates, becomes the winning bidder and now has her (on loan) until she tires of him (or he runs out), and another high bidder comes around (who often has been waiting on reserve anyway). It doesn't take a rocket scientist to figure that out.

11. Damn, would you look at this broad! She should know you can get a man with sex, but you won't keep him. And he should know, you can get a woman with money, but you never really had her.

12. Look at those two dummies. That's lust, not love. Love has a ton of impersonators. You may think you finally have it, but it's really something else.

13. Bad-ass Bebe's kids! Parents who don't raise their children deserve whatever their children do to them once they're grown.

14. Ah, another white person with a "Save Darfur" shirt. White people aren't all bad. But why are we so quick to jump to the defense of *the whole*, when it's only a small minority of em who are down for us?

15. Damn. Look at those Black helicopters. World War III ain't far away. I'm not scared.

16. Look at these old-ass dudes talking like kids. Some of us never became men. Backtracking and doin it right is not a bad move.

17. Being low on funds is temporary. Being poor is lifelong.

18. Ugh. Beauty is inside. But some folks are just tough to look at.

Try it for yourself. Take 30 minutes today to sit outside, somewhere public, and observe people. See what you can learn, just from watching people interact and go about their daily lives. You'll be amazed by how much a man can learn when he just shuts the f*ck up and pays attention.

A man's ability to learn from others helps him avoid making the same mistakes as everyone else.

THE MOVE BOMBING

MOVE was a mostly-Black organization started in 1972 by John Africa and Donald Glassey in Philadelphia. The organization preached a "back to nature" lifestyle and spoke out against social injustices. On May 13, 1985, the Philadelphia police engaged MOVE in a gun battle at the house they shared on 6221 Osage Ave. The police then dropped a C-4 explosive on the roof of the MOVE residence. The resulting fire destroyed the entire block, killed eleven MOVE members, and left 250 area residents homeless. Ramona Africa, the only adult MOVE survivor, was convicted of riot and conspiracy and served seven years in prison, before winning a $1.5 million judgement against the city. No government official or police officer has ever faced any criminal charges for the deaths.

It all seems pretty cut and dry. But, even though the important parts are clear and undeniable, there are many parts of the MOVE story that have been told many different ways, depending on who was doing the telling.

Side A:

According to one side, MOVE members were filthy, obnoxious, and disruptive, and used their communal residences to terrorize their neighbors and the rest of the hard-working community. The first MOVE residence was a constant disturbance to the community. Members didn't bathe, and didn't use running water, so the stench of human waste was everywhere. After the city began issuing warnings, MOVE members put their neighbors in a panic by marching around their house with rifles. When police tried to clear the house by force, an officer was shot by a gun traced back to MOVE member Phil Africa. Following this event, Philadelphia Mayor Frank Rizzo had the house demolished as it was deemed uninhabitable due to health code violations.

MOVE then relocated to a second house on Osage Avenue, where they continued their harassment of local residents. The Osage Avenue houses were connected, and their shared roofs formed a convenient jogging track for MOVE. Neighbors woke up to sounds of the MOVE physical training program through their bedroom ceilings in the early morning. This disturbance was soon joined by MOVE's loud speaker system, broadcasting political rants for hours at a time that were laced with profanity. In addition, the MOVE organization's emphasis on "recycling" contributed to a heavy waste pileup both in and out of the house, and the stench was growing. As a matter of fact, members of MOVE had begun training the large wharf rats that were in and out of their house as a means with which to intimidate or annoy their unfriendly neighbors.

During a failed attempt to serve an arrest warrant for four MOVE members at this house, police responded to shots fired and became engaged in a gun battle with the organization. Fully aware of the massive amount of firepower held at the MOVE home, the police commander decided to disable a "bunker"-type structure on MOVE's rooftop with a satchel of explosives, referred to as an "entry device." Barrels of gasoline in the MOVE residence soon led to the tremendous destruction that followed.

But it's not that simple…

Side B:

According to the other side, it was a completely different story. MOVE members began transforming their views towards a Black Panther Party-style philosophy of armed self-defense only after police jailed three members and attacked their home in the Powelton Village section of Philadelphia in 1977, killing a young child named Life Africa. MOVE members began protesting, and using loudspeakers to inform the community about the injustices being committed. In response, the Philly police engaged in a year-long siege on the MOVE residence.

The mayor ordered a blockade of the immediate neighborhood, in order to prevent food and supplies from reaching MOVE. However, since the blockade was announced in advance, supporters were able to bring in large supplies of food. MOVE members had also secretly dug a tunnel through to Powelton Ave., outside the police perimeter.

The year-long siege came to a head on Aug. 8, 1978, when officers fired hundreds of rounds of ammunition into the basement of the MOVE house, where members had retreated. When Officer James Ramp was found dead following the gunfire, nine MOVE members were charged with the murder, even though evidence indicated that the bullet that killed Ramp could not have been fired from the MOVE house.

Within 24 hours of the assault, police completely destroyed the MOVE home, along with any evidence that would support the MOVE members' defense. Three police officers who brutally and publicly beat MOVE member Delbert Africa after the shootout were acquitted.

After the relocation, MOVE members fortified their new house to prevent further attacks. They also began crusading aggressively for the release of the MOVE 9. This confrontation with the city and the police reached boiling point in May of 1985. At dawn on May 13, 500 police officers evacuated the neighborhood. Soon after, they surrounded and attacked the house with over 10,000 rounds of ammunition in 90 minutes. They also used small explosive charges and water from fire department hoses in an attempt to penetrate the house, fully aware that several children were inside.

Four months before this siege, a special agent of the FBI had given the Philadelphia police bomb squad 30 blocks of C-4, the most lethal of military plastic explosives. On the afternoon of May 13, a police helicopter dropped a bomb containing C-4 on the roof of the MOVE home on Osage Avenue.

Although fire trucks were present, and their water cannons were already in use as a weapon against MOVE members inside, the resulting fire was allowed to burn for 45 minutes before fire hoses were turned on. By then, the blaze was starting to devour the entire block. MOVE members who attempted to escape from the rear of the building were shot at by police. Six MOVE adults and five children were killed. Only Ramona Africa and a 13-year-old boy named Birdie Africa escaped the fire.

Today, 6221 Osage Ave has been turned into a Philadelphia police station. Ramona Africa remains an outspoken political activist. Birdie Africa, who was illiterate and had never owned a toy at the time of the bombing, is now an Army sergeant on the other side of the fence. MOVE's most well-known supporter, Mumia Abu Jamal, now on Death Row, is an accomplished activist and author. But what really happened?

To help you decide, here are the words of survivor Ramona Africa:

> The government has used the media to try to convince people that what happened on May 13, 1985 was because of complaints from neighbors, but that is absolutely ridiculous. When has this government ever cared about Black folks complaining about their neighbors? Look at 8th & Butler. How long have those people been complaining about the drug traffic and the drug wars? They cannot even let their children sit outside in the summer because they are afraid that their children will be shot to death! Did they drop a bomb down there? Are they giving that area the kind of attention that they gave Osage Avenue? It's ridiculous to think that a handful of Black people can complain about their neighbors and get the FBI, the U.S. Justice Department, the state and local government involved.

What do you think really happened that day, and on the days leading up to it? What led you to that conclusion?

How can you see past the "he-said/she-said" to figure out the truth in anyone's story?

When you watch the news or hear about personal conflicts, how can you avoid being misled?

**There are always three sides to a story:
Side A, Side B, and the Truth**

MOVIES TO SEE

The Lord of the Rings Trilogy; 300

The *Lord of the Rings* may be long as hell, but it's interesting because it tells the story of all the white tribes in ancient Europe coming together as one to keep out all the Black and brown people from nearby countries. This is how "white people" came to be.

Just think about it. All the good guys were different kinds of white people. All the bad guys were brown and Black. Some of them looked like Muslims, some of them had dreads, and some of them even looked like Asians. Just so you know I'm not making this up, the story was written by a racist professor of Old English (as in European studies, not the malt liquor).

300 is more of the same. A white fantasy version of how they fought off all the Black, brown, and yellow people that they thought were getting too close to Europe. Why do they make all of us look like gremlins and goblins in these movies? I guess that's what they think of us. At least in this one, the Persian leader Xerxes is big and Black and says he's God…except they made him out to be a total queer.

10 LESSONS FROM THE CLUB

Like I've said before, you can find a lesson anywhere…if you're looking. Here are 10 life lessons I learned in the club. Not that any of this stuff ever happened to me, of course.

1. Enjoy yourself

You've got $60 to your name. You've been working double-shifts all week. You need a break. So you go to the club. What are you here for? Tell yourself that you're here to take somebody home, and you've got a 1 in 100 chance of being successful. Tell yourself that you're just here to have fun, and you've got a 1 in 3 chance of being successful. You decide. Once you step in, there's plenty of fine women to choose from. But you've decided you're just going to have fun. If they want to be a slut and come home with you, that's just an added bonus. And guess what, when you come off like you're just tryin to enjoy yourself, and don't care about hoes…that's when the hoes seem to like you more.

Live out your intentions.
What you put out is what you get back.

2. Don't think she won't go for it

There she goes. Now, she may be bad. She may be so fine that she'd make a gay man's mouth water. And she may be dressed better than everyone in there. And she may be sitting or standing still like she has no plans on dancing…or talking to a knucklehead like you. But you won't know for sure until you step to her.

Don't assume; find out.
Believing and knowing aren't the same thing.

3. Ask and see

There's actually plenty of superfine women in here who haven't met anybody the whole night because most of the men were intimidated. The few that tried were too drunk or too stupid. Maybe you're only a little drunk and a little stupid. And maybe she'll give you a chance. I've learned that some of the girls that look "stuck up" standing still are just waiting for someone to do the right thing. Just step up and tell her what you'd like to do. If she says no, cool. Nothing lost. If she says yes, you win.

The squeaky wheel gets the oil.
Every journey begins with taking one step.

4. Make sure things are clear before proceeding

"Wen Tzu always thought three times before taking action. Twice would have been quite enough."
Confucius (551-479 B.C.)

You've chosen. And the girl you're eyeing is dancing on this dude like she's doin $20 lap dances. And she's letting him slap her ass, palm her chest, and all sorts of other ungodly things. Now you want your turn. The next song comes on and you're ready to squeeze in behind her. Next thing you know, ol' girl is pushing you off, dude is looking at you crazy, and security is about to crush you. Turns out she's his wife. And he's the owner of the club. Next time, ask first.

Look before you leap.

5. Handle confrontation appropriately

So dude is upset. He's not a little punk kind of guy either. He's either been hittin the gym, or hittin some steroids, and that's probably how he ended up hittin something as fine as ol' girl. Now he's about to hit you. You think fast. He's loud and angry, so you neutralize him with the opposite. You give him dap, and apologize in his ear, and let him know you meant no disrespect. You tell him he's a lucky man and move on.

Fire needs ice; Ice needs fire.
Every situation has a smart way to handle it.

---

6. Pick your battles

But as you move on, the security dude keeps grillin you. What's his problem? You're not a chump, so maybe he got the wrong idea when you didn't knuckle up with the last guy. So you step to him and ask him what the problem is. He tells you that his mother just died, and he's only working to pay for her funeral...and he's not in the mood to talk. He says if you have a problem with how he's looking, the two of you can definitely "handle that." So, he's pretty unstable, you figure. He's going to snap at any minute. And you don't want to be around when he does.

Foresee the consequences.
Sometimes your next step isn't the best step.

---

7. Anything can happen at any time

So you walked away from another one unscathed. You're feeling pretty cool now. You've had a few drinks and you feel relaxed. All of a sudden six people fall on top of you. As you hit the ground hard, some girl steps in your eye trying to run away. That crazy bouncer from a minute ago throws somebody else on top of you. The gun you snuck in the club goes off in your pants. Now you have no penis.

You should have been more alert, and watching out for that fight that just broke out. If you had been paying attention, you would have been able to get out of the way in time. But it's too late to worry about that, because now you have no penis.

Pay attention to your surroundings.
Sleep is the cousin of death.

---

8. Know when to stop

"Now your life is leavin yo body, for drinkin too much Bacardi/
You should've known when you started..."
Eightball and MJG, "You Don't Want Drama"

Let's say you avoided getting crushed, trampled, and having your penis shot off. You're feeling good, but a few more drinks will have you feeling even better, right? But you're taking straight shots, and passing bottles around with your homeboys. Pretty soon, every girl on two legs looks like a supermodel, and even the girl with only one leg seems like she could be fun. But you can't approach them, because every time you try, you trip over somebody and damn near fall. You're sweating like fat people in the summer, and your breath smells like throw-up and berries.

Somebody passes you just one more cup, and you take it. One sip later, everything in your stomach is now on the floor…and on your clothes. Try being smooth now.

Know your limits.
Too much of anything is not a good thing.

---

9. Fools die over pride

So you're trying to stumble your drunk ass to the bathroom to wipe down enough to go home. But you trip over a girl doing a split and crash into the club owner again. Seems you tripped over his girl, made him spill his drink on himself, and accidentally stabbed him with your stainless steel medallion. He's obviously upset. But you're mad too, because he was in your way. And, in your mind, he's the reason for all your problems tonight (not you). So you let him know that you're about to beat his ass. He asks you to come outside with him. You're ready to fight. No, scratch that, you're ready to do him with that 380 in your pants. As soon as you get outside and reach for it, he kicks you in the forehead, takes your own gun from you, and shoots you with it at point blank range. Turns out his day job is as a police officer. Now you're dead, and he still gets the girl.

Don't ever lose your composure.
Uncontrolled emotions lead to big problems.

---

10. She's not that cute

Let's just say you never threw up on yourself. Let's say you got that superfine girl you would have been too scared to talk to. Not only did you get her number, you got her to come to breakfast with you. You're feeling like a king, aren't you? You're ready to make some magic happen as soon as you leave the Waffle House. That is, until you get into the bright lights of the parking lot and realize that ol' girl is really a man.

Don't believe everything you see or hear.
Anything that seems *too good* to be true…usually is just that.

RACISM IS ALIVE

On December 22, 1984, Bernard Goetz, a white middle-aged electronics repairman, boarded a New York City subway train as he may have any other day. Except today, four Black teenagers approached him. Goetz became nervous. When one of them asked for five dollars, he was sure he was being mugged. Goetz drew a snub-nosed .38 revolver from his quick-draw holster and began firing at the youth.

He hit Troy Can'ty, 18, in the chest; James Ramseur, also 18, in both the arm and the chest; and Barry Allen, 19, caught a slug in his back as he

---

attempted to run away. As the train conductor, hearing the shots, pulled the train to a screeching stop, Goetz approached the fourth boy, Darrell Caby, 18, saying, "You don't look too bad. Here's another." With that, he squeezed the trigger again and shot Caby in the spinal cord, instantly paralyzing him.

Goetz was a fugitive for ten days following the incident. During the manhunt for the "Subway Vigilante," tons of white callers phoned into radio stations to voice their support for Goetz. Goetz finally turned himself in and confessed on videotape. He described the events, still emotional but not a bit repentant: "My problem was I ran out of bullets. I was going to gouge out one of the guy's eyes with my keys. I was vicious. My intent was to kill them."

His fans shared his idea. They weren't content that these four boys were hospitalized – one of them paralyzed from the waist down and succumbing to permanent brain damage – they wanted the boys dead. Whites from all over showed their support in every way imaginable: They sold and wore T-shirts emblazoned with Goetz face and the words, "Thug Buster" and "New York Loves Ya, Bernie!" They put up graffiti and bumper stickers praising him. Radio talk show callers applauded him for "doing the city a huge favor." There were even several offers to pay his bail.

Goetz, who had been carrying a lethal weapon illegally, had attempted to viciously murder a group of four youth carrying only screwdrivers, which Goetz had not yet even seen. During Goetz's trial, the boys were depicted as savage murderous criminals, and Goetz as an innocent white citizen only hoping to defend himself against these young Black predators. James Ramseur, based on his words and body language, was described as an obvious thug, with one of the ten white jurors later confessing that Ramseur "gave her nightmares."

Goetz was ultimately found not guilty on seventeen of the eighteen counts, excluding the one charge of illegal gun possession, for which he served less than a year in prison before being released. Years after the trial, Goetz remarked of his four victims:

> They represented the failure of society…Forget about their ever making a positive contribution to society. It's only a question of how much a price they're going to cost. The solution is their mothers should have had an abortion.

It later turned out that Goetz had also loaded his gun with illegal ammunition – "dum dum" slugs – meant to do the maximum of bodily damage, and that he had – over the years – made several racist comments like those above. Since then, Goetz has put in his bid to run for mayor of New York City, started a company he named Vigilante

Electronics, appeared in movies, and spoken out publicly for animal rights.

> "A snake, if allowed to live, will only sting someone else."
> Lost-Found Muslim Lesson #2

Racism and discrimination are very simple, but not in the way that we are taught. We are taught that racism just means the dislike of another group, and therefore anybody can be a racist. That's simply not how it is.

There are two forms of discrimination: Institutional discrimination and Individual discrimination. Institutional discrimination is the systematic practice of maintaining an unfair power structure like the one we have in America. In a nutshell, institutional racism is white supremacy, the global ideology that whites should be in a position of power over all people of color. After all, everywhere whites have ever been, they -and their values – are THE supreme authority on everything.

On the other hand, anybody can be a victim or perpetrator of individual discrimination. A white person can treat a Black person like dirt, but a Black person can do the same thing to a white person, and after all these centuries of racism and suffering, many frustrated Black people are quick to do so when given the opportunity. But individual discrimination perpetrated by a Black person is not representative of a system of actual power.

Think about: A Black principal may run a school and think she's the H.N.I.C. But if she treats a white student badly, that bigger system of institutional discrimination is going to come down on her head, and she'll be replaced in no time. A Black CEO can run a billion dollar company and think he's Superman. But if he tries to *only* hire Black people, or – even worse – he starts giving money to Black organizations like the Nation of Islam, pretty soon he's going to come under fire and his company will start losing all that white money that helped make him rich. On the other hand, **everything white people do is reinforced by the system**, *except* fighting on the side of Black people.

Racism is Alive

Wait, before I explain, don't tell me you think racist attitudes and practices are disappearing? Please. That's not how this society works. This society is founded on exploitation of "others." For that to change, there would need to be a complete revolution. That's why the 60s were such a scary era. A revolution may have actually happened. Fortunately, white people introduced us to heroin and acid, the hippie movement and "free love," and all the tension eventually dissipated.

Anyway, if you want proof, you can't judge from what white people say in public. These days, it's not PC to talk that way. It appears downright crude and uncivilized to speak of "niggers" and returning to slavery. Rather, the same ideas are now coded with vernacular like "the working class," "low-income neighborhoods." and "welfare reform."

If you want to know what white people *really* think, you'd have a hard time finding examples, since most white people even deny their *own* racist attitudes. But check out any message board discussing a controversial issue related to people of color. You can even look at the comments to any YouTube video on Black history. You may be shocked. Or check out the YouTube clip on the "Wiener Circle" in Chicago. Or what about the secretly recorded conversations where we hear powerful people saying what they really think about us? Or what about everyone from Kramer to Don Imus to "Dog the Bounty Hunter"? Do you think those people are just "special" cases? No, they're just the ones dumb enough to get caught.

IF YOU'RE NOT OUTRAGED YOU'RE NOT PAYING ATTENTION

White people love to think that racism is not specific to them. History tells us otherwise. No other population has systemically engaged, enslaved, and exploited every other population with which it has come in contact. Yes, there have been wars since man has had things to dispute over. But systemic exploitation? No other population group has made it their mission to canvas the globe, even its most distant outposts, and claim ownership. Not only of the land, but of its ruling class and its economy.

No other people have used religion as a means of convincing native populations of their own inferiority, only to be followed by subjugation. As the saying goes, "First, they had the Bible and we had the land. Now we have the Bible and they have the land." What's amazing is that this methodology has been their M.O. for thousands of years. Even before Christianity!

Examining the globe as a whole, it's evident who the ruling class is worldwide. Focusing on any particular country will reveal that the ruling class is either white, or elected and controlled by whites. In any country where the local population will strongly resist white leadership, whites have installed "puppet" governments. This is why sub-Saharan Africa is doing so bad even today. It has nothing to do with the inability of the people.

This is also the reason why there's currently a war in the Middle East. Sure, there's oil at stake. But let's not ignore the fact that the Middle East represents the last stronghold of ethnic independence against white cultural imperialism and economic exploitation. The Muslims, unified through Islam and repulsion of "Western (meaning white) values (whatever that means)" were the single most dangerous force on the planet since the Black Power movement was crushed in the 1970s.

To deny racism is itself racist. To deny that whites represent the ruling class everywhere...is racist. Because you KNOW it's true. To act as if whites aren't given preferential treatment and privilege damn near everywhere is as racist as perpetuating these practices oneself.

Whites are borne into a life where the "world is your oyster," and they don't have to fear discrimination, incarceration, poor education, or a lack of opportunity for social mobility. According to one study, even a poor white ex-con was hired over five highly qualified Black candidates for a tech position.

To deny these realities is racist. If you are the beneficiary of ill-gotten gains, and you have neither shrugged off the illegitimate privileges of such a corrupt system, then you too are a *passive participant* in the system. The Germans who watched idly as the Nazis inflicted atrocities on the Jews were just as guilty for their apathy. If you are one of the few white people who vehemently opposes racism and exploitation, give up what your family has passed down to you as a result of the above, and dedicate yourself to fighting for the freedom of others. Otherwise, I don't believe you.

Eliminating racist practices does not eliminate white supremacy and its agenda. The Civil Rights movement only served to force racist thinking into the underground. Covertly, racism thrives, everywhere from suburbia to corporate boardrooms to Iraq. What are you fighting?

Solving a problem doesn't mean ignoring what caused it.

REVIEW

The principle for this chapter was **Reconsider and Reevaluate**: Seek understanding. Find clarity, vision, and perspective on yourself, life, and the world.

Here are the principles and lessons we covered in this chapter:

Ambition
With enough drive and ambition, anyone can become their own boss.
Anticipation
Whatever is done in the dark will one day come to the light. Whatever you do, make sure it is something you wouldn't mind everyone knowing about.
Approach

Be aware of your situation, and set up your approach with that in mind.
Appropriateness
Fire needs ice; Ice needs fire. Every situation has a smart way to handle it.
Causality
There is no better aid to clarity in life than understanding the law of cause and effect.
Clarity
Getting caught up in appearances is the fastest road to disappointment.
There are always three sides to a story: Side A, Side B, and the Truth
Understanding is seeing things for what they really are, not what they appear to be.
Consequences
Foresee the consequences. Sometimes your next step isn't the best step.
Look before you leap.
There are consequences for every move you make, and every action you take.
Discretion
Know better, do better.
Know your limits. Too much of anything is not a good thing.
Evaluation
Consider the messenger before you consider the message.
Intention
Live out your intentions. What you put out is what you get back
Interpretation
Everything can be a learning opportunity if you let it. The world unfolds in layers of meaning. Keep looking and you'll see it all around you.
Investigation
Don't assume; find out. Believing and knowing aren't the same thing.
Obligation
Find a teacher; be a teacher.
Orientation
A man's orientation in the game of life plays a major role in whether he wins or loses.
The squeaky wheel gets the oil. Every journey begins with taking one step.
Think for yourself, or be a slave to others' imagination.
Understand your position. Play your role accordingly.
You either look inward or outward for what you want.
Perception
Pay attention to your surroundings. Sleep is the cousin of death.
Perceptiveness
A lesson can be anywhere. Some you find, some find you.
A man's ability to learn from others helps him avoid making the same mistakes as everyone else.
Life is chess. Learn from the game.
Problem-Solving
Solving a problem doesn't mean ignoring what caused it.
Realization
Many have dreams, but few choose to wake up and work hard enough to make them real.
Restraint
Don't ever lose your composure. Uncontrolled emotions lead to big problems.
Self-Acceptance
The man who has been taught not to like himself is doomed to destroy himself.

Self-Awareness
Don't be self-conscious; be self-aware.

Skepticism
Don't believe everything you see or hear.
Anything that seems too good to be true...usually is just that.

Take a break.
Put this book down for a minute.

Do NOT go back to reading this book until you do one (or more) of the following things:

- ❏ Call somebody who is going through some rough sh*t and make sure they are okay.
- ❏ Eat something that your body is telling you it needs, or drink some water.
- ❏ Wrestle, spar, or slapbox someone to make sure you "still got it."
- ❏ Take a walk through your neighborhood and see if somebody needs help with something.
- ❏ Clean up a part of your house, or organize some f*cked up part of your life.
- ❏ Tell somebody about this book and what you're learning. Invite them to come read it.
- ❏ Give this book away to somebody who needs it and get another copy for yourself.
- ❏ Cook something good, and make enough to share. Invite people.
- ❏ Check yourself out in the mirror and pick something to improve.
- ❏ Identify ten positive things about your life and stop forgetting them when you're stressed.
- ❏ Tell somebody you love them, cause it might be your last chance.

This has been a PSA from 360 and SDP.
Once you're done, carry on.

Habits and Addictions

C R E A T E   A   C U L T U R E   O F   S U C C E S S

"Watch your thoughts, for they become words. Choose your words, for they become actions. Understand your actions, for they become habits. Study your habits, for they become your character. Develop your character, for it becomes your destiny."

Your culture, or way of life, is the sum total of your behaviors, attitudes, and every action that you engage in so repeatedly that it's become second nature to you.

The choices you make take on a life of their own, and they produce a culture of either success or failure. Ultimately, it's up to you. In choosing which actions and attitudes you will make yours, you decide the way you'll live. You choose your habits. You choose your addictions.

That element of choice is the single most important factor in your life. It's bigger than the household you were raised in, the money your family had, the education you received, the environment you grew up in, or the problems you were born into.

All of those factors are important, but they take a backseat to the driver: You. You are the sole controller of your destiny, and the goals you set are attainable, regardless of your circumstances. However, depending on the pace you set and the direction you take, you may or may not make it to your desired destination.

So it's about more than just what you want or why you want it. It's about how you're going to get there. The life you live is up to you. And regardless of whether you 'get it how you live' or 'live how you get it', the mindset you adopt is up to you. So who is the biggest influence on your lifestyle? You.

QUIZ FOUR: VALUES AND PRIORITIES

1. **The most important things in my life are...**
   a. my family, my friends, and my loved ones.
   b. money and women.
   c. my values and the issues I'd fight for.
   d. studying, learning, and spreading ideas.

2. **In life, I most need...**
   a. love, peace, and happiness.
   b. food, clothing, and shelter.
   c. freedom, justice, and equality.
   d. knowledge, wisdom, and understanding.

3. **I'm most impressed by a person who has...**
   a. a large, strong family.
   b. more money than me.
   c. been a political prisoner.
   d. written books.

4. **The best college major for me would be...**
   a. Fine Arts.
   b. Business.
   c. Political Science.
   d. Philosophy.

5. **My favorite hobby is...**
   a. spending time with others.
   b. getting paid.
   c. activism and community service.
   d. reading or writing.

6. **One thing I hope I never do (from this point on) is...**
   a. hurt somebody I really care about.
   b. go broke.
   c. forget about my people or where I come from.
   d. forget everything I have learned.

7. **If I landed on a deserted island, I would...**
   a. begin missing my people immediately.
   b. gather up food first.
   c. explore the island first.
   d. think up a plan first.

Explanation

Okay, I've been pretty hard on you so far. For the last three chapters, there was basically only one correct answer, right? If the descriptions for the other three seemed harsh, they were there in the early chapters to make it clear how f*cked up we really are. At this point, we can move on to other ways of looking at things.

Mostly As: The "Family Men" These answers describe someone who puts their loved ones before everything. They will often sacrifice in order to help others. However, these people can get caught up in being "social" and "having fun," and not doing anything else with their lives. For many of these people, they don't have a purpose for their lives, so they spend most of their energy keeping people happy. Unfortunately, these people sometimes cannot equip their own families with the needed mindset for survival in this corrupt world. These people must work harder on developing an agenda, or purpose, for their lives.

Mostly Bs: The "Businessmen" These answers describe someone who is all about getting paid. Whether they lose themselves and everyone else in the process isn't important for many of these people. For others, they see money as an immediate solution to their problems, and those of people they care about. They believe that "making it" financially will solve it all. Oftentimes, these people become successful, but rarely do they have lives of true significance. These people must work harder on seeing past the dollar signs, and looking at what's "really" going on around them.

Mostly Cs: The "Activists" These answers describe someone who is all about making a change in the world. One of the strong points of this lifestyle is that these people are sincerely inspired to do something about what is wrong. However, these people can often lose sight of friendships, relationships, and even personal responsibilities, while "fighting" for their cause. These people must work harder on maintaining balance in their lives, while continuing to refine their strategy for change.

Mostly Ds: The "Philosophers" These answers describe someone who is in love with ideas. They often lack a practical approach, and cannot apply their ideas in a realistic fashion. Often they become disenchanted with the world and other people, because the real world is very different from the world of ideas. These people must work harder on staying in touch with their people, and not confusing what "should be" for "what is."

The Fourth Principle

"Create a Culture of Success" means: Transform a strong vision into a strong lifestyle and long-term agenda.

What You'll Learn

- How the things we take for granted may be killing us slowly.
- Which of our four possible paths is the only one that won't result in failure.
- Which laws are the most important.
- How to break the cycles that are destroying us and our communities.
- What white people can actually do to help.
- How to deal with a criminal charge, a dysfunctional family, women, and our own bad habits.
- How to tell if you have an anger problem…and what to do about it.
- When to go with the plan, and when it's best to "do you."

WHAT A WASTE

You may not know it, but you probably live closer to a toxic waste site than you think. You also probably live in an area where air and water pollution standards are being seriously violated. The chances are good that your environment is making you sicker as we speak.

A confidential memo by the Environmental Protection Agency revealed that even they considered this environmental racism "one of the most politically explosive environmental issues yet to emerge." The EPA planned to spin the issue by pursuing positive publicity in Black and Hispanic-centered publications, until the memo revealing their plan was leaked to the media.

Sixty percent of the total Black population in the United States (as well as 60 percent of the Hispanic population) live in communities with one or more uncontrolled toxic waste sites. A majority of Blacks and Latinos in the U.S. live in areas where two air pollution standards are violated, compared to only one-third of whites. According to Michael Novick, "study after study has also shown a clear pattern of hazardous and other waste facilities most commonly being located in existing African American, native and Chicano communities."

For example, in Houston, Texas, all of the municipal landfills and six out of eight incinerators were placed in Black neighborhoods between the 1920s and 1970s. From 1970 to 1978, three out of four privately-owned landfills were also placed in the Black community. Although the

Black community only represented 28% of Houston's population, they had 82% of the trash.

The community around the nation's largest hazardous waste landfill, in Emelle, Alabama, is 95 percent Black. The landfill, which operates in the heart Alabama's "blackbelt," accepts hazardous wastes from the 48 contiguous states and several foreign countries.

According to a 1983 General Accounting Office study, three of four offsite hazardous waste landfills in EPA Region IV (eight Southern states) were located in mostly Black communities. Today, 100 percent of the hazardous waste in the region is dumped in the Black community, as reported in "Dumping in Dixie." But blacks make up only 20 percent of the region's population.

The same pattern holds true across the country. A 1984 report prepared for a California state agency identified Black and Hispanic communities as better candidates for trash-burning power plant sites. A study by the NAACP showed that Blacks are 50% likelier to live near a commercial toxic waste facility. The Commission for Racial Justice has found that three of every five Blacks live in communities with abandoned toxic waste sites.

The number one environmental health threat to children is lead in older housing. More than 40 percent of American homes still have lead-based paint in them. But low-income children are eight times more likely than those of affluence to live where lead paint causes a problem, and Black children are five times more likely than white children to suffer from lead poisoning, according to the Centers for Disease Control and Prevention (CDC).

Recent studies supported by the National Institute for Environmental Health Sciences suggest that a young person's lead burden is linked to lower IQ, lower high school graduation rates and increased delinquency.

What are the things you do, or are around often enough to influence you? What kind of influences are they?

Name the five most influential people in your life. How do they influence you?

Be aware of your influences. Like anything else, you can be poisoned by constant exposure.

MOVIE TO SEE

The Day After Tomorrow

An Inconvenient Truth is a good DVD documentary if you want facts on how white people are destroying the Earth, but it's kinda boring. *The Day After Tomorrow* tells the story of what could happen any day now as a result of the same sh*t. The best part is the end, when the world's tables are finally turned.

21 DAYS

It takes 21 days to make a habit. Three weeks. Almost anything you do consistently for that period of time will become habitual. It's as if you are programming yourself to do something without thinking by doing it over and over again.

I've tried it for myself plenty of times. I've changed the way I walk, the way I get dressed in the morning, how I eat, even how long I watch TV. People who've read *How to Hustle and Win* have told me they've used this advice to do everything from losing weight to quitting smoking. I even went on a slouching fast that literally made me an inch taller by the 3rd week (You probably slouch more than you know!). Repetition creates habit. Why do you think people who have been locked up or in the military act like they are still programmed to make their beds a certain way or hide their toilet paper like an inmate is still going to steal it?

If you part your hair a certain way every day for a period of time, it will eventually start growing out that way until you start brushing it the opposite way. If you start catching yourself every time you say a word like "nigga," in three weeks you won't be saying it by accident any more. It's like a plant being cultivated to grow and produce fruit. You can nurture it with the right elements and bring forth good fruit, or you can water it with poison and produce death.

> "Ill habits gather to unseen degrees –
> As brooks run to rivers, rivers run to seas."
> John Dryden (1631-1700)

This information is helpful for two reasons:

First, you can purposefully program yourself to adopt new behaviors in less than a month. If you want to stop wasting money, limit your spending for 21 days. After then, you'll notice that your spending habits have changed. The new behavior will now be in place without you having to think about it anymore.

> "The unfortunate thing about this world is that the
> good habits are easier to give up than the bad ones."
> W. Somerset Maugham

Second, you can program yourself without wanting to. If you smoke weed regularly for three weeks, guess what? You've got a weed habit now. I don't care if you never smoked before. In three weeks, you'll have a habit that's hard to shake. You can hang around people with more money than you and overspend for almost a month. After that, you're stuck with spending habits you may not be able to afford. Once the money runs out, you're going into shock. That's when you need another 21 days to reprogram yourself.

Bottom line:

When you're around others, either you influence them, or they influence you. So, be aware of how you're changing. Watch your thoughts, they become your actions. Watch your actions, they become your habits. Watch your habits, they become your culture. Watch your culture, it becomes your life.

Cultivate yourself or be cultivated.
If you can't train yourself, you'll never be in charge.

YOU ARE WHAT YOU DO

Tray did his best to appear calm when he spotted Black Smoke in the grimy strip club where Tray spent most of his Saturdays. Black Smoke, a street-hustler turned label-owner, was Tray's favorite rapper.

Seated at a corner table with some of the Black Money crew, Smoke was back in DC for the first time since he was shot at for his Lamborghini in 2006. It appeared that maybe he was trying to play it cool this time around. Tray paid the bouncer to let him and one of his stripper friends through the ropes and occupied a table nearby. He sent a bottle of Patron over, nodded, and that's when Smoke acknowledged him. When Tray came over he told his homegirl to sit with Smoke. Smoke wasn't interested.

Tray wasn't deterred. He bought drinks for everyone at the table and started talking to Smoke about music. Tray was trying to get into the music business, and he was willing to do whatever it took. Smoke was in the middle of dismissing him when – out of nowhere – a man appeared, his fitted cap pulled low over his eyes, his fists balled up, and it was clear that he wasn't a fan. Tray was the closest one to him. Before anyone could respond, Tray stood up.

Bam! **Tray slapped him so hard that the dude – much bigger than Tray – actually fell back and hit the ground.** Tray walked over to him while he was getting up, dragged him by his neck to the exit, and threw him outside. When he came back to the table, everyone's jaws were still open. Smoke was impressed. He told Tray he wanted him to be his "DC man," and act as an extended member of the Black Money family. Tray was in.

But it wasn't going to be what he thought. Tray's musical dreams never took off. As a matter of fact, Tray never even got in the studio. Instead, whenever Black Smoke and the crew came through DC, Tray was called in as "security." When someone in Black Money had a problem in DC, Tray was called in as an "enforcer." Instead of an artist, Tray had become, as they said, one of the "goonies."

That may seem bad enough, but what was worse was that Tray wasn't even a gangsta to begin with. You see, he had saved up that money he spent on Smoke and the others at the strip club that night. So when they'd expect Tray to cover the tab, he was usually left with bills that it took him months to pay off. And the guy he slapped, well that was Tray's old childhood friend. Since the 3rd grade, Shawn would do anything if you gave him enough money. As he grew up, Shawn never grew out of that behavior, mostly because that was his reputation, and people kept finding crazy things to pay him for. When someone wanted to stash their drugs at someone else's house, they used Shawn. When someone had a stolen credit card and needed someone else to go in the stores and make the purchases, they used Shawn. When Tray had the bright idea to "stage" the ass-whupping in the stripclub, it only made sense to call Shawn.

> "One does what one is; one becomes what one does."
> Robert von Musil (1880-1942)

But now Tray was the fool. He was being called in to "enforce" on people he wouldn't even go against in his dreams. Finally, he was promised his "big deal" if he could just handle this one last drug beef. Only six months after having met the Black Money crew, Tray was found dead. Nobody ever found out who was responsible. The dealers who killed him had paid someone else to do it.

What was Tray's first mistake?

What could he have done to change his situation once he was halfway in?

How often do people get jammed up by creating reputations they can't live up to?

How often do people get jammed up trying to live up to a reputation that others created for them?

**Be careful of how easily a reputation develops.
Whatever you do once, you'll be expected to do again.**

THE FOURTH PATH

A young brother recently told me that he felt like it was impossible to make it out of poverty "unless you were one of the good people." He said the "bad people only end up dropping out and going to jail," while the good boys do okay but are considered "lame" and get picked on mercilessly. He was talking about what Anne Ferguson calls the two types of Black males in schools: The Schoolboys and The Troublemakers.

So which path is better? Being a Schoolboy or a Troublemaker?

Azeem

Azeem grew up in Apartment 203B of the Winter Hill Housing Projects in inner-city Cleveland. His mother was a former crack user, who now spent a lot of her time drinking. All he knew was poverty. Roaches in the cereal box, hand-me-down clothes, uncles who were in and out of jail, etc. Azeem's father had been around when he was very small, but after losing his factory job, he'd turned to drugs and went M.I.A.

Azeem went to school completely unprepared. He often hadn't slept much the night before, sometimes hadn't bathed, and his clothes were consistently wrinkled or stained. His mother was rarely home, and as a result, his homework was never checked, and he never had school supplies. The teachers scolded him and the other students picked on him. Not only was Azeem unprepared physically, he couldn't understand much of what was being taught. The parts that he did understand he didn't find interesting.

By the time he was eight, Azeem had learned to fight in order to shut up the other kids. By the time he was eleven, he'd been kept back twice, and had completely lost interest in school. Azeem just didn't see how school would help him in life, seeing his uncles – some of whom had finished high school – working at dead end jobs in fast food.

So when he turned fifteen he stopped going. He hooked up with some of the older drug dealers in his neighborhood and started hustling. Before long, he was making good money and got a small apartment with an older partner of his. Azeem could finally afford brand name clothes and fresh sneakers, and he only needed to be able to work a scale and count. He was doing really well for himself and had just bought a car when his entire ring was brought in on drug charges. Not only was there a ton of evidence against him, some of his homeboys were snitching on him to save themselves. Azeem, not knowing better, chose an unskilled lawyer who not only cost him all the money he'd saved up, but also got him a conviction and a sentence of six years.

Shahid

Shahid grew up in Apartment 306C of the Winter Hill Housing Projects. Like Azeem, Shahid grew up in poverty to a single mother who was also a former drug user. His father was behind bars doing a long bid for an armed robbery he had committed when Shahid was still an infant. In their part of Cleveland, the number of men who were unemployed made crimes like this – and the prison rates – commonplace.

Shahid also knew all about poverty, and had known little else. By age ten, the furthest he had ever traveled was to the other end of Cleveland. However, by the same age, Shahid was in the honors program at his school and was expected to participate in the statewide spelling bee. Turned away by the other boys in the neighborhood, Shahid turned to books and dug in deep. He studied every night, amidst the occasional popping of gunshots and wail of sirens.

While the other boys fought and hustled outside, Shahid stayed in and worked on his reports and projects for school. Coming from such a limited background, a lot of the work was tough for him, but he was a model student and the teachers loved him. They did their best to protect him from bullies like Azeem, but Shahid usually had to run home to avoid the older boys in his neighborhood.

Shahid believed the teachers when they told him that education and hard work would equal success, and he was convinced that his dedication would land him a good job one day. So Shahid didn't just work on his assignments, he worked to please his teachers as well. He stayed late after school grading papers and cleaning up the class. During school, he could be counted on to snitch on students who were cheating or planning to cut class, and the teachers rewarded him with praise and compliments.

But when Shahid finished high school, his family didn't have the money to send him to college, and he hadn't done well enough on his SATs to get a full scholarship. Shahid, now 19 and needing money to support himself, reluctantly took a job at McDonald's. Shahid got stuck in a rut after getting his girlfriend pregnant. Dealing with a family now, Shahid couldn't even afford the thought of college, and never got out of working in the service industry.

Marcus

"I cannot tolerate Black exploitation of Black people any more than I can tolerate it from white people."
Louis Farrakhan

Marcus grew up in Apartment 406A of the Winter Hill Housing Projects. Marcus's story starts the same as that of Shahid. However, Marcus excelled past Shahid in both academics and kissing up to the school staff. As a result of him being such a polite, respectful student, one of Marcus's high school teachers went out of his way to get Marcus a scholarship to a local college.

It is here that Marcus's story takes a turn away from that of Shahid. Marcus finished college at the head of his class. He was recruited by several large corporate firms, and took the position with the best salary and benefits. Marcus was now making good money simply by using his intelligence to develop programs and increase profits for his company. His company turned out to be the one that had once run several manufacturing plants in the Cleveland area, but had shut them down to increase profits.

It turned out that this was one of the main reasons why there were so many poor and unemployed people in Cleveland. Marcus's company was now in the process of tearing down the Winter Hill Housing Projects to make room for more profitable housing. The families there would be forced to relocate outside of the city or become homeless. This was  going to be especially difficult for the many who didn't have cars to get around. Perhaps Marcus knew all this, but either he'd long forgotten or simply couldn't risk speaking up. He enjoyed the money he made in his position, and he wasn't interested in jeopardizing it for anything.

Marcus simply did what he was told, and didn't protest. He was most happy when he was pleasing his superiors, something he'd been doing almost all his life. With his assistance, the company was able to displace all of the residents of the Winter Hill Housing Projects, including Marcus's own mother. Most of the former residents were relocated to a community built adjacent to a toxic waste site. Not surprisingly, many of them developed diseases from the effects of living so close to hazardous chemicals. Marcus's mother was diagnosed with cancer the day he was awarded his promotion.

So, who was successful? After reading this, it probably looks like none of them. That makes everything look pretty hopeless, huh?

Not really, in this book (both parts), I plan to show you a fourth path. Because, yes, those three paths did turn out to fail, all in their own ways. In the ghetto, we usually take one of those three paths:

Like Azeem, we rebel against everything in society and turn to crime, only to end up dead or in jail

Or like Shahid, we try our best but don't have much to work with, so we end up working some dead-end jobs in a dead-end life

Or like Marcus, we make it out of the hood, become highly successful, but only end up serving the interests of the white people that made us miserable to begin with

Even the rappers and ballplayers that "make it big" end up being pawns in a game for people that don't care about them. So, if almost everyone ends up a slave one way or the other, what's the way out? What's the fourth path?

Fight slavery. Fight for freedom. Dedicate your life to challenging what's wrong about society, and the world. That way, even if you end up dead, in jail, or in a minimum-wage job, it was with a purpose. You didn't perish in vain. And if you do become successful, which usually happens with people who have the determination to fight, and the intelligence to know how to fight, then you can look at yourself in the mirror and not hate yourself like Marcus probably does.

There is always another way.

LAW AND ORDER

The 42 Declarations of Ma'at

What do you think the crime rate was in Ancient Egypt? Blacks then lived at one of the highest stages of civilization without a need for prisons or police. How? The people of ancient Egypt lived by a code, known as Ma'at.

Ma'at was the Ancient Egyptian concept of divine order — governing law, morality, and justice. In later Egyptian mythology, Ma'at was made into a goddess. Ma'at was seen as being charged with regulating the stars, the seasons, and the actions of both mortals and the gods, after she had set the order of the universe from chaos.

Thus the Egyptian citizens subscribed to a set of guiding principles which would be used to declare the righteousness of their lives upon their death. These are the "42 Declarations of Ma'at" according to the ancient *Egyptian Book of the Dead*:

I have not committed sin.	I have not swindled offerings.
I have not committed robbery with violence.	I have not stolen from a God.
I have not stolen.	I have not told lies.
I have not slain men and women.	I have not carried away food.
I have not stolen food.	I have not cursed.
	I have not closed my ears to truth.

I have not committed adultery.
I have not made anyone cry.
I have not felt sorrow without reason.
I have not assaulted anyone.
I am not deceitful.
I have not stolen anyone's land.
I have not been an eavesdropper.
I have not falsely accused anyone.
I have not been angry without reason.
I have not seduced anyone's wife.
I have not polluted myself.
I have not terrorized anyone.
I have not disobeyed the law.
I have not been excessively angry.
I have not cursed a God.
I have not behaved with violence.
I have not caused disruption of peace.
I have not acted hastily or without thought.
I have not overstepped my boundaries of concern.

I have not exaggerated my words when speaking.
I have not worked evil.
I have not used evil thoughts, words or deeds.
I have not polluted the water.
I have not spoken angrily or arrogantly.
I have not cursed anyone in thought, word, or deed.
I have not placed myself on a pedestal.
I have not stolen that which belongs to a God.
I have not stolen from or disrespected the deceased.
I have not taken food from a child.
I have not acted with insolence.
I have not destroyed property belonging to a God.

The Only Laws that You Can't Break

The Universe is written in the laws of mathematics. Almost all ancient and modern scientists have said this, in one way or another. Understanding these laws, and living by them, puts you in harmony with the grand scheme of things. Until you do this, you're going "against the grain" and bound to run into problem after problem. Every system in the universe, no matter how big or small, is governed by the same laws or principles. And guess what is at the very center of it all? You. Just think about it:

← The atom	← The Black Family →	The solar system →
(Protons, Neutrons, and Electrons)	(Man, Woman, and Child)	(Sun, Moon, and Stars)

Living Mathematics (Spoken Word)

Yeah, I used to do poetry and spoken word. Don't laugh. It's good therapy. You should try it. But you might suck. Here's a piece I once did on the mathematics of our condition.

I wish we weren't divided like this...
Fighting for a fraction of a pie in the sky that don't exist.
Instead of makin money in multiples with these million-dollar brains,
We droppin like flies, subtracted from the game.
Stuck in hell, or stuck in the cell, add it to our pain,
That's why we f*ckin yell, tragedy's our name
Our daddies became missing from the equation early
Now we lookin for answers, like we 12 when we 30
I wish we could see it wasn't always like this...

Once African mathematicians and scientists,
Now American gangsters and hustlers, tryin to live...
Born into a dirty game, dyin as kids.
Dead men walkin, that's what slavery did to Black heros
Told they were nothing, absolute zeros
Told they were less than nothing, became negative
Passed it down, passed it around, it was inherited
American dream, minus us, plus Satan
American nightmare...Black man awakened
All it takes is one man, takin a stand not to fall
Change begins instantly, the equation gets solved.

The RBG Code

There are other sets of laws that act as guidelines for life, and not rules on what someone is not "allowed" to do. By observing these guidelines, you avoid problems for yourself and others. In the streets, many speak of a "G Code" but few can tell you what it involves, besides "not snitching." After all, principles like "no harm to women and kids" and "family first" are considered old and outdated by those who have no idea what the game is really even about, in the first place. Unfortunately, it's these same idiots who set most of the trends that our people are following now. This is why something like an RBG Code is essential these days. You can interpret RBG as "Red, Black, and Green," "Revolutionary But Gangsta," or whatever suits your tastes. The bottom line is that no matter what your hustle, you are bound first to being a Black man up against a system that is set to destroy you. For that reason, this code belongs to everyone in that struggle. Here are the five basic principles of the code, as Stic.man, of the rap group dead prez, explains:

1. No snitching.
Self explanatory. Integrity and honor is the foundation. Without it we are our own worst enemies.

2. Protect your self, family, and community at all times.
Study martial arts, security, armed self defense, participate in anti-police brutality watches and campaigns, support political prisoners, study up and practice the best healthy lifestyle you can. Love your body, protect it, and feed it good things. Feed your children the best healthy things you can. Use wisdom before violence. But definitely handle yours when absolutely necessary. Preventing harm is better than reacting to it.

3. Each one, teach one.
Stay humble. Learn constantly. Always re-evaluate what you think you know. Don't force your ideas on others. You live them and be the example. People ain't stupid; if they see it working for you, they have the ability to follow your example, if they choose to. Learn skills that are useful to your real life and goals. Read. Write. Speak. Have monthly goals for new skills you want to acquire. Share what you learn with those who want to learn what you have.

4 Be organized.

Turn dreams into plans, and plans into realities, by organizing the steps (write them down), and staying focused and disciplined 'til you reach your goal. Don't do nothing without thinking it through all the way to victory, step by step. Plan, grind, reassess the plan. Grind = Succeed.

5 Be productive.

Make money moves. Make power moves. Don't let another day go by without using all your energy to get your plan in motion. Don't be idle. Get up, get out, and hustle. Proof is in the pudding. Respect comes from showing and proving. What you wanna see happen in the world is up to who? You.

Memorize, internalize, and live this sh*t. These is just codes coming from the streets, from the people. No matter what hood, the struggle is all the same.

Some laws are guidelines for the best life, not rules for what you can't do.

American Law

Of course, observing our OWN codes alone won't save us. We ain't in Egypt anymore, so Ma'at won't fly in a criminal court. In America, if you don't know the laws, you're going to find yourself in a jam sooner or later. As they say, "Ignorance of the law is not an excuse."

How well do you know your laws? I have several volumes of the *Official Code of Georgia* in my home library. When I've been in a jam, I've been able to consult myself for legal advice. To this day, I've never been convicted of any wrongdoing. Only once have I ever paid a lawyer, and that was because my career was on the line, and I couldn't afford to take any chances.

My brother Wise is even more adept when it comes to the law. I can't count how many times he's been in and out for only a day or less. How? He not only researches the laws and his rights, but he knows the game on a higher level. You see, most people in power belong to fraternal organizations like the Freemasons. Wise would go into a courtroom and engage the judge in a silent display of Masonic ritual that most observers wouldn't notice or understand. After he's done standing in a certain stance, folding and crossing his arms a certain way, and nodding in certain directions, he gets a slap on the wrist and no jail time. When that doesn't work, he's made sure that he had everything set up so that there was no way they could justifiably keep him.

So what do you know?

The Black Panther Party

The Black Panther Party was founded in Oakland, California in 1966 by Huey P. Newton and Bobby Seale. Initially, the BPP called for armed resistance to racist oppression in the interest of Blacks receiving justice. Their Ten Point Program stated the BPP's agenda:

1. We want power to determine the destiny of our black and oppressed communities.
2. We want full employment for our people.
3. We want an end to the robbery by the capitalists of our Black community.
4. We want decent housing, fit for the shelter of human beings.
5. We want decent education for our people that exposes the true nature of this decadent American society. We want education that teaches us our true history and our role in the present-day society.
6. We want completely free health care for all black and oppressed people.
7. We want an immediate end to police brutality and murder of black people, other people of color, and all oppressed people inside the United States.
8. We want an immediate end to all wars of aggression.
9. We want freedom for all Black and oppressed people now held in U. S. Federal, state, county, city and military prisons and jails. We want trials by a jury of peers for all persons charged with so-called crimes under the laws of this country.
10. We want land, bread, housing, education, clothing, justice, peace and people's community control of modern technology.

In May of 1967, in one of the first highly public Black Panther events, Bobby Seale, with 23 men and six women all carrying guns, marched into the California Legislature to protest a pending gun control bill whose language was aimed directly at the party's openly armed members. "There were 30 or 40 press following behind me and all these legislators ducking under their desks," he said. "Of course we had loaded weapons, and we ended up on the floor of the Legislature, and I looked at these guys under their desks and said 'Sorry you guys, we're in the wrong place, we wanted the spectator section.'"

Since the group had done its research into California weapons law, no one was arrested for carrying the guns, but members were charged with disturbing the peace. Seale got six months on a misdemeanor charge.

Seale, now 70, said one of the first things the Black Panthers did was follow the police around and observe their actions. "It was a real thing to have this discipline with our (physical education) classes and then showing them how to clean their guns and then to have 14 members with black leather jackets patrol the police," said Seale. "We always had only one person do the talking, and we knew all the gun laws."

The United States Constitution and the Bill of Rights

Let's begin with the basics. The United States Constitution is the supreme law document in this country. It is basically the Bible when it comes to law, as in no legal decision should contradict it or go against it. The Constitution and its later Amendments dictate how American government is supposed to run today. When a court is about to make a decision that would go against it, critics call that idea "unconstitutional."

In a nutshell, you should know the Constitution to know what is and is not allowed on a national level in this country. As for each state, of course, they make their own laws. The part of the constitution you'll need most is the Bill of Rights. These ten rights are guaranteed by the United States Constitution, and until the "War on Terror" strips us of all our constitutional freedoms, they are still valid. They are:

> **Did You Know?**
>
> In New York, the penalty for jumping off a building is death.
> In Massachusetts, it is illegal to go to bed without first having a full bath.
> In West Virginia if you run over an animal, you can legally take it home and cook it for dinner.
> In Kentucky, it is illegal to carry ice cream in your back pocket.
> Know your laws!

I. Right to Freedom of Speech, Religion, Press, Assembly, and to Petition the Government and Ask for Changes
II. Right to Own Weapons and Form a Militia
III. Government Cannot Force you to House Soldiers
IV. No Unreasonable Search and Seizure of People, Homes, or Property
V. Right to Due Process (the right to a fair trial, to not be tried more than once for the same crime, and to not have to speak and incriminate yourself at a trial)
VI. Right to a Speedy, Public Trial by Jury of Peers (also the right to a lawyer, to be told what crime they are accused of, to face their accuser, and to question witnesses)
VII. Right to Trial By Jury (people who have a disagreement about something worth more than $20 have the right to a jury trial)
VIII. Right to Non-excessive Bail, nor Cruel and Unusual Punishment
IX. Right to Other Protections Not Stated in the Bill of Rights
X. Powers the Constitution Does Not Give to the Federal Government are Reserved for the States or the People

I've included a primer titled "What To Do If You're Stopped By The Police" in the Appendix. It's worth memorizing, or at least keeping a copy on hand. And if that doesn't satisfy for your hunger for this kind of information, you can find even more at:

http://flag.blackened.net/daver/anarchism/stopped.html

Know the laws; know your rights; know the system or be its victim.

THE CYCLES OF LIFE

In his memoir *Cooked: From the Streets to the Stone, From Cocaine to Foie Gras*, world-renowned Chef Jeff Henderson writes about his experience as a major crack dealer before he was sentenced to 18 years in prison.

The following is an excerpt from his book, describing his method for laundering his drug money:

> I knew this girl Paula who ran a check-cashing place. On the first and fifteenth of every month everyone would cash their welfare checks. The night before, I'd go to her crib and trade a hundred grand in singles, tens, and twenties for the clean fifties and hundreds that she had just gotten off the money truck. I'd kick her a little taste and my money would be clean. I'd have the crisp bills that were easier to make deals with, and her customers would get the money that my people had gotten off the streets. Of course, within a week, many of the customers of the check-cashing place would bring their county money back to our crack houses and we'd take that money right back to the white man, buying all the flashy sh*t a hustler had to have. And, if we're caught, the DEA takes all our sh*t and sells it back at auction. It's a f*ckin game.

Let's review the cycle:

💣 Drugs are widely available in the poor communities

💣 Poor people, suffering from problems in society, become drug addicts and buy drugs with welfare and social security money, leaving little left to provide for their children

💣 Young men grow up poor and neglected, seeing they have little and others have so much

💣 These young men pursue the American Dream by selling drugs to get rich

💣 Drug dealers spend most of their money on material things purchased from white businesses and end up owning very little, but showing off so much they can't stay under the radar

💣 Drug dealers are easily caught and, not having saved enough money for lawyer fees, are quickly funneled into the prison system

💣 The prison system brings in billions of dollars in revenue, while the drug dealers' possessions are auctioned off by the government

💣 The government uses taxpayers' money to fund agencies and programs that are geared to stop the spread of drugs, but only incarcerate drug dealers

💣 Meanwhile, other government agencies are bringing drugs into the country and putting them in the hands of local distributors

💣 Drugs become widely available in more poor communities

💣 Cycle repeats

I can break it down even simpler:

- ☠ We sell dope because we're poor and miserable.
- ☠ The dope makes the community worse, while we spend our money on frivolous bullsh*t.
- ☠ Because of us, more children are born poor and miserable.
- ☠ Cycle repeats.

Or as Kanye West put it, "Crack dealer buy Jordans, crackhead buy crack, and the white man get paid offa all a dat."[7]

When you think about it, there's many other "cycles" in the hood, besides the ones in the drug game. Here's ten of them:

The Cycle of Fatherlessness

On "Amen," Lil Wayne is damn near cryin when he raps:

> All I know bout my real dad is that he had money/ No bank account, that brown paper bag money/ Yeah he might hit me off with a little brag money/ But the nigga still wouldn't be a dad for me/ But look how I turned out, I hope he glad for me/ But that's why when I see him, I acts mad funny/ Cause he's a joke to me/ Don't message, don't call, don't talk to me

We all know how this one goes. You ain't have a daddy growin up. You swore you'd never do that when you had a kid, because you know how f*cked up it feels. Then you f*ck up and get somebody pregnant, and it's time to be a man. But you had no idea how that fatherhood sh*t feels. And you've never been shown HOW to be a father. And you got stuck with an ignorant female who you can't keep a stable relationship with, in the first place. You ain't even done runnin the streets yet! So what do you do? You run. Just like your daddy did.

Or, you try your best to be there...but you can't get out the streets. So you get locked up before your child finished grade school. Just like your daddy did.

The Cycle of Teenage Pregnancy

This goes hand in hand with the above. And teenage pregnancy ain't just about females. It takes two to do that dance. And I don't know if the clinics stopped passin out free condoms, but I'm willin to bet you that you'd have a hard time findin somebody young with one these days. As if HIV wasn't more popular in the hood than a white girl with a big butt. But later for diseases. Let's look at why some of our grandmas are 35. If your mama and daddy had you when they were teenagers, they did two things for sure:

1. They f*cked.

2. They f*cked you up.

Think about it, how good you think a kid can do raising another kid? Sh*t, most kids I know can't even raise the blinds. And what happens as a result? The mama's mama raises the kid, who grows up thinkin that this silly sh*t is okay. Then what? He or she does the same thing his parents did.

The Cycle of Addiction

Any drug running through your body when you conceive a child (whether you the man or the woman) goes into your baby somehow. If you're an alcoholic, your baby's got a wino gene. If you toot powder, you better start saving up to put your kids in rehab. And if your kids see you doin ANY kind of drug, it's a really good chance they'll be doin it too. And they'll probably start it younger than you did.

The Cycle of Debt

I know some people who've got their car in their mama's name, and their phone in their baby's name. Why? Cause our credit sucks (Check yours at www.freecreditreport.com). We don't learn how to manage money from school or our parents, so we end up deep in debt by the time we're 21. We pass on both the debt and the bad spending habits to our kids. Not only that, but bad money management is infectious between friends and relationships as well.

The Cycle of Abuse

"Children have never been good at listening to their elders, but they have never failed to imitate them."
James Baldwin

If you seen your mama getting her ass whupped, you're bound to have some issues. Unless you're working hard to avoid doing everything you've seen wrong in your childhood, you're gonna end up beatin up your girlfriends too. And one day, one of their kids is gonna kill you like you wanted to do when you were a kid.

And don't even get me started on sexual abuse. Do you know how many of our young men and women are still suffering because of some pervert relative or family "friend" (Visit www.familywatchdog.us for a list of the sex offenders in **your** area, plus photos)

The Cycle of Miseducation

Parents who had a hard time in school do one of two things: (1) They push their kids to do better than they did, or (2) they don't give a f*ck and the kids can tell. Either way, it's rough showin your kids how to do their homework when you don't get it your damn self. As a result, uneducated people have uneducated kids. And uneducated people also attract uneducated friends. Finally, uneducated people go into lines of work that uneducated people are qualified for, which don't pay enough money to send anybody to college.

The Cycle of Retaliatory Violence

"A tooth for a tooth, an eye for an eye," they say. Martin Luther King said that philosophy would leave everybody blind. I guess it would, huh? When you think about the gang wars in L.A., the only way there could ever be truces was when the gangs decided NOT to retaliate for one of their dead.. That's the only way it stops. Otherwise the cycle continues until the bloodshed consumes everybody. Sometimes the only way is to sit down with the other side and agree not to take it to the next level. I didn't say it was easy, I just said it was the only way.

The Cycle of Recidivism

"It's like a cycle, niggas come home, some'll go in/ Do a bullet, come back, do the same sh*t again."
Nas, on Raekwon the Chef's "Verbal Intercourse"

In a nutshell, recidivism means the same as being a repeat offender. Once you get accustomed to doin dirt, it's hard to go legit, because the money ain't as fast and easy, and the life just ain't as exciting. But once you've got a felony on your record, it gets even harder to break the cycle. By then, your options are limited to the kind of tough jobs that employ convicts, or making money in the street again. And then, you're playing with the "Three Strikes" law, and that's where the cycle will stop for anybody who keeps coming back.

The Cycle of Disease

HIV, Herpes, Syphilis, even Cancer from second-hand smoke. We get it, we pass it around. It's like we're playing hot potato, except you *always* get burned. You know you doin bad when you get gonorrhea from a girl who slept with a guy who slept with a girl who got that same damn gonorrhea from *you* six months ago. (Now go get tested)

The Cycle of Femininity

I hate talking about this one. It always makes people get real uncomfortable. If you're not ready to face the facts, just skip this part. But if you are, let's be all the way real. Most of us were raised by women. Either daddy wasn't around, daddy wasn't strong, or daddy didn't really give much of a f*ck. As a result, we grew up under our mamas, grandmas, aunties, and cousins. Meanwhile, the men were falling victim to the grave, the jail, or drug addiction. With the number of strong Black men in our communities droppin faster than Superhead's bottom jaw, we spent a lot more time influenced by women than we did by men. Some turned out gay in the aftermath. Others

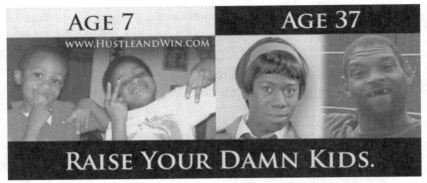

continued to act as men, but respond emotionally, as women do. Even though we see anger as strong and manly, getting angry over petty sh*t is a feminine trait. Jumping to conclusions: feminine trait. So is gossiping and backbiting. And all those wild emotions are not traits of a strong Black man. So we try to mask those qualities by hiding our emotions, even from ourselves. It does no good. We still have no idea how to handle things as a man. If only daddy had stuck around (See *Part Two*, "Whippin Ass and Feminine Ways").

But there's hope. There's ways to break these cycles and others. All that you need to do is find the tipping point. The tipping point is the point where there is enough good present to bring about a change in the whole picture. According to a sociologist named Thomas Crane, for Black teenagers, when the percentage of "role models" in a community falls below five percent, dropout rates and other problems more than double. But when people who can be considered role models make up five percent or more of the community, dropout rates, teenage pregnancy, drug usage and juvenile crime begin to decline. All you have to do is be part of that 5%. And **it doesn't take much to be a role model.** You just have to be a respectable dude that's NOT falling victim to the cyles of bullsh*t. And by not falling victim to the cycles, you become part of the process of change that breaks the cycles as a whole.

Break the cycles of self-destruction, or be broken by them.

A LIFE OF REGRETS

> "Men of ill judgment often ignore the good that lies within their hands, till they have lost it."
> Sophocles

Faheem Najm was young when he learned about regrets. He had taken the batteries out of the satellite navigation system on his father's boat. He needed them for his Walkman. Little did he know, this selfish but petty act could have cost his father's life. When Mr. Najm didn't come home that night from a solo boat excursion, the family thought the worst. Young Faheem believed that he had killed his father...just to listen to music. How could such a small, selfish act have such dire consequences?

Faheem's father finally made it home the next day. He had waited until daylight to use the position of the sun to guide him back to shore. This experience would scare Faheem away from the water for the rest of his life. Now an adult, Faheem is known to most as T-Pain. He owns a fleet of cars and even his own personal jet, but he remains one of the few Florida celebrities who don't do boats.

> "Awaitin call, from his kin not the coroner
> Phone in my hand, nervous, confined to a corner
> Beads of sweat, second thoughts on my mind
> How can I ease the stress and learn to live with these regrets?
> This time... stress... givin this sh*t up... f*ck"
> Jay-Z, "Regrets"

Have you lost anyone close to you? Have you ever wondered, what would you have done if you knew in advance? Have you ever thought about what you could have done to prevent it?

Or have you ever done something that seemed small to you, but resulted in some serious damage in someone else's life? Have you thought about what you could've done differently?

Or have you made a mistake in your own life that you wish you could go back and fix?

Do you beat yourself up over, thinking about you could have, would have, or should have done?

Do you find yourself still thinking about these mistakes, no matter how much time has passed since then? Well, you're not alone. Most of us live life with regrets. We have things we wish we'd done and things we wish we'd said. Some of us can't get past thinking about all the chances we missed to do something that could have made things turn out different.

After the break-up of N.W.A., Dr. Dre and Eazy-E had a relentless back and forth beef, while Dre and Ice Cube refused to speak to each other. This went on until the day that Dre and Cube learned their former partner was dying of AIDS. The former N.W.A members could now only express their sorrow and love to a man on his deathbed.

OUR LIVES BEGIN TO END THE DAY WE BECOME SILENT ABOUT THINGS THAT MATTER.

> "Jerry Heller tried to make his escape
> I had to bounce, while other niggas got raped
> Same niggaz turned around and said f*ck me
> No F*CK YOU cause I'm down with Chuck D
> And I'm 'bout to do a movie up, a classic
> When I hit the screen, nigga it was magic
> Never thought I'd see Eazy in a casket
> Thanks for everythang, that's on everything"
> Ice Cube, "Growin Up"

After the break up of the Hot Boys, B.G. never had a kind word for Baby, though Baby had been something of a father figure and mentor to all of the young rappers in the group. B.G.'s hatred remained intense until the day Birdman lost his sister in a car crash, when he could finally offer his condolences and a truce.

> "Out of all the niggas I was with when I was doin wrong
> 3 in the fed, 1 doin life, and 2 dead and gone
> Knew there was more to life than sellin blow and chopper bustin
> But what's the good in knowin better if I ain't tell 'em nuttin?"
> T.I., "Still Ain't Forgave Myself"

How would it feel to be one of those multi-millionaire celebrities who spends most of his time in the spotlight promoting bullsh*t...pushing Black people towards things he's not even about...and then – at the climax of your career – to get brought down by the same white folks you helped? Now you're in jail (or dead) wishing you never played into that bullsh*t they wanted you to rap about. As Tupac said:

> If we really are saying that rap is an art form, then we gotta be more responsible for our lyrics. If you see everybody dying because of what you're saying, it don't matter that you didn't make them die, it just matters that you didn't save them.

Jay-Z said something similar about Hurricane Katrina on "Minority Report":

> Silly rappers, because we got a couple Porsches/ MTV stopped by to film our fortresses/ We forget the unfortunate/ Sure, I ponied up a mill, but I didn't give my time/ So in reality, I didn't give a dime/ Or a damn, I just put my moneys in the hands/ Of the same people that left my people stranded/ Nothin' but a bandit, left them folks abandoned/ Damn, that money that we gave was just a band-aid

So how much time are YOU going to waste looking back and thinking about what you could have done? The best time is always NOW. If you can save somebody, save them now. If you can prevent something, prevent it now. If you can tell him to slow down, tell him now, and tell him why. If you want the beef to end, end it now. If you want to reconcile – whether with an old enemy, a parent who's almost a stranger, or a past relationship gone sour – do it NOW. Otherwise, you'll only have regrets.

Don't live with regrets. The best time is now.

JUVENILE "JUSTICE"

> "Martin Lee, innocent, he ain't even have a chance
> They beat him in that boot camp 'til he died in that ambulance
> That boy was only fifteen years old, f*ck what they say he did
> So tell me how I'm 'posed to feel when police killin' kids?"
> Rich Boy, "Let's Get This Paper"

Martin Lee Anderson was 14 years old when he was murdered. However, he wasn't killed by another young Black male, as we're so used to hearing in the news. On his first day at the Bay County Sheriff's Office Boot Camp in Florida, Martin collapsed while performing a series of strenuous exercises. He was then restrained and severely beaten by 7 guards while a nurse watched. He died the next day. A year later, the courts decided that Martin's death was no one's fault, and all 8 boot camp employees were acquitted. Martin had only been sentenced to boot camp for violating his probation by trespassing onto school grounds and taking his grandma's car.

Nationwide, African-American youth represent 15% of the youth population. But they also represent 26% of juvenile arrests, 44% of youth who are detained in juvenile facilities, 46% of the youth who are judicially waived to criminal court, and 58% of the youth admitted to adult state prisons. In fact, 12% of Black adolescent males go to adult prisons, while only 1.2% of white adolescent males go to adult prisons.

The National Council of Crime and Delinquency reported that Black and Hispanic youths are more likely than white youth to be arrested, held in jail, sent to juvenile or adult court for trial, and convicted. Like Black and Hispanic adults, they are also given harsher prison sentences.

Black youths are more than six times as likely as whites to be sentenced to prison by juvenile courts. When charged with violent crimes, Blacks are nine times more likely to be sentenced; for drug offenses, Blacks are sent to prison an astounding 48 times more often than whites charged with the same crimes.

To make matters worse, the nationwide recidivism rate among teen offenders averages 82 to 83 percent. Black youth are not only arrested and sentenced more than anyone else, but once they're in, they're probably never going to stay out for long...ever again.

Have you been in already? If not, what are your chances of getting twisted, based on what you do on a daily basis right now? If you've already been in, how much have you changed in your life so that your chances of going back are close to zero?

And if you haven't changed anything, what kind of game do you think you're playing?

It's difficult, but not impossible, for a man to break free of a cycle he begins at an early age.

THE CYCLES OF HISTORY

"Those who do not learn from history are bound to repeat it."
George Santayana

History runs in cycles as well, except with a slight twist. I'll explain.

The past is a way to predict the future, because people and places may not return, but the principles never go away. The same sh*t that happened in 2000 BC is happening in 2000 AD. And the people who succeed are the ones who can see the patterns. The people who fail in these times are the people who get caught off-guard and have no clue about what's going on. I've been able to predict damn near everything Bush and his buddies have done with their War in the past few years. Why? Because they did the same sh*t in World War II. Don't believe me? Just read up on it.

Back then, they called them kamikaze pilots. Now they say "suicide hijackers." Back then, the Japanese were trying to unite with Black people and they had to be crushed. Now, it's the Muslims and Arabs who they have to destroy. Back then, Hitler bombed his own building to blame the people he wanted to attack. Now...well we know that part, don't we?

But even though there are cycles to see, they aren't full circles that end where they began. That would mean we are repeating history. That's not what happens. Instead, history is renewed, like the growth of new skin in the place of dead cells. In that way, it's like a spiral.

The principles remain the same, but things get bigger, or smaller, or better, or worse. Often, things look like they're progressing, but a closer examination will show you that nothing has changed. The key is being able to look at what was "really" going on THEN, and what's "really" going on now. Keep in mind, the more things change, the more they remain the same.

One good example of this is when we look at race relations. We are constantly told things are getting better for Black people. But when you really think about it, the only things that have "really" changed are that white people are better at hiding their racism, and Black people feel more comfortable with being sh*tted on.

How do we miss this? Easy, we miss the patterns. We miss the cycles. We miss the spiral. We end up repeating our own mistakes instead of renewing our approach and doing something different, using the knowledge we SHOULD have gained the LAST damn time we went through that type of sh*t. Here's another example.

Gangster Rap

Flashback to the late 80s. With the help of several white music industry executives, gangster rap became the "next big thing." At first, groups like NWA rapped about the problems in the ghetto and the forces that caused them. They called it "reality rap." But after Ice Cube left and stopped writing for the others, NWA was influenced by manager Jerry Heller and interest groups like the Jewish Defense League more than anything else. Before long, they had left out the political content and went hard about sex, violence, and little else. Other acts that followed and copied the format did the same.

The rise of gangster rap effectively crushed the rising popularity of the "conscious" hip hop movement of the late 1980s. Artists like Public Enemy, X-Clan, Poor Righteous Teachers, KRS-One, Rakim, and others who rapped about social issues and uplifting Black people were very popular during this era. After the rise of gangster rap, the white-run music industry was able to change the attitude of young Black people from fighting for change to fighting each other for nothing. They did it through music.

Then, with the emergence of new artists like Nas and Wu-Tang Clan, the public once again started becoming interested in "righteousness" and "Black Gods," words they kept hearing on the radio. To crush this, the music industry unleashed a new trend in hip-hop: "shine" rap. Sometimes also called bling rap, shine rap was heavy on materialism and empty on substance. Rappers talking about jewelry and cars soon outnumbered even those rappers talking about guns and crime. In the Black community, sales of platinum went up. Homebuying and other solid investments were ignored.

Fast forward to the late 90s. Southern club music took the world by storm. Although "crunk" music and "snap" music were more about dancing than anything else, they continued the trend of rappers getting rich saying absolutely nothing. At the same time, "trap" music boasted unrealistic claims of big-time drugdealing, while rarely mentioning the bad parts of the game.

20 years after leaving NWA, Ice Cube had something to say about the progress of hip hop, when interviewed recently on *Flow TV* (www.Flow.tv):

> I just think rap and the hip hop nation period has used rap to escape they problems and not to confront or analyze or even discuss or even expose they problems.
> The money, partying, clubs, sex, clothes, you know, just all these things that make us feel good, and not talk about the stuff that make us feel bad. It seem like we on a treadmill sometime, you know, we runnin,

runnin, runnin, but not goin nowhere. You know, we makin strides, but we not makin' progress.

And I believe that there's been a conscious effort by government to leave us behind if we can't keep up, and to dumb us down, so we are forever the cheap labor of the world. So, you know, I think all those things are in play, and I think it's up to us to get ourselves out this situation.

So, what's next? If you've been paying attention, you'll see that rap lyrics are finally going back to telling the truth, and Black people are once again starting to wake up to the racism that never really went away. So what's next?

If you study histoy, you'll know what's happened in the past, and what's coming in the future. You'll even be able to see what will emerge in your own future. And you'll hopefully be smart enough to do it better this time, instead of repeating the old mistakes.

History repeats itself, but we have to renew it, not repeat it. You'd be a fool to keep doing it the way it's already been done.

How to Deal With a Criminal Charge

I've been stopped and searched dozens of times. I've been arrested plenty of times. I've even been to trial a few times. I've never been convicted. I've always been smart enough to handle things successfully. If you're smart enough to read this book, you should be too. Here's some tips:

1. If you are interrogated, don't admit to anything. Even if they say your partner snitched, keep your mouth shut. That "he told on you, now tell on him" is the oldest trick in the book. Wait for a lawyer.

2. Depending on how strong the evidence is, weigh out your options with your lawyer. If you feel you have to plead out, plead out. But keep in mind, that evidence often isn't as strong as they make it seem IF you got a decent lawyer. And sometimes a plea deal (with the wrong lawyer) could be the worst move to make. That's why Plies said:

    > Money talk and bullsh*t walk a thousand miles/ You ain't got a paid lawyer, then don't go to trial/ Crackers owe each other favors, they'll swap ya out/ "You give us him, we'll give you him" Know what I'm talkin' 'bout?/ Nigga took thirty years on a cop out/ [How the] f*ck you get thirty years for breakin' in a bitch house?/ Crackers playin' a dirty game, boy, this sh*t wild"

3. Keep in mind that there are dozens of things the police and courts can do wrong. Any one of these things can result in you being acquitted. Learn them and look out for them.

4. If you choose to fight, do your legwork. Don't rely on your lawyer alone. If they're a public defender, they're overworked and probably won't even meet you until the day of your trial. Unless, that is, you go see them first. Meet with them and do as much work on your part as you can.

5. That means find your witnesses. That includes people who saw the incident in question, as well as character witnesses who can vouch for you as a person. If you're a good-for-nothing bastard, don't bother looking for character witnesses.

6. Write down exactly what happened. Read up on similar cases. Study the law now (it's better than studying it from the jail library). Meet with your lawyer and discuss what you can offer them to help their case. They want to win too, they just don't have the time to do everything Johnny Cochrane would.

7. If you are convicted and sentenced, do your time with your head up. Finish a degree or something. I know I can't tell a man what to do if he's facing twenty years, but you're a dummy if you go on the run for a six month charge. Living as a fugitive is NOT easy, and it's NOT fun. I don't recommend it.

8. Before you get out, make sure you know what your plans are, and follow through once you're out.

9. Make seeing your probation officer a top priority. He or she may be an asshole, but they're an asshole with the power to send you back. I'd advise you not to smoke or be around anyone (or anything) you shouldn't. But if you can't quit smoking, at least have the sense not to smoke before seeing your P.O., and drinking that detox juice like you supposed to.

10. Find a job. I don't care if it's fast food. Beggars can't be choosers. Employment gives people like your P.O. faith that you're not back doin dirt to survive.

11. Don't repeat the cycle. I know it's hard going legit with a felony on your record, but there are agencies that help ex-cons find jobs. It's all about how bad you want to do something different.

Life is never hopeless. There are successful ways to handle any situation.

REVOLUTIONARY LOVE

The immortal Che Guevara (see *Part Two*) on being a revolutionary:

> Let me say, with the risk of appearing ridiculous, that the true revolutionary is guided by strong feelings of love. It is impossible to think of an authentic revolutionary without this quality... One must have

a large dose of humanity, a large dose of a sense of justice and truth, to avoid falling into extremes, into cold intellectualism, into isolation from the masses. Every day we must struggle so that this love of living humanity is transformed into concrete facts, into acts that will serve as an example.

I started with this quote because having a love for the people, a love for yourself and for your own, a love that compels a man to fight to protect others, that kind of a love is the realest love there is. Most of us don't know the depths of a love like this, so we satisfy ourselves with flimsy relationships characterized by puppy love, lust, or infatuation.

I've done all that. But my love now is a revolutionary love, and the woman I love now is dedicated to the same principles I am willing to fight and die for. As a result, our bond is stronger than the previous loves I've experienced, many of which – you'll see – weren't really even loves at all.

On the Single Life
Journal Entry: July 16, 2006

I've come to some realizations over the past few weeks. I recently came out of a committed relationship. People usually say a month isn't enough time to truly be over and done with something as deep as this last relationship. Healing and closure take time. Am I fully over it? Maybe not. I've learned from my past that hindsight often makes present perception appear as error in retrospect. Thus I take no authority to say that I am sure about something in the present. In other words, what seems so NOW, may seem so ignorant later. I can still say, however, that I am almost sure I have moved on.

But the single life? It's different now.

I have come to some realizations and conclusions. For one, I was in a relationship of prospects and possibilities, not reality. I had great expectations for what lay ahead, while struggling through the hell of the present. Oftentimes, the carrot at the end of the stick, the pot of gold at the end of the rainbow, is what kept me going. It's true that with the things you LOVE, you will have to go through some HELL, to see it come out RIGHT...but sometimes we love the WRONG things. And nothing right will come out of that.

There are many false loves out there. Loving someone for:

- how they make you feel
- how they look

- what they do for you
- sexual gratification
- what they may become in the future
- your idea of who you *think* they are
- the things they say, or
- just for the fact that they accept you...

...these are not examples of true love.

True love is selfless and not based on self-serving motives. Looking at another person, or relationship, as an "investment" is not loving them *in the now.*

In the past, I loved rarely, but when conditions were right, I raced full speed ahead. Of course that led to a lot of dissatisfaction and grief. As intelligent men, we often strive to change our women by "teaching them." Given, an intelligent man will want to teach everybody, but we are often especially demanding and insensitive when it comes to the transformation of our women. People only truly change and grow on their own. If you want a woman to come into the knowledge of self, supply the demand. Don't demand and supply.

In addition, I've never enjoyed the roller coaster of emotions involved with being in love. I've realized though, upon accepting and "loving" your own (our people as a whole), we suffer less from the whims of individual, personal love. I am a lot more understanding and accepting of the unique strengths and shortcomings of the women I meet these days. I have actually begun getting to know women without sizing them up for wifey or Earth material. I haven't even taken the opportunities I've encountered for sex because I'm already aware of the impending disappointment of empty sex.

See, in my previous relationship, I learned to love someone who wasn't my physical type. Not to say she was ugly, but she did nothing for me in purely physical terms, ie, no "lust factor." The gratification of sex was solely in the bond we shared and the emotions involved. It was sex as a byproduct of love, not love as a byproduct of sex.

So now, I won't get much out of casual sex. I'm less enthusiastic about the girls who are my "type" body-wise and more keen on the compatibility of our personalities. This is somethin I didn't consider enough in the past. Looks aren't enough, brains aren't enough, what matters is whether y'all smile at the same things or not, or whether y'all will work for the same things.

Also, I've learned to examine a little more closely the emotional and psychological baggage of the people with whom I deal. A lot of people are in denial, and negative emotions like fear, insecurity, mistrust, anxiety, depression, etc...These are relationship killers. And they kill slowly. You won't know why your woman is always upset. Sometimes it isn't you. I'm not perfect, but I'm not anything like the men I've heard my female friends describe. For the longest, I couldn't get why my head was always on the chopping block for something or other. In the end, it's not always us. Sometimes it really is them.

Now if you're the kind of dude who cheats on your girl, is on the DL, beats her, never comes home, or smokes crack in secret, we are not in the same boat. I'm referring to the good dudes who get in bad relationships with hurt women who've been with bad dudes. What can you do? You learn and move on. Will it happen instantly? Of course not, but wisdom is treatment and understanding is the cure.

Until you're ready to tackle "real love" and a "real relationship," use the advice in the next section.

**Real love takes time...and a lot of trial and error.
If you're not ready, don't play with it.**

22 GUIDELINES FOR DEALING WITH WOMEN

In an upcoming book, we'll be able to get a deeper on women, love, and relationships. Until then, here are some basic guidelines for dealing with the opposite sex:

1. **First things first.** Straighten yourself out first. Get your mind right, get your money right. When you've got that, pussy comes to you. And when you're ready, the right woman will also.

2. **Don't rush.** Most men don't meet "Miss Right" until their late 20s, or mid 30s. Until then, you're bound to go through a gang of "learning experiences" that will prepare you. **You don't buy every car you test drive, so don't marry the first girl you love.**

3. **Watch where you stick that thing.** It's only one to a customer. If you're scared of what you might catch or what kind of bullsh*t baby mama she'd be, then don't even worry bout the condom breaking. Just leave that pussy alone.

4. **Pay attention.** Watch women. Listen to them. Ask them what they think and what they like. Adjust your game so you ain't sellin apples to people who want carrots.

5. **Be confident.** Nobody wants a loser. Being "that dude" starts with believing in yourself. A woman wants a man she believes in, and

that's why a thug can take a girl from a good-hearted nerd in a minute.

6. **Let her choose you.** You don't need to compete. If she knows what she wants, and you're it, all you have to do is show her. F*ck fighting for her attention.

7. **Don't choose no dumb fine broad.** Forget fine. Worry bout the dumb. The dumb will make you forget about the fine in no time, anyway.

8. **Your girl gotta have somethin goin on for herself.** Don't choose no broke, dropout broad with a perfect ass. The ass won't last, but the brokeness will.

9. **Make sure y'all have somethin in common to talk about.** If y'all ain't interested in the same things, it's not gonna work. If you really want to go to Africa and she thinks Africa is made of mud, you're gonna be miserable.

10. **Make sure she wants the best for you.** Any girl who doesn't want you to stop smokin, or stop hustlin, don't really give a f*ck about you. She's using you for the short term homey. Get wise.

11. **Step your game up.** Don't chase young girls. They're simple and don't want much…actually they don't even know what they want. You look like a molestor holding hands with a girl 5 years under you. Try an older woman and see if you can hang.

12. **Strap up.** I don't give a f*ck if you love her. Strap up. Ain't no pussy so good that it's worth a slow death.

13. **Don't buy her.** If she expects you to pay for everything, you're a trick. You might as well just go get a prostitute. It's cheaper, and they don't argue.

14. **Leave them white girls alone.** That's it.

15. **Don't let a woman screw up your life.** If she's got you beefin with your brother, give her the boot. A good woman don't bring drama with her.

16. **Don't change.** Any woman will try to change you, but won't respect you if you change every time she says so. Grow up at your own pace. A bad woman will try to turn you from a schoolboy to a fake thug in a minute, or from a real thug to a pretty boy. Meanwhile, your boys are looking at you like a sucker.

17. **Do the right thing.** If she say no, respect the no. If you slip and make a baby, don't run. If she's sick, go see her just as fast as you would if it was a booty call.

18. **Check out the tree the apple fell from.** If her mama is fat, maybe you better hide the Twinkies from your girl. If her mama is a no-good thief, maybe you should watch your wallet at night too.

19. **Karma can be a bitch.** If you keep sh*ttin on people, it's only natural you'll get sh*tted on too. Treat people with respect. Even if you're just f*ckin, don't lie to em. If you got 8 girls, don't act like you're Mr. Faithful.

20. **Don't lose sleep.** If she's gonna cheat, she's gonna cheat. If you think she's cheatin, why you even with her? Do what you supposed to, and choose right, and you won't have to worry about her doin bullsh*t behind your back.

21. **Read a book.** It don't hurt to be educated. Even a chick who likes thugs would rather have a smart thug than a dumb one.

22. **Make sure you've found your "better half."** Not a new mother to be spoiled by, or a daughter you need to raise.

Good relationships are built on sound principles.
And good relationships are the key to a good life.

EAT TO LIVE

The following is an excerpt from an April 2001 *ABC News* article titled, "Woman Contracts Parasitic Worm in Her Brain from Pork Taco":

> What sounds like science fiction was all too real for Dawn Becerra, who found a parasitic worm lodged in her brain after eating a pork taco while vacationing in Mexico. Doctors at Arizona's Mayo Clinic in Scottsdale believe the taco contained Taenia solium, a parasite that is surprisingly common in Latin American countries, and is often transmitted by eating undercooked pork. Becerra said the snack made her ill for three weeks. And soon after, she began suffering seizures.
>
> …Doctors at the Mayo Clinic discovered Becerra had neurocysticercosis – a lesion in her brain, caused by the parasitic worm. Last November, she was told that if she wanted to live a normal, seizure-free life, she would need surgery.
>
> …As an egg, the worm attached itself to the intestinal wall, and eventually moved into her blood stream and to her brain, said Dr. Joseph Sirven, who operated on Becerra.
>
> …"All of a sudden, I realized they were going to cut open my brain, and take a worm out of my brain" she said.
>
> …"The fascinating part about this is that it's much more common than people think," notes Sirven.
>
> …The World Health Organization says neurocysticercosis is a common cause of epilepsy in Africa, Asia, and Latin America.[8]

Uh, it's 2008, and people still eat pork?

Of course, there are a lot bigger problems for us to deal with, but pork is a good one to talk about, because it not only makes us sick, but it says a lot about the way we still think. Here's the way most people who still eat pork think about those nasty chunks of disease:

      1. It tastes good.

      2. It hasn't killed me yet.

      3. It can't be THAT bad for me.

But we could start cooking rats in curry sauce, or sh*t in barbecue sauce, and say the same thing. The pig has been unclean and unhealthy since its appearance on the planet, and it will always be that way. It was never even meant to be used as food, after all.

Let's go over some basics:

- The pig has only one stomach and very limited excretory organs. Other animals, like cows, have much more in their bodies to help them digest their food. The pig doesn't. That means the pig is full of sh*t.

- The pig is a scavenger, so it eats "any kind of food, including dead insects, worms, rotting carcasses, excreta (including their own), garbage and other pigs."

- The pig is so nasty inside, it's the only animal that you can feed poison and not kill it.

- The pig doesn't have pores to sweat. That's why it rolls in the mud or feces to keep cool. That's also why all of the filth in the pig stays inside of it.

- Every holy book and religion has put the pig down as filthy and unclean. From Ancient Egypt, to the Old Testament (Leviticus 11:7,8, Genesis 1:29, Isaiah 65:2-4, Isaiah 66:15-17) to the Qur'an (Surah 2:172-173, etc.), even down to the New Testament, where Jesus sends demons out of a man and into a herd of pigs.

- The Honorable Elijah Muhammad taught that the pig was used around 2000 B.C. to clean out the filthy caves where the Europeans lived then. In more recent times, pigs have been bred to clean the streets of early Spain, and the sewers of Chicago. This works, because pigs will eat anything nonstop, including feces.

- A diet heavy in red meat, especially pork, is one of the most significant factors behind the high rates of cancer, heart disease, high blood pressure, arthritis, and diabetes in the Black community. Want a cure for cancer? Stop eating bullsh*t. That's a start.

More Black men die from eating the wrong foods than they do from homicide. But when do these problems start showing up? When it's too late. At some point, you're just sick as hell, taking pills, and the doctor says "stop eating red meat." Doctors tell women the same thing when they're pregnant, which makes you wonder: If it's that bad for you when you're pregnant, isn't it always bad for you?

Pig meat contains:

- Excessive quantities of histamine and imidazole compounds, which lead to itching and inflammation.

- Sulphur-containing mesenchymal mucus, which leads to swelling and deposits of mucus in tendons and cartilage, resulting in arthritis, rheumatism, etc. Sulphur also helps cause firm human tendons and ligaments to be replaced by soft mesenchymal tissues like the pig. The sulphur also causes the degeneration of human cartilage.

- High levels of dangerous cholesterol and saturated fat, which leads to gallstones, obesity, and heart disease.

- The Taenia sodium worm, a tapeworm found in the flesh. They occur in human intestines and are not only capable of spreading to other organs, but are incurable after passing a certain stage.

- The Trichinae nematode worm – which causes trichinosis. Trichinosis is a disease one gets from eating pork that is undercooked. Then there's cramps, aches and stiffness, later nausea and vomiting; and then headaches and nervous disorders. The Trichina worm is able to burrow through tissues and invade neighboring organs or go straight into the bloodstream. After this point, they are often known to invade the brain or nervous system, as in the story above. Approximately 1 in 6 people in the U.S. and Canada has trichinosis and may not know it.

- Plenty of other fun critters like the kidney worm, the lungworm, the thorn-headed worm, and the roundworm.

There are also diseases common to the pig, like:

- Genital papilloma

- Infectious porcine encephalomyelitis (or Teschen disease, porcine poliomyelitis, Talfan disease, or picornavirus)

- Swine erysipelas

- Hog cholera (or swine fever)

- Hemophilus influenza (or swine influenza, swine flu, hog flu)

- Swine plague, enzootic pneumonia, swineherd's disease, and swinepox

With some of these diseases, the animal (and the humans affected by eating their meat) may show no symptoms at all.

During slavery, the slave owner and his family cast their leftovers and unused parts to the slaves. The slaves, having only cornmeal and weeds to eat, used the meat scraps to turn something into nothing. The slaves found ways to eat the intestines, the ears, faces, genitals, tail, feet, and even the brains of the pigs. But once slavery was over, we were conditioned. Just like the freed slaves kept their slave religion, they kept their slave food.

The most ironic part is that most Blacks – before slavery – had never eaten pork or prayed to a white Jesus. Today, pork and pork products are in damn near near everything. For example, the gelatin used to make Jell-O comes from boiling pig bones and stripping them of collagen.

This nasty, sick sh*t is a 10-billion-dollar industry. Why do you think that – even though there's thousands of Americans sick every day from eating it – we never hear how bad it is for us? It's simple: The FDA worries about how much money something is making before it worries about what it's doing to the stupid people who don't read…or don't care. That's why the FDA's guidelines for packaged foods require:

- No more than 50 insect fragments or 2 rodent hairs per 100 grams of peanut butter.

- No more than 10 fruit fly eggs in 100 grams of tomato juice.

- No more than 150 insect fragments in an 8-ounce chocolate bar.

In fact, a December 2005 Ohio University research study found that Americans unintentionally eat 1 to 2 pounds of insect parts a year.

That's also why, even though we know eating red meat like beef and pork leads to cancer and heart disease, pork is promoted as the "Other White Meat." Pork is NOT a damn white meat.

A lot of people will tell you, my grandpa ate pork and he's 76. But they leave out the fact that their grandpa is in a f*ckin wheelchair or on dialysis. Even if their pork-eating grandpa is in good health, what about their grandma and auntie, who both have ankles so swollen they look like slouch socks, and need five medications every day just to KEEP living?

So let's be real. Pork ain't gon kill you today. Not even next week. But neither will heroin. In life, things have short-term consequences and long-term consequences. You can't ignore the long-term effects of something just because nothing's happening in the next two weeks. It ALL catches up with you sooner or later. And who wants to die slow and painful over a Bacon Cheeseburger?

All decisions have long-term consequences.
Think long-term more than you think short-term.

WHO ARE YOU FIGHTING?

I could spend 20 pages talking about how ignorant we look constantly fighting and feuding with each other. I'm talking about everyone

from the millionaire celebrities to the preachers to the dudes on the block. If you've heard of Willie Lynch (See "Mental Illnesses in the Black Community") you should understand how this all started. But it's 2007, and we still can't come together. Goddamn. I'm not going to spend 20 pages on this issue, though, because someone else did it real well. Here's David Banner's second verse on "B.A.N. (The Love Song)":

> This is for the Bloods and this is for my Crips/ Throw your sets up, one Nation in this bitch/ We so quick to kill each other in the hoods where we from/ But we hide the AKs when them f*ckin Feds come/ When there's a pedophile that's lurkin round where we stay/ We turn our f*ckin cheek and let them faggots walk away/ But God gave me a vision, and now a thug sees/ What would happen in the hood if the Vicelords and the Gs/ All came together, blue and red flags/ Raisin a nation of Black men, but ain't it sad/ We got too many cowards that'll let them bullets fly/ Cause they'd rather get paid, and watch the young kids die/ You motherf*ckin...BITCH ASS NIGGAAA

I couldn't have said it better myself. But this ain't just about the gangs. It's about everyone of these motherf*ckers who can't see the real problem we're facing out here...and it ain't each other. If we could come together – just for one year – don't you know every hood across America would change? Don't you know that ALL of America would have to change? Don't you know that the whole world would rise up with us and the *entire* world would change?

You're all in the same slaveship. Instead of worrying about the man
next to you, worry about who is on top of both of you.

RACE TRAITOR

The chances are good that you have a couple of white friends. Or you're one of the 17 white people who bought this book. I've got something to share with you either way.

Frederick Douglass, after publicly separating himself from the white abolitionists he once worked for, said: "No people that has solely depended...upon the efforts of those, in any way identified with the oppressor...ever stood forth in the attitude of Freedom."

I agree. I don't want to be down with white people, and I don't need any white people down with me. BUT I don't hate white people. In fact, you *could* be down if you were white...but it'll take some time for me to tell you how.

When I posted a MySpace blog about the Jena 6 (See "The White Tree"), I got dozens of positive comments from Black people. Only one white person responded, and this is what she said:

> I feel like you have turned other white people's hatred for Black people against all of us. I am very well aware that there is still racism all over the world, and that not much has changed in the last few decades...
>
> I think what is happening to those children in Louisiana is horrible. And I think the white people should have strict consequences for their hate crimes. But you make it sound as if you feel that Blacks should stay away from whites. Is that how you feel? You are taking the racism that these whites have displayed and telling Blacks to do the same. Basically you are telling them they are wrong for being friendly with whites, or for loving us. Don't hold an entire race responsible for what people are doing in Louisiana...
>
> Please don't turn on all white people for what some have done. We are not all fake. We are not all full of hate... I know my opinion is only that of a lowly white bitch, but I couldn't stop myself from spilling my feelings. You have a celebrity status. So, please don't use it to teach people to hate. Even after your people have been wronged. You should be teaching people to overcome.

She even validated herself by explaining how she was married to a Black man, and described a time when she felt like the police were discriminating against her because she was stopped while driving through a Black neighborhood. She was being completely sincere. Since then, I've realized that many white people, especially the ones who think they are "liberal-minded" think like this. So here was my response:

> First, I don't think of you as a "lowly white bitch." I'm above looking at people like that. I think what you've said has a lot of thought and consideration put into it.
>
> However, I must continue to disagree with your position. There is a fundamental dynamic you must understand. That is, there are different levels of discrimination/racism. There is "interpersonal discrimination" and there is "institutional discrimination."
>
> The first one, anybody can experience, as you have. I could refuse a white person a job because they are white, and that would be interpersonal discrimination. But the system would eventually come

down on me and stop me, or persecute me for it. Institutional discrimination is so much bigger than you and your family.

It is the overarching system, a global system of white supremacy, a system that dictates and governs the affairs of most of this world. You cannot escape it. You, as a white woman, cannot run from your privilege and your participation in this system of oppression UNLESS you are willing to fight and die for the dismantling of that system. Because if you do NOT take that stand, you as a white woman, give it your silent consent, especially so because you – in many ways – continue to benefit from it.

There is an online journal I've come across lately, www.racetraitor.org. The premise of their publication is that "treason to whiteness is loyalty to humanity." The authors and editors, presumably white people, see "whiteness" as a construct...a symbolic representation of "otherness" to people of color. Those who are "white" are inherently against those of color. It is part and parcel of being "white," just as being "royalty" means you are part of a system of rulership, regardless of what you do in your personal life.

Until I see white people fighting and dying to dismantle the oppressive systems of the world, I will continue to view them as passive participants and beneficiaries of a wicked system. And I don't mean fighting to save some lemurs in Africa (instead of the people) because that's just another dynamic of racist thinking as well. I appreciate your response. I hope you can see where I'm coming from.

Needless to say, she never responded. Now, you may be thinking, "Supreme, it sounds like you have a problem with ALL white people!" If you read my response, you can see that's just not true. I say a lot about white people throughout this book, but I have a degree in history, a home library with over 1,000 books in it, and have traveled all over the world. I'm not making ANY of this up. Anything I say is backed up by historical or political fact. And my goal isn't to bash ALL white people.

However, I'm not taking sides with a group of white people just because they want to help give clothes to poor refugees. I don't consider a white person "cool" just because they never said the word nigger, or because they listen to hip hop. I don't give a f*ck if they even have those funky-looking dreads.

What I want to know is "What are you doing to stop white supremacy?" Because if you ain't doin nothing about THAT, then you're part of the problem. I see a lot of white people saying they're against racism, but I don't see too many who will give away their family's money because the money came from slavery. I saw a bunch of white Americans and Europeans when I went to Africa. But they weren't hanging out with the brothers and sisters like I was. They were going to the beach (the same beaches where the slave-ships waited), or playing with the animals on safari. Even when I saw some white people on my visit to the slave dungeons, they all left as soon as the guide started talking about how horrible slavery was.

So show me some people who are out there trying to change the system, and fighting alongside Black people, and they'll be cool with me. Show me someone ready to lose their life for the struggle of people of color, and they're all right with me. It's not like there's never been such a thing.

In the 1960s, the Black Panthers worked closely with a white radical group known as the Weather Underground. The Weathermen were a mostly white underground organization dedicated to social change, by any means necessary. They were outspoken critics of "white skin privilege" and advocates for racial identity politics.[9] As the unrest in poor black neighborhoods intensified in the early 1970s, Bernardine Dohrn said, "White youth must choose sides now. They must either fight on the side of the oppressed, or be on the side of the oppressor."

Now what side are most white people on today? Just think about it, the US is only about 12% Black. Now, when someone white is truly being punished unfairly (rare), you'll see about 12% of the protestors are Black, at least if it's something we all know about.

But usually white folks don't have much to protest about, besides saving the hippos, stopping the war, or gay rights. And the US is about 70% white. But were 70% of the Jena 6 protestors white? Why not?

The truth is, even white people are scared of other white people clowning them for taking sides with Black people. So I don't expect much from them. But don't expect me to bite my tongue either, when I'm telling the truth.

If you're white and you want to be a part of the struggle, you need to stop fighting on behalf of trees and birds, and start studying what happened to people like the Weathermen and the Symbionese Liberation Party (look them up), as well as the "anti-racism" movements that are still alive in some parts of the U.S. and Europe today.

For the people of color: Out of all the white people you're "down with," how many are really "down" for you?

For the 17 white readers: Are willing to fight and sacrifice to fight white supremacy? Can you accept white supremacy as being a very real and powerful system that affects everyone, including you? Are you prepared to have your family and friends cut you off for your dedication to non-white people and their survival? If so, you're alright with me. If not, go read *The Heart of Whiteness: Confronting Race, Racism And White Privilege* by Robert Jensen or *White Like Me: Reflections on Race from a Privileged Son* by Tim Wise...to start.

**We must only "pledge allegiance"
to those who will fight with us and for us.**

How to Survive a Dysfunctional Family

I thought I'd provide a brief guide for young people suffering from FUH Syndrome (F*cked Up Household):

1. Remember, they're only human. They can't be perfect, and will probably never even get close. Your job is to do better than them.

2. FUH Syndrome can either make you incredibly strong or incredibly weak. Victim or victorious, it's up to you.

3. Sick people can have kids. But sick people's kids don't have to be sick too.

4. Sometimes you just have to accept people for who and how they are, and deal with their craziness the best you can without becoming crazy yourself.

5. People who are full of chaos inside create chaos around them, and spend more time blaming others than solving the issues within. It's not always your fault.

> **Did You Know?**
> President Thomas Jefferson had a Black mistress named Sally Hemmings, who was also one of his slaves. Sally Hemmings had children by President Jefferson, and they have many living descendants today.

6. Sometimes you can substitute. When a parent is failing at their job, find somebody decent who can fill in some of the gaps.

7. We all know the children of alcoholics usually end up alcoholics, and children of abusive relationships end up beating their girlfriends as well. But break the cycle. If it's what's killing your family, don't make it a part of your life.

8. Running away works for some people, but it also creates other problems (like getting food, clothing, and shelter).

9. Depression is a long, winding road that only goes downhill. Final destination: suicide. So don't even take that path. Force yourself to look at the bright side of life.

10. Find someone worse off than you. Counsel them and be their support. It will make you feel better in many ways.

11. Avoid confrontations. You know you can't win arguing with certain kinds of people, so don't bother. Swallow your pride, and take it in stride.

12. If you have to, avoid interactions unless necessary. Sometimes it's best just not to cross paths. That doesn't mean you have an excuse to post up on the block all day. Be productive with your time away.

13. Too much control is not a good thing, but neither is too much freedom. An unstructured home produces laziness and failure, which are often just as bad as a home that's run like a prison. So discipline yourself if no one else will.

14. Find a hobby. Whether you're rapping, drawing, or building robots, there are ways to turn all that frustration and stress into creative energy.

Life is never hopeless. Even the worst environments can produce the best people, so long as they are strong enough to make it out.

MURDERING FOUR DEVILS

Shaka Zulu

In the 19th century, the Zulus would be one of the few African peoples who managed to defeat the technologically superior British Army, at the Battle of Isandlwana. Shaka Zulu not only replaced the weapons and shields of his people with more effective designs, but he introduced military tactics and formations that the British had never encountered before, especially not among African people. Further, those who chose to join Shaka Zulu, as most did, had to give up their tribal affiliations. They not only joined the Zulu; they became Zulus.

Strong discipline and close combat distinguished Shaka Zulu's army. To toughen his men he had them give up their leather sandals, having them train and fight in bare feet, often covering more than fifty miles a day in a fast trot in order to surprise their enemies. One of the most notable features of Shaka's military leadership is that, in his conquests, he spared no one, even children. Seeing their potential as future rivals, Shaka Zulu intended to leave no opportunities for retaliation.

What can we learn from the historical example of the great Shaka Zulu?

Western Psychology

According to Freud, the human mind is composed of three main components: the Id, the Ego, and the Superego. The Ego represents the Self, and the Id are the primitive urges that fuel our subconscious desires to f*ck, flight, and find food. On the other hand, the Superego is the higher consciousness of man that directs him to

Did You Know?

The word 'gymnasium' comes from the Greek word gymnazein which means 'to exercise naked.' If you're wondering what the Greek teachers did with their young male students while they were naked, I'm sure you can figure it out.

"do the right thing" and follow his morals and values.

Greek Philosophy

The Greek philosopher Aristotle said Man has a primitive animalistic side to him, a side that operates purely off instinct, and like an animal, only desires to eat, drink, sleep, sh*t, fight, and f*ck. The logical side of man is where the rational decisions get made, and where the weaker side is tamed and disciplined.

Entertainment

Think about the old cartoons and movies where the main character has a devil on his shoulder or sneaking around somewhere, trying to convince him to do something he shouldn't do. Eventually, the guy has to flick the little devil off his shoulder or ignore him until he disappears.

Buddhism

The Buddha taught that the only way to attain salvation and find true peace was to rid ourselves of negative emotions by relinquishing our "worldly desires." After letting go of these attitudes, we could see clearly and find happiness.

The Quran

Islam teaches that there are three kinds of jihads, or struggles: the political jihad that occurs between groups of people, the interpersonal jihad that occurs between individuals, and the internal jihad, which is the struggle within self. Muhammad made it clear to his followers that the greatest jihad was that which occurs within oneself.

The Bible

Sloth. Wrath. Gluttony. Greed. Jealousy. Hatred. Lust. Sound familiar? Those are the Seven Deadly Sins in the Bible. Why are they deadly? These are the kind of issues that will end up killing you...some can take you off this planet in one fell swoop, while others will destroy you slowly. Some of us don't even know that we're killing ourselves! Well, once you know, then what? What do you do with something that's going to kill you? You destroy it!

The Bible also tells several stories of evil spirits infesting men, particularly the story of a man who is named Legion because he has that many evils within him. In the parable, Jesus expels these evil spirits and sends them into a herd of equally filthy swine who go plunging into the ocean to their death.

When you think about the word "spirits," it can mean a lot of things. It can refer to emotional attitudes (I'm in good spirits today, They broke his spirit, etc). It can also refer to strong alcohol. And what happens to people when they drink strong alcohol? All of those emotions come out!

The Moorish Science Temple

The lessons of Noble Drew Ali's Moorish Science Temple taught that the lower self of the Black man, was what kept him from acting in the nature of his true self, his higher self, God.

The Nation of Gods and Earths

In the 120 Lessons of the Nation of Gods and Earths, there is a lesson that brings up the murder of four devils. What Allah taught his young Five Percenters was that these four devils weren't necessarily people, but they symbolized the vices of man. Gods and Earths don't teach that the devil himself is within the Black man, only that the weaknesses that produce a devil are in us. Allowed to grow and mature to the point of permanence, we become (mentally) like the devil himself.

Review

Some of us are addicted to a pill, a powder, or a plant, and we can't admit it. Some of us are chasing money like it can buy happiness (but we stay miserable). Some of us are extremely insecure or full of hatred for others (really ourselves). Some of us really, really, really, like sex...to the point where we'll f*ck anything with a hole in it...if we're desperate enough.

And sometimes, we can't reconcile with these weaknesses, so we justify them. We talk about our bad habits like they're cool and not really a problem...knowing in our hearts that we're killing ourselves. Most of us glorify our sexual exploits, ignoring how many bad experiences we've had...or how sex has never really made us happy for more than a few minutes. Most of us will spend our lives struggling with our inner demons, and some of us never win.

The simple fact of life is that everybody has weaknesses. We all have internal vices. We each have our own dogs to walk. And your issues aren't the same as your best friend's, so this is a war you've got to wage on your own...you can find support, but you'll never find anyone to fight this fight for you.

What can we do? The first step is to identify your weaknesses. Name your devils, the most significan't vices you have (right now). Seriously.

My vices/weaknesses are: _____

Now, these are the issues that come up again and again in your life. You may not even be aware of them. That's the nature of a snake. But if you allow a snake to live, it will sting you again and again. It will probably end up killing you because you let it.

So cut the grass low and the snake's heads will show. Ask people what your vices are and be ready to hear some things you may not like. For some of us, they're pretty obvious issues like our addictions and dependencies. But even those kinds of issues have layers, as we've learned. Sure, you might chase a lot of pussy. But why? What creates that need in you, to a greater extent than it does in other people? Sometimes you can't kill the snake because you *think* you're cutting off its head, but you're just whacking at its tail.

No, you kill it, and leave nothing left. Until the day that happens, you live every day with the intent in mind to kill that snake/devil every time it tries to rear its ugly head. You've got to go past when Jesus said, "Get thee behind me, Satan!" and kill that motherf*cker.

Ways to kill a snake	Ways to kill a vice
Suffocate it	Never allow it to breathe/develop
Overfeed it	Indulge it until you've had too much to want anymore
Poison it	Allow a bad experience to turn you off from it
Cut off its head	Work actively to eliminate it
Burn the field and replant	Start everything about yourself anew
Kill the babies	Eliminate related thoughts and behaviors

The greatest struggle is within.
Eliminating your bad habits may be the hardest thing you do,
but it is certainly one of the most important.

DO YOU HAVE AN ANGER PROBLEM?

I can name a dozen vices, bad habits, and weaknesses that keep Black men from achieving greatness. There's irresponsibility, which comes from growing up realizing your life was f*cked up before you even got here...so what the hell is there that you can do about it? There's foolish pride, which comes from our desire to be more than what we are because we feel so small in this bitter world...only to make things worse for ourselves. There's petty envy and jealousy which result from a combination of being raised mostly by women and never having enough to feel satisfied with our lives. There's even greed, which comes to many of us because we hate having so little and are constantly told having more will make us happy.

But there's one weakness that will destroy you faster than any of the above. It's not lust. It's not sloth. You know what it is: Anger.

Think about it…we kill each other over anger. We lose our jobs due to anger. We end up doing life in prison after one fit of anger. We are f*ckin angry.

Why? Look around, and it's obvious. We're all pretty cool as little kids (unless we were abused from an early age). But by the time we hit 3rd or 4th grade, we're hip to the game. We know the teachers are lying about how useful and helpful the bullsh*t they're teaching is…We know adults are lying when they say school and hard work will equal success (and all we see around us is broke-ass adults)…We know the world is lying to us with its promises of freedom, justice, and equality. The Black man in America knows he's f*cked from an early age.

That does some things to you, whether you know it or not. For one, it creates an "I Don't Give a F*ck" attitude (See "Who Gives a F*ck?"). For another, it makes us angry with ourselves, angry with each other, and angry with the world. We never really figure out how to take our anger out on the people who put us in such a f*cked up predicament in the first place, so we lash out at the closest ones to us. First, we torture our mothers for bringing us into such a f*cked-up life and giving us so little with which to defend ourselves. Nine times out of ten, our mothers are completely unprepared to raise Black boys in a world set out to destroy them. Many of them have no idea what it will take to keep us from becoming yet another victim. It's not their fault…they simply don't have a magic formula.

After we've burned our bridges with our families, we end up going to war with anyone who we feel wrongs us in any way. Step on my shoes or pass me without saying "Excuse me," and it's on. We aren't dying over Jordans, we're dying because we are angry with our lives and the world steadily sh*ttin on us, and the dude who stepped on our Jordans was just that last straw of disrespect that broke the camel's back.

There's nothing wrong with being angry about a f*cked-up situation. That's natural. What's wrong is to take that anger out on people who had nothing to do with it. What's wrong is to ignore what you are doing to make your situation f*cked up, while blaming everyone else. What's wrong is to throw your life away because you're angry. Instead of wasting your life over something the news reporters will call "trivial" and the church folks will call "ignorant," here's the number one thing you need to do, followed by several other suggestions to help you deal with anger.

1. Figure out why you're angry, and who you're angry with. Leave other people out of it.

2. When you're angry, tell people before they start bothering you and making things worse.

3. Breathe and count. Before you do something stupid, breathe and count for at least 20 seconds. You'll avoid a lot of drama this way.

4. If you're going to destroy something, make sure it doesn't belong to someone else. Your anger has nothing to do with them.

5. If you feel like violence is the only option, weigh out the consequences. Will you get away with murdering someone in the street? Doubt it.

6. Listen to some music, write something, or work out. Turn your negative energy into something else. If nothing else works, jog until you're tired.

7. Find someone you can talk to when you're stressed or pissed. Look at what they do that calms you down.

8. When you finally figure out what you've been so mad about all your life, deal with it like a real man.

**Of all our vices,
anger destroys the fastest.**

I SMOKE, I DRINK

My Perspective

I started drinking when I was about 13, beginning with secret trips to the basement where I'd found some dusty bottles of Jack Daniels Whiskey. The first few sips were like torture, but I grew used to it with every new trip that I made. When I got into malt liquor the next year, I had such a high tolerance for alcohol that it took a whole 40 ounce to get my 14-year-old ass a decent buzz. Drinking seemed to make the pain go away...at least temporarily. When I started smoking, weed did about the same thing. So I spent most of my teenage years drinking and smoking. Even when I stopped smoking weed, I couldn't let go of cigarettes.

I had tons of bad experiences along the way. I blacked out a few times. I did some things I regret. I responded with violence at times when I was too drunk to defend myself well. I think I even ruined a few friendships and relationships. And I did a gang of stupid sh*t that just didn't make

> **Did You Know?**
> Even a small amount of alcohol placed on a scorpion will make it go crazy and sting itself to death.
> Smoking is a billion dollar industry, even though it is known to kill half of its customers. In fact, the United States produces more tobacco than it does wheat.
> Whatever the father or mother is smoking or drinking (before and during pregnancy) becomes part of the newborn's system.

any sense. I always laugh when people say weed helps them think, because that says so much about what kind of mind they're working with. As Project Pat raps on "Purple":

> Niggas'll ride, and get high, wit' they tags out/ Police'll spy, pull 'em over, wit' they badge out/ You know that's dumb, you got guns wit the bags out/ The windows full of smoke, e'erybody passed out

But it wasn't going to stop. I even coughed up blood once or twice from my smoking habit. Even after that, I continued. I was stuck. I was still miserable. But worst of all, now I felt like I couldn't function sober. And I felt anxious and uneasy when I hadn't had a cigarette. I – like the rest of my friends – had a "chemical dependency." Just like the addicts we were serving.

As with religion, weed, tobacco, and alcohol are drugs we use to deal with the daily pain and stress of living in a state of constant failure and oppression. Why wait til we're 21 to drink, or "say no to drugs" when life is f*cked up and promises never to change? Why avoid cigarettes when you believe you're more likely to die from a bullet than cancer? As Lil Wayne raps on "Monsta":

> And a nigga drink like the late Fred Sanford/ And a nigga smoke like there is no cancer/ And I know this world is so cold and deceiving/ But I keep my head up like my nose is bleedin

I simply couldn't see through the clouds of smoke and the blur in the bottle. I couldn't see that my way of escaping the pain was actually making the pain worse day by day. I looked at weed and liquor like they were my medicine, when they were just making me sicker. But I couldn't see that, because I was never sober long enough to think seriously about my life and what I was doing. Many days, I hated what my addictions were doing to me. I hated how I felt, but I felt that I needed them still. I couldn't get away, even though I told other people I could. In a way, the liquor and the weed were taking control of me.

> "You niggas try to solve problems by smokin' weed
> But you only gettin' high, and ya problems become big
> But ain't nothin' but some Nike Airs comin' to a sleeper"
> Project Pat, "Purple"

That was the real problem. I was losing interest in reality. I didn't want any part of the bullsh*t anymore. I was even intoxicated in school. In fact, I failed Driver's Ed because I'd drive drunk on the simulator. When I brought liquor to school, I was flagrant with mines. While some people concealed theirs in bottles, I'd pour gin into a half-empty Sprite can and hope nobody knew the smell was coming from me. I was pretty stupid and wild, and it was mostly because I was losing touch with reality. Of course, no one was there to try to tell me any different. No one stepped to me like Wu-Tang Clan's "A Better Tomorrow" and said:

> You can't party your life away, Drink your life away/ Smoke your life away, F*ck your life away/ Dream your life away, Scheme your life awa/ Cause your seeds grow up the same way

When I got to college in Atlanta, I heard the stories of people who failed out by "partying" too much. That stuck with me, because I had barely gotten out of high school myself. By the time I left Jersey, I was drinking by myself, which is a sure sign that now you've got a problem.

It took a few years for me to get rid of all my vices. But I began by quitting hard liquor and weed. It was hard for the first few weeks, but I found other things to do with my free time. I knew I was doing the right thing when I began seeing life so much clearer than I ever had. I was focused. I still got stressed, but I found other ways to handle it. I went from dependent to independent. And once I did that, I began to see that the misery I was trying to escape wasn't just my problem. I started seeing that we're all suffering. And I became determined not to run from that pain, but to fight it head on like a man.

So, in a way, I didn't become a man, until I stopped letting other things have power over me, and I took control of myself.

Frederick Douglass' Perspective

According to Frederick Douglass, his experiences in slavery taught him about how Blacks were kept in their conditions through methods that continue to work today. He recalled that the slaves were given their only vacation on the days from Christmas to New Year's, and these "holidays" were spent in many different ways.

> "The money you spend for whiskey will run a government."
> Malcolm X

The "sober industrious ones" would keep busy through their days off, finding ways to make money, acquire food, or help themselves by making tools or clothes. Even smaller groups would secretly plan escape attempts or rebellions. But most slaves were too brainwashed to see free time as a time to "get free." After all, as Douglass explained, "We regarded this time as our own by the grace of our masters, and we therefore used it or abused it as we pleased."

So, while a few worked to improve their lives in their time off, and even less worked to pursue true freedom, most slaves behaved like...well, slaves. Douglass recalled:

> The majority spent the holidays in sports, ball-playing, wrestling, boxing, running, foot-races, dancing, and drinking whisky, and this latter mode was generally most agreeable to their masters.
>
> A slave who would work during the holidays was thought by his master undeserving of holidays... Not to be drunk during the holidays was disgraceful.

We were induced to drink, I among the rest, and when the holidays were over we all staggered up from our filth and wallowing, took a long breath, and went away to our various fields of work, feeling...glad to go from that which [we thought was] freedom, back again to the arms of slavery...

It was about as well to be slave to master, as to be a slave to whisky and rum. When the slave was drunk, the slaveholder had no fear that he would plan an insurrection, or that he would escape to the North. It was the sober, thoughtful slave who was dangerous and needed the vigilance of his master to keep him a slave.[10]

The weak need a drug to escape temporarily, only to come back to their misery. Feeling stronger, but now inebriated, they're unable to see clearly enough to fight what is causing their misery.

So, what's your drug of choice? And how is it helping you?

Instead of destroying yourself, destroy what's destroying you.

WHY THE POOR STAY WEAK

"Every man thinks God is on his side. The rich and powerful know he is."
Jean Anouilh

When Communist scholar Karl Marx said, "Religion is the opiate of the masses," he meant that poor people everywhere use religion to help them get through the misery of being poor and powerless....like a drug (opium). Rich people usually don't pay too much mind to religion, because they don't have those kind of problems. It makes you think, who do you think gives us the drug that keeps us from wanting to rise up and change our miserable conditions?

Let's do a quick review of history:

Historically, the people in power have controlled the idea of God as well as what the God wants. They've used religion as a method of social control. They make up a belief system that tells everyone else how to behave...or ELSE. This is how it begins.

Then, the common people follow this kind of thinking because they don't like thinking for themselves. Some of them are scared to challenge or question these ideas. After all, the belief system threatens them for thinking with their own minds!

The common people then turn to the God of the ruling class for their salvation. They figure, "If it works for them, and they are successful, then I should follow it also."

Poor people who cannot get out of poverty and desperation need SOMETHING to give them hope. If reality can't offer it, fantasy will.

Opiates like heroin and morphine are both narcotics and sedatives. Not only do they reduce pain and suffering, but they provide feelings of ecstasy and happiness. In the same way, religion gives suffering people their only glimpses at happiness.

The people in power continue to exploit the masses in the name of their religion, like drug dealers who don't use their own product, but get rich off the weaknesses of the users.

"Religion is excellent stuff for keeping common people quiet."
Napoleon Bonaparte

Anywhere people are oppressed, they usually believe there is a better future waiting for them in the afterlife. So suffering is a rewarded, as long as you don't fight back, which is usually not promoted in the religion.

Sometimes, to enhance the emotional appeal of a religion, a charismatic personality is attached to the belief system, no matter how much the religion has been perverted from what that person intended. These

figures offer a cult-like following their central figure, almost a father figure, who will listen, support, and save. All without ever being there.

As a result of beliefs like this, the common people become increasingly delusional, and are willing to believe anything they are told by the ruling class.

This is great for the ruling class, who uses it to their advantage to continue to oppress them and take away their freedoms, with their consent.

At some point in this downward progression of society, another reformer emerges from the common people, attempts to teach them of their true history, provide them a real value system, and encourage them to resume the fight for their freedom and self-determination.

This individual is usually killed, jailed, or declared insane by the ruling class he would have otherwise exposed and overthrown.

After an extended period of time has past, when discussions of the above individual become "safe" again, the ruling class makes him a hero…for everyone. His original intent and agenda become clouded and the ruling class twists his message to conform to their desires.

Eventually a new religion is built around this martyr. And the cycle continues.

↓

BACK TO THE BEGINNING!

To sum it all up: The whole idea of a God in the sky, Christian or otherwise, doesn't help people save themselves from their suffering. No matter your religious background, relying on a God who "works in mysterious ways" won't fix your problems.

Now, let's deal with our present-day reality and think about the following:

The same people who gave us our present idea of God used religion as a way to keep us servile and passive while they took our land, our rights, and our people.

Europeans have used religion in this same way everywhere they've gone and taken over. Everywhere in the world where white people have gone and set up colonies, later taking over the region completely, they've first sent in missionaries to win the people over.

> Draw the white Jesus picture you remember from your early childhood here.

"Peep the description of historian Josephus:
'Short, dark, with an underdeveloped beard' was Jesus
He had the Romans fearing revolution
The solution was to take him to court and falsely accuse him
After being murdered by Pilate, how can it be,
these same white Romans established Christianity?"
Ras Kass, "Nature of the Threat"

In some instances, they had no intentions of appearing benevolent. They forced conversion, although the idea of "civilizing the savage" and "cleansing the pagan" was still the lie they used to justify their terror. During slavery, they stripped Black people of their language, their culture, and their knowledge of God, often inflicting brutal punishments on those who rebelled.

Instead, they gave us their God, which looked like them (and it usually still does), and made us think they were closer to God than us (oh, we were so wrong!). They also told us that slaves who fought slavery went to Hell, while slaves who took their whippings on Earth would receive a "pie in the sky" when they died. We didn't realize that Hell was right there on that American soil.

Over 400 years later, we still believe in the same porkchop religions, with a few minor changes here and there. Black and Brown people are so crazy about their religions that we are willing to fight and kill each other for the same beliefs that were used to put us in slavery.

White people hardly believe in their own religion, its God, or its ethical principles. In the name of Christianity, they have ordained slavery, went to war and killed millions of innocents, and persecuted and tortured thousands of people. Meanwhile, the average church session at a white church is about 45 minutes, and white people are rarely seen waiting for God or Jesus to save or help them. Now look around in YOUR community!

They say, on every block in the ghetto, there's a hope house and a dope house...and they both sell the same thing.

Look around and tell me I'm wrong. Not only can you buy drugs within 100 feet of any church in the hood, but I can guarantee there's a liquor store on the next block....maybe even next door.

> "People go to church for the same reasons they go to a tavern: to stupefy themselves, to forget their misery, to imagine themselves, for a few minutes anyway, free and happy."
> Mikhail Aleksandrovich Bakunin (1814-1876)

Yes, the church does do a few good works here and there. Every pastor and reverend is not a thief or liar. Many of them have very good intentions. But it's pretty hard to find a church that's not keeping the congregation asleep and dreaming...or should I say "fiending." Of course, they can't wake the people up if they plan on keeping the huge building and everyone's salaries. Not to mention the luxury cars and mansions.

So what's your drug of choice?

Religion is a drug for the poor and weak.
The powerful use it to keep things the way they are.
We must be more realistic in finding solutions to our problems.

NO PRICE BETTER THAN FREE

It's said that Black people can't turn down anything free. I think white people know that. I'm sure there were a couple of white folks on the slave ships, yelling to the people on the shore: "Free bracelets! Free shiny bracelets and chains!" Next thing you know, there was a stampede.

That's a joke. Well, not completely (see "Greed and Ignorance"). But the point is: Nothing worth having is actually free. Everything comes with a price.

Sex? Well you already know the prices on that are rising daily. Even if she ain't chargin, you're gonna spend time, pay attention, and it'll cost you a few gray hairs before you get there.

I've heard that they're even gonna start chargin for air too. Well, I hope those fat people that be breathin real hard are gonna pay more than my skinny ass.

If you really think about it though, air isn't free. Your lungs have to work to get it. It doesn't just come to you with no effort on your part. And that's how it is with everything. Either there's a cost, or a catch.

If something seems too good to be true, there's probably a catch.

If something seems like a decent deal, you'll still need to put in some work. The following items will show you how to get the most out of life when you've got the least in your pocket. But if you're lazy, or you put everything off until never, you might as well not even waste your time reading this section.

Free Food

There's better ways than eating out the trash, you know. And I don't mean going to the local soup kitchen for a free meal. Of course, there's scams like dining at a restaurant only to slip out before the check, or slipping some hair, a bug, or a piece of glass in your food so you won't even be asked to pay. But there's also free food available at the kind of meetings they hold in hotels. Many places like Dunkin Donuts will also give you their unsold food at the end of the day, if you are nice to the people working there. After all, places selling fresh-baked bread can't sell old food. If all else fails, hit a mall and eat every free sample you can get.

Free Education

You can start out at the library and build your whole world from there. I'm not exaggerating. I know people who were homeless, hanging out at the public library all day. The next time I saw them, they had started some sort of business with their knowledge. It's not impossible. Also, there are programs, organizations, and community colleges that won't cost you a dime to attend. Kantis Williams, the author of *Playing Your AGame*, talks about how he was able to get 3 college degrees without ever paying a dime. If you put in your work, you can even go to Harvard for free. If all else fails, you can attend the cultural events in your city, which are usually a good source of helpful knowledge.

Free Housing

I know a couple of people who have squatted in empty houses and buildings for months at a time. It's usually not very safe, but neither is sleeping on a bench. Some abandoned buildings still have running water and electricity, so you may be doing okay for a while. You can also hang out in places like the airport for a night or two. If all else fails, you could always hook up with a fat girl with her own spot. At least you'll be warm.

Free Money

There's scholarships, grants, stipends, and loans available for all kinds of things. Matthew Lesko even has a *Free Money* series of books. If you're not gifted enough to figure out how to get THAT kind of money, there's other ways beside hustling and crime. As my brother Justice recalled about his experience in high school:

> I learned that it was easier to ask four people for a quarter – and get it – than to ask one person for a dollar. A quarter is nothing. But it adds up. So every day, I'd work up a dollar and gamble in back of the school during lunch. Most of the time, I'd come to school with nothing and leave with $20. I didn't risk anything because it wasn't even my money. And when I won, I could pay everyone back, which made them feel good about lending me money.

Free Entertainment

I'm not talking about sneaking into concerts and movie theaters, though I think we've all done something like that before. There are dozens of free events happening in your city every week. And chances are that you can broaden your horizons by being there. If you like rap, hit a spoken word event instead of a concert. If you like lookin at women, hit a fashion show instead of the strip club. If all else fails, go to the park and attend a stranger's family reunion.

Free Miscellaneous

I could tell you how to get free gas, free electronics, free clothes, free studio sessions, free groceries, free pets, and free condoms, but if I have to tell you, that's probably the reason why you don't have sh*t now. If you want something out of life, you got to do some leg work. Get off your ass and go get it. If you don't know where to get it, learn how to ask the right questions and find out how and where to get it.

Nothing worth having is free. But putting in the right amount of thought, time, and work will save you from spending money.

GUERILLA WARFARE

The Vietnam War is one of the few military conflicts in which the U.S., with its superior military, has lost. The war began with the revolutionary Communist forces of North Vietnam attempting a takeover of U.S.-supported South Vietnam. This conflict, lasting from 1959 to April 30, 1975, concluded with the victory of the North Vietnamese military after more than 15 years. How did a poor, mostly "jungle" army of soldiers, common people, and teenagers, defeat the United States military?

There were several factors involved: Strategy, Involvement, Weaponry, and Intelligence. The common thread of all these elements was resourcefulness. The Vietnamese were not rich, nor were they heavily trained. They didn't have missiles and rockets, and some fighters didn't even have guns. But through resourcefulness, they were able to overcome all odds.

Strategy

To begin, war was to be waged on all fronts: diplomatic, ideological, organizational, economic and military. The strategic basis for revolution was known as Dau Tranh. Dau Tranh was divided into military and political spheres:

Political Dau Tranh

Dan Van: Action among your people: This element involved the Viet Cong motivating and educating their old soldiers for the fight, as well as the common people, whose participation and support they would need

Binh Van: Action among enemy military: This element involved the Viet Cong working to discourage enemy soldiers and lower their morale and desire to fight. They were able to make many enemy soldiers leave their armies, some of whom even joined the Viet Cong.

Dich Van: Action among enemy's people: This element involved an effort to sow discontent, defeatism, dissent and disloyalty among the enemy's population. Part of this involved the Viet Cong bringing in reporters to show the media the terrible atrocities of the Vietnam War. When Americans at home saw this bloodshed and violence, millions stopped supporting the war and protesting.

Military Dau Tranh

These phases could overlap and coexist.

Preparation (organization and propaganda phase)

Guerrilla warfare (small groups with small arms doing big things with little money)

General offensive (conventional war phase involving tanks, etc.)

As part of the final stage, emphasis was placed on the Khoi Nghia, or "General Uprising" of the masses, joining with the liberation forces. This uprising of the masses would sweep away the imperialists and their puppets who would already be sorely weakened by earlier guerrilla and mobile warfare.

The Viet Cong employed extensive ground warfare. In previous wars, the U.S. military had marched and attacked in large formations. In Vietnam, soldiers were faced with a new kind of fight. The Viet Cong attacked enemy soldiers in small battles, many of them surprise attacks in the jungle. This was known as guerilla warfare (guerilla being Spanish for "small war"). In guerilla warfare, the Vietnamese knew their terrain better than the foreign soldiers, and these used this knowledge to their advantage.

The Viet Cong also fought many battles "hugging" their enemies, or fighting so close to enemy troops that American planes avoiding dropping bombs for fear of killing their own.

Even in retreat, the Viet Cong employed many effective strategies:

Fragmenting (splitting up into small groups)

Dispersing (leaving when discovered, sometimes dropping packs to delay enemy forces who stop to inspect them)

Hiding (within underground tunnels and bases or hidden camps in the jungles)

Deceiving (using decoy attacks to misdirect the attention of enemy forces)

Delaying (rear units turning on enemies to fight while others escaped)

The Viet Cong also created extremely complex and intricate tunnel systems over vast regions of South Vietnam. The tunnel system was built over 25 years, beginning in the 1940s. The tunnels allowed the Viet Cong to invisibly control a large rural area. The tunnels were an underground city with living areas, kitchens, storage, weapon factories, hospitals, and command centers. Sometimes, they were several stories deep and could house up to 10,000 people. These people lived underground for years. They had wedding ceremonies underground, as well as giving birth and going to school. Essentially, the only time they came out is at night to tend their crops.

For the troops, these tunnels were fighting bases, capable of providing continuous support. The bases were well hidden from American spotter planes, and in the remote swamps and forests there were fewer problems.

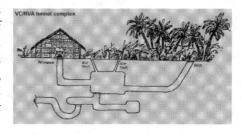

The planning and construction of these tunnels took an incredible amount of thought and effort. People dug into the hard clay with hand tools. Each villager in the region had to dig three feet of tunnel a day. There was even a handbook that specified how tunnels were to be built. They installed vents in order to hear approaching helicopters. Smaller vents were used for air. Of course, there are also many hidden trap doors and bamboo-stake booby traps.

Cu Chi, only one of the largest tunnel systems, is a massive network, with almost two hundred miles of tunnels. Various hidden trapdoors lead below the Earth's surface, past guarded chambers, to long passages. Tunnels branched off in some areas to lead back to the surface or to other secret entrances. Some entrances were even masked beneath a stream. The tunnels not only allowed guerrilla communication, but they allowed surprise attacks, even within the U.S. military bases. In response, the U.S. bombed much of the region.

Involvement

Successful guerilla warfare requires the involvement of all segments of the population. In addition to the troops of formally trained professional soldiers, the Viet Cong also trained local guerrilla units. The guerilla units were responsible for surprise attacks, ambushes, and jungle warfare. Wealthy people and business owners provided supplies and money, sometimes secretly. Farmers and peasants also were involved, and contributed however they could, whether by providing food, supplies, or intelligence. Even local women, many of them prostitutes became part of the wartime efforts. These courageous prostitutes offered themselves to the men of invading enemy troops so they would not rape the innocent women and children of the villages.

At first, local guerrillas were given only a basic minimum of military training, but they often received advanced training as they progressed. There were dozens of hidden centers – many of them underground – all over South Vietnam for leadership training, weapons training, and communications training. To make sure that the guerrillas understood why they were fighting, all training courses included political instruction.

In addition to this training, other strategies were used to develop all those involved:

Three-Man Cells: All soldiers were grouped into three-man cells. These allowed for mutual support and assistance among soldiers, as well as monitoring. By creating strongly-linked groups of three, the Viet Cong discouraged their soldiers from defecting or betraying their unit.

Criticism and Self-Criticism: "Criticism and self-criticism" sessions were conducted on a daily basis to improve discipline, control and cohesion. Individuals had to confess to their own faults or errors, as well as weak or incorrect thoughts. Leaders critiqued individual soldiers, who in turn were critiqued by their comrades. A soldier had to admit to his faults and weaknesses in order to grow.

Weaponry

By the mid-1960s, most main force Viet Cong troops were armed with Chinese AK-47 rifles. Since mortars were cheaper than large guns, they were used extensively. The Viet Cong also used a range of effective Soviet and Chinese light and medium machine guns, and occasionally heavy machine guns. As the heavier guns were rare, Viet Cong learned how to disable American helicopters with rifles by shooting at the blade rotors.

Local forces designed primitive weapons that were often extremely dangerous, such as "punji traps." Punji traps were small pits dug into the ground. The floor of this trap is covered with punji stakes, which can easily pierce the sole of a leather boot. These spikes were coated in animal feces to cause infection and blood poisoning.

The swinging man pit was heavily camouflaged and located on jungle trails. It had a weight beam pivoted so that when the pressure plate is pushed down, the other spiked end swung upwards. This force then plunged the spike into the victim's chest, ensuring a messy, fatal wound.

Trip wires were commonly used by guerrillas to delay the enemy, assist in ambushes, or set off other traps. The bamboo whip was set off by a trip wire. It was a shoot of bamboo under tension, and set with poisoned spikes positioned chest-high.

Another weapon set off by the trip wire was the spiked ball. The trip wire released a heavy mud ball set with spikes. The combined height of the release and the force of gravity cause severe wounds, usually in the head and shoulder area.

Many weapons, including booby traps and mines, were homemade in villages. The materials ranged from scavenged tin cans to discarded wire, but the most important ingredients were provided by the enemy, in the form of dud American bombs and shells scattered around the Vietnamese countryside. After the air-raids, local volunteers retrieved the duds and began creating new weapons.

Some traps used artillery shells and bullet cartridges, such as the 12.7mm machine gun bullet. It was set in a bamboo shoot in long grass, with its primer resting on a nail. The tip of the bullet barely protrudes from the earth. As a foot presses down, the device is set off. The bullet explodes to shatter the enemy's foot.

The resourceful Viet Cong also created explosive booby traps, made from powder-filled coconuts, mud balls, grenades in tin cans, and old bicycles.

Intelligence

The Viet Cong also used resourceful means of gathering intelligence on the enemy. Some examples include:

- A bicycle repairman on the road that reported on military traffic

- A farmer counting the number and type of aircraft that landed and took off on the airstrip near his fields

- A peasant woman outside her hut reporting on the size and composition of enemy troops by pre-arranged signal, when they approached.

How did the Viet Cong involve everyone in the community? Why didn't they reject some people as useless or unimportant? Why didn't they stick to only other poor people?

How did the Viet Cong use what little they had, and make the most of it? How can we do the same in our daily lives and hustles for success?

What strategies did the Viet Cong use that other armies, like that of the U.S., did not? How did this help them?

The most successful are the most resourceful. Your survival depends on how well you can use what you have to do what you must.

DETERMINED IDEAS

According to the Honorable Elijah Muhammad, the white race was produced as the result of a system of selective breeding carried out by Black people. The Black people, he taught, were under the direction of a Black scientist named Yacub.

In short, the story of Yacub begins over 6,000 years ago near the holy city of Mecca. Yacub was born into a society where 30% of the people were dissatisfied with the leadership of Mecca. Even among these people, who were all Black and Brown, there was internal strife, conflict, and tension.

Upon adulthood, Yacub seized the opportunity to rally up the dissatisfied segments of the society and have them follow him. He taught that he would bring about a new society, even a new world. He spoke out against the king, and promised changed. Thousands of people joined him. The king told Yacub he could not continue this kind of teaching in or near Mecca, but that he would allow Yacub to have control of a small island in the Aegean Sea.

Yacub took with him nearly 60,000 of his followers and began setting up his new society according to the strictest of rules and regulations. Yacub regimented a system of birth control and eugenics which was meant to produce a new kind of people, a people that had never been seen before. On his island, Yacub only allowed marriages between people whose blood tests indicated that they could produce lighter children. Any others were rejected and told that their blood tests said they were not compatible.

He mandated that the married couples produce children in rapid succession, but that only the lighter-complexioned babies were kept. All the darker babies would be killed by a pin in the head or by being abandoned in the woods. The mothers of the aborted babies were told lies and made to believe that the children had gone off to a heaven in the sky, where they were happily waiting.

Yacub didn't build prison houses for his people. Should anyone of Yacub's followers disobey his commands, or reveal the secret of what was happening, the penalty was death. Naturally, everyone complied for fear of the consequences.

Then one day, Yacub himself passed away. But his followers had been trained so well, and indoctrinated so fully into Yacub's teaching, that they continued without his direction. After following this process of selective breeding for 48 generations, over 600 years, Yacub's followers finally produced a generation of people with white skin and blue eyes, which are completely recessive traits.

According to Elijah Muhammad, Yacub's plan has continued for over 6,000 years of the white man's rule over the planet. In fact, looking at history, you can see that white people have used the same methods and techniques everywhere they've gone.

Well, what about you? How far into the future can you plan?

Are you where you planned to be five years ago? Did you even have a plan five years ago? Do you have one now? How detailed is it?

How many factors have you taken into consideration? Is it a pipe dream or a fantasy? Or is it realistic, allowing for the chances that things can – and will – go wrong (quite often)?

As they say, people don't plan to fail – they fail to plan. If you haven't done so already, come up with a five year plan for yourself. Write it down. Check back on it regularly and see how you're doing. If your plan is strong enough, you won't even need to check it after a while…it will simply be flowing smoothly.

A strong plan can continue without the planner.

WHO YOU WITH?

There are three main types of relationships between living things in nature. They are commensal, symbiotic, or parasitic. Keeping in mind that human beings are living things operating by the laws of nature, it makes sense that these same relationships occur between us.

Commensal Relationships (benefit/nothing):

One example of a commensal relationship in nature is the small pea crab living inside a mussel. The pea crab receives shelter and food, while the mussel merely tolerates its presence.

Another example is the small pea-brained girlfriend who lives inside your house, but doesn't pay any bills. She receives shelter and food, while the muscle-headed man (you) only gets sex, which doesn't really pay any bills.

Symbiotic Relationships (benefit/benefit):

The sea anemone where Nemo's family lived demonstrates an example of this relationship. In exchange for the benefits an anemone receives from the cleaning activities of clownfish and tiny cleaner shrimp, the sea anemone provides a home for these creatures instead of stinging them with its tentacles.

Skin parasites can be terrible for fish. On coral reefs, large fish line up at familiar "cleaning stations," spread their fins and open their mouths. The resident cleaner wrasse, a tiny fish that feeds on small parasites and dead tissue, diligently picks off the above, and gets a good meal in exchange for its service.

I hate washing dishes. I know that when I cook, if I invite over my brother True Master to eat, he'll wash the dishes. He gets to eat good, I get my dishes washed.

Parasitic Relationships (benefit/harm):

For example, the crustacean Sacculina spreads funguslike strands throughout its host crab's body to extract nutrients, weakening or eventually killing the host crab.

My partner Marcus was in a relationship with a real needy chick named Deborah. Deborah sat at home all day eating chips and ice cream and sh*t, watching cable. When Marcus came home from work, Deborah didn't cook him sh*t or rub his back – she complained. She was depressed and miserable, and couldn't help but make him miserable too. Eventually, her negativity brought him down and he was miserable every day too. He never put her out though, because he was stuck. It was probably the pussy. Anyway, I think he's dead now.

Look at your own relationships, whether with family, friends, girlfriends, business partners, etc. Which relationships are symbiotic? Good. Which ones are commensal? Well, depending on who is benefiting, that's not bad. Now...which ones are parasitic? Why are you still in those relationships?

If your relationships aren't healthy, find new relationships.

BLACK SKATEBOARDER

Stevie Williams grew up poor in a rough neighborhood in Philadelphia. While most of his peers were getting into hip hop and basketball, a young Stevie became interested in skateboarding. He got his first skateboard at 11 and it wasn't long before he was never seen outside without it. But a Black skateboarder wasn't the most common sight in the neigborhood where Stevie grew up. So, while he was picked on for "trying to be white" by many Black people, he and his friends were taunted by the whites at the local skate arena as "dirty ghetto kids." That didn't stop him, however.

At 15, Stevie Williams put all his chips in. He left home for San Francisco where other skateboarders were making it big. His goal was to use his impressive skills to gain sponsorship and recognition as a pro skateboarder. But instead, Stevie found himself homeless and sleeping on the streets. Though he often didn't even have food to eat, Stevie continued skating daily, and earning a strong reputation in the skating community.

Today, Stevie Williams is a professional skateboarder, with plenty of sponsors paying him for his talent. The biggest of those sponsors is Reebok, which entered into a multi-million dollar partnership with Stevie's company to produce clothing and footwear. The name of the company? Dirty Ghetto Kids.

"We got called dirty ghetto kids," Williams told the press. "So I thought: 'OK, let's show you what Dirty Ghetto Kids can do.' And now those same people who were laughing and calling me that, they see the name because it's so big you can't miss it."

Williams, the first professional skateboarder on Reebok's roster, went against the grain and went out on a limb to pursue his dream:

> I wanted to be my own (man)...So I did it...I have put my life on the line for this. I jumped right in the flame and it was hot. I go back to San

---

271

Francisco sometimes and I'll be riding round in my car and think: "I used to sleep on that bench."

So what does a Black skateboarder have to do with you? Everything. Stevie's story isn't just a story of success by following an unconventional path. Stevie's story does highlight his success, but to fully understand it, you have to think about what became of the other people in his story. Specifically, what happened to most of the people who laughed at Stevie when he was pursuing his dream? What did the people who discouraged him do with their lives? If you've ever lived in the ghetto, you know the most likely answer, because the ghetto doesn't have a very high success rate.

Stevie's story reminds us that we often must venture off on our own, and go against the grain, in order to find our calling and achieve success. At other times, we must be the only man in the crowd to do what is right, or say what must be said. And in other moments, we will simply have to fight alone, because everyone has deserted us or turned against us. *In an inhuman environment, you owe it to yourself to be your own man.*

> "Do not separate yourself from the community.
> In a place where no one behaves like a human being, you must strive to be human."
> Rabbi Hillel

It's hard though. Many of us can't accomplish something that sounds so simple. The strength of the crowd is like a tidal current, and we get swept up in and swallowed alive. Not knowing what it is to be our own man, we either venture off and forget our roots, or we stand still and forget ourselves. As T.I. rapped on "Prayin for Help":

> So many niggas done left out of the hood/ Instead of givin back, they stayed for theyself/ So many playin theyself/ Instead of readin, educatin they self

It's unfortunate, but it's true that most people just can't do what is right for themselves. In a crowd of 100, only 5 can truly be their own man. I hope you're one of the five.

What dreams and ideas have you dismissed because of other people's opinions?

How many times have you let other people convince you not to pursue something you were interested in?

Do you worry about what other people will think, before you think about what you want for yourself?

Be your own man.
Allowing others to decide your life's path is a sure way to failure.

OUTCASTS

"Humanity's most valuable assets have been the non-conformists. Were it not for the non-conformists, he who refuses to be satisfied to go along with the continuance of things as they are, and insists upon attempting to find new ways of bettering things, the world would have known little progress, indeed."
Josiah William Gitt

The Black Untouchables of India

Over 3,000 years ago, India was a Black civilization. In fact, the ancient Greek historians called India "eastern Ethiopia" because the people there looked exactly the same as the Black people of the Ethiopia in Africa. The Black people of India built an amazing civilization, complete with paved roads, flushing toilets, and a working sewage system.

They also lived in peace...that is, until 1500 BC, when white invaders calling themselves Aryans came in and took over by force. They destroyed the towns, murdered the warriors, and raped the women and children. Once they had control of India, they set up a new society and a new religion...both by their rules.

They created something called a caste system based on skin color. According to this system, known as the *varna* system ("varna" meaning color), the white Aryans put themselves on top as "Brahmins" (the priest caste), and put the other people underneath them. The people born of rape had brown complexions, and were higher up than the darkest people, who were at the bottom as "Sudras" (the slave caste).

But there was another group of people in Indian society. These people weren't even included in the caste system. These were the people who refused to be a part of the new system, and continued to fight against the Aryans. Or they ran off into the jungles to live free like the Maroons would do during American slavery. These people were left out of the caste system and treated like outcasts. They were murdered, beaten, raped, and robbed, not only by the Brahmins, but by the other castes as well.

"No one can make you feel inferior without your consent."
Anna Eleanor Roosevelt (1884-1962)

The caste system remains in place in India today. The outcasts of the caste system are still there as well. These Black people are probably darker than anyone reading this

> **Did You Know?**
> India used to be the wealthiest country in the world until the British invasion in the early 17th Century.

book, and they have probably experienced more racism than most of us as well. They have chosen to stick together and continue to fight. In India, they were called the "Untouchables," because they were considered too impure to touch or be around. But they call themselves Dalits, meaning "unbroken," because their spirits are unbroken. The

Dalit are considered the largest Black community in the world outside of Africa. To this day, they continue to be treated as badly as Blacks in America in the 1950s. If another Indian was to kill a Dalit, they'd probably get away with it easily! It's that bad for them. But the Dalit refuse to blend into a corrupt system that wasn't designed for them. Like the Maroons, they refused to be a part of some bullsh*t.

Would you be willing to suffer and sacrifice, just to stick to your values and what you know is right?

Would you join the Dalits or the Maroons, or would you rather try to "get in where you fit in"?

Jim Jones and the Suicide Cult

The original Jim Jones started out as a preacher in Indiana in the 1950s. He built a following by manipulating followers to believe anything and everything he told them. He claimed to be an incarnation of Jesus, Akhenaton, Buddha, Lenin, and Father Divine and performed bogus "miracle healings" to attract new members. Thousands of Blacks and whites joined the white preacher's racially integrated church, the Peoples Temple. They called Jones "Father" and believed that their movement – and Jim Jones himself – represented the solution to the problems of society.

In 1977, Jones and almost 1,000 members of the Peoples Temple moved to the jungles of Guyana after the IRS began investigating the church for tax evasion. Once Jones and the others moved to their Jonestown settlement, former members finally began to come forward. Until then, they had lived in fear of leaving the cult. Jones had made them give away their belongings and cut off all contact with their families and friends, leaving them nothing to return to if they left.

But some could take it no longer. They fled and told authorities about the brutal beatings they endured or witnessed, as well as a mass suicide plan. However, since most of Jones' followers were Black and poor, no one believed them.

On November 18, 1978, *it happened.*

913 of the inhabitants of Jonestown (including 276 children) died in a mass suicide, ordered by cult leader Jim Jones. Some followers obeyed Jones' instructions and drank cyanide-laced grape Flavor Aid. Others were injected with cyanide or shot to death. Jones himself was found dead sitting in a deck chair with a gunshot wound to his head. Only a few survivors lived to tell the tale.

What would you have done? Would you have left or would you have been too worried about being ridiculed for leaving?

Why is it so easy to be followers, but so rare that we think for ourselves?

Being left out of something isn't always a bad thing.

TROUBLEMAKERS

There was an island where a group of people was creating havoc. The king of the island rounded them all up and said, "What is your problem? Why don't you want to follow the laws that have been set?"

They replied, "We just want to do our own thing!"

The king then said, "You can do your own thing, but you just can't do it here. So I'll provide you with what you need and you can do what you wish on that island over there."

So they set out in their boat with their provisions. Halfway through the trip through the ocean, one man stood up and took out an awl from his pocket and began digging into the bottom of the boat. The others looked at him for a moment and then paid him no mind...until the boat started taking on water. They all screamed at the man, "You're going to sink the boat! What the hell are you doing?!" The man looked up from his work and replied, "I'm just doing my own thing...I'm doing me."

Needless to say, they threw him overboard![11]

You can't always do as you please, nor can you let others do whatever they want in your company.

THEY DON'T WANT YOU

> "It's all about the real nigga, I keeps it real, nigga
> And won't sell out for Girbaud or Tommy Hilfiger"
> Scarface, "Smartz"

Once popular '80s jeans designer François Girbaud made a small comeback in the last few years, but it was with the wrong kind of people.

The Black kind.

"Somewhere, the company was running too much in some direction, too much in hip-hop stuff," Mr. Girbaud, 62, told Transom radio. He was wearing a black-collared shirt over baggy black jeans, which were adorned with a single drooping silver chain that smacked against his knee as he walked and talked.

Girbaud complained:

> To be just connected in the hip-hop stuff is other brand; there is people like Russell Simmons or Damon Dash or Puff Daddy or all this kind. I'm not the rap people. Sure, we introduced the baggy jeans, we introduced stonewashed and all this stuff in the 60's or 70's, I never target just to be ethnic. It's stupid.

NOW

WWW.HUSTLEANDWIN.COM

THEN

"BRAND NAMES"

But Girbaud didn't stop there; he claimed he walks "through projects today" and all he sees are "the same five-pocket jeans." He went further: "I have to talk like that"- he flashed a gang hand-sign – "and speak like that" – he flashed another gang hand-sign – "and move like that" – he grabbed his crotch – "and it's ridiculous!" Yeah right. I guess if you ever see an old-ass old white man walking through the projects in some Girbauds, it may be Francois himself. Whoop his racist ass.

This attack came just weeks after we learned how the people at Cristal champagne feel about their new Black buyers. Asked by a magazine if the association between Cristal and the "bling lifestyle" could be detrimental, Cristal's director Rouzaud replied: "That's a good question, but what can we do? We can't forbid people from buying it. I'm sure Dom Perignon or Krug would be delighted to have their business." **Translation: "F*ck off, niggers!"**

They Don't Want Your Business!

Non-Urban Dictate. Three words that basically mean a company is not interested in the Black Consumer. An NUD label means that a company does not want their marketing and advertising materials placed in media that claim an urban (meaning Black) audience as their main target.

Starbucks	America West Airlines	Mondavi Wines
Jos. A Bank	HBO – Apollo Series	
CompUSA	Paternal Importers	Builders Square
Weight Watchers	Calico Corners	Don Pablo
Keebler	OMScot	Lexus
Life Savers	Pepperidge Farms	Aruba Tourism
Continental Airlines	Ethan Allen	Ciba Vision
Northwest Airlines	Busy Body Fitness	Kindercare

Grady Restaurant   Eddie Bauer

Jay-Z as we know, led a pretty successful Cristal boycott in the Black community. A lot of hip hop clubs no longer stock Cristal, and now offer Dom Perignon and Krug instead. The last time someone sent over a bottle of Cris to Jay, he poured it on the floor of the VIP.

But how do you know Dom Perignon likes Black people? How many dollars do you think they put back into the Black community? When is the last time ANY of the brands which seem to LOVE Black people (Lincoln, Chevy, Coca-Cola, etc.) PROVED it? The truth is, these brands don't care about you any more than the brands with NUDs. They just need your money and they know it.

Like a politician who relies on the Black vote to get elected, Lincoln isn't selling cars in the white community. White people don't buy their sh*t any more. But Black people do. So now their ads have hip-hop music, and brag about "all the chrome" they added to their trucks.

I'm not saying that we should make all of our clothes and ride homemade skateboards to work. I'm the last person to say something like that. I drive a Mercedez-Benz, but I don't brag about it. I don't wear Benz t-shirts and look for new ways to celebrate the f*cking Benz company. And I damn sure didn't pay full price for my car. All I'm saying is that we need to stop suckin these companies's dicks, especially if they spend most of that time pissin on us anyway.

I think we should hold the companies we support to a higher standard. Make them support charities and fundraisers in the hood. Make companies like Evisu spend money to help the Black community, while putting companies like Girbaud and Cristal damn near out of business. We did it with Hilfiger, didn't we?

If wearing $200 "Dirty Nigger" wristbands was the hottest new style, would you jump on the bandwagon and wear three at a time?

How hard is it for you to avoid following trends?

What will it take for us to think harder about how and where we spend our money?

Stop trying to be accepted where you're not wanted, and buying into what isn't for you.

REVIEW

The principle for this chapter was **Create a Culture of Success**: Transform a strong vision into a strong lifestyle and long-term agenda.

Here are the principles and lessons we covered in this chapter:

Change

Break the cycles of self-destruction, or be broken by them.

Don't live with regrets. The best time is now.

History repeats itself, but we have to renew it, not repeat it.
You'd be a fool to keep doing it the way it's already been done.

It's difficult, but not impossible,
for a man to break free of a cycle he begins at an early age.

There is always another way.
Even when the circumstances appear to offer you no choice, you have a choice.

Collectivity

We must only "pledge allegiance" to those who will fight with us and for us.

You can't always "do your own thing,"
nor should you let others do whatever they want in your company.

You're all in the same slaveship. Instead of worrying about the man next to you,
worry about who is on top of both of you.

Consistency

A strong plan can continue without the planner.

Be careful of how easily a reputation develops.
Whatever you do once, you'll be expected to do again.

Direction

Be your own man. Allowing others to decide your life's path is a sure way to failure.

Life is never hopeless. Even the worst environments can produce the best
people, so long as they are strong enough to make it out.

Discipline

All decisions have long-term consequences.
Think long-term more than you think short-term.

Cultivate yourself or be cultivated. If you can't train yourself, you'll never be in charge.

Instead of destroying yourself, destroy what's destroying you.

Real love takes time...and a lot of trial and error.
If you're not ready, don't play with it.

The greatest struggle is within. Eliminating your bad habits may be
the hardest thing you do, but it is certainly one of the most important.

Independence

Being left out of something isn't always a bad thing.

Stop trying to be accepted where you're not wanted, and buying into what isn't for you.

Inflence

Religion is a drug for the poor and weak. The powerful use it to keep things the
way they are. We must be more realistic in finding solutions to our problems.

Be aware of your influences.
Like anything else, you can be poisoned by constant exposure.

Interaction

If your relationships aren't healthy, find new relationships.

Order

Know the laws; know your rights; know the system or be its victim.

Life is never hopeless. There are successful ways to handle any situation.

Some laws are guidelines for the best life, not rules for what you can't do.

Resourcefulness

Nothing worth having is free. But putting in the right amount of
thought, time, and work will save you from spending money.

The most successful are the most resourceful. Your survival depends on
how well you can use what you have to do what you must.

Guns and Ammo

IDENTIFY YOUR STRENGTHS

"The strongest people in the world aren't the most protected; they are the ones that must struggle against adversity and obstacles — and surmount them — to survive."

Without the aid of guns, knives, steroids, or a gang of thugs riding with you, you alone are infinitely strong. Within you there is the infinite potential for unprecedented greatness. As said before, the decision is up to you to act on that potential or let it wither away and die within you. All of us were born great, but few of us live great.

What are your strengths?

It may be these strengths and talents that one day propel you to greatness. Then again, there may be some undiscovered part of you that will only emerge when you are ready to see it and develop it.

But the conditions we live in give us an overwhelming feeling of powerlessness. We see life as a series of problems rather than opportunities, and because we are tired of struggling, many of us quit halfway through.

Out of these feelings of powerlessness and hopelessness, we develop other emotions, attitudes, and behaviors that further our self-destruction. We show our immense frustration with our oppression when we fight and act out, when we escape into the highs of various drugs, when we zone out completely and give up on being successful.

But in doing so, we reinforce our powerlessness even further.

Instead, we can reverse the cycle by denying our fears and cultivating the infinite power within us.

QUIZ FIVE: INFLUENCES AND AWARENESS

1. What percentage of network news about Black people is negative in tone?
   a) 8%
   b) 60%
   c) 50%
   d) 25%

2. How many poor Black families and poor white families are there in America?
   a) 5 million black families, over 2 million white families
   b) 3 million black families, 3 million white families
   c) Over 2 million white families, 5 million black families
   d) 4 million black families, 5 million white families

3. What is the best predictor for whether a student will score well on the SAT?
   a) Family income
   b) Gender
   c) Race
   d) Private school attendance

4. How much money does a full-time worker making minimum wage make compared to the poverty line for a family of three?
   a) $2,000 more than the poverty level
   b) $500 more than the poverty level
   c) $2,000 less than the poverty level
   d) $500 less than the poverty level

5. What are the median net financial assets per Black family (net worth minus car and home equity)?
   a) $0
   b) $7,000
   c) $36,000
   d) $145,000

6. What are the chances of a Black high school basketball player making the NBA?
   a) Over 24,000 to 1
   b) Over 7,600 to 1
   c) Over 2,400 to 1
   d) Over 760 to 1

7. What are the chances of a Black college senior on the basketball team making the NBA?
   a) 1,500 to 1
   b) 150 to 1
   c) 15 to 1
   d) 1.5 to 1

8. How much prison time do Blacks receive for drug and weapons violations, compared to whites convicted of the same crime?
   a) The same amount of time
   b) 5% less time
   c) 5% more time
   d) 50% more time

9. What percentage of America's drug users are Black, and what percentage are white?
   a) 50% Black, 35% white
   b) 25% Black, 50% white
   c) 12% Black, 50% white
   d) 12% Black, 70% white

10. In terms of drug usage, from ages 12 to 34...
    a) Blacks and whites are equally likely to have tried drugs
    b) Blacks are four times as likely to have tried drugs as whites

c) Blacks are less likely than whites to have taken drugs

d) Blacks are twice as likely as whites

11. Asia has the largest population (3,879,000,000 people). Europe has 727,000,000. North America: 501,500,000. What is the human population of Africa?
   a) 204,500,000
   b) 379,500,000
   c) 32,000,000
   d) 877,500,000

12. What percentage of the world population is white?
   a) 15%
   b) 28%
   c) 42%
   d) 73%

13. What percentage of the world population is *not* Christian?
   a) 82%
   b) 70%
   c) 45%
   d) 23%

14. What was the total spending power of Blacks in America in 2006?
   a) $100 million
   b) $500 million
   c) $5 billion
   d) $800 billion

15. How much of the above amount stays in the Black community, or is spent with Black-owned business?
   a) 5%
   b) 15%
   c) 50%

d) 85%

16. What percent of white Americans have at least one Black ancestor?
   a) 5%
   b) 30%
   c) 50%
   d) 19%

17. In 1997, what percent of voting-age Black men could not vote because they were in prison or because they have been convicted of a felony?
   a) 1% or 104,000 Black men
   b) 3% or 312,000 Black men
   c) 14% or 1,460,000 Black men
   d) 50% or 5,200,000 Black men

18. What region of the U.S. has the highest concentration of Black residents?
   a) The Northeast
   b) The Midwest
   c) The Southwest
   d) The Southeast

19. What percent of the population of Washington D.C., our nation's capital, is Black?
   a) 10%
   b) 25%
   c) 43%
   d) 60%

20. How many tigers are there in Africa?
   a) 3,500
   b) 480
   c) 0
   d) over 1 million

Answers

1. B	4. C	7. C	10. C	13. B	16. B	19. D
2. C	5. A	8. D	11. D	14. D	17. C	20. C[12]
3. A	6. B	9. D	12. A	15. A	18. D	

0-4 Correct: Damn! I'm not saying damn, you're stupid, because I'm sure you're not. If you've made it this far in the book, you can't be stupid. Assuming, of course, that you're actually reading it and not just flipping around. I'm saying damn because your score lets you know how much you've been "lied to, hoodwinked, bamboozled, and led astray," as Malcolm would say. Damn, ain't it crazy?

5-10 Correct: Good job! I'm impressed. If this were a test, you'd have an F, but in a world so full of lies, you're actually doing better than most people. I read somewhere that one-third of Americans (of all races) can't identify where America is on a map. So if you can get 7 or 8 questions right on a quiz like this, I think you're ahead of the pack. Now keep learning and researching.

11-17 Correct: Great! You're an inspiration. I'm pretty damn sure you have to be an intelligent person to know this much, especially since this information is not taught in schools. Either that, or you're a hell of a good guesser. Either way, more power to you. You're on the right track, one way or the other.

18-20 Correct: Wow. Wow is right. Either you're a well-read and highly-informed super-genius...or you're a pathological liar. I'm gonna go with liar. I mean c'mon now, I spent hours researching some of these questions, and I have a damn doctoral degree. You mean to tell me you just "knew" all this? Who are you trying to prove something to? You frontin for a book? It's a damn shame when you can't even be honest with a damn inanimate object.

The Fifth Principle

"Identify Your Strengths" means:

Find your power within, in life, and in the world...and focus on developing it.

What You'll Learn

- What we can learn about manhood from killer ants, Tupac Shakur, and the real hustlers behind the movie, Paid in Full.

- How to understand your subconscious mind and its workings.

- Why we just don't seem to give a f*ck anymore.

- How our gangs began…and what has changed since then.
- Why rappers just aren't telling the truth anymore.
- When to "let it go"…and when to "go hard."

AT LEAST SHOOT THE FENDER

It was a damp evening in November. Our U-Haul truck cruised down I-20 West, clattering and bouncing as Born Culture drove a little more carelessly than one should when you're at the helm of a huge truck. I didn't mind. I was feeling a good caffeine buzz, as I had just finished a huge cup of Mountain Dew from the Citgo.

Some of my brothers had finally persuaded me to move in with them, ending a year-long period of my homelessness. During that time, I had lived out of two trash bags while most of my belongings remained in a storage unit. I didn't have my license yet, so Born Culture was driving the truck back to the storage unit so we could get my furniture.

At some point, Born swerved and cut off a car. I didn't notice until I heard horns blaring at us from behind and then to our left. Born thought it was funny that they'd gotten so mad, so he swerved in front of them again. I laughed, not just because it was funny, but because Born Culture is usually a really meek, humble guy. Moments later, a late-model Chevy pulled up along side us and the dude in the passenger seat was going nuts. He was cursing up a storm, telling us he wasn't "no pussy nigga from the South."

"I'm from L.A.!," he screamed, "Real G's! We don't play that sh*t!"

I looked at Born Culture for a moment in disbelief. Then I took my 32 oz. cup, now only filled with ice, reached across Born Culture, and tossed the contents directly into dude's face while calling him a bitch. Almost every ice cube hit him dead in the face, and I think he swallowed his cigarette. It was pure comedy.

But then they pulled back up alongside us and now dude had a gun out. He was waving it at us wildly and now he was really talking some cash money sh*t. This time he was making some serious threats. All this while speeding along on a state highway. I could look at this guy and tell he wasn't serious. A real gangster wouldn't be talking anymore. I didn't have mine on me, but I felt safe dealing with this loser. I told Born Culture to lean back so that he was out of the line of fire and yelled out the window, "Pussy, if you was serious, you'da dumped by now!"

He screamed something else, still trying to play tough.

"But you got your gun out and you ain't gone do sh*t! You weak!"

Still no gunfire.

Pathetic. But he was still talking sh*t.

So I took my cup, with whatever little ice was left in it, and I chucked it at the Chevy, followed by the lid and straw. When the cup hit their windshield, the car swerved and they nearly lost control.

They got off at the next exit without saying another word.

If you're not a tough guy, aren't you better off not playing tough?

How embarrassing is it to get "outed" for who you really are, when you spend most of your time acting and pretending?

Why can't people be themselves?

Be yourself. Don't act tougher than you really are. Especially when you're only tough on your own people.

KILLER ANTS

The fan-shaped formation moves steadily forward like a monstrous black tide. It is nearly 15 feet wide and made up of at least 100,000 ants, working together as a single hunting unit. A big scorpion scuttles out from under a log with an ant, several thousand times smaller, clamped onto its leg. It frantically tries to shake off its attacker with aimed strikes of its stinger, but the ant hangs on. The ant grapples at the floor with hooked feet, and releases a chemical signal from a pair of special glands. Within seconds, hundreds respond to the call, and the scorpion soon vanishes below a seething throng of black ants. Within minutes, little trace of the once-mighty scorpion remains.

Like Black people lost in the wilderness of North America, the Siafu ants do not have a permanent home. African driver ants, or "Siafu" in Kiswahili, live in colonies, but unlike most ants, constantly remain in movement. Unlike North American ants, when they do form anthills, they are only temporary, lasting a few days up to three months. Each roaming Siafu colony can contain over 20 million individuals.

Like true warriors, the Saifu ants hunt at night, and hide in holes in the ground and in trees during the day. They shift locations regularly as the insect, rodent, and sometimes lizard prey is exhausted. In some areas, the Siafu hunt all night and day. Blind, they follow their other senses for guidance.

Like their North American counterparts, there is a soldier class among the worker ants. The soldier Siafu are larger, with a very large head and pincer-like jaws. Their jaws are so strong that the native Masai people of East Africa place them on broken skin to hold wounds together when there is a large cut or gash. These Siafu will hold on so strong with their terrible bite that you can pull them off by the body but the heads will remain attached.

In traveling from their lair to the hunting grounds, the Siafu form foot-wide highways of ants. The Siafu will also shift their formation into much wider fans when they are actively hunting. The marching Siafu's columns are arranged so that the smaller ants are flanked by the larger soldier ants on the outer edges of the column. The giant soldier Siafu stand on their back legs and take defensive positions along the path, allowing the weaker Siafu to run freely in the corridor in between.

> "When spider webs unite, they can tie up a lion."
> Ethiopian proverb

The long columns of marching ants will fiercely defend against anything that crosses their path. In fact, some people have seen Siafu form terrifying rolling balls as large as a basketball. These rolling balls of Siafu may have actually been small animals engulfed in thousands of attacking Siafu. People even claim that these fierce warriors will climb up inside the trunk of an elephant and bite it to attack, eventually overcoming it with millions of Siafu. Large animals and even people have been found dead, covered in Siafu, and being picked away to the bone. As long as you get out of their way, however, you are safe.

Siafu, although aggressive and painful, are not seen as a pest or a threat by the Masai. They know that if the Siafu swarm into your house or farm, they will eat all of the other ants, roaches, spiders, and everything else that slithers crawls or creeps, and then leave as they came. A colony of Siafu can eliminate as much as 2 million pests a day. For that reason, the Siafu are both fear, respected, and admired.

Why is it that ants can work together in ways that we cannot?

What could we accomplish if we put our personal differences aside to work together?

Alone we are weak, but together we are mighty.

TUPAC LIVES

With over seventy-five million albums sold to date, Tupac Shakur is the highest selling rap artist of all time. More importantly, however, Tupac was one of the realest rap artists of all time.

Tupac Amaru Shakur was born June 16, 1971 to mother Afeni Shakur just one month after her acquittal on more than 100 charges of "Conspiracy against the United States government and New York landmarks" in the New York Panther 21 court case. His stepfather Mutulu Shakur and godfather Geronimo Pratt were also established freedom fighters who later became political prisoners.

Tupac's first album, *2Pacalypse Now*, was loved by the Black community, but the American powers that be did not approve. Vice President Dan Quayle stated that Tupac's album had "no place in our society." What was Tupac doing wrong? He was reporting on the problems affecting the Black community. It was these problems that have no place in our society. But being the son of a Black Panther, one of his earliest songs being named "Panther Power," Tupac was on a watchlist very early in his career.

> "And the raps that I'm rappin to my community shouldn't be filled with rage?
> They shouldn't be filled with same atrocities that they gave me?
> The media they don't talk about it, so in my raps I have to talk about it,
> and it seems foreign because there's no one else talking about it."
> Tupac Shakur

In 1991, Tupac was brutally beaten by officers who accused him of jaywalking. He survived and filed a lawsuit against them. He won the suit and was awarded $42,000.

Following the controversy surrounding his second album, in October 1993, Tupac witnessed a Black man being harassed by two white men. He came to the brother's defense and was met with guns drawn on him. Tupac shot one in the leg, and one in the ass. It later turned out that they were off-duty police officers, they were drunk, and they had been threatening Tupac with a seized gun stolen from the evidence locker. When charges were dropped, Tupac became one of the few young Black men to have shot a police officer (two, actually) and not gone to jail. This made the second time he'd gone against the police and won.

Of course, the powers that be were determined to take Pac down by this time. Tupac kept pushing forward with his music. Tupac's reinvention of the word "Nigga" as Never Ignorant, Getting Goals Accomplished, was his introduction of the concept of "Thug Life." To Tupac, Thug Life stood for "The Hate You Gave Little Infants F*cks Everybody."

Tupac envisioned a *Thug Life* album series featuring songs by gang members and drug dealers trying to shed their street hustles to get into legitimate business making music. He declared that the dictionary definition of a "thug" as being a rogue or criminal was not how he used the term, but rather he meant someone who came from oppressive or squalid background and little opportunity but still made a life for themselves and were proud.

> "My music is not for everyone.
> It's only for the stong-willed, the [street] soldier's music.
> It's not like party music – I mean, you could gig to it, but it's spiritual.

My music is spiritual. It's like Negro spirituals,
except for the fact that I'm not saying 'We shall Overcome.'
I'm saying that we are overcome."
Tupac Shakur

In December of 1993, Pac was charged with sexually abusing a woman in his hotel room. Even though she had voluntarily given him oral sex on a club dance floor the night before, and had consentual sex with him earlier that night, when she returned, she blamed Tupac for rape. Pac was asleep when the woman came back (or was sent back?) and his crew allegedly forced themselves upon her.

After at least three more run-ins with the law, Tupac was robbed and shot five times – twice in the head – while with four other men in front of a recording studio in Manhattan. None of the other men were harmed. It was November 30, 1994, the day before the verdict on the sexual abuse case, and Tupac came into the courtroom in a wheelchair. Of course, he was found guilty of three counts of sexual abuse, including "sexual abuse (forcibly touching the buttocks)". In sentencing Shakur to one-and-a-half years in prison, the judge described the crime as "an act of brutal violence against a helpless woman." The police did little to investigate his shooting.

While in prison, Pac continued reading, writing, and building with other freedom fighters, stating that he had built with "every Five Percenter" in the prison. After this, Tupac began saying a lot more about the white "devils" who were making life so hard for the Black man.

After his release from prison, Pac began working for Suge Knight and recording with Death Row Records. Mostly as a result of Suge's comments, and hype from the American media, there developed significan't tension between Death Row and Bad Boy Entertainment. The media turned this conflict into an East Coast-West Coast beef, which was picked up and further escalated by young hotheads who didn't know better.

Tupac lived just long enough to record and oversee the production of his Don Kiluminati album. Pac issued the album under the name Makaveli, an homage to Niccolo Machiavelli, whose book "The Prince" he'd been reading heavily. Tupac was also able to oversee the design of his final album cover, which depicted him as a Black Jesus crucified on a cross. Some people say that the blurry emblem atop the cross is a small Universal Flag of the Nation of Gods and Earths (the Five Percenters).

"To me, I feel that my game is strong.
I feel as though I'm a shining prince, just like Malcolm,
and I feel that all of us are shining princes, and if we live like princes,
then whatever we want can be ours. Anything."
Tupac Shakur

On September 7th, 1996, Tupac left the Mike Tyson fight in Las Vegas riding in a convoy besides Suge Knight, who was driving. At about 11 pm, another vehicle pulled up beside theirs and unleashed a flurry of shots, several of which hit Tupac. While at the hospital, individuals working with Death Row began receiving calls that there were more shooters coming up to the hospital to finish the job. Pac's people called for police protection, but none was sent.

All the while, the media was hyping up the shooting as further escalation of the East-West War, as they called it now. The Notorious B.I.G was blamed, but denied any involvement. Shortly after the accusations, Biggie was murdered as well. Following these two deaths, a string of murders on both coasts ensued. Pac's close childhood friend and member of The Outlawz, Kadafi, was in the convoy when the shooting happened and indicated to police that he might be able to identify the assailants, but he was killed shortly thereafter in a housing project in Irvington, New Jersey. Fortunately, a full-fledged East-West War never materialized, no matter how much the American media wanted it to.

> "It always happens, all the niggas that change the world die.
> They don't get to die like regular people, they die violently."
> Tupac Shakur

To this day, over ten years later, little attempt has been made to solve the murder of Tupac Amaru Shakur and no suspects have been apprehended. Instead, the legacy of Tupac lives on. There are foundations promoting the ideas he believed in, college courses teaching about his life and his philosophy, books and movies documenting his impact, and hundreds of rappers who claim his influence. Tupac is most likely your favorite rapper's favorite rapper.

> "I expected to die. At no time before the trial did I expect to escape with my life.
> Yet being executed in the gas chamber did not necessarily mean defeat.
> It could be one more step to bring the community to a higher level of consciousness."
> Huey P. Newton

Michael Eric Dyson said he "spoke with brilliance and insight as someone who bears witness to the pain of those who would never have his platform. He told the truth, even as he struggled with the fragments of his identity." SUNY English professor Mark Anthony Neal argued that Shakur was an example of the "organic intellectual" expressing the concerns of a larger group. Neal also said that the death of Shakur left a "leadership void amongst hip-hop artists," describing Tupac as a "walking contradiction", a status that allowed him to "make being an intellectual accessible to ordinary people." In essence, Pac made it so gangstas and thugs could be intelligent and revolutionary.

Tupac is alive. Not in the physical sense, but in the sense of an idea that can't be killed. That idea is one that the government attempted to destroy since he first emerged on the scene. It took them several years and several attempts, but even after cutting him down just as he was reaching his prime, he lives on.

Tupac was killed at 25. If we'd lost Dr. King, Jesus, or even Barack Obama at 25, we'd have lost nobodies. Imagine what Tupac could have developed into by the time he was 30 or 35.

Now imagine what you could do.

You can't kill an idea.
As long as people continue to see it, a vision is indestructible.

YOUNG MONEY

Part I

Manager: Look guys, we called you in because the label heads don't like the new song.

Label A&R: You guys are going to have to save that for a mixtape or something. It's not going on the album.

Yung Murda: What's wrong with "It's a Trap"? Everybody said they really felt it.

Lil Baby: We need a song like that. It's bout how bad things are in the dope game, and in the ghetto period.

Manager: That's not you guys's sound! That's not what the fans want!

Label A&R: It's not what we had in mind for you guys. It's just not your image.

Manager: What about a "Grind that Pussy" Part Two? Or something like "Gone on that X" or "Got Mo Money Than You"? Those would all be hits! Classics!

Label A&R: The buying public wants party music. They don't want no KRS-One sh*t. They don't want no Public Enemy sh*t. All that sh*t is played out. Do you guys want to go broke?

Lil Baby: Man, we ain't tryin to be no Public Enemy. We ain't even preachin. We just tellin' it how it is. Every song can't be about cars and money and getting f*cked up!

Yung Murda: Sh*t, we ain't even really got all that sh*t! We waitin' on checks from y'all!

Label A&R: And you'll never have anything either, if you're making depressing music that no one can dance to.

Manager: Look guys, you know I'm like a father to you, and I wouldn't steer you wrong. You guys have an image, a reputation, you know? You gotta come off hard and flashy. That's what the people want. When's the last time you seen something like "It's a Trap" on 106th and Park?

Yung Murda: You're right.

Manager: Just go in that studio and record another hit. That's all the truth they need. When they see y'all doing good, pushing that new Lamborghini through the projects, they'll know they can make it too.

Label A&R: Listen to him. He's telling you the truth.

Lil Baby: Aight, but "It's a Trap" is goin on the mixtape.

Label A&R: Sure, whatever.

Part II

Look at the following list of rappers:

Hurricane Chris	Dem Franchize Boys	Soulja Boy
Shop Boyz	Crime Mobb	Young Hot Rod
Gucci Mane	Sean Kingston	D.G. Yola
Huey	Young Berg	Montana Da Mac
D4L	Bow Wow	Lil Retard

Okay, I made up the last guy, but here's the question: What do they all have in common?

First, the obvious: They've all put out hit singles in recent years. Millions of people have listened to them, or still are listening to them.

Second, they're all young and clueless, and have **nothing to say.**

I'm not saying that out of hate, I'm saying that out of straight up honesty and genuine concern. Almost of all of the new rappers coming out in the past few years have been under 25. Their songs and dances have caught fire across the nation, and you can't turn on the radio or BET and not catch the same 10 songs every few minutes.

The stupid part, I'll explain. It's not that I'm mad at young rappers for coming out and tryin to make money. I understand that a lot of these kids have been trying to make it big for a long time…maybe even 4 or 5 months! But whether or not they're one-hit wonders, people love them. And I'll admit it, the songs, or at least the beats and the hooks, are really catchy.

As far as the contents of the lyrics, most of them will tell you in a heartbeat that they don't really care about being considered "lyrical." They're just trying to make party music. Don't believe me? Watch BET. Count how many times you hear "in VIP" or "in the club." You might hear it in every song.

The thing you need to understand, though, is why they're so popular. You may not realize it, but the record labels are going crazy trying to push out these young artists one after the other. They don't do any artist development with them, so they don't care if they're one-hit wonders or not. The record labels know young people, Black and especially white, are going to go out and get the albums.

They also know that these young rappers aren't going to go against the grain, and say anything "controversial." They're just going to rap about cars, money, hoes, clothes, shows, and how tough they are. A rapper under the age of 25 who is rapping bout being in the streets probably has never done a serious jail-bid.

A young rapper from the ghetto usually hasn't matured enough to understand why things are so bad in the ghetto. They haven't grown up enough to want to say something about it. They don't feel responsible enough to care about helping anyone that's dealing with the same bullsh*t they grew up with. They don't know the power they have, and so they are powerless.

Then again, a lot of these kids come from good families (eg., Bow Wow), and were recording their first songs in studios that their daddies paid for (eg., Crime Mobb). That doesn't stop them from playing tough, in between their songs for the girls (eg., Sean Kingston). It's an image…actually, it's a formula. You buy into it, so they keep selling it.

But back to the labels and the people in power. By avoiding rappers who have something to say, the people in power know that they can keep young Black audiences asleep and dumb too. This generation is growing up without any awareness of how bad the struggle is, and how much fighting needs to be done. All we hear about is going hard for cars, money, clothes, and hoes…at any cost. And let's not forget that we keep hearing about how it's better to stay high and drunk.

The record label heads and the managers tell these young, impressionable rappers, "Don't say anything about white people" and "Just keep making party songs." And they do what they're told. It's a damn shame to be platinum at 21, and you're still a slave.

Part III

Just check out the way 16-year old Soulja Boy responded to some deep interview questions posed to three up-and-coming artists:

AllHiphop: What do you believe contributed to Hip-Hop swerving in this [negative] direction?
Red Café: There aren't any A&Rs. One party song and an album without any substance. We aren't selling the lifestyle anymore we are just selling the dance move. The artist has no identity, just one single.

Music is focusing all their energy and budget on one artist that has one record that they believe to be a hit. It might be a hit for the radio but it isn't doing anything for the culture or the artist in terms of longevity or revenue.

Soulja Boy: *No comment.*

Rich Boy: I believe that someone put out a track like that and everyone saw that it did well and jumped on that formula. It's like a casino where someone wins the jackpot. Now, everyone has a recording studio. It's comparative to everyone playing the slot machines trying to win the jackpot. Yeah, everyone has talent but it is supposed to be a creative art.

AllHiphop: Which rappers contributed to this change?

Red Café: Like I said, it isn't really the rapper, it is the people behind him, the people teaching them how to complete an album. The people should make sure there are three or four of those kind of tracks before they jump the gun and release the album.

Soulja Boy: *No comment.*

Rich Boy: Cash Money, No Limit, Master P, and Puffy. They showed the fruits of their labor on videos of cars and jewelry they purchased. People watching the videos were like, "Damn, those are nice things."

Nuff said. You've got 14 million hits on Myspace and nothing to say. But it's not that he's actually stupid. He's obviously a genius at marketing himself. But he's still playing the game the way they gave it to him. (But see *Part Two*, "Since Part One")

Did you realize that it's been almost two or three years since we've heard anything on the radio or BET that talks about how bad things are? That talks about what needs to change? That talks about how hard the dope game actually is?

Where are the Tupacs?

And if you do music, what are you doing that's so different?

When people are listening, have something to say.

STOP CRYIN'

Because of the blood diamond trade and other corruption caused by Europeans, many parts of Africa continue to suffer from civil wars. Many of the victims are children. When Ishamael Beah was 14, he was recruited into the Sierra Leone Army. He later described his first experience at the front line:

> When we got there we were in an ambush, the rebels were attacking where we were in a bush. I did not shoot my gun at first, but when you looked around and saw your schoolmates, some younger than you, crying while they were dying with their blood spilling all over you, there was no option but to start pulling the trigger. I lost my parents during the war, they told us to join the army to avenge our parents.

In Uganda, rebel forces are engaged in a civil war with the government. These rebel forces kidnap children from villages they raid and force them to join with them. One 16-year-old girl testified to the cruelties she endured when a boy tried to escape:

> ### Did You Know?
>
> If our world were shrunk down to a village of only 100 people:
> 80 of them would have bad living conditions
> 70 would be uneducated
> 50 would be underfed
> Only 1 would have a higher education
> As the Geto Boys rapped years ago, "The World is a Ghetto."

> One boy tried to escape, but he was caught. They made him eat a mouthful of red pepper, and five people were beating him. His hands were tied, and then they made us, the other new captives, kill him with a stick. I felt sick. I knew this boy from before. We were from the same village. I refused to kill him, and they told me they would shoot me. They pointed a gun at me, so I had to do it. The boy was asking me, "Why are you doing this?" I said I had no choice. After we killed him, they made us smear blood on our arms. I felt dizzy. They said we had to do this so we would not fear death, and so we would not try to escape.

Another child soldier, Ibrahim, told his story at 16:

> The first time I went into battle I was afraid. But after two or three days they forced us to start using cocaine, and then I lost my fear. When I was taking drugs, I never felt bad on the front. Human blood was the first thing I would have every morning. It was my coffee in the morning... every morning.

There are 41 countries, from Peru to Burma to Uganda with active child soldiers. None of these countries are populated by white people. Most of them are run by people whom the U.S. helped put in power. All of these countries are poor.

Let me ask you a question. Do you still feel sorry for yourself?

Just think about it. How bad are you REALLY doing? Are you doing so bad that you can't help yourself, or are you just looking for an excuse to be sorry and hopeless? Are you doing so bad that you can't afford to help the next man up?

My Story

If you don't already know, my family is from India. I was born in Jersey, and never really got too deep into Indian culture. I was a Jersey kid, and I thought I was bad.

The first time my mother brought me to India, I was six. I lost a race to another kid in this village, and I kinda threatened him. Well, I told him that I would come back with a gun and shoot him...which is considered a threat in India, I guess. Anyway, that didn't go over very well with the people of the village, so we ended up leaving there earlier than we planned.

The next time my mother brought me with her to India, I was 14 and I was the one feeling threatened. It was all clearly my fault, however. I went to India, a "third-world" country, expecting to maintain the "thug" posturing I'd picked up on the streets of Jersey.

Let me explain something to those of you who have never been out of the country. The world is a ghetto. And these dudes in the poverty-stricken majority of our planet ain't playin. The white man got these people dying by the minute. They have nothing to lose. They will strip you BARE.

I don't care how tough you think you are. If a dozen rappers can get robbed in Brixton, London (I can name a few of your favorites), just imagine what would happen if you walked down the wrong alley in Trenchtown, Jamaica or Sao Paolo, Brazil.

India is no different. The word "thug" actually comes from the "thuggee" cult of India, a gang of bloodthirsty thieves who would abduct, rob, and sacrifice their victims to the Black goddess Kali. What's more gangsta than that? A chain with a spinning medallion? I don't think so.

Of course, I wasn't aware of any of this when I hopped on that plane. Our layover in London was as dull as London should be, complete with persistent fog and light rain, gray skies, and bland food. We stopped by the palace and I wanted to kick one of those guards with the big furry hat, but I was with mom-dukes and didn't want to embarrass her. Within a few hours of landing in London, we had to return to the airport and begin the torturous 99-hour flight to India. The flight was so long I think I actually completed puberty in mid-air.

Upon arriving and stepping into the airport, I felt instantly out of place. There I was, fresh Nike baseball cap, bright, short-sleeve racing shirt, baggy blue jeans, and my cleanest pair of sneakers. They weren't the Payless XJ1000's either. I think I'd persuaded mom to buy the fifty-dollar Fila's by this time.

Having to beg so hard just for some $50 sneakers made me think I was poor. But "poor" is a relative word, and I learned that fast. Looking around, all I saw was abject poverty. In the airport, I mean. We weren't even outside yet. There were beggars stationed throughout the New Delhi airport like the airport in Vegas has slot machines.

Working our way through baggage claim, customs, and eventually outside, the smell from the streets hit me like a sack of sh*t. With that exact force of impact, AND that exact smell. A taxi driver hurried my mother and me into his little sedan, and with minimal negotiation between him and my mother, we sped off. I couldn't understand much of what he was saying. I just thought the driver was a psychopath, because he was weaving and winding through the heavy New Delhi traffic as if there were no rules of the road in India. I'm still not sure if there are any, or if it's just every man for himself.

Pushing about 80 on the crowded city street, we passed hundreds of storefronts and businesses, their walls and windows covered with dust from the poorly paved roads. Along the wider sidewalks in the commercial district there were rows of shacks where the homeless people had set up their living quarters. And there were thousands of them.

Assembled from three or four large sheets of sheet metal, they seemed to provide little protection from the heavy rain, but I guess they were better than sleeping under the scorching hot sun, as many others were doing. From my first look, it appeared that the lepers and the animals slept outdoors. Animals...that was at least where part of the smell came from. Chickens, goats, and monkeys, oh my.

When we finally arrived, we were in a rural town on the outskirts of the big city. I was so hot I was about to pass out. I didn't want to sit around in my aunt's stuffy apartment, so I decided to venture out and explore the town on my own. My goal was to find a cool bottle of Coca-Cola – or something – before I died.

As I walked, a startling realization slowly crept into my consciousness. As I passed rows of shirtless, dark-skinned Indian men with sneers on their faces and suspicious eyes checking me out, it dawned on me:

I was the sucka.

I was the out-of-town sucka that was about to get got. These dudes were sitting in the dirt, many of them barefoot, all of their clothes dirty or torn, and every last one of them had an ice-grill for me. When they saw me, all they saw was "American money." And by the cold glare in their eyes, the pain in their faces, the cuts and muscles across their otherwise thin, bony frames, I could tell that they had nothing to lose.

I came to slums of India thinking I was a thug. At any moment, a few of these third world thugs could have dragged me out to an alley somewhere and cut my head off with one of the machetes I saw a few of them carrying. Now, that's gangsta.

I made the same observations in every third world country I've visited since then. I've been to Ghana, Thailand, Mexico, and the Dominican

Republic, among other places. In all those places, poverty is some real sh*t.

There are open sewers, homes with no doors, ten people forced to share one room, no running water, rats and dogs everywhere, and the boys you see in the *City of God* are real. Those boys that kill for candy in the movie *Hostel* are real. The boy soldiers in *Blood Diamond* are real.

The hoods in the rest of the world are nothing to play with. I don't care who you are. You don't have a ghetto pass for Sao Paolo, Brazil. They will gut you. And for less than five dollars, because five dollars can feed a family there.

> "The one-eyed man is grateful only when he sees a man who is totally blind."
> Nigerian proverb

So the next time you want to cry about how broke you are, or how bad you got it, keep in mind that there are whole communities in the Phillipines living on top of trash dump sites. The families there survive completely off other people's trash. Imagine the dinner you'd eat there.

When it rained heavily there some time ago, there was a "dumpslide" that buried hundreds of people alive in the garbage they were living on top of. Think about that. Think about the children in Africa that are kidnapped by rebels and forced to kill their families and join a militia. Imagine the kind of issues you'd have then. Appreciate what you've got, homey, because – to somebody else – you have a damn lot.

To get an idea for yourself, go get a passport and visit your brothers and sisters in another country anywhere in the world. For something a little less expensive, go rent any of the following movies:

Born in Brothels (about the children of prostitues in India)

The Devil's Miner (about child labor in Bolivia)

Blood Diamonds (the actual documentary)

Rabbit Proof Fences (about Australian Aborigines)

**Millions of people have it worse than you.
Get over yourself.**

MOVIES TO SEE

Blood Diamond; Lord of War; Hotel Rwanda; Cry Freedom; The Constant Gardener; The Last King of Scotland; City of God; The Last Samurai
Some pretty good, popular films based mostly in Africa, South America, and Asia. Most of them are about some pretty deep issues. But the crazy part is that none of them could have been made as major films without

their being a white boy as a main character…except *City of God*. And if you liked *Blood Diamond*, you need to watch the DVD documentary *Bling*.

BLOODS AND CRIPS

While in prison, Cle "Bone" Sloan started reading a book about Los Angeles history that said, "Out of the ashes of the Black Panther Party came the Crips and the Bloods and the other gangs." That got him interested. He started asking questions of his fellow Bloods, only to see that "a lot of bangers didn't know the history of how the gangs started" and resolved to educate himself.

That's what led Sloan to become director of *Bastards of the Party*, the story of the origins of the Bloods and Crips in L.A.

"I discovered that we come from a revolutionary background," said Sloan.

The Great Migration

Gangs first appeared in Los Angeles in the late 1940s, when Blacks started to move from the south into the mostly white Los Angeles area. White gangs would prey on Blacks and any other people who would move into their cities. Even when Blacks were living together in their own communities, white gangs would come in at night to rob, rape, and beat whoever they found.

If you have a hard time understanding that, read any book on the history of gangs in America. If you're lazy, just go see the movie *Gangs of New York*. The first gangs in America were all white.

Later, many of the violent white gangs would be legitimized by becoming political parties and organized crime syndicates.

But the Black groups that emerged to protect their women and children from the white gangs never solidified into such strong organizations. Nonetheless, they came very close.

When the Black Panther Party emerged, and the Nation of Islam became popular throughout America, many Black groups began developing using the same ideas. Though they could be considered gangs, which many of them remain today, they could have also become revolutionary armies.

Origin of the CRIPS

Stanley "Tookie" Williams grew up in South Central Los Angeles in the era of the Black Panthers and other revolutionary groups. Black groups were conscious about racism and police brutality because they'd already had plenty of run-ins and clashes with so-called law enforcement.

In the neighborhood where Tookie lived, there were already small gangs that stole from the residents. He wanted something done about it, but he and his friends were too young to join the Black Panther Party.

In late 1969, there was a South Central L.A. community meeting place called Community Relations for an Independent People. The center attracted many young people, as a place to hang out and talk about the kind of issues Tookie wanted to deal with. In 1971, at 16, Tookie and his 15-year-old friend Raymond Washington banded many of these youths together as a gang organized to protect the community. The acronym of the center itself became the name of their group: C.R.I.P.s.

In those early days, the street clothes of the CRIPs reflected its main influence: the Black Panthers.

In 1973, after many young warriors joined this new set, its leaders tried to steer it back to its community service roots. They published a new CRIP Constitution, and defined themselves as: Community Reform Inner-Party Service (CRIPS). These members, many of them fresh out of jail where they had studied books on the Black struggle, pledged to serve their people, instead of exploiting them as white people had done.

> "I don't bang for the color or the land. I bang for the principles and for the honor."
> Tupac Shakur

In the "Purpose and Objectives" segment of the new Constitution, the reoriented CRIPS wrote:

> We are a party that's purpose is to serve our communities in general.
> Our services will be to provide therapy to social ill, guidance in
> struggling to correct those ills, and love and peace for our community.

The CRIPS began to grow and spread from the Eastside to the Westside to Compton and beyond. By 1979, the CRIPS had grown from a small, good, neighborhood gang to a massive group with sets all across the state of California. As they grew rapidly, with no way to keep checks on what was taught in the new sets, members lost focus on the original mission. According to Mumia Abu-Jamal, "In essence, the CRIPS became exactly what they were fighting against, gang bangers."

The rise of the CRIPS fueled the rise of a rival group, the Bloods. The Bloods were also influenced by the Black Panthers, as well as the teachings of Islam. In fact, the popular term "Damu," is a Swahili word, meaning "blood."

If you read up on the history of the Vicelords, the Gangster Disciples, the Black P. Stone Nation, or almost any gang born in the 60s or 70s, you'll find the same thing.

Asian gangs and Hispanic gangs developed in the same way. At first, they were organized resistance to outside threats. By outside threats, I mean the local whites who would terrorize immigrant communities. But as times passed, revolutionary gangs like the Young Lords Party and the Red Guard Party (who worked hand in hand with the Black Panther Party) gave way to gangs with no direction and no focus. These Asian and Hispanic gangs began fighting not only the Black gangs, but each other as well.

Since the late 1960s, the Five Percenters remained one of the only active street groups consuming gang members and often entire gangs (like New York City's Chiefs, Chaplains, Tomahawks, and the infamous Decepticons), and converting them to positive orientations. Members of the Latin Kings, Netas, CRIPS, Bloods, Vicelords, GDs, and many other gangs have turned their lives around by turning to groups like the Five Percenters, the Nation of Islam, the POCC, the RBG Movement, the People's Army, and the New Black Panther Party.

In recent years however, the lack of direction in the Black community has led to:

1. copycat gangs, modeled on the structures of the gangs that came before them, typically funded by hustling, and

2. neighborhood gangs, serving as surrogate families for youth with nowhere else to go, and a need to belong to something, so long as it is strong and aggressive (not passive like the church).

Introduction of Guns and Crack

Since Oscar Danilo Blandon Reyes' Colombian supplier was Ross' source for the cheap cocaine that flooded the streets of South Central Los Angeles in the mid-1980s, the *Mercury News* dubbed Blandon "the Johnny Appleseed of crack in California – the Crips' and Bloods' first direct-connect to the cocaine cartels of Colombia."

According to Mumia Abu-Jamal, the original mission of the CRIPS didn't spread when the gang spread:

> What has spread, from coast to coast, is nihilism, anger, anti-Black violence, and the economic engine of the drug business, which is but a chemical weapon against Black communal life.

But some are waking up, and trying to redirect their focus:

> Sanyika Shakur, once a CRIP, now a Black nationalist, asks rhetorically, "Had we not begun as predators of New Afrikans [Blacks] would we have been allowed to last this long?" He announced, in 1993, the reformation of the CRIPs into the Clandestine Revolutionary Internationalist Party Soldiers. (I doubt there will be many rap videos about those kinda gangstas!). Every few decades, such street groups try

to reorganize, reform, and resurrect themselves, but something gets in their way.

Guess what gets in their way? I'll give you ten seconds. If you still can't get it, you need to see "Soulja 4 Life."

Current Conditions

At 45, Mr. Tookie Williams had been on death row for 19 years. Since being imprisoned, he has left the leadership of the CRIPS, began community activism and education efforts, written children's books, and been nominated for a Nobel Peace Prize. Two years before his 2007 execution, he said:

> For a long time I shied away from my own redemption. I was worried what others would think of me. Would they think Tookie had gone soft? That was my concern. I used to think that not to gang bang was a sign of weakness.
>
> Many of today's youth feel as I did in the past. But now I know better. A legitimate redemptive effort to change yourself takes arduous discipline to succeed. So making a positive transition in your life is a sign of strength, never weakness.

Rough estimates suggest that there were at least one million gang members in the United States in 2000. It appeared that, with the destruction of the Black family, and the persistence of drugs and guns in our communities, that number was not decreasing.

Imagine if all that manpower was harnessed? Considering that these young people, Black, brown, yellow, and even white, are mostly frustrated with their conditions and willing to do anything, imagine what kind of a military power there is in the ghettos of America. If the Black leaders were less concerned about telling the youth to pull up their pants, and more concerned with working WITH these youth, we would have a full-scale revolutionary army on our hands.

In fact, that is exactly what white America feared in the 1960s, and this threat was the ONLY reason why they gave up Civil Rights. They weren't convinced by King's promise of peace. They were SCARED of the threat of WAR. Groups like the Panthers, the Mau Maus, the Black Liberation Army, Robert Williams' followers, and many others had the government SHOOK.

But what's going on with our young people now? They're not fighting for us. They're fighting each other.

Mumia concludes about the mindset of our young "soldiers" today:

> They are mindnumbingly materialistic, sexist, and revel in the imagery of violence against their communities. And, as our loving fascination for things expands, our caring about people decreases.
>
> Things matter. Bling matters.

Videos project, not our wealth, but our inherent poverty, for it is only poor people who feel the *need* to flash; for the truly wealthy have learned that to flash is the sign of the nouveau riche; those to whom wealth is newly acquired.

Moreover, there is a deadly twist in the lure of gangsta life; it opens the door to prison, or the grave, and feeds the containment industry – the prison industrial complex, the institutional descendant of slave plantations, that feeds on Black pain and Black loss.

Meanwhile, the biggest Gangsta on the planet, the U.S. Empire, gobbles nations like bon-bons, invades countries like crossing the street, and treats the Constitution like toilet paper.

Now, that's gangsta!

Or, as David Banner recently said in a *Billboard* interview:

America points the fingers at young black men when the biggest gangster is unfolded in the war. When I [the President] say, "I don't care what you think about this war, I'm going to continue," that's gangster. For the president of the United States to say, "You've got 24 hours to get out my country," that's gangster. If I come to your country and say I just discovered it, though you've been here for years, that's gangster. They brought Africans to this country and done stripped them of their language, their culture. We lost our traditions 'cause they beat it out of us. That's gangster.

What were the goals and objectives of the first gangs?

What has caused us to lose sight of that vision?

Whose goals and objectives are we serving by fighting against each other?

What will it take to get back to the original program?

Develop a focus and stick to it. There's no point in climbing halfway up a mountain, only to let yourself slide off.

KILLING A MAN

I had the gun off safety with one in the chamber. Aimed straight between his eyes, I was milliseconds away from popping him. One in the head, ready to put one in his head. All I'd have to do was squeeze the trigger with just enough pressure to put the hammer in motion, but not so much pressure that my hand would jerk and I'd miss.

I was hot. I was screaming. I had jumped out from behind that bush with murder on my mind. There was almost nothing between me, him, and his brains on the pavement at this point. He was begging me not to shoot, pleading something I couldn't even fully understand. I couldn't even understand his words. I was that hot. At the last moment, one of my brothers stopped me. We could handle this another way, he proposed. He was cool-headed, the way I usually am in tense situations like this one, and I listened. To make a long story short, I didn't kill a man in the middle of the street that night.

Before that night, the last time I had seriously seen myself killing someone, I was completely cool and calm. It was going to be premeditated weeks in advance and planned down to the last detail. As they say, "Revenge is a dish best served cold." And I was cold enough to give people freezer burns at this point. I was in murder mode. Not the angry "heat of the moment" kind of murder, but the "shoot you and smile" kind of murder. I just couldn't get all the details of my plan to fall into place the right way. For one thing, I was broke and didn't have my own car yet. Leaving a murder scene to wait on the bus just didn't seem practical. And I knew better than to ride with someone else, because you can't trust anybody to keep their mouths shut these days.

There were other problems too, like trying to figure out dude's exact routine without the money to pay someone who could get all those details for me. After all, I needed to get into his house so I could make it look like a suicide. But nothing was working out. And again, I had brothers in my ear tryin to talk some sense into me. As time dragged on, I realized it just wasn't gonna go down.

Since then, I've grown up. I don't even put myself in those kind of situations to begin with. And murder isn't even in my vocabulary now. If something should happen now, I promise you, I guarantee you, it will be self-defense.

As I look back on those two experiences, though, I learned a lot from them. I learned that you can't kill a man unless you're "all the way" there. I was, but fortunately, other factors kept me from going through with it. That's different from the time when I was six, making death threats I didn't even understand.

There are people who have put guns to my head who I could tell were half-assing it just as bad as I was at 6 years old. They weren't anywhere near the right mode or frame of mind to murder me. That's why you can still get punched in the mouth with your gun out. Because if you're not all the way hot, or all the way cold, you can't follow through. You can't do it, because you're not ready to go hard. You've got to be all in. Otherwise, you'll hesitate. And as Jay-Z said, "You know what they say about he who hesitates in war? He who hesitates has lost."

You don't want to have a gun out, only to freeze up when it's pull the trigger time. When that wrist locks up, it's game over. You better hope you can walk away with only shame to worry about.

The same with life, you can't half-ass anything. Either go hard, or don't go. Either be all the way in, or don't step forward. Either be all in or all out. Don't straddle the fence, or hop back and forth. You really shouldn't go to extremes, but I'd rather deal with someone who sees life in only black and white than someone who's half-cocked on everything.

Don't half-ass anything.
Either do it or don't. Be about it or not.

PAID IN FULL

Over twenty years before "making it rain" became the catchphrase for every cornball with a few singles, AZ, Rich Porter, and Alpo were throwing $50s in the air everywhere they went. The stories of these three cocaine legends are a true-life testimony to the few paths one can take in this dirty game. As Killer Mike says, it's "Jail, Hell, or the Hospitel."

Path 1: AZ

In 1983, the movie *Scarface* came out, and the story of Tony Montana and his lust for money and power inspired youth in ghettos throughout the country. That same year, a Colombian cocaine supplier approached Azie Faison – pronounced "AZ" – about selling cocaine, and the rest was history. By 19, Azie was a cocaine "wholesaler" in Harlem, regularly earning from $40,000 – $100,000 a week.

Azie had also teamed up with childhood friend Rich Porter and later Alberto "Alpo" Martinez, the three of whom would later become legends in New York. The trio lived like kings, flashing expensive jewelry and luxurious cars throughout the streets of Harlem.

But it didn't last long. In 1987, a kick-door invasion of Azie's stash house left three dead and three others critically injured. Azie himself was shot nine times in the robbery attempt, including two times in the head at point-blank range. With his head bust open like a cantaloupe, the robbers left him for dead.

Yet, miraculously, he survived.

Azie described the experience in his autobiography, *Game Over: The Rise and Transformation of a Harlem Hustler*:

> "Open the safe, nigga! Open the f*ckin' safe now, or I'm gonna kill everybody in this bitch! Hurry up, motherf*cka..." That's the last thing he said before he hit me hard in the head with the butt of his gun, causing blood to flow into my eyes. Shaking with fear and numb from the pain, I tried to respond: "Look, man...The blood is blinding me. I can't see! I don't have no money in the safe anyway. Just let everybody go...I'll get you some money. They don't got nothin' to do with this."
>
> I was on my knees, bent over, with blood pouring out of my head. I felt no pain; I was numb. This was my judgment day – payment for all my sins. God lost patience with me. Instead of listening, I ignored the

Lord's warnings and turned my back on Him. I heard His voice throughout the years, but I wasn't sure it was Him. So there I was. My head was spinning, my heart was pounding, and my eyes were stinging from the sticky blood pouring into them.

Stumbling around in pain, I managed to clear some blood from my eyes using my shirt. What I saw took my breath away: Five people, including my aunt and my best friend, were tied up in my aunt's bedroom. They were handcuffed and lying facedown, pleading for their lives. By nightfall, my aunt, her friend, and my best friend were pronounced dead. Two more people survived, but they sustained serious wounds. As for me, I took two shots to my head at point-blank range, and seven more: one to my neck, another in my shoulder, and the rest in my leg. I was shot nine times. I saw a bright light and my body felt like it was rising toward the light.

"We're losing him, we're losing him. He won't make it." The paramedics who rushed me to the hospital had no reason to believe I'd survive. In fact, I didn't survive...at least the old me didn't. On that day, the old me was killed so a new me could be reborn.

After his near-death experience, AZ didn't follow the path most others would (that is, claiming to have "found God," acting like they're "saved," and soon after going back to doing wrong).

Instead, he left the drug game to embark on a mission to disavow his former life and steer youth away from the path he chose. In 1989, he formed a rap group composed of street hustlers whose lyrics told the story of life from the eyes of drug dealers.

Following the tragic murders of his friend Rich Porter and his little brother Donnell Porter, Azie began working on a movie about his life, which eventually became 2002's *Paid in Full*. Around the same time, he teamed up with street documentarian Troy Reed to produce the documentary about his life called *Game Over*.

In 2002, Azie also teamed up with educator Agyei Tyehimba to work on his life story. His goal was to tell the truth about the drug game, especially how it destroys the fabric of families and communities. The result was the book *Game Over: The Rise and Transformation of a Harlem Hustler*.

Path 2: Rich Porter

While childhood friend Azie Faison worked in a neighborhood dry cleaners, Rich Porter began his rise to drug dealing at 12 years old. By the early 80s – the height of Reagan's "War on Drugs" – Rich Porter was rich.

Unlike his low-key counterpart Azie, Porter was known for his flamboyance and high-profile lifestyle. As early as 16, Rich could be seen on Harlem streets showing off his brand new BMW. Before long, his love of cars led to a large fleet of luxury vehicles, some of which he even gave away. People said Rich never wore the same outfit twice and kept a garage in Manhattan filled with dozens of high-end cars.

AZ and Rich may have been drug dealers, but in other ways, they were honorable men. Whenever possible, they gave generously to the poor and the homeless. And they weren't proud of what they did.

On DJ KaySlay's "The Truth," LL Cool J rapped about his experience with the three:

> A seventeen-year reign, simple and plain/ When I ruled the rap game and all my peers sold cocaine/ 1-3-2 Uptown, when Rich Porter told me/ "See you can push a new car, it's different for a rap star"/ And AZ was givin' 50s to the homeless/ They never bragged about it: "L, we don't condone this"

But in the life they chose, honor and good deeds guaranteed nothing. Rich Porter was murdered by two associates in January of 1990. One of those two men was his friend Alpo. The cause? Drug money that Porter supposedly owed Alpo.

Path 3: Alpo

Since joining up with Rich and AZ, Alpo had developed a reputation as a serious force to reckon with, an enforcer with enough money and power to terminate lives and careers of any who opposed the trio.

> "And Alpo ordered guys to slaughter guys
> And the whole Harlem was in tears when Rich Porter died.
> Wasn't no bummy crew, had money true, packed dummies boo
> Had niggas scared to death to even walk past 1-3-2"
> Cam'ron, "I Remember When"

While Rich was known for showboating, and AZ was considered cool and calculating, Alpo was regarded as reckless and trigger-happy. But who would think that this enforcer would turn on his own brother?

In 1992, Alpo was arrested and convicted on several charges, including the murder of Rich Porter. Hoping to reduce his prison term, Alpo cooperated with authorities as an informant. He provided information on dozens of people, leading to several long convictions for former friends and associates.

Recently Alpo talked about killing his good friend in *F.E.D.S.* magazine:

> My man Gary shot him twice, but Rich didn't die so than I shot him. I know he felt something because I had to pry his hands off the doorknob. Did I kill Rich? Yes. Yes, I did kill Rich, but it wasn't personal. It was business.

Recently asked by DJ KaySlay if he could change one thing, Alpo said it would have been killing his friend Rich.

Even with the many people he sold out to the authorities, Albert "Alpo"

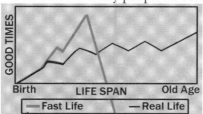

Martinez isn't coming home anytime soon. At the date of this writing, Alpo is still serving a life sentence for various drug charges and 13 homicides, including the murder of his friend and partner Rich Porter.

In a game like this, there's not many ways to become truly successful. Even the illusion of success, manifested in the fast money, fast cars, and faster women – is short-lived. It comes fast, and it goes fast, as you can see in the graph above. Of course, the best idea is to start out with, and stick to, a legitimate hustle, but life isn't a fairy tale. As Jay-Z says on Memphis Bleek's "My Mind Right": "It ain't about Rich and 'Po, nigga, it's bout rich and po' (poor)." But we miss that reality for the illusion they show us, and we go hard after all the wrong sh*t.

Many of us have gotten ourselves so deep into this life that it's hard to see a sensible way out. All I can say is, if the fourth path is too tough (see "The Fourth Path"), take the first path in the story above. If you don't make your way out of this game like AZ, it's almost guaranteed you'll end up like Rich or Alpo.

When you're in a situation that's known to never go right, get out before you become another sad story.

HOW TO GET SMART IN 17 EASY STEPS

1. **Read this book.** You don't have to read it from front to back. You can hop around. But read everything in here, and you'll know more than many people twice your age.

2. **Research.** As you read this book, or any book, look up people, places, and events that you want to know more about. Also, look up the meanings of any words you're not familiar with.

3. **Read daily.** You can start out small, like *Don Diva Magazine* or the graphic novel *Sentences: The Life of M.F. Grimm*, but if you keep at it, you'll feel comfortable reading Chancellor Williams or Cornel West in no time.

> "The man who does not read good books has no advantage over the man who *can't* read them."
> Mark Twain

4. **Write.** Writing improves reading, just as reading more makes you a better writer. Keep notes on things you're studying, keep a journal on your life and thoughts, or just keep a sheet of paper handy to

write random things down as they come to you. And start now, not once you're locked up and have no choice.

5. **Change what you take into your body.** The food you eat and the other chemicals you put in your body affect the way your brain works. If you can't keep a clear head or a decent memory, it's time to quit something.

"It's time for us as a people to start makin' some changes.
Let's change the way we eat, let's change the way we live,
and let's change the way we treat each other.
You see the old way wasn't working,
so it's on us to do what we gotta do, to survive."
Tupac, "Changes"

6. **Look deeper.** When things are happening, look for the answers to "why" and "how." If you don't know how something works, find out.

7. **Question everything.** When you are told something, or you see something on TV or the news, ask yourself whether it could be untrue. Look into what someone's goal is in telling you something.

8. **Use the Internet.** Get off Myspace, Facebook, and Youtube. Start using the Internet to research, find information, and discover resources.

9. **Don't be scared.** It takes courage to think differently. The easy way is to think what everyone else thinks. When you begin thinking for yourself, you have to get smart enough to defend your ideas.

10. **Go to school.** You may not believe in what they're teaching, but most people won't believe in you if you can't show that you're smart enough to get your degree. Chances are, you'll learn something useful there.

11. **Don't be a couch potato.** Even if you're not ready to watch the Science Network, the History Channel, and PBS, think about the messages in the shows you do watch.

12. **Talk to people smarter than you.** I'm not saying you have to spend all your time with nerds and geeks. Just find a few people who have something to teach you, and spend some time with them as often as you can.

13. **Study what you're doing.** If you want to be a rapper, read a book on the music industry and how it works...so you don't get screwed. If you like guns, learn everything you can about them. At least you'll

have something to talk about when people are having an informed conversation.

14. **Attend speeches given by intelligent people**. It doesn't have to be a lecture on opera music. There are plenty of opportunities to hear people speaking on prisons, hip hop, starting businesses, and other topics that may mean something to you.

> "Thinking is the hardest work there is, which is probably why so few engage in it."
> Henry Ford

15. **Play mind games.** And I don't mean messing with people's heads. Activities like crossword puzzles, sudoku, and chess offer needed exercise for the brain. If that feels too nerdy, start problem-solving in the real world. All around you, there are plenty of opportunities to use critical thinking skills and get your wits razor-sharp.

16. **Get a smart girl.** A dumb girl will only keep you dumb, or make you dumber. Your best bet is a college girl (even if you're still in high school) or a college graduate. If not, at least make sure she reads (and not just books by Eric Jerome Dickey and Omar Tyree).

17. **Ask.** There's nothing wrong with asking questions. It's much more dangerous to go through life trying to do everything without knowing how to do it. You'd be surprised how much you can learn just by asking the right person the right question.

It's no longer smart to be dumb.
It's dumb to be dumb, so get smart or die.

PAWNS IN THE GAME

A few nuggets of information on our friend, Crack:

"Crack" was named for the snaps and cracks it makes when heated and smoked.

Reports of crack usage surfaced in L.A., San Diego, Houston, and in the Caribbean as early as 1981. The first crack house was discovered in Miami in 1982. Crack hit Detroit by 1985, New York by 1986, and Chicago by 1988 before expanding into small cities by the 90s.

The Reagan administration's massive social service cuts and the end of many manufacturing jobs caused unemployment rates to skyrocket. Meanwhile, it became easier to distribute the drug (due to government "help"), generating unbelievably large sums of money for dealers.

> "See when the Reaganomics era was poppin' off/
> We used to get that inconceivable guap"
> Busta Rhymes, on Rick Ross' "Hustlin'" (Streets Remix)

Before long, territory disputes and other factors led to unprecedented violence in the Black community. Guns also became much easier to get a hold of, at this time.

Crack spread like wildfire due to notorious dealers and crews like New York's Alpo, Pappy Mason, the Wild Cowboys, and The Supreme Team; New Jersey's Pretlow Brothers and The Family; Philadelphia's Junior Black Mafia; L.A.'s Freeway Rick; D.C.'s Rayful Edmonds; and Detroit's Young Boys, Inc. and Latin Counts.

Crack was used to crush the growing Black consciousness movement, as well as the rise of hip hop. As Rodrigues says in Jamel Shabazz's *A Time Before Crack*: "Former b-boys and alpha males became street generals and traded in hip hop for a shot at being the next Tony Montana."

Crack was the first drug primarily sold by Black men and used by Black women (there were 98,000 Black female users by 1992). Rodrigues continues: "Young women who were once beautiful and vivacious were transformed into skinny, toothless, painful sights. In no time they began turning tricks for rock, giving birth to the 'crack whore,' which in turn gave birth to the 'crack baby.'"

> **Did You Know?**
> You don't technically "cook" crack? You actually just heat it enough to dissolve the coke and sodium bicarbonate so that you change the cocaine hydrochloride into its smokeable bicarbonate or carbonate salts. You then can cool it to precipitate out the cocaine and then separate or further heat it to a gentle boil to evaporate the remaining water. So as you can see there is no cooking, just dissolving, and if you choose, evaporation.

Sex for crack became commonplace, even leading to sex orgies that some drug dealers would videotape, which may have been the precursor to the "Girls Gone Wild" movie phenomenon.

Crack addicts went from prostituting themselves to pimping their young daughters (and sons), which led to the rise of molestation, pedophilia, and sexual abuse in the Black community

From 1979 to 1990 (the rise of the Crack Era), the percentage of Black men sent to state and federal prisons increased 14%.

Crack also led to the rise of single parent households, due to the high incarceration rates of Black males. During the same time period, teenage pregnancy also rose significantly.

As violence overwhelmed the inner cities, middle class Black people relocated their families to the suburbs, further straining already tense class divisions between middle class Blacks and poor Blacks. However, the illicit wealth being attained by the crack dealers, in an era where other Blacks were struggling under the economic pressures of

Reagonomics, made drug dealing and drug use especially appealing to Black youth.

After many Black people started getting rich dealing in heroin and cocaine, in 1973, the State of New York passed a set of "Rockefeller drug laws," after sending 713 people to prison for drug crimes in 1973. By 1992, using these tough new laws, the state was imprisoning 11,000 new drug offenders every year.

For those not on the wrong side of the fence, the criminal justice system is a $70 billion dollar industry. Even major corporations benefit from

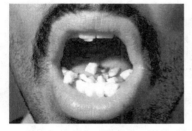

the use of cheap prison labor, in a form of slavery allowed by the 13th Amendment.

Poor, isolated white towns suffering from high unemployment benefit from the building of new prisons to house Blacks. There, uneducated, racist rednecks can become C.O.s and once again get paid to control powerless Blacks, as in slavery. As Baruti has said, "Again, our fall facilitates their rise."

Also, federal programs and organizations geared to fight the "war on drugs" make a ton of money, using our tax dollars. When exactly will this war be won? And why is it that Blacks are the main ones targeted, even though white people are just as deep (if not deeper) into the drug trade?

Finally, the people who import and assist the incoming shipments of drugs into our country are getting extremely rich. If you dig deep enough, you can see the many high-ranking people – including former presidents (even Bill Clinton) – who were/are involved.

According to a report by the U.S. Sentencing Commission on Cocaine and Federal Sentencing Policies, sentencing for crack cocaine offenders is six times longer than that for that for cocaine offenders with equivalent drug quantities. Defendants – mostly Black – trafficking crack received an average of over 64 months, or slightly more than five years. On the other hand, those caught trafficking cocaine – mostly white – received an average sentence of only 13 months.

Powder cocaine (mostly used by whites) and crack cocaine (mostly used by Blacks) contain roughly the same amount of the drug per gram. According to the Rockefeller Laws, being convicted of possession of how much of either drug will get you a mandatory minimum sentence of 5 years in jail under federal law?

❑   500 grams of powder or 500 grams of crack

❑ 5 grams of powder or 50 grams of crack

❑ 500 grams of powder or 5 grams of crack

❑ 5 grams of either powder or crack

If you picked the third choice, congratulations! You know the rules of the game. Now the question is, are you dumb enough to keep playing?

This game isn't simply unfair. This game is designed for you to lose.

YOUR SUBCONSCIOUS MIND

Your subconscious mind is very busy. Even when you don't know you're thinking, you're thinking. While you may be cool and calm on the outside, inside, you may be feeling fear, guilt, shame, lust, greed, doubt, or thousands of other things. The problem is: Either you know it and won't admit it, or you don't even know it. Becoming aware of your subconscious mind is like going beneath the surface of the ocean. Sometimes you'll find treasure, and sometimes you'll find some nasty, icky sh*t you wish you never saw. Either way, you need to know, because your subconscious mind plays a role in every decision you make, and every thought you think.

Here's a few examples:

Example One

Situation at Hand: Some joker just bumped into me in the club and spilled some of his drink on my shirt. There's a little stain, so I gotta stop him and get at him bout it.

Conscious Thoughts: This nigga just ruined my favorite shirt. Matter fact, he just ruined my night with this bullsh*t. He lookin all stupid right now, so I gotta set him straight. He's payin for this shirt, one way or the other: either out his pocket or out his ass. It's the only right thing to do.

Subconscious Thoughts: Damn, this nigga is big as hell. I don't want to knuckle up over this cheap ass shirt from Target, but my niggas is watchin. If I don't at least bark on him, I'ma look like a pussy. I hope he's a bitch and don't want to fight, cause then all of my clothes are gonna be f*cked up.

Example Two

Situation at Hand: Tay-Tay's second cousin – twice removed, on his stepdaddy's side – Maurice, just got jumped by them boys down on 79th St. The goons are piling up into a car and they're on the way to come pick me up to handle things.

Conscious Thoughts: I'm ready. I don't give a f*ck! I ain't whupped a nigga ass in weeks! These niggas don't know who they just f*cked with! They gon be sorry when they find out!

Subconscious Thoughts: Who the f*ck is this nigga Maurice? I don't even know his ass. Sh*t, I hardly even f*ck with Tay-Tay! Anyway, I'm on goddamn probation, and my P.O. is just waitin to violate me. I don't need this. These crazy niggas always tryin to go out and f*ck somebody up for some kinda reason. But half the time, I gotta do most the fightin, and they just be waitin to get a cheap hit in while a nigga's down. I need to find an excuse not to go. Maybe I'll go drink that sour milk and get sick.

Example Three

Situation at Hand: My best female friend, Sheronda, is mad at her boyfriend, who is usually really good to her. She's telling me all about it, so she can get it off her chest.

Conscious Thoughts: I'm gonna tell her to leave dude alone. He's a good dude sometimes, but he's not good enough for her. She needs to know that she can do better. I'm gonna show her how he's not the man for her. A real man, like me, would never do the sh*t he did…uh, whatever that is.

Subconscious Thoughts: Damn, this is my chance. I been wantin to blow Sheronda's back out for years, but dude always been in my way. I respected that sh*t long enough. He's a good dude, but he's not gonna cockblock me today. I know I wouldn't do her right if I had her, but I only want her for tonight!

Example Four

Situation at Hand: I'm dating a white girl.

Conscious Thoughts: I don't care about Megan's race. Megan is good to me. She never brings me around her parents, and we can never talk about Black issues, but she's not a racist. After all, she loves me. And I love her, not because she's white, but because she's better to me than any Black girl I ever met.

Subconscious Thoughts: I got a white girl, I got a white girl, I got a white girl! Nyah nyah nyah nyah nyah!

Example Five

Situation at Hand: I met this dude on the train who was talking about "revolution." He was dark as hell, with some rough-ass dreads and some African-lookin clothes.

Conscious Thoughts: This nigga is a weirdo. All that Black "Back to Africa" sh*t ain't for me. I'm tryin to get paid, and I bet this nigga is broke. I ain't heard a word he was sayin. Let me see if there's somethin good on BET.

Subconscious Thoughts: I'm scared of the sh*t this man is talkin about. It makes me feel real small to feel like everything I know and believe in...is wrong. He looks weird, but what he was saying made sense...but I didn't want to admit it in front of all them people. I need to stop thinkin about it. I know: Let's see what's on 106th and Park.

Summary

Sometimes, our subconscious mind holds our deepest, darkest desires. We don't want to admit to some of the things we think, but they're there. Unless you bring them to the surface and deal with those thoughts (and why you have them) they'll eat away at you. This can continue for years and years...until something bad happens one day. By then, it'll be too late to turn back and fix what was wrong.

Other times, our subconscious mind wants to do what we know deep down is the right thing to do. That's what we call our conscience, and even the foulest of people have one. It may be buried deep, but it nags at us when we're doing something we don't feel right about. In these cases, you need to recognize what you're REALLY thinking, and be the man you really want to be.

Be aware of your subconscious thoughts.

THE GREATEST...

The most destructive habit	Worry
The greatest joy	Giving
The greatest loss	Loss of self-respect
The most satisfying work	Helping others
The ugliest personality trait	Selfishness
The most endangered species	Dedicated leaders
Our greatest natural resource	Our youth
The greatest "shot in the arm"	Encouragement
The greatest problem to overcome	Fear
The most effective sleeping pill	Peace of mind
The most crippling disease	Excuses
The most powerful force in life	Love
The most dangerous "friend"	A gossiper
The world's most incredible computer	The brain
The worst thing to be without	Hope
The deadliest weapon	The tongue
The two most power-filled words	"I Can"

The greatest asset	Determination
The most worthless emotion	Self-pity
The most beautiful attire	A look of confidence
The most prized possession	Integrity
Our worst enemy	Ourselves

Greatness in the way you live results in a great life.

BLOOD DIAMONDS

How many people had to die for that chain or bracelet?

According to www.realdiamondfacts.org, every year about 300,000 carats of diamonds are mined with slave labor in rebel-controlled regions of West Africa. These diamonds are then sold to fund civil wars that exploit child soldiers and destroy millions of lives. Those blood diamonds then end up in American and European jewelry. The movie *Blood Diamond* was based on what's really happening.

As Kanye West said on the remix of "Diamonds from Sierra Leone":

> Good Morning, this ain't Vietnam, Still/ People lose hands, legs, arms for real/ Little was known of Sierra Leone/ And how it connect to the diamonds we own/ …These ain't conflict diamonds, is they Jacob? Don't lie to me mayne/ See, a part of me sayin' keep shinin'/ How? When I know of the blood diamonds/ Though it's thousands of miles away/ Sierra Leone connect to what we go through today/ Over here, it's a drug trade, we die from drugs/ Over there, they die from what we buy from drugs/ The diamonds, the chains, the bracelets, the charmses/ I thought my Jesus piece was so harmless/ 'til I seen a picture of a shorty armless/ And here's the conflict/ It's in a Black person's soul to rock that gold/ Spend ya whole life tryna get that ice/ On a Polo rugby it look so nice/ How could somethin' so wrong make me feel so right, right?

(Oh, you know Kanye ain't allowed to rap like that no more!) Anyway, that one verse tells a lot of the story of blood diamonds, also known as "conflict diamonds." But even diamonds that are conflict-free aren't problem-free. Even when people aren't being killed over the diamond trade, lives are lost in other ways. For example, children work as slaves in the diamond mines of the Republic of Sierra Leone. The craziest part about this is that Sierra Leone was originally established by the British as a home for freed West African slaves. These diamonds are not considered "blood diamonds," so they can be readily exported to

Antwerp and other locations where they are polished and make their way to your local department store or jeweler.

And if your diamond is a cheaper diamond or gem (which it probably is if you bought it in the hood), it may have been cut or polished by bonded children in India.

After all this, what's it worth once you get it? You don't know how many arms and legs got chopped off for it, or how many families were killed, or how many poor children got worked to death behind it, but it's...what? It's sparkly? It makes you feel like somebody? Does it really make you happy at the end of the day? Man, you can't even resell it without losing most of your money! And there's so many people wearin fake ones, no one cares what you paid for yours!

Basically, homeboy, you playin yourself...only at the expense of a lot of other people.

I'm just waiting for the day when a rapper says, "Nigga I stay in these icy-ass stones/straight from them slave niggas in Sierra Leone/ Gyeaah!"

That's the day when I start shootin.

(Note: Since the 2008 publication of *How to Hustle and Win*, The Game and several others have actually bragged on record about wearing blood diamonds.)

Diamonds ain't forever. Our lust for more and more "things" only makes things worse for more and more of us.

MOVIE TO SEE

Be Cool

Kinda silly, but it highlights some of the silliness that is very real in the music industry. Unlike *Hip Hop Dynasty* or *CB4*, which do the same thing, *Be Cool* goes further and offers some smart commentary on race and power throughout the film.

WHO GIVES A F*CK?

> "We rollin' deep in this bitch so f*ck y'all niggas,
> I got that dirty south wit me, I don't give a f*ck!"
> Lil Jon & The Eastside Boys, "I Don't Give a F*ck"

You know how any song, with a hook like "F*ck You" or "F*ck them Other Niggas" can make everybody in a club or a party go crazy? Put on the right song, and even the dudes in wheelchairs got their middle fingers in the air, elbowin people in the nuts. Why is that?

Anybody seeing that can tell that it seems like we got a lot of anger and frustration to get out of our systems. And we don't care what anybody thinks about us or our way of expressing ourselves. We've got some rage to get out of our system.

It's been this way for a while now. Whether you were slamdancing to Onyx back in the 90s, or pushin hatas off in the South, you've seen Black clubs lookin a lot like white moshpits. And to this day, if you go to the type of clubs I go to, you know ain't nothin changed.

When DJ Khaled's "I'm so Hood" came on in any club in Atlanta, chaos erupted once Plies came on spittin, "Damn my P.O.! Ya'll can tell her I said it! Violate me if she want, [she] gon have to come catch me!" Why? Because he was simply telling everyone "I...don't...give...a F*CK." And 90% of us can relate to that on some level. Whether you know it or not, every poor person of color has feelings of "I don't give a f*ck" or "f*ck the world" somewhere under their surface. I'll explain.

If you pay attention, when any song comes on that's saying "I don't give a f*ck" or "f*ck the world" it's about to go down. We get buck, get wild...even the good guys got their middle fingers in the air, and the bad guys are stompin a stranger out...Where did all this rage come from?

> "We ain't gon stop until some devils die up in the audience
> Word up, push them to the floor
> Put your foot in his guts, a sample, watch a fool get trampled
> Shoot a pistol in the air, make it so security can't handle"
> Three Six Mafia, "I Bet You Won't Hit a Muthaf*cka"

Simple. We weren't just saying "f*ck the world" because we felt like we could. We meant it. The truth behind why is buried deep in our collective psychology.

After so many years of being the abandoned generation of an already exploited people, we just don't give a f*ck any more. We sincerely don't give a f*ck about this world that never gave a f*ck about us. Even Young Buck wasn't happy with how his album *Buck the World* got its final title: "I really just wanted to have the middle finger on there. I wanted to name my album "F*ck the World," but they wouldn't let me name it that."

> "I'm thugged out / F*ck the world 'cuz this is how they made me"
> Tupac, "Life of an Outlaw"

Do you get it? If you've ever said "F*ck the world" I know you do. If you ever just held your middle fingers up in the air, to no one person in particular, I know you do. If you ever just wanted to tear some sh*t up, I know you do.

I'm here to tell you that it's natural to feel this way when you are fed what we've been fed. We were born into the pain that made us feel this way. As Ice-T recalled in his book, *The Ice Opinion: Who Gives a F*ck?*:

"Who gives a f*ck?" is one of the first questions a kid will ask himself growing up in the ghetto. He'll look around at the broken-down buildings, the shabby projects, the cracked schoolyard playgrounds, and it doesn't look like anybody gives a f*ck. He'll watch mean muthaf*ckas in patrol cars rolling around the neighborhood, and they won't give a f*ck. Everybody he sees is just trying to survive; they are just trying to make it over to another day.

This is his view from here. To understand where the rage and defiance in inner-city kids come from, you have to understand the attitude of people when they're down. Even a strong-willed kid will have a difficult time giving a f*ck when everywhere he looks, the cops, the schools, and the people outside the ghetto reinforce his feelings of hopelessness.

This hopelessness consumes us. We lash out in rage, anger, and frustration as a result. The same way old folks release their misery and despair by crying and falling out in church, we nut up and act a fool in the club the night before. However...The key to making sense out of all this is to escape the cycle of suffering and venting.

> "To be Black and conscious in America is to be in a constant state of rage."
> James Baldwin (1924-1987)

We must learn to channel this rage and use it to destroy what is weak in our lives and our communities. We don't need to put our middle fingers down. We just need to remember who to point them at, as Plies does in his video for "100 Years."

> "Since they don't give a f*ck, I don't – Feel what I'm saying?"
> Kastro on Tupac's "They Don't Give a F*ck About Us"

From a man with money like Young Buck, to the broke teenager on the corner, all of our attitudes have been shaped by this wretched system. Even those of us who haven't given up on "making it" have started to look at the rest of the world, even other Black people, like they have nothing to offer us or tell us. When you look around, even when we ain't waving a middle finger in the air, we're waving a middle finger in the air.

And then what?

Young Black men everywhere are full of rage and frustration. Only once you know where all that comes from, will you be able to have the power to change it.

TO BE CONTINUED

This is the where the stories end...for now.

As I said in the introduction, there's no way I could take you full circle in one book. That one book would have literally been over 600 pages long, and I knew very few people would try reading a book that long. But I knew we could all handle the meal if I split it into two courses.

Now that you're done with the first 300 pages, how do you feel?

Do you sense the changes that are occurring in the way you think and the way you live? You may not see it yet, but it's already begun.

Are you ready for the next steps?

The second part to this book goes deeper, hits harder, and will produce even stronger thoughts and reactions in you. *Part One* is, in many ways, just the preparation for the ideas in *Part Two*. *How to Hustle and Win, Part 2: Rap, Race, and Revolution* continues the journey, and takes the reader through the final five stages of development towards total success.

You can look in the back of this book to get an idea of what else you can look forward to in *Part Two*...as well as what you can do *now*.

REVIEW

The principle for this chapter was **Identify your Strengths**: Find your power within, in life, and in the world...and focus on developing it.

Here are the principles and lessons we covered in this half of the chapter:

Compassion
Millions of people have it worse than you. Get over yourself.
Focus
Develop a focus and stick to it.
There's no point in climbing halfway up a mountain, only to let yourself slide off.
Inspiration
When people are listening, have something to say.
Timing
When you're in a situation that's known to never go right, get out before you become another sad story.
Total Dedication
Don't half-ass anything. Either do it or don't. Be about it or not.
True Power
Alone we are weak, but together we are mighty.
Don't act tougher than you really are.
It's no longer smart to be dumb. It's dumb to be dumb, so get smart or die.
Young Black men everywhere are full of rage and frustration. Only once you know where all that comes from, will you be able to have the power to change it.
Truth
Be aware of your subconscious thoughts.
This game isn't simply unfair. This game is designed for you to lose.
You can't kill an idea.
As long as people continue to see it, a vision is indestructible.
Values
Diamonds ain't forever. Our lust for more and more "things" only makes things worse for more and more of us.
Greatness in life results in a great life.

This is just the first half of Chapter Five. This chapter and its lessons are resumed and completed in *How to Hustle and Win, Part 2: Rap, Race, and Revolution*.

Afterword

STILL NOT THE END

I hope you don't feel like I left you hanging. The other half of this book is already done, I swear. I'm not trying to stall by cutting it short. As you read this, *Part Two* (titled *How to Hustle and Win, Part 2: Rap, Race, and Revolution*) is available in stores or via www.HustleAndWin.com.

Either way, here are some closing thoughts on *Part One*. As you know, I wrote these books hoping to share some of the game I've learned from life and the many mentors, coaches, and teachers I've met along the way. Many of these lessons I had to learn the hard way. While I'm hoping you won't have to go through the same, I know you're going to have to fail a few more times before you get it right. Life is the best teacher, so long as you're smart enough to learn something everytime you fail. Hopefully, this book will show you the lessons to look out for, as well as how to find other lessons in your daily life.

I'm confident that we can change the world. And when I say "we," I'm not talking about a group of politicians or wealthy people. I'm talking about the leaders who will emerge from poverty, abuse, and nothingness...as our most incredible leaders always do. I'm talking about a tidal wave of change that will start off small, before eventually growing to a critical mass that can't be ignored. I'm talking about people continuing to be followers...but following people like *you*, instead. I'm talking about the entire world looking our way and saying, "Here is a people who have been enslaved, exploited, and nearly exterminated, and yet they rise up in a way that the world has never seen. We must salute them, support them, and come together in solidarity with them...and rise up as well." I'm talking about change from the bottom up.

There is nothing about our people that ever truly dies. Even as the critics scream "Hip Hop is Dead," I see dozens of rappers bringing hip hop back to life. I see rappers being honest again, and talking about what is really going on in our bitter world. I see rappers becoming bold and defiant, unafraid to talk about racism once again. If rappers can tell the truth again, I know that our people will be able to see it again.

At the same time, I see our young people seething with anger. Either they express it openly with their "I don't give a f*ck" attitudes, or they hold it in and burn quietly, hoping that they can make it to the next day without killing themselves somehow. I know what they're angry about even when it's clear that they do not. But I know that anger can be turned around and channeled into the most unstoppable force for change. I know, given discipline and a desire for change, a man who hates his twisted life will become determined to change not only his life, but the lives of everyone around him. All he needs is a vision. I wrote these books to provide that vision.

I wrote these books for the fatherless and abandoned, the poor and the persecuted, the tired and humiliated, the raging and self-destructive, the confused and alienated. I wrote this book for people who don't look for their answers in the Bible anymore, so they missed *Psalms 82*, where it tells them:

> How long will you defend the unjust and show partiality to the wicked?
> Defend the cause of the weak and the fatherless;
> Maintain the rights of the poor and oppressed.
> Rescue the weak and needy;
> Deliver them from the hand of the wicked.
> They know nothing, they understand nothing.
> They walk about in darkness;
> All the foundations of the earth are shaken.
> I said "You are Gods. You are all Sons of the Most High.
> But you will die like mere men;
> You will fall like every other ruler."
> Rise up, O God, judge the Earth;
> For all the nations are your inheritance.

I didn't write to nobodies and nothings. I wrote to the Gods who will one day judge the Earth and inherit all nations. I wrote to challenge and inspire, while making sure I didn't venture too far away from day-to-day reality. I didn't have many other audiences in mind when I wrote, so forgive me if I said something that just didn't sit right with you. I'm a scholar now, but I wasn't thinking scholarship when I wrote this. I was thinking *solutions*.

On the other hand, if this book was *above* your head, read it again. You'll get it. And with that said, I hope I've done my job.

Until next time.

— Supreme Understanding

Appendixes

ABOUT THE AUTHOR

Before I begin with the other resources, I figured I'd give you an idea about the person who wrote this book. I've said plenty about my life throughout this book, but if you happen to be reading this section first, I'll just give you my life story – the highlights, at least – as a list:

I almost wasn't born
I grew up in a FUH
I stayed in trouble in school
I ran away from home
I was raised by the hood
I hated my life
I was expelled from high school
I was told I wasn't college material
I got jumped
I jumped people
I got robbed
I robbed people
I bought drugs
I did drugs
I sold drugs
I sold guns
I sold forged documents
I sold pussy
I was harassed regularly by the police
I have been arrested
I have been to jail
I have been under surveillance
I have been at gunpoint
I have had people at gunpoint
I have been in stand-offs
I set myself on fire
I almost drowned
I almost electrocuted myself
I almost killed myself
I jumped rooftops for fun
I wanted to find myself
I was run over by a car
I drank until I blacked out
I smoked til I coughed blood
I cried til I couldn't cry again
I lost friends to drugs
I lost friends to jail

I lost friends to the gun
I lost friends to the truth
I almost lost my own mind
I found knowledge of self
I had a car blow up
I had health problems
I totaled a few cars
I had my own apartment at 17
I had my lease terminated at 18
I was homeless for a year
I bought my first house at 20
I owned almost a million $ worth of real estate by 24
I racked up a half a million dollars worth of debt
I lost houses to foreclosure
I had no credit at 18
I had great credit by 22
I had terrible credit by 26
I stayed in school
I graduated from college with honors
I caught a case and beat it
I got my doctorate at 26
I sat in a burning building and kept eating
I traveled across the US via Greyhound at 18
I traveled to Asia, Africa, and Europe, and the Islands
I got lost in the wilderness
I camped out in the woods
I lived in a rural village
I tried skiing, horse-riding, mountain-climbing, and white-water rafting
I moshed in a heavy metal concert
I hurt a lot of people

I was a rapper
I hung out with the industry and found out it was empty
I was a spoken-word artist
I was a graphic artist
I was a photographer
I hung out with models and found out they were empty
I enjoyed plenty of meaningless pussy
I attempted several meaningful relationships
I endured plenty of break ups
I "managed" a dancer
I enjoyed plenty of crazy nights
I smutted plenty of smuts
I suffered plenty of crazy mornings
I was engaged
I endured abortion
I endured miscarriage
I stopped a couple of murders
I took custody of a 15 year old "son" at 23
I started over 7 businesses
I started a non-profit
I was recognized and awarded as an activist and educator
I toured Japan as an esteemed guest of the government
I did professional lectures and presentations
I finally found myself
I volunteered countless hours
I talked to hundreds of youth
I started a family
I got my money right
I got my money clean
I wrote a book about it all

Black-On-Black Violence: The Psychodynamics of Black Self-Annihilation in Service of White Domination by Amos N. Wilson

Blaming the Victims by. Edward W. Said & Christopher Hitchens

Blood in My Eye by George Jackson

Blueprint for Black Power by Amos Wilson

Breaking the Chains of Psychological Slavery by Na'im Akbar

Breaking the Curse of Willie Lynch: The Science of Slave Psychology by Alvin Morrow

Broken Alliance by Jonathan Kaufman

By Any Means Necessary by Malcolm X

Capitalism and Slavery by Eric Williams

Chains and Images of Psychological Slavery by Na'im Akbar

Chemical and Biological Warfare by Steven Rose

Chosen People from the Caucasus by Michael Bradley

Christopher Columbus and the African Holocaust by John Henrik Clarke

Community of Self by Naim Akbar

Confessions of an Economic Hit Man by John Perkins

Countering the Conspiracy to Destroy Black Boys by Jawanza Kunjufu

Culture Bandits by Dr. Del Jones

Do You! by Russell Simmons

Echoes of the Old Darkland: Themes from the African Eden by Charles S. Finch

European Holidays: An Afrikan Genocide by Dr. Ishakamusa Berashango

Faces at the Bottom of the Well by Derrick Bell

Facing Mount Kenya by Jomo Kenyatta

Fall of America by Elijah Muhammad

Freedom and Unity: Uhuru Na Umoja by Julius Nyerere

From Babylon to Timbuktu: A History of the Ancient Black Races including the Black Hebrews by Rudolph R. Windsor

From Columbus to Castro by Dr. Eric Willams

From Niggas to Gods by Bro. Akil

From Superman to Man by J. A. Rogers

From the Browder File: Survival Strategies for Africans in America by Anthony T. Browder

General History of Africa by UNESCO

God, the Bible and the Black Man's Destiny by Ishakamusa Barashango

God, the Black Man and the Truth by Ben Ammi

Herbally Yours by Penny C. Royal

History and Culture of Africa by Dr. John Henrik Clarke

Holler if You Hear Me by Nathan McCall

How Europe Underdeveloped Africa by Walter Rodney

In Search of Enemies: The Clash of Race by Haki Madabuti

Intellectual Warfare by Jacob H. Carruthers

Keepin it Real by Kevin Powell

Know Thy Self by Nai'm Akbar

Know What I Mean? By Michael Eric Dyson

Last Year of Malcolm X: The Evolution of a Revolutionary by Geroge Breitman

Lies My Teacher Told Me by James Loewen.

Life and Times of Frederick Douglass by Frederick Douglass

Lost Cities of Africa by Basil Davidson

BLACK INVENTORS (INVENTIONS A-L)

Philip Emeagwali	Accurate Weather Forecasting	1990
Frederick Jones	Air Conditioner. Patent # 2475841	July 12, 1949
J.F. Pickering	Air Ship	1892
James S. Adams	Airplane Propelling	
Granville T. Woods	Auto Cut-Off Switch	January 1, 1839
G. Cook	Auto Fishing Device	May 30, 1899
Andrew Beard	Automatic Car Coupling Device	1897
Richard Spikes	Automatic Gear Shift	February 28, 1932
Elijah Mccoy	Automatic Lubrication System (For Railroad/ Heavy Machinery)	July 2, 1872
Jan Matzelinger	Automatic Shoe Making Machine	1883
Garrett Morgan	Automatic Traffic Light	November 20, 1923
W. H. Richardson	Baby Buggy	June 18, 1899
J. Ross	Bailing Press. Patent # 632,539	Sept 05, 1899
L.R. Johnson	Bicycle Frame	October 10, 1899
A.P. Ashbourne	Biscuit Cutter	November 30, 1875
Charles Drew	Blood Plasma Bag	Approx. 1945
L. F. Brown	Bridle bit. Patent # 484,994	October 25, 1892
Sara E. Goode	Cabinet Bed	1885
A.E. Long	Caps For Bottles And Jars	1898
A.C. Richardson	Casket-Lowering Device. Patent # 529,311	November 13, 1894
Darryl Thomas	Cattle Roping Apparatus	
Henry T. Sampson	Cellular Phone	July 6, 1971
Lloyd A. Hall	Chemical compound to preserve meat	
A.C. Richardson	Churn. Patent # 466,470	February 17, 1891
J.A. Sweeting	Cigarette Roller	1897
Benjamin Banneker	Clock, Almanac	Approx. 1791
G.T. Sampson	Clothes Dryer	June 6, 1862
Ellen Elgin	Clothes Wringer	1880s
G.W. Murray	Combined Furrow Opener and Stalk-Knocker.	April 10, 1894
J.H. White	Convertible Sette (A Large Sofa)	1892
R.P. Scott	Corn Silker	1894
G. E. Downing	Corner Cleaner Attachment.	February 13, 1973
G.W. Murray	Cotton Chopper. Patent # 520,888	June 5, 1894
G.W. Murray	Cultivator and Marker. Patent # 517,961	April 10, 1894
S.R. Scratton	Curtain Rod	November 30, 1889
William S. Grant	Curtain Rod Support	August 4, 1896
J. Robinson	Dinner Pail. Patent # 356,852	February 1, 1887
Manley West	Discovered compound in cannabis for glaucoma.	1980-1987
O. Dorsey	Door Stop	December 10, 1878
J. W. Reed	Dough Kneader and Roller. Patent # 304,552	September 2, 1884
Lawrence P. Ray	Dust Pan	August 3, 1897
Willie Johnson	Egg Beater	February 5, 1884
Lewis Latimer	Electric Lampbulb	March 21, 1882
Elbert R. Robinson	Electric Railway Trolley	
Alexander Miles	Elevator and safety device for elevators.	October 11, 1887

Rufus Stokes	Exhaust Purifier Patent #3,378,241	April 16, 1968
P. Johnson	Eye Protector	November 2, 1880
George Alcorn	Fabrication of Spectrometer. Patent # 4,618,380	October 21, 1986
G.W. Murray	Fertilizer Distributor. Patent# 520,889	June 5, 1894
C.V. Richey	Fire Escape Bracket. Patent # 596,427	December 28, 1897
J.W. Winters	Fire Escape Ladder	May 7, 1878
Thomas J.Martin	Fire Extinguisher	March 26, 1872
L.C. Bailey	Folding Bed	July 18, 1899
Brody & Surgwar	Folding Chair	June 11, 1889
W.B. Purvis	Fountain Pen	January 7, 1890
O.A. Fisher	Furniture Caster	1878
A.L. Rickman	Galoshes	1898
B.F. Jackson	Gas Burner	
Garret A. Morgan	Gas Mask	October 13, 1914
G. F. Grant	Golf Tee. Patent # 638,920	December 12, 1899
R. F. Flemming, Jr.	Guitar	March 3, 1886
Lydia O. Newman	Hair Brush	November 15, 18--
C. J. Walker	Hair Care Products	1905
Walter B. Purvis	Hand Stamp	February 27, 1883
Alice Parker	Heating Furnace	1918
Paul E Williams	Helicopter	
J. Ricks	Horse Shoe	March 30, 1885
W.H. Sammons	Hot Comb	1920
Philip Emeagwali	Hyperball Computer	April 1996
Augustus Jackson	Ice cream	1832
Alfred L. Cralle	Ice Cream Scooper. Patent # 576,395	February 2,1897
S. H. Love	Improved Vending Machine. Patent # 1936515	November 21, 1933
Henry Single	Improved Fish Hook. Sold later for $625	1854
Philip Emeagwali	Improved Petroleum Recovery	1990
S. H. Love	Improvement to military guns.	April 22, 1919
A.C. Richard	Insect-Destroyer Gun	February 28, 1899
B. F. Cargill	Invalid Cot. Patent # 629,658	July 25, 1899
Dr. Charles Drew	Blood Banks	1940
Sarah Boone	Ironing Board	December 30, 1887
F.J. Loudin	Key Chain	January 9, 1894
H.A. Jackson	Kitchen Table	
Michael C. Harvey	Lantern	August 19, 1884
L.A. Burr	Lawn Mower	May 19, 1889
J.S. Smith	Lawn Sprinkler. Patent # 581,785	May 4, 1897
J. Thomas White	Lemon Squeezer	December 8, 1893
Phillip Downing	Letter Drop Mailbox. Patent # 462,096	October 27, 1891
J. H. Robinson	Lifesaving guards for Street Cars.	April 25, 1899
Lewis H. Latimer	Light Bulb Filament	
W.A. Martin	Lock	July 23, 18-

How to Win Friends and Influence People

This is simply a concise summary of a *very* useful book. Read it. *Use it.*

Part One – Fundamental techniques in handling people:

1. Don't criticize, condemn or complain.
2. Give honest and sincere appreciation.
3. Arouse in the other person an eager want.

Part Two – Six ways to make people like you:

1. Become genuinely interested in other people.
2. Smile.
3. Remember that a person's name is to that person the sweetest and most important sound in any language.
4. Be a good listener. Encourage others to talk about themselves.
5. Talk in terms of the other person's interests.
6. Make the other person feel important – and do it sincerely.

Part Three – Win people to your way of thinking:

1. The only way to get the best of an argument is to avoid it.
2. Show respect for the other person's opinions. Never say, "You're wrong."
3. If you are wrong, admit it quickly and emphatically.
4. Begin in a friendly way.
5. Get the other person saying "yes, yes" immediately.
6. Let the other person do a great deal of the talking.
7. Let the other person feel that the idea is his or hers.
8. Try honestly to see things from the other person's point of view.
9. Be sympathetic with the other person's ideas and desires.
10. Appeal to the nobler motives.
11. Dramatize your ideas.
12. Throw down a challenge.

Part Four – Be a Leader

A leader's job often includes changing your people's attitudes and behavior. Some suggestions to accomplish this:

1. Begin with praise and honest appreciation.
2. Call attention to people's mistakes indirectly.
3. Talk about your own mistakes before criticizing the other person.
4. Ask questions instead of giving direct orders.
5. Let the other person save face.
6. Praise the slightest improvement and praise every improvement. Be "hearty in your approbation and lavish in your praise."
7. Give the other person a fine reputation to live up to.
8. Use encouragement. Make the fault seem easy to correct.
9. Make the other person happy about doing the thing you suggest.

THE SEVEN HABITS OF HIGHLY EFFECTIVE PEOPLE

Another summary of a book that can seriously help you.

1. Be Pro-active. You can either be proactive or reactive when it comes to how you act about certain things, and we're not talking skin cream. Being "proactive" means taking responsibility for everything in life. When you're reactive, you blame other people and circumstances for obstacles or problems. Man is different from animals in that he has a mind, which gives him self-awareness. He has the ability to detach himself and observe his own self, think about his thoughts. This attribute gives man the power not to be affected by his circumstances. Thus, man takes the initiative to create whatever he wants to occur in his life.

2. Begin with the End In Mind. This chapter is about setting long-term goals based on "true-north principles". The idea here is to formulate a "personal mission statement" to document your idead of what your true purpose is in life. The author sees visualization as an important tool to develop this. Basically, see where you want to be, and work out a roadmap to get there.

3. Put First Things First. This chapter presents a framework for prioritizing work that is aimed at long-term goals, at the expense of tasks that appear to be urgent, but are in fact less important. Successful delegation deals with finding the right people to do the right jobs, and checking on them the right way.

4. Think Win/Win. This chapter describes an attitude where mutually beneficial solutions are sought, that satisfy your needs as well as others. In the case of a conflict, both parties can meet on common ground and compromise.

5. Seek First to Understand, Then to be Understood. Basically, try to see it their way first. Giving out advice before having empathetically understood a person and their situation will usually result in your advice being rejected. You've got to let them see that you feel where they're coming from, and it actually matters to you. Working communication isn't about waiting until someone is done talking to say what you were going to say anyway. Working communication is about seeing what everyone is really trying to say.

6. Synergize. To "synergize" describes a way of working in teams. Some of the important qualities of true teamwork are effective problem solving, collaborative decision making, and accepting (and valuing) your differences. Everyone has different strengths, and if put together correctly, the result of the teamwork will exceed the sum of what each of the members could have achieved on their own. "The whole is greater than the sum of its parts."

7. Sharpen the Saw. This idea focuses on balanced self-renewal. Basically, this means you regain your ability to grind and put in hard work by carefully selecting recreational activities or "fun" that doesn't take away from what you're striving to accomplish. "All work and no play makes Jack a dull boy."

ARTISTS DON'T MAKE MONEY FROM RECORD DEALS

By Wendy Day from Rap Coalition

Who is the incredible bonehead who said rappers make mad loot? Wrong, wrong, wrong, wrong, wrong!! Because the fans expect their favorite artists to be crazy paid and livin' large, this puts an incredible amount of pressure on the artists to appear wealthy. And it's not just the fans; I can't tell you how many times I've been out with rappers along with people in the industry, and the industry slobs have expected the artists to pick up the dinner check. I've even seen people cop an attitude if the artist doesn't pay for everything. This is small minded and ignorant because the artist is ALWAYS the last to get paid. Everyone gets their cut first: the label, the manager (15%- 20% of all of the artist's entertainment income), the lawyer (by the hour or 5%-10% of the deal), the accountant (by the hour or 5% of all income), and, of course, the IRS (28% to 50% depending on the tax bracket).

Once an artist releases a record, the pressure is on to portray a successful image to fans, friends, families, and people around the way. People expect the artists to be well dressed, drive an expensive car, etc. Think about it. Don't you expect artists "to look like artists?" Would you admire Jay-Z as much if he drove a busted old 1990 Grand Am instead of that beautiful, brand new, top of the line Bentley?

Sadly, when an artist gets signed to a label deal, especially a rap artist, he or she receives somewhere between 8 and 13 points. What that means is 8% to 13% of the retail sales price, after the record label recoups the money it puts out (the advance, the sample clearances, the producer advances, usually half the cost of any videos, any cash outlays for the artists, etc.). The artist has to sell hella units to make any money back. Here's an example of a relatively fair record deal for a new rap artist with some clout in the industry and a terrific negotiating attorney:

ROYALTY RATE: 12%

We're going to assume that there are 3 artists in the group, and that they split everything equally. We're also going to assume that they produce their own tracks themselves.

> Suggested retail list price = $10.98
> less 15% packaging deduction (usually 20%) = $9.33
> gets paid on 85% of records sold ("free goods") = $7.93

So the artists' 12% is equal to about 96 cents per record sold. In most deals, the producer's 3% comes out of that 12%, but for the sake of brevity, in this example the group produced the whole album, buying no tracks from outside producers, which is rare.

Let's assume that they are a hit and their record goes Gold (although it is rare that a first record blows up like this). Let's also assume they were a priority at their record label and that their label understood exactly how to market them. So they went Gold, selling 500,000 units according to SoundScan (and due to the inaccuracies in SoundScan tracking at the rap retail level, 500,000 scanned probably means more like 600,000 actually sold).

GOLD RECORD = 500,000 units sold x $ .96 = $480,000. Looks like a nice chunk of loot, huh? Watch this. Now the label recoups what they've spent: independent promotion, 1/2 the video cost, some tour support, all those limo rides, all those out of town trips for the artist and their friends, etc.

$480,000
-$100,000 recoupable stuff (NOT advance)
$380,000
-$ 70,000 advance (recording costs)
$310,000

Still sounds OK? Watch... Now, half of the $380,000 stays "in reserve" (accounting for returned items from retail stores) for 2 to 4 years depending on the length specified in the recording contract. So the $70,000 advance is actually subtracted from $190,000 (the other $190,000 is in reserves for 2 years). Now, there's also the artist's manager, who is entitled to 20% of all of the entertainment income which would be 20% of $310,000, or $62,000. Remember, the artist is the last to get paid, so even the manager gets paid before the artist.

So the artists actually receive $19,333 each for their gold album, and in two years when the reserves are liquidated, IF they've recouped, they will each receive another $63,000. IF they've recouped. Guess who keeps track of all of this accounting? The label. Most contracts are "cross-collateralized," which means if the artist does not recoup on the first album, the money will be paid back out of the second album. Also, if the money is not recouped on the second album, repayment can come out of the "in reserve" funds from the first album, if the funds have not already been liquidated.

Even after the reserves are paid, each artist only actually made 50 cents per unit based on this example. The label made about $2.68 per unit. This example also doesn't include any additional production costs for an outside producer to come in and do a re-mix, and you know how often that happens.

So each artist in this group has received a total of about $82,000. After legal expenses and costs of new clothing to wear on stage while touring, etc, each artist has probably made a total of $75,000 before paying taxes (which the artist is responsible for – remember Kool Moe Dee?). Let's look at the time line now. Let's assume the artists had no jobs when they started this. They spent 4 months putting their demo together and getting the tracks just right. They spent another 6 months to a year getting to know who all of the players are in the rap music industry and shopping their demo. After signing to a label, it took another 8 months to make an album and to get through all of the label's bureaucracy. When the first single dropped, the group went into promotion mode and traveled all over promoting the single at radio, retail, concerts, and publications. This was another six months. The record label decided to push three singles off the album so it was another year before they got back into the studio to make album number two. This scenario has been a total of 36 months. Each member of the group made $75,000 for a three year investment of time, which averages out to $25,000 per year. In corporate America, that works out to be $12 per hour (before taxes).

WHAT TO DO IF YOU'RE STOPPED BY THE POLICE

From the American Civil Liberties Union

To fight police abuse effectively, you need to know your rights. There are some things you should do, some things you must do and some things you cannot do. If you are in the middle of a police encounter, you need a handy and quick reference to remind you what your rights and obligations are.

The following information is produced by the American Civil Liberties Union, an organization that fights to protect the constitutional rights of all people. They hope that you print these pages and carry this information in your wallet, pocket, or glove compartment to give you quick access to your rights and obligations concerning police encounters.

THE BASICS

Think carefully about your words, movement, body language, and emotions.

Don't get into an argument with the police.

Remember, anything you say or do can be used against you.

Keep your hands where the police can see them.

Don't run. Don't touch any police officer.

Don't resist even if you believe you are innocent.

Don't complain on the scene or tell the police they're wrong or that you're going to file a complaint.

Do not make any statements regarding the incident. Ask for a lawyer immediately upon your arrest.

Remember officers' badge and patrol car numbers.

Write down everything you remember ASAP.

Try to find witnesses and their names and phone numbers.

If you are injured, take photographs of the injuries as soon as possible, but make sure you seek medical attention first.

If you feel your rights have been violated, file a written complaint with police department's internal affairs division or civilian complaint board.

What you say to the police is always important. What you say can be used against you, and it can give the police an excuse to arrest you, especially if you bad-mouth a police officer.

You must show your driver's license and registration when stopped in a car. Otherwise, you don't have to answer any questions if you are detained or arrested, with one important exception. The police may ask for your name if you have been properly detained, and you can be arrested in some states for refusing to give it. If you reasonably fear that your name is incriminating, you can claim the right to remain silent, which may be a defense in case you are arrested anyway.

You don't have to consent to any search of yourself, your car or your house. If you DO consent to a search, it can affect your rights later in court. If the police say they have a search warrant, ASK TO SEE IT.

Do not interfere with, or obstruct, the police – you can be arrested for it.

IF YOU ARE STOPPED FOR QUESTIONING

1. It's not a crime to refuse to answer questions, but refusing to answer can make the police suspicious about you. If you are asked to identify yourself, see paragraph 2 above.

2. Police may "pat-down" your clothing if they suspect a concealed weapon. Don't physically resist, but make it clear that you don't consent to any further search.

3. Ask if you are under arrest. If you are, you have a right to know why. If not, you are free to go.

4. Don't bad-mouth the police officer or run away, even if you believe what is happening is unreasonable. That could lead to your arrest.

IF YOU'RE STOPPED IN YOUR CAR

1. Upon request, show them your driver's license, registration, and proof of insurance. In certain cases, your car can be searched without a warrant as long as the police have probable cause. To protect yourself later, you should make it clear that you do not consent to a search. It is not lawful for police to arrest you simply for refusing to consent to a search.

2. If you're given a ticket, you should sign it; otherwise you can be arrested. You can always fight the case in court later.

3. If you're suspected of drunk driving (DWI) and refuse to take a blood, urine or breath test, your driver's license may be suspended.

IF YOU'RE ARRESTED OR TAKEN TO A POLICE STATION

1. You have the right to remain silent and to talk to a lawyer before you talk to the police. Tell the police nothing except your name and address. Don't give any explanations, excuses or stories. You can make your defense later, in court, based on what you and your lawyer decide is best.

2. Ask to see a lawyer immediately. If you can't pay for a lawyer, you have a right to a free one, and should ask the police how the lawyer can be contacted. Don't say anything without a lawyer.

3. Within a reasonable time after your arrest, or booking, you have the right to make a local phone call: to a lawyer, bail bondsman, a relative or any other person. The police may not listen to the call to the lawyer.

4. Sometimes you can be released without bail, or have bail lowered. Have your lawyer ask the judge about this possibility. You must be taken before the judge on the next court day after arrest.

5. Do not make any decisions in your case until you have talked with a lawyer.

IN YOUR HOME

1. If the police knock and ask to enter your home, you don't have to admit them unless they have a warrant signed by a judge.

2. However, in some emergency situations (like when a person is screaming for help inside, or when the police are chasing someone) officers are allowed to enter and search your home without a warrant.

3. If you are arrested, the police can search you and the area close by. If you are in a building, "close by" usually means just the room you are in.

We all recognize the need for effective law enforcement, but we should also understand our own rights and responsibilities -- especially in our relationships with the police. Everyone, including minors, has the right to courteous and respectful police treatment.

If your rights are violated, don't try to deal with the situation at the scene. You can discuss the matter with an attorney afterwards, or file a complaint with the Internal Affairs or Civilian Complaint Board.

WHAT DO YOU DO NOW?

You're done already? Great. Now relax. Breathe. Let everything sink in. Reread whatever you think you need to look at again. Don't get all excited and start slapping people in the face for not knowing half of what you know now.

Instead, here's what you can do now:

- Tell people about this book and the ideas in it.

- Send copies to people who need this in their life.

- Put the lessons in this book into practice in your daily life.

- Develop a plan for how you're going to create changes in your life and the world around you.

- Make it a habit to find at least one lesson a day in your life's experiences.

- Look for lessons from this book in your daily life and the lives of others you know.

- Start eliminating your bad/weak habits, beginning with those most destructive to you.

- Build your leadership skills and destroy your fear.

- Think about constant themes found throughout this book (ideas or facts that keep coming up) and ask yourself why?

- Pick up *Part Two* as soon as you're able to.

- Add on, by sending us your praise, comments, or suggestions for improvement.

- Share your success stories with us.

- Leave positive reviews of the book at Amazon.com and other sites.

You can reach us by mail at:

Supreme Design
PO Box 10887
Atlanta, GA 30310

Or you can visit us online at **www.HustleAndWin.com**

WHAT TO EXPECT IN
HHW PART TWO

Lessons from the true stories of:

Che Guevara	Lil Wayne
Tupac Shakur	The Jena 6
Steve Biko	Haile Selassie I
The Real Rick	Bob Marley
Ross	Philly's Black
Rebel Slaves	Mafia
Bumpy Johnson	Samuel Jackson
Allah (Clarence	Frank Lucas
13X)	Hugo Chavez
Fred Hampton	Saddam Hussein
NWA	Dave Chappelle
Rodney King	...and dozens
Mike Vick	more

As well as chapters showing you:

- How to have your money make you more money

- How to overcome against any odds or obstacles

- The true story behind American holidays

- How to deal with the police

- How to discipline your mind and your body

- 11 ways out of the hood

- What kind of leadership style you have

- How to get pussy...and how to get love

- Why Black men are becoming more and more feminine

- How to set goals and accomplish them

- How we can accomplish *true* social change

And dozens of other true stories, rare facts, hidden truths, thought-provoking commentaries, and practical life lessons that anyone can use.

If *Part One* made you think...*Part Two* takes you even further.

Available NOW at...

WWW.HUSTLEANDWIN.COM

HERITAGE PLAYING CARDS

THE WHOLE WORLD
IN THE PALM OF YOUR HAND

54 Full Color Playing Cards and Educational Booklet

Why bother with a dull deck of plain cards when there's Heritage Playing Cards?

Not only is this deck perfect for any game you can think of, it's also an amazing conversation starter and an incredible educational tool! Featuring 54 hand-painted images of indigenous people from every corner of the globe, this deck is like a world tour in a box!

In any given hand, you might find an Egyptian pharoah sharing the company of a Chinese merchant, a Pawnee chieftain, a Mayan priest and an Indian folk dancer!

The enclosed booklet offers details on the cultures represented on every card, a history of how playing cards came to be, and a selection of traditional card games from around the world! This deck can be used to teach number concepts, world cultures, geography, history, and multicultural education.

With Heritage Cards, you've found tremendous value in a tiny box!

HAVE CHILDREN? THEN PICK UP

REAL LIFE IS NO FAIRY TALE

A STORY OF RESILIENCE AND POSITIVE THINKING

Real Life is No Fairy Tale is the inspirational story of one child's resilience and optimism in spite of the many struggles that often accompany urban poverty. Tony's attitude towards life is what makes the difference.

It seems almost nothing can bring him down, until a school bully makes Tony reconsider his positive outlook.

Children of all ages will be in awe at the beauty and authenticity of both the words and images. The story is composed entirely in verse, and the images are brilliantly rendered full-color illustrations. Review questions covering vocabulary, comprehension, and critical thinking are presented at the end.

About the Enhanced CD:

The included disc provides a wealth of resources to accompany the book. These resources are designed to help parents, educators, and of course the readers themselves. In a CD player or computer, you can play a narration of the text in two versions, one set to an original musical score, and the other is read without music. The disc also contains the captioned video of the story, as well as lesson plans, graphic organizers, worksheets, mazes, crossword puzzles, and other printable activities. These resources will significantly extend the relevance of Real Life is No Fairy Tale in any home or classroom.

AVAILABLE NOW

Browse the art, listen to the audio, watch clips, and find out more at…

WWW.NOFAIRYTALE.COM

THE HOOD HEALTH HANDBOOK

A PRACTICAL GUIDE TO HEALTH AND WELLNESS IN THE URBAN COMMUNITY

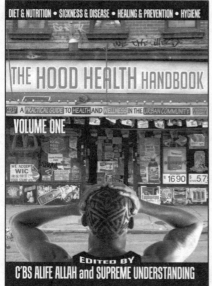

How can you attain optimum health with minimum resources? This book shows us how, in plain English. *Hood Health* is an anthology of over health experts from urban communities throughout the U.S., including fitness gurus, dieticians, personal trainers, and holistic practitioners, offering practical health solutions to common health problems. The text was edited by C'BS Alife and Dr. Supreme Understanding and supervised by a panel of licensed physicians.

TOPICS INCLUDE

❏ Why We're So Sick
❏ Fast Food vs. Real Food
❏ Weight Loss without Crash Diets
❏ Chemicals in our Homes & Foods
❏ Home Remedies that Work
❏ Traditional vs. Western Medicine
❏ Treating ADHD, Depression, and Drug Addiction

❏ Food Budgeting and Preparation
❏ Preventing and Treating Diabetes, Cancer, and Heart Disease
❏ How to Quit Smoking
❏ Urban Survival and First Aid
❏ Chemical Genocide and Environmental Racism
❏ Herb/Vitamin/Mineral Guide

WWW.HOODHEALTHHANDBOOK.COM

What should you do now that you're done reading?
Here are some suggestions:

❑ Complete any activities mentioned in this book, especially the discussions. See any of the films mentioned, but with others.

❑ Tell somebody about this book and what you've learned. Invite them to come read it. Don't let them steal the book.

❑ As another option, let them steal the book. It might help them.

❑ Mentor some young people or teach a class using this book as a handbook or reference.

❑ Talk about this book online, but don't stay on the Net forever.

❑ Join an organization or group that discusses concepts like the ones in this book and get into those discussions.

❑ Leave this book away somewhere it will be picked up and read.

❑ Identify the people in your community who could use a copy of this book. If they're people would want to buy a book like this, let em read a few pages and see if they can afford to buy a copy.

❑ If they're people who don't normally buy books – but you know that givin em a copy could change their life – give em a copy and tell em to come see you when they're ready for another one. This is why you can order copies at wholesale rates at our site.

We hope this helps you keep the knowledge contagious.

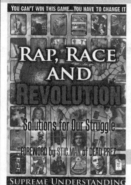
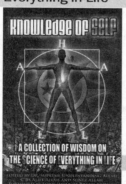

The Hood Health Handbook, Volume One (Physical Health)

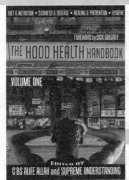

Edited by Supreme Understanding and C'BS Alife Allah, Foreword by Dick Gregory

Want to know why Black and brown people are so sick? This book covers the many "unnatural causes" behind our poor health, and offers hundreds of affordable and easy-to-implement solutions.

CLASS	PAGES	RETAIL	RELEASE
PH-1	480	$19.95	Nov. 2010

ISBN: 978-1-935721-32-1

The Hood Health Handbook, Volume Two (Mental Health)

Edited by Supreme Understanding and C'BS Alife Allah

This volume covers mental health, how to keep a healthy home, raising healthy children, environmental issues, and dozens of other issues, all from the same down-to-earth perspective as Volume One.

CLASS	PAGES	RETAIL	RELEASE
MH-1	480	$19.95	Nov. 2010

ISBN: 978-1-935721-33-8

A Taste of Life: 1,000 Vegetarian Recipes from Around the World

Edited by Supreme Understanding and Patra Afrika

This cookbook makes it easy to become vegetarian. In addition to over 1,000 recipes from everywhere you can think of, plus over 100 drink and smoothie recipes, this book also teaches how to transition your diet, what to shop for, how to cook, as well as a guide to nutrients and vitamins.

CLASS	PAGES	RETAIL	RELEASE
W-1	400	$19.95	Jun. 2011

ISBN: 978-1-935721-10-9

La Brega: Como Sobrevivir En El Barrio

By Supreme Understanding

Thanks to strong demand coming from Spanish-speaking countries, we translated our groundbreaking How to Hustle and Win into Spanish, and added new content specific to Latin America. Because this book's language is easy to follow, it can also be used to brush up on your Spanish.

CLASS	PAGES	RETAIL	RELEASE
0-1	336	$14.95	Jul. 2009

ISBN: 978-0981617-08-4

Locked Up but Not Locked Down: A Guide to Surviving the American Prison System

By Ahmariah Jackson and IAtomic Allah
Foreword by Mumia Abu Jamal

This book covers what it's like on the inside, how to make the most of your time, what to do once you're out, and how to stay out. Features contributions from over 50 insiders, covering city jails, state and federal prisons, women's prisons, juvenile detention, and international prisons.

CLASS	PAGES	RETAIL	RELEASE
J-1	288	$24.95	Jul. 2012

ISBN: 978-1935721-00-0

The Science of Self: Man, God, and the Mathematical Language of Nature

By Supreme Understanding and C'BS Alife Allah

How did the universe begin? Is there a pattern to everything that happens? What's the meaning of life? What does science tell us about the depths of our SELF? Who and what is God? This may be one of the deepest books you can read.

CLASS	PAGES	RETAIL	RELEASE
I-4	360	$29.95	Jun. 2012

ISBN: 978-1935721-67-3

When the World was Black, Part One: Prehistoric Cultures

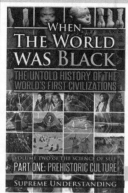

By Supreme Understanding
Foreword by Runoko Rashid

When does Black history begin? Certainly not with slavery. In two volumes, historian Supreme Understanding explores over 200,000 years of Black history from every corner of the globe. Part One covers the first Black communities to settle the world, establishing its first cultures and traditions. Their stories are remarkable.

CLASS	PAGES	RETAIL	RELEASE
I-3	400	$24.95	Feb. 2013

ISBN: 978-1-935721-04-8

When the World Was Black, Part Two: Ancient Civilizations

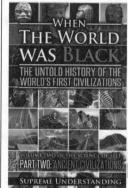

By Supreme Understanding

Part Two covers the ancient Black civilizations that gave birth to the modern world. Black people built the first urban civilizations in Africa, Asia, Europe, and the Americas. And every claim in these books is thoroughly documented with reputable sources. Do you want to know the story of your ancestors? You should. We study the past to see what the future will bring.

CLASS	PAGES	RETAIL	RELEASE
I-3	400	$24.95	Feb. 2013

ISBN: 978-1-935721-05-5

When the World was Black, Parts One and Two (Hardcover)

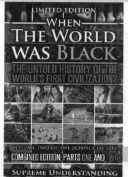

By Supreme Understanding

An incredible limited edition that combines Part One and Part Two into a single book, cased in an embossed clothbound hardcover and dust jacket. Autographed and numbered, this collector's item also includes both sets of full-color inserts.

CLASS	PAGES	RETAIL	RELEASE
I-3	800	$74.95	Dec. 2013

Only available direct from publisher.

Black Rebellion: Eyewitness Accounts of Major Slave Revolts

Edited by Dr. Sujan Dass

Who will tell the stories of those who refused to be slaves? What about those who fought so effectively that they forced their slavers to give up? Black Rebellion is a collection of historical "eyewitness" accounts of dozens of major revolts and uprisings, from the U.S. to the Caribbean, as well as a history of slavery and revolt.

CLASS	PAGES	RETAIL	RELEASE
P-3	272	$19.95	May 2010

ISBN: 978-0-981617-04-6

The Heroic Slave

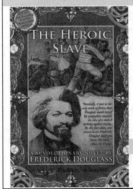

By Frederick Douglass

Most people don't know that Douglass wrote a novel...or that, in this short novel, he promoted the idea of violent revolt. By this time in his life, the renowned abolitionist was seeing things differently. This important piece of history comes with *David Walker's Appeal*, all in one book.

CLASS	PAGES	RETAIL	RELEASE
P-3	160	$19.95	Apr. 2011

ISBN: 978-1-935721-27-7

David Walker's Appeal

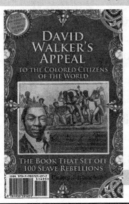

By David Walker

This is one of the most important, and radical, works ever published against slavery. Rather than call for an end by peaceful means, Walker called for outright revolution. His calls may have led to over 100 revolts, including those described in *Black Rebellion*. This important piece of history comes with Douglass' *The Heroic Slave*, which it may have helped inspire.

CLASS	PAGES	RETAIL	RELEASE
P-3	160	$19.95	Apr. 2011

ISBN: 978-1-935721-27-7

Darkwater: Voices from Within the Veil, Annotated Edition

By W.E.B. Du Bois

This book makes Du Bois' previous work, like *Souls of Black Folk*, seem tame by comparison. *Darkwater* is revolutionary, uncompromising, and unconventional in both its content and style, addressing the plight of Black women, the rise of a Black Messiah, a critical analysis of white folks, and the need for outright revolution.

CLASS	PAGES	RETAIL	RELEASE
I-4	240	$19.95	Jun. 2011

ISBN: 978-0-981617-07-7

The African Abroad: The Black Man's Evolution in Western Civilization, Volume One

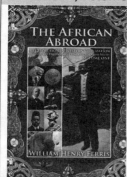

By William Henry Ferris

Who would think a book written in 1911 could cover so much? Ferris, chairman of the UNIA, speaks up for the Black man's role in Western civilization. He discusses a wealth of history, as well as some revolutionary Black theology, exploring the idea of man as God and God as man.

CLASS	PAGES	RETAIL	RELEASE
I-5	570	$29.95	Oct. 2012

ISBN: 978-1935721-66-6

The African Abroad: Volume Two

By William Henry Ferris

The second volume of Ferris' epic covers important Black biographies of great leaders, ancient and modern. He tells the stories of forty "Black Immortals." He also identifies the African origins of many of the world's civilizations, including ancient Egypt, Akkad, Sumer, India, and Europe.

CLASS	PAGES	RETAIL	RELEASE
I-5	330	$19.95	Oct. 2012

ISBN: 978-1-935721-69-7

From Poverty to Power: The Realization of Prosperity and Peace

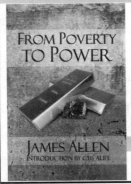

By James Allen

Want to transform your life? James Allen, the author of the classic *As a Man Thinketh,* explores how we can turn struggle and adversity into power and prosperity. This inspirational text teaches readers about their innate strength and the immense power of the conscious mind.

CLASS	PAGES	RETAIL	RELEASE
I-3	144	$19.95	May 2010

ISBN: 978-0-981617-05-3

Daily Meditations: A Year of Guidance on the Meaning of Life

By James Allen

Need a guidebook to a productive and healthy year? This is it. James Allen delivers another great work in this book, this time offering 365 days of inspiration and guidance on life's greatest challenges. This book includes sections for daily notes.

CLASS	PAGES	RETAIL	RELEASE
C-3	208	$19.95	Apr. 2013

ISBN: 978-1-935721-08-6

The Kybalion: The Seven Ancient Egyptian Laws _

By the Three Initiates

Thousands of years ago, the ancients figured out a set of principles that govern the universe. In *The Kybalion*, these laws are explored and explained. This edition includes research into the authorship of the book, and where the laws came from.

CLASS	PAGES	RETAIL	RELEASE
C-4	130	$19.95	Oct. 2012

ISBN: 978-1-935721-25-3

Real Life is No Fairy Tale (w/ Companion CD)

By Sujan Dass and Lord Williams

Looking for a children's book that teaches about struggle? Written for school age children, this full-color hardcover book is composed entirely in rhyme, and the images are as real as they get. Includes a CD with an audio book, animated video, review questions, and printable worksheets and activities.

CLASS	PGS	RETAIL	RELEASE
CD-4	36+	$16.95	Jun. 2010

ISBN: 978-0-9816170-2-2

Aesop's Fables: 101 Classic Tales and Timeless Lessons

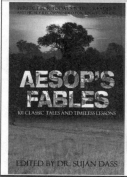

Edited by Dr. Sujan Dass

What's better to teach our children than life lessons? This easy-to-read collection of classic tales told by an African storyteller uses animals to teach valuable moral lessons. This edition includes dozens of black-and-white images to accompany the timeless fables. Color them in!

CLASS	PAGES	RETAIL	RELEASE
CD-3	112	$14.95	Feb. 2013

ISBN: 978-1-935721-07-9

Heritage Playing Cards (w/ Companion Booklet)

Designed by Sujan Dass

No more European royalty! This beautiful deck of playing cards features 54 full-color characters from around the world and a 16-page educational booklet on international card games and the ethnic backgrounds of the people on the cards.

CLASS	PGS	RETAIL	RELEASE
CD-2	16+	$14.95	May 2010

UPC: 05105-38587

Black God: An Introduction to the World's Religions and their Black Gods

By Supreme Understanding

Have you ever heard that Christ was Black? What about the Buddha? They weren't alone. This book explores the many Black gods of the ancient world, from Africa to Europe, Asia, and Australia, all the way to the Americas. Who were they? Why were they worshipped? And what does this mean for us today?

CLASS	PAGES	RETAIL	RELEASE
C-3	200	$19.95	Jan. 2014

ISBN: 978-1-935721-12-3

Black People Invented Everything

By Supreme Understanding

In *The Science of Self* we began exploring the origins of everything that modern civilization depends on today. In this book, we get into specifics, showing how Black people invented everything from agriculture to zoology, with dozens of pictures and references to prove it!

CLASS	PAGES	RETAIL	RELEASE
I-3	256	$29.95	Feb. 2020

ISBN: 978-1-935721-13-0

The Yogi Science of Breath: A Complete Manual of the Ancient Philosophy of the East

By Yogi Ramacharaka

A classic text on the science of breathing, one of the most ignored, yet important, aspects of our physical and emotional health. This book has been used by both martial arts experts and legendary jazz musicians. This edition explores the "secret science" of breath, and where its mysterious author learned such teachings.

CLASS	PAGES	RETAIL	RELEASE
PH-4	112	$14.95	Apr. 2012

ISBN: 978-1-935721-34-5

How to Get Our Books

To better serve our readers, we've streamlined the way we handle book orders. Here are some of the ways you can find our books.

In Stores

You can find our books in just about any Black bookstore or independent bookseller. If you don't find our titles on the shelves, just request them by name and publisher. Most bookstores can order our titles directly from us (via our site) or from the distributors listed below. We also provide a listing of retailers who carry our books at www.bestblackbooks.com

Online (Wholesale)

Now, you can visit our sites (like www.supremeunderstanding.com or www.bestblackbooks.com) to order wholesale quantities direct from us, the publisher. From our site, we ship heavily discounted case quantities to distributors, wholesalers, retailers, and local independent resellers (like yourself – just try it!). The discounts are so deep, you can afford to GIVE books away if you're not into making money.

Online (Retail)

If you're interested in single "retail" copies, you can now find them online at Amazon.com, or you can order them via mail order by contacting one of the mail order distributors listed below. You can also find many of our titles as eBooks in the Amazon Kindle, Nook, or Apple iBooks systems. You may also find full-length videobook or audiobook files available, but nothing beats the pass-around potential of a real book!

By Mail Order

Please contact any of the following Black-owned distributors to order our books! For others, visit our site.

Afrikan World Books
2217 Pennsylvania Ave.
Baltimore, MD 21217
(410) 383-2006

Lushena Books
607 Country Club Dr
Bensenville, IL 60106
(800) 785-1545

Special Needs X-Press
927 Old Nepperhan Ave
Yonkers, NY 10703
(914) 623-7007